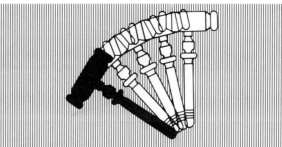

CONTRACTS

DANIEL WM. FESSLER
Professor of Law
University of California, Davis

author: *Alternatives to Incorporation*
for Persons in Quest of Profit (3rd Edition)
co-editor: *Cases and Materials*
on Contracts (with Loiseaux)

Published and Distributed by:
CASENOTES PUBLISHING CO., INC.
1640 Fifth Street, Suite 208
Santa Monica, CA 90401
(310) 395-6500

Second Edition, 1996
First Printing, 1996

ISBN 0-87457-176-6

With the introduction of *Casenote Law Outlines,* Casenotes Publishing Company brings a new approach to the legal study outline. Of course, we have sought out only nationally recognized authorities in their respective fields to author the outlines. Most of the authors are editors of widely used casebooks. All have published extensively in respected legal journals, and some have written treatises cited by courts across the nation in opinions deciding important legal issues on which the authors have recommended what the "last word" on those issues should be.

What is truly novel about the *Casenote Law Outlines* concept is that each outline does not fit into a cookie-cutter mold. While each author has been given a carefully developed format as a framework for the outline, the format is purposefully flexible. The student will therefore find that all outlines are not alike. Instead, each professor has used an approach appropriate to the subject matter. An outline on Evidence cannot be written in the same manner as one on Constitutional Law or Contracts or Torts, etc. Accordingly, the student will find similar features in each *Casenote Law Outline,* but they may be handled in radically different ways by each author. We believe that in this way the law student will be rewarded with the most effective study aid possible. And because we are strongly committed to keeping our publications up to date, *Casenote Law Outlines* are the most current study aids on the market.

For added studying convenience, the *Casenote Law Outlines* series and the *Casenote Legal Briefs* are being coordinated. Many titles in the *Casenote Legal Briefs* series have already been cross-referenced to the appropriate title in the *Casenote Law Outlines* series, and more cross-referenced titles are being released on a regular basis. A tag at the end of most briefs will quickly direct the student to the section in the appropriate *Casenote Law Outline* where further discussion of the rule of law in question can be found.

We continually seek law student and law professor feedback regarding the effectiveness of our publications. As you use *Casenote Law Outlines,* please do not hesitate to write or call us if you have constructive criticism or simply would like to tell us you are pleased with the approach and design of the publication.

Best of luck in your studies.

CASENOTES PUBLISHING CO., INC.

CASENOTE LAW OUTLINES — SUPPLEMENT REQUEST FORM

Casenotes Publishing Co., Inc. prides itself on producing the most current legal study outlines available. Sometimes between major revisions, the authors of the outline series will issue supplements to update their respective outlines to reflect any recent changes in the law. Certain areas of the law change more quickly than others, and thus some outlines may be supplemented, while others may not be supplemented at all.

In order to determine whether or not you should send this supplement request form to us, first check the printing date that appears by the subject name below. If this outline is less than one year old, it is highly unlikely that there will be a supplement for it. If it is older, you may wish to write, telephone, or fax us for current information. You might also check to see whether a supplement has been included with your *Casenote Law Outline* or has been provided to your bookstore. If it is necessary to order the supplement directly from us, it will be supplied without charge, but we do insist that you <u>send a stamped, self-addressed return envelope.</u> If you request a supplement for an outline that does not have one, you will receive the latest *Casenotes* catalogue.

If you wish to request a supplement for this outline:

#5010, CONTRACTS by Fessler ● (Second Edition, First Printing, 1996)

please follow the instructions below.

● **TO OBTAIN YOUR COMPLIMENTARY SUPPLEMENT(S),** *YOU MUST FOLLOW THESE INSTRUCTIONS PRECISELY IN ORDER FOR YOUR REQUEST TO BE ACKNOWLEDGED.*

1. **REMOVE AND SEND THIS ENTIRE REQUEST FORM:** You *must* send this *original* page, which acts as your proof of purchase and provides the information regarding which supplements, if any, you need. The request form is only valid for any supplement for the outline in which it appears. *No photocopied or written requests will be honored.*

2. **SEND A STAMPED, SELF-ADDRESSED, FULL-SIZE (9" x 12") ENVELOPE:** *Affix enough postage to cover at least 3 oz.* We regret that we absolutely cannot fill and/or acknowledge requests unaccompanied by a stamped, self-addressed envelope.

3. **MULTIPLE SUPPLEMENT REQUESTS:** If you are sending supplement requests for two or more different *Casenote Law Outlines,* we suggest you send a return envelope for each subject requested. If you send only one envelope, your order may not be filled immediately should any supplement you requested still be in production. In that case, your order will not be filled until it can be filled completely, *i.e.,* until all supplements you have requested are published.

4. **PLEASE GIVE US THE FOLLOWING INFORMATION:**

Name: _____ Telephone: (___) ___ - ____

Address: _____ Apt.: _____

City: _____ State: _____ Zip: _____

Name of law school you attend: _____

Name and location of bookstore where you purchased this *Casenote Law Outline:* _____

_____

Any comments regarding *Casenote Law Outlines?* _____

_____

CASENOTES PUBLISHING CO., INC., 1640 Fifth Street, Suite 208, Santa Monica, CA 90401
TELEPHONE (310) 395-6500 ● FAX (310) 458-2020

CASENOTE™ LAW OUTLINES

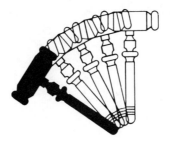

CONTRACTS

In memory of Joseph M. Snee, S.J.
from one who was privileged
to be his student.

INTRODUCTION TO THE SECOND EDITION

What you have a right to expect from these materials: In the jargon of legal education, this is an "outline." From it you should expect to find a summary statement of the major rules of contract law as well as examples of their application. This goal is common to all outline writers. But I have undertaken to do more. A quarter of a century spent working with students in first-year contracts courses has presented ample opportunity to note the repeated problems which this discipline presents for many intelligent people. These materials have been developed in the attempt to anticipate some of the more recurrent problems and assist you in getting the feel ("hang" would be the more trendy term) of this most interesting of subjects.

Any subject, including the common law, is much easier to understand and remember if it can be learned from the perspective of common sense: Most students who consult sources beyond the assigned casebook have little difficulty discerning the specific rules being discussed in the assigned case or cases. Anxiety enters the picture when the student feels unable to relate these individual rules to an emerging "big picture." Scripture has it that, in this life, we are condemned to see as through a glass darkly. Many first-year students would be delighted if that were the only challenge. Instead they read cases which seem to relate to the contents of a darkened room with the description being uttered in a foreign tongue! If your background is similar to the one I brought to the first-year study of law, it ill prepared you to make immediate sense of such an experience. No person in my family had ever been a lawyer, and few were thrilled with the prospect that I might become one.

What I needed was an overview, something I could not supply from direct or vicarious experience. Without it, this subject can seem unfathomable; a jumble of rules with exceptions and, to border on the perverse, exceptions to the exceptions! It is the unconventional goal of these materials to assist you in forming this big picture; to give you a common-sense appreciation of the problems the law is confronting so that you can see the rules as attempted solutions. Thus from time to time (usually at the beginning of a major subject) you will encounter a note entitled **"Problems in perspective."** Seen in the context of these notes to the reader, most of the rules of common law contracts should make common sense. Many will vindicate your expectations of common decency. The first edition introduced these notes and that perspective. Surveys conducted by the publisher report that they are considered very helpful. The number of such notes has been expanded in this second edition.

What these materials are not: If you are a first-year law student, please understand that neither this nor any outline is a substitute for reading and briefing the assigned cases. While an outline can assist in framing the big picture and in gaining a quick knowledge of the content of rules, cases offer the best illustration of the way in which human beings manage to generate the problems which we attempt to resolve by application of the rules collectively known as the "law of contracts." Your goal is to become a solver of human problems. To do this, you must develop an instinct for spotting them in a client's tale of woe. This instinct is developed through the study of cases, each of which is a true story of problems which often reflect human misery. Cases do something else. Each provides an example — sometimes faulty — of legal reasoning. Here is the attempt of the judge or judges to appreciate the human plight and select appropriate rules. The art of the advocate is to cast the human problem in such a manner as to attract the application of "friendly" rules which will produce an outcome favorable to one's client.

My final disclaimer comments on the obvious. An outline is neither a hornbook nor a treatise. In lesser or greater detail, these important works aim to provide the reader with an historical appreciation of the origin of rules and to relate those rules to important cases. In common with much modern law review writing, some of these reference works also have the ambition of imposing a philosophical model on contract law. You will find none of that here. My goal is the more modest one of relating the content of rules to an appreciation of problems. Whether that job has been done in a manner agreeable to philosophy or politics is for each reader to decide.

The first year in perspective: Contracts is a study of human promises and the consequences of disappointing the expectations which those promises have reasonably generated in the mind of the person to whom the promise was given, the "promisee." Because it is centered on the giving, keeping, and breaching of promises, contracts has long been distinguished from other subjects which form the core of the first year.

Torts is focused on the obligations imposed as the price for living in a collective society. Hence we speak of "duties" owed to others to refrain from intentional or negligent behavior which injures their physical selves, their reputations, or property. Property, too, is a classical first-year subject. Think of it as the "mine" and "thine" ordering of that same collective society. Criminal law features infractions against the order of society or the person or property of another which threaten collective security. Procedure, be it civil or criminal, relates all of these substantive rules to the manner in which they are posed and then advanced through the judicial process.

In each of these areas society has determined the rules of "fair play." This is also true in contracts but with an important added dimension. Here, alone, are individuals afforded the luxury of inventing the nature of obligation where none would otherwise exist. They do this by giving or exchanging promises.

The natural division of the subject: As a study of promises, contract law breaks down into seven natural subjects. While the editor of the casebook you are using may have elected to mix the order, a few minutes spent with the table of contents will reveal a course fashioned out of seven topics.

1. **The agreement process:** the law of offer and acceptance, and the role of ambiguity of language or mistakes of the traders as precluding the formation of an agreement.

2. **The qualities of a contractual relationship:** the doctrine of valuable consideration and its substitutes.

3. **Barriers to contractual status:** defenses to the formation of a bargain or the enforcement of its terms.

4. **The allocation of risk inherent in the bargain:** the law of conditions — express, implied in fact and implied at law.

5. **The rights and duties of nontraders:** intended third party beneficiaries; assignees of rights and delegates of duties.

6. **Excusable nonperformance:** the law of impossibility, economic impracticability, and frustration of purpose.

7. **The consequences of breach:** the affirmative duties of the aggrieved party and the remedial rights which accrue to that party.

Using these seven topics we can follow the parties through the formation of a private bargain and the qualification of that bargain for the legal status of a contractual relationship. Next we examine the nature of the performance obligations created by that contract. Are they matters of absolute obligation or conditional promises? Most contracts affect the legal status only of the parties, but the terms of the bargain, or subsequent conduct of either or both of the traders who formed it, may impose rights or duties on nontraders. It is here that we examine the status of the intended beneficiary as well as the potential presence of assignees of rights and delegates of duties. If the bargain of the parties has qualified for contractual status, and the performance obligations have become a matter of current duty (either there were no conditions or the conditions have been satisfied or excused), a failure or refusal to perform *may* be legally privileged. If the contract duty has become objectively impossible, commercially impracticable or there has been frustration of purpose, performance has been excused. If none of these doctrines apply, a failure to perform as promised constitutes a breach. Here we must examine two final topics: the affirmative obligations of the aggrieved party (generally to mitigate her damages) and the remedial rights which accrue to that party either at law or in equity.

Selecting the appropriate rules: The sketch outlined in the preceding paragraph is the beginning and end of a contracts course. But as you travel this journey, please be aware that there are two competing sets of rules to govern each of these topics. The first is the common law, and it is potentially applicable to every bargain or attempted bargain. The competitive rules are statutory, and for our purposes are mainly concentrated in Article 2 of the Uniform Commercial Code. A determination of which set of rules applies to any given fact pattern is made on the basis of the subject matter of the attempted exchange.

The common law: Unless a particular transaction falls within the scope of an applicable statute, the rules of contract law consist of judge-created precedent enunciated over hundreds of years. While much of the earliest precedent is probably lost in time and would today appear as foreign to our society as the costume of the Middle Ages, contract law as you are studying it has been quite recognizable for at least two hundred years. The major reason that it has endured is that it adapts to new customs, mores, and technology. For this reason the rule on any given issue may be in a state of transition with majority and minority positions. As a law student you will have to be content that in many areas there may be no clearly "correct" answer.

The Sales Article of the Uniform Commercial Code: If the subject matter of the attempted exchange is the purchase or sale of *goods,* the seven critical subjects of contract law will be defined by the terms of a statute which has now been enacted in fifty of the fifty-one American jurisdictions. Louisiana is the sole exception. The goal of this statute has been to make uniform throughout the United States the law governing commercial transactions. While much of its content parallels that of the common law, in major areas the provisions of Article 2 dramatically reform, or resolve disputes within, the common law. Invariably, the result is to simplify and make certain the legal rules while affording the traders maximum flexibility in structuring their relationship. Because the statute aims to facilitate the commercial relationships of professional traders, these major reforms generally require that "goods" constitute the subject matter of the attempted exchange and that both parties be "merchants." Each of these is defined by the Code.

"Goods" are defined in U.C.C. § 2-105 to include all things (including specially manufactured goods) which are moveable at the time the contract is formed. "Goods" also includes growing crops and the unborn young of animals. Anything attached to the land, but which is to be removed or severed from the realty, also constitutes "goods" and the contract of sale is governed by Article 2. Examples would include oil and minerals as well as structures which are severed or removed from the land. (U.C.C. § 2-107)

The concept of a "merchant": U.C.C. § 2-104 defines a merchant in terms of both presumptive knowledge of the customs and practices of the marketplace and skill in dealing in that environment. Thus a merchant is any person who deals in goods of the kind or otherwise affirmatively claims possession of the skill and knowledge of one who has such a livelihood.

As a consequence of these definitions, every lawyer must make two important preliminary determinations with respect to every agreement or attempted agreement: do "goods" constitute the subject matter; and, if so, are both traders "merchants"? If the subject matter is not "goods" but instead is real property, personal services, or the sale of intangibles, Article 2 has no application and, aside from occasional statutory inroads, the rules on formation, performance, excuse, and breach are all taken from common law. If the subject matter involves goods, but the traders are not merchants, Article 2 applies, but few of the major revisions of the common law are effective. In this outline, every reference to Article 2 presupposes goods as the subject matter and merchant traders on both sides of the exchange unless a broader coverage is specifically mentioned.

A word about the Restatement of Contracts: Depending on the content of the casebook adopted in your course and the preferences of your instructor, you may hear much or little about the Restatement. If it is a matter of emphasis in your experience you probably already know more about the work and its origin than I will seek to briefly summarize. If not, you will want to take in these basic points so as to render intelligible the not infrequent citations to the Restatement in American common law decisions.

The Restatement of Contracts is the work product of the American Law Institute (ALI), a society of several thousand practicing lawyers, sitting judges, and legal academics. The goal of the Institute is to study the content of decisional law with a view to noting its strengths and weaknesses in serving the needs of the contemporary society. Acting upon such studies, the Institute then prepares what it terms "restatements" which seek to express the approved rules in a clear "black letter" statement followed by examples contained in what is termed a commentary section. To the extent that the Institute feels free to depart from merely reporting majority positions and to substitute in its "black letter" statements rules which are minority views or (less frequently) the invention of the Institute, a "restatement" is more akin to an idealized portrait than a realistic photograph of the common law.

These restatement efforts are undertaken by experts termed reporters, and their work is first reviewed by a larger group of interested members who are members of the council. Only when the preliminary draft by the reporter or reporters has received the support of the council is it debated at annual meetings of the members of the Institute. Once adopted by the members, the work is printed and widely distributed as the Restatement of the Law of _____. The initial Restatement of Contracts was one of the earliest accomplishments of the Institute. It was completed in 1932. The exploding volume of case law and the rapid change experienced in society following the Second World War prompted calls for a revision in the Restatement of Contracts. Such an effort was begun in 1962, and the Restatement (Second) of Contracts was published in 1981. A prominent feature of the revised work is the extensive use of analogies to the content of the Uniform Commercial Code as recommended reforms in the content of the common law.

The Restatement is not the "law" in any jurisdiction. Unless and until a provision of the Restatement is adopted by the courts of a given jurisdiction, it is merely a persuasive expression of what the members of the Institute would like the law to be. Notwithstanding its dependence upon judicial adoption, the various Restatements have had significant influence upon the development of decisional law in this country, as is attested by the references in cases you are reading in contracts and other common law fields.

Daniel Wm. Fessler
Professor of Law

King Hall
University of California, Davis
February, 1996

TABLE OF CONTENTS

TC

NOTES

NOTES

CAPSULE OUTLINE

CAPSULE OUTLINE

CHAPTER 1: THE AGREEMENT PROCESS

CO

I. **THE PROCESS OF AGREEMENT — THE MANIFESTATION OF MUTUAL CONSENT: Whether by words, deeds, or a combination thereof, the parties must form an agreement by consenting to the same terms at the same time. They accomplish this by the process of offer and acceptance.**

 A. **Express and Implied Contracts Distinguished by the Manner of Manifesting Assent**

 1. *Express contracts:* If the offer and acceptance are manifested by oral or written words, the resulting bargain is said to constitute an express contract.

 2. *Implied contracts:* If the mutual assent of the parties is manifested by conduct, rather than oral or written words, the resulting bargain is deemed an implied-in-fact contract.

 B. **Quasi-, or "Implied-at-law" Contracts:** Both express and implied-in-fact bargains form "true contracts" in that each evidences an objective manifestation of mutual assent to be bound by the terms of the agreement. By contrast, a quasi-contract (also termed an "implied-at-law" contract) is a device created by the common law to avoid unjust enrichment of a person who has received and retained valuable goods or services under circumstances in which it is socially reasonable to expect payment.

II. **THE OFFER**

 A. **At Common Law:** Courts insisted upon an express manifestation of the intent to form the present bargain which incorporated an express articulation of the essential terms. Communication to a clearly identified individual or class of persons as "offeree" was also required. A manifestation which failed to satisfy any one of these elements was too indefinite to constitute an offer irrespective of the intention of the would-be offeror.

 B. **Under the U.C.C.:** The Code does not define the term "offer." However, provisions of Article 2 make it clear that a less formal or exacting attitude exists respecting the manner in which the three elements of intent, content, and communication may be established.

 C. **Elements of an Offer**

 1. *Intent:* The offeror must utter such words, acts, or a combination of the two, which would convince a reasonable person standing in the shoes of the offeree that an opportunity had been extended to create a present contract.

 a. Proposed relationship must be formed in the present.

 b. Duties of performance created by present promises may be fixed in the future.

2. *Fact patterns raising issues of present intent*

    a. *State-of-mind problems:* If the factual setting reveals that the party charged with making an offer spoke in anger, in jest, or in a state of hysteria, the presence of an offer is in serious doubt.

    b. *Social setting:* Sometimes the social relationship or setting which forms the context of a promise or statement can defeat the reasonable expectation that it is an offer of a present contract.

    c. *Preliminary negotiations:* If the presence of an offer is disputed in the wake of business discussion, a court must decide if the parties merely discussed potential future business, or transacted present business.

        (1) Significance of language: The language of a controverted statement will be subjected to a reasonable interpretation.

        (2) Significance of the setting: Frequently as important as the words used is the setting of their use.

        (3) Offers addressed to the public: It is possible for a statement to be reasonably interpreted as an offer of a present contract to a member of the public.

    d. *Auctions:* Whether placing an item "on the block" constitutes an offer to sell or merely an invitation to persons attending the auction to make offers to purchase depends upon whether the auction was "with reserve" or "without reserve."

3. **Essential terms:** Either by express content or within the realm of permissible implication, the offer must articulate the essential terms of the proposed bargain.

    a. *The common law:* The classical common law insisted that an offer express a definite articulation of the "essential terms." A failure to do so meant that no matter what the intention of the orator, the proposal was too indefinite as a matter of law to constitute an offer.

        (1) The essential terms amounted to an identification of the parties, a description of the subject matter, the time for performance, and the price.

        (2) Total silence of both parties as a source of implication to trade on a reasonable term.

    b. *The U.C.C. reforms:* In an attempt to facilitate contract formation, the Code has abolished common law formation rules respecting attempted contracts for the sale of goods.

        (1) Under § 2-204(1) there is no emphasis upon the offer as having to impart the content of the essential terms.

CO

(2) The failure of the parties to identify the content of one or more essential terms by their words or deeds is not fatal under § 2-204(3).

c. The position of the Second Restatement clearly seeks to promote common law reform in the direction of U.C.C. positions on formation.

d. *Major limitation on the ability of any court to imply a "reasonable term."* If the parties sought to fix the content of an essential term but did so in a confusing or ambiguous manner, a reasonable term may not be implied and the bargain fails owing to indefiniteness.

(1) Requirement and output contracts are not indefinite. If the quantity term is measured by the seller's output or the buyer's requirements, modern courts do not regard the bargain as too indefinite. In either instance the quantity term is the output generated by the seller or the requirements realized by the buyer in the course of a good-faith operation of their respective business efforts.

(2) U.C.C. position is in accord with the modern common law.

e. *Agreements to agree in the future respecting the content of an essential term:*

(1) U.C.C. flexibility regarding an "open price" term: Under § 2-305 the parties, if they so intend, may form a present contract for sale even though the price is not fixed.

(2) In the event that the parties opt for the agreement to agree in the future, or to have the term fixed by agreed-upon machinery, a present contract is formed, although both traders and a reviewing court will have to await future events to ascertain the price term.

(3) If the agreed-upon machinery should fail to set the future price, whether formation will be defeated depends upon the earlier intent of the parties.

(4) If the original agreement had featured mutual promises to agree on a price term in the future, and one of the traders should become disillusioned and seek to frustrate formation by refusing to agree, formation will not be defeated and a court will imply a reasonable price.

4. *Communication:* There must be communication of the intention to form a present contract and the essential terms to an intended offeree.

a. Performance of an act, which would otherwise accept an offer to contract in the unilateral mode by one who is ignorant of the offer cannot form a bargain.

b. Indirect, or second tier, communication is effective if offer was intended for public.

D. Legal Significance of an Offer: An offer creates in the offeree the capacity to form a bargain by a timely and effective acceptance.

E. Duration or Life of an Offer: The power of the offeree to create a bargain requires that she complete the acceptance before the offer has expired either (1) by its own terms, (2) by operation of law, or (3) by act of the parties.

1. *Expiration or revocation is governed by terms of the offer.*

2. *Duration of an offer which contains no expiration or revocation provision*

   a. *Computation:* Computation of a reasonable time is made with reference to the nature of the subject matter and the condition of the market forming the context of the proposed bargain.

   b. *U.C.C. terminology and concepts:* Section 1-204 introduces and defines the term "seasonably." An action is taken seasonably when it is performed at or within the time agreed or, if no time is agreed at, within a reasonable time.

3. *Termination by operation of law:* An outstanding offer is terminated by operation of law in any of the following circumstances:

   a. *Incapacitation of the offeror:* Death, insanity or legal incapacity of the offeror revokes any outstanding offer even though the offeree is ignorant of knowledge or reason to know of these developments.

   b. *Destruction of the subject matter prior to an effective acceptance.*

   c. *Supervening illegality of the subject matter.*

4. *Termination by act of the parties:* At any time prior to acceptance, the offeror is free to revoke the offer. If the offeree attempts an acceptance but fails to mirror the terms of the offer, at common law she has blundered into a "rejection/counteroffer," in which case the original offer has been revoked by operation of law.

   a. *Revocation:* An offer is inherently revocable at any time prior to acceptance.

      (1) Revocation — how accomplished: If, prior to acceptance, the offeror communicates withdrawal of the offer to the offeree, the offer has been revoked.

      (2) Indirect communication effective: If the offeree acquires reliable information that the offeror desires to withdraw the offer, there can be no effective acceptance.

      (3) Revocation of offers to the public are effective if the offeror has made

reasonable efforts to reach the same audience to whom the offer had been extended.

    b. *Offers which have been reenforced are not revocable:* There are three exceptions to the general rule that an offer is inherently revocable prior to acceptance.

      (1) Formation of an option contract which renders the offer irrevocable during the time fixed by the terms of the option contract.

      (2) An offer which has induced foreseeable reliance on the part of the promisee has become irrevocable.

      (3) A merchant's written "firm offer" is irrevocable.

    c. *Termination as a consequence of the offeree's response to an outstanding offer:* Rejection by the offeree, or any attempt to vary or add to the terms of the offer in the course of an attempted acceptance, terminates the offer as a matter of law.

III. **THE ACCEPTANCE: An acceptance consists of an expression of present, unequivocal, unconditional assent by the offeree to each and every term of the offer. This expression must be communicated to the offeror at a time prior to revocation or termination of the offer. The U.C.C. has made radical change in the rules respecting the content of an effective assent if the subject matter of the attempted exchange is the sale of goods.**

    A. The Elements of an Effective Acceptance: The person seeking to accept an offer must be an "offeree." The content of the offeree's response must express agreement to the terms of the offer within the parameters defined by law, and there must be an effective communication by that person of those terms to the offeror during the life of the offer.

      1. *Status as an offeree:* Only a person intended by the offeror may create and effective acceptance.

        a. *Offer extended to the public:* Unless restricted by the terms of the offer, a proposal to form a bargain extended to the public may be accepted by any person who has acquired direct or indirect knowledge of its terms.

        b. *Offer extended to an agent:*

          (1) If the offeror knows that the person to whom she is extending the offer is the agent of another, that agent's principal qualifies as an offeree.

          (2) Undisclosed agency: The undisclosed principal of an undisclosed agent is not an offeree.

c. *Offeror's mistake as to identity of offeree*

    (1) If the dealing is face to face, an offeror must accept the consequences of his own mistake.

    (2) If the dealing was not face to face the offeror's mistake may preclude formation.

2. ***Content of the offeree's response:*** In order to form a bargain an offeree must express agreement with the terms of the offer within the parameters defined by law.

3. ***The common law's requirement of a mirror-image acceptance:*** At common law the content of an effective acceptance must be a literal mirror image of the terms, and only the terms, of the offer.

    a. *Rationale for the mirror-image at peril of a rejection/counteroffer rule:* The justification of this extraordinary rule was protection of the offeror. If she made a proposal which was not accepted because the offeree attempted to vary its terms, it was felt that the offeror should be immediately free to propose the transaction to some third person without worry that the original offeree might change his mind and make a mirror-image acceptance.

    b. *Common law limitations on the rejection/counteroffer rule*

        (1) Offeree's request that the offeror consider variant terms is not a rejection/counteroffer.

        (2) A response by the offeree which makes explicit a term implicit in the offer is not a rejection/counteroffer.

        (3) Revival of the original offer: If, in the wake of a rejection/counteroffer, the offeror remanifests an intention to trade on the terms of the original offer, that offer is once more open to a mirrored image acceptance.

4. ***The offeree's response under the U.C.C.***

    a. *The U.C.C. position:* The operation of the rejection/counteroffer rule has been dramatically curtailed if goods are the subject matter of the attempted exchange.

        (1) Neither the offeror nor the offeree obliged to assume the risks inherent in formation under § 2-207(2): The offeror may make an "iron clad offer," or the offeree may respond with an explicit rejection/counteroffer.

        (2) Impact of additional or different terms in a purported acceptance of an offer to purchase or sell goods: At common law such a tactic would trigger the rejection/counteroffer rule. Under § 2-207(1) this result is clearly repealed by statute. Such a response will create an

CO

executory contract. The only issue will be the fate of the offeree's terms.

(3) Terms of the resulting bargain: The language of the Code appears to distinguish between the fate of "additional" as opposed to "additional or different" terms.

(4) Fate of additional terms depends upon whether they work a "material alteration" in the bargain as framed in the offer.

(5) Fate of "different terms" contained in an attempted expression of acceptance has triggered disagreement among courts attempting to interpret and apply § 2-207.

(6) Relevance of conduct: Notwithstanding additions, contradictions, or omission in the writings otherwise relied upon to reconstruct the offer and acceptance, if the conduct of the parties recognizes the existence of a contract, and a reviewing court can somehow reconstruct the essential terms, contract status is achieved.

B. Determining the Moment of Formation: Classical contract analysis envisioned two distinct formation patterns. If the offer and acceptance each contained a promise of performance, the exchange of promises formed a bargain in the bilateral mode. If the offer contained a promise but also specified that the acceptance was to take the form of the offeree's performance of a designated act or endurance of a stipulated forbearance, formation was in the unilateral mode.

1. *Formation in the bilateral mode:* A promise standing against a responsive promise creates a bargain in the bilateral mode.

   a. *The deposited acceptance rule:* If the formation of a bilateral bargain was accomplished other than in face-to-face negotiations, a problem arose as to the moment the offeree's acceptance could bind the offeror to the terms of the executory contract.

      (1) The common law began from its classical premise that the offeror was in complete control not only of the terms, but also of the circumstances in which he would expose himself to contract liability.

      (2) Concept of implied authorization: If the offeror had utilized a mode of communication in extending the offer and had been silent with respect to the offeree's mode of acceptance, the common law concluded that there was an implied authorization for the offeree to utilize the same channel of communication.

      (3) The "mail box rule": The contract is formed upon dispatch of the offeree's acceptance using any explicitly or impliedly authorized channel of communication. This rule imposed all risk of delay and loss upon the offeror.

      (4) Today's "deposited acceptance rule": If the offer has been extended

by the use of a channel of remote communication, the offeree is impliedly authorized to use any reasonable channel for communicating her acceptance.

(5) If the offeree did not use an authorized channel of communication, a bargain may still be formed, but the acceptance is effective only upon receipt by the offeror.

(6) Self-protective strategies for the offeror: The easiest way for the offeror to protect himself is to stipulate in the offer that he must receive the acceptance by a certain date or else it is not effective.

b. *Silence as acceptance:* Absent a "duty to speak," the offeror may not impose upon the offeree a risk that his silence may be deemed an effective acceptance. A "duty to speak" may arise from:

(1) Previous dealings; or

(2) Conduct of the offeree in retaining the goods tendered under the terms of an explicit offer.

c. *Crossed communications*

(1) Crossed acceptance and revocation: Under the majority view, a revocation by the offeror is only effective upon receipt by the offeree.

(2) Rejection followed by acceptance: If the offeree changes his mind and manages to send an overtaking acceptance which is the first communication received by the offeror, a bargain is formed.

(3) Acceptance followed by retraction or repudiation: If the acceptance was effective upon dispatch by virtue of the deposited acceptance rule, it is too late for either party to unilaterally withdraw.

2. *Formation in the unilateral mode:* Where the offer specifies that acceptance is to take the form of the rendition of some specified act or, endurance of some forbearance, formation is in the unilateral mode.

a. *Moment of formation is achieved when the offeree completes performance of the specified act or endures the specified pattern of forbearance.*

b. *Peculiar risks faced by the offeree:* Until the offeree has completed his attempted acceptance he faces the peril that the offer may be revoked.

c. *Rules designed to protect the offeree*

(1) Positive bias of the law in favor of bilateral formation: Unless the offeror is very explicit that acceptance must take the form of an act or forbearance rather than a promise to so act or forbear, a reviewing court will construe the offer as inviting acceptance in the bilateral mode.

CO

(2) U.C.C. solution: If the offer is one to buy goods, § 2-206(b) declares that it "shall be construed as inviting acceptance either by a prompt promise to ship or by the prompt or current shipment. . . ."

(3) Offer irrevocable once offeree begins to perform: Once the offeree has begun to perform the requested act or endure the stipulated forbearance, the contract is not formed, but the power of the offeror to revoke is suspended.

d. *Risks to the offeror who elects to bargain in the unilateral mode*

(1) Offeree who commences performance is not bound to complete it.

(2) The "unilateral contract trick": In some common law decisions, an offeree who responded to a buyer's offer to purchase by the shipment of nonconforming goods could claim that there had been defective acceptance rather than a breach of a resulting contract. Such a result is now precluded by the U.C.C.

e. *Notice to the offeror:* As a general rule acceptance is achieved upon completion of the offeree's act of acceptance; no notice to the offeror of this fact is required.

(1) Power of offeror to protect self: The offeror may make the giving of notice the final element of the offeree's act of acceptance.

(2) Notice of completed performance at peril of discharging the offeror's promissory obligation under an implied condition subsequent: If the offeror was unlikely to acquire independent knowledge of the offeree's acceptance, and the offeree as a reasonable person should have realized this, some courts have held that failure to give notice triggers an implied condition subsequent. A contract has been formed, but the promissory obligations of the offeror were discharged by the offeree's failure to provide notice.

f. *U.C.C. solutions*

(1) If the seller reacts to the buyer's offer to purchase goods by sending goods which fail to meet the buyer's reasonable expectations, the seller has both accepted the offer and breached the resulting bargain.

(2) This result can be avoided by the seller if at the time he ships nonconforming goods, he notifies the seller that the shipment does not conform to the terms of the offer but is being offered merely as an accommodation.

(3) An offeree who elects to begin performance as a mode of acceptance must notify the offeror within a "reasonable time" of such commenced effort or else the offeror may treat her offer as having lapsed.

IV. THE IMPACT OF AMBIGUITY AND MISTAKE AS POTENTIALLY PRE-CLUDING THE FORMATION OF A BARGAIN

    A. Ambiguity — When Language Betrays: If a word or phrase used by the parties to identify a term of their bargain is susceptible of more than one reasonable meaning or interpretation, and the parties subjectively attach divergent meanings, their bargain is plagued by ambiguity.

        1. *Impact of ambiguity in the language of the bargain:* If the ambiguity goes to an essential term of the exchange, and each party — having attached a different meaning — had developed equally reasonable expectations, the misunderstanding is fatal to formation.

            a. *Irreconcilable and equally reasonable expectations of the parties defeat formation of a bargain.*

            b. *Court forbidden to overcome omission by implication of a reasonable term.*

        2. *Ambiguity classified as "latent" or "patent"*

            a. *Latent ambiguity:* If, at the formation stage of offer and acceptance, the parties employ a term unaware that it is susceptible of more than one reasonable meaning and each attaches a different meaning, their bargain is flawed by latent — hidden — ambiguity. Latent ambiguity, if it reaches an essential term, is fatal to formation.

            b. *Patent ambiguity:* If the parties frame their bargain using terms which they either know or, as reasonable persons, ought to know are susceptible of more than one reasonable meaning, the ambiguity is patent — obvious. Patent ambiguity, if it attaches to an essential term, is fatal to formation.

            c. *One party at fault:* If, at the formation stage, one of the parties is aware that a term of her offer has more than one reasonable meaning, while the offeree is innocent of such appreciation, the ambiguity is not fatal.

                (1) If the knowing offeror is subjectively aware that the offeree's innocent interpretation differs from the one she intends, formation is accomplished.

                (2) If the knowing offeror employs without definition a term or word which has more than one reasonable meaning, and makes no inquiry of the intention or state of mind of the offeree the offeror is also at fault.

            d. *Role of the "reasonable person":* If a particular trader is subjectively unaware of the ambiguous quality of specific contract language, but a reasonable personwould have recognized such a quality, modern courts regard this as an actionable specie of negligence.

CO

e. *The status of the novice trader:* Whether a novice trader may evade the imputation of the knowledge and skill normally imputed to a "reasonable person" depends upon whether he discloses his neophyte status at the formation stage.

f. *Burden of proof:* Faced with a defense of a claimed different understanding, the plaintiff must prove that: (1) there was no subjective misunderstanding; or (2) if there was, that the defendant was at fault; or (3) the defendant was responsible for failing to preclude the misunderstanding while plaintiff had no such opportunity. If the traders are equally innocent, or equally at fault, neither can sustain this burden.

g. *U.C.C. provisions:* The concepts of course of dealing, usage of trade, course of performance, and practical construction would be used by a court to determine the scope of reasonable behavior if the attempted bargain involved the sale of goods.

   (1) These Code sections emphasize that previous conduct between the parties may be used as a common basis of understanding in interpreting the words of the parties.

   (2) Usage of trade must be proven as with any other fact.

   (3) If there is conflict between course of dealing and usage of trade, the course of dealing — representing the specific history of these parties — governs.

   (4) Finally, under Sec. 2-208(3), a course of performance may be used to show that subsequent to formation, one party became aware of the misunderstanding and the interpretation being given by the other and acted in such a manner as to acquiesce. Such behavior would be taken as a *waiver* or *modification* of the term or a dispute as to its meaning.

B. **Mistake:** In mistake fact patterns the problem is not that the words used by the parties are ambiguous, but rather than they do not convey the subjective intent which would have been entertained but for a mistake by either or both of them. In another variation, the mistake is committed by some third party who has attempted communication services which ought to have facilitated rather than sabotaged the process of formation.

   1. *Mistakes of the parties:* The common law distinguishes fact patterns in which both traders are mistaken from those which feature the blunder of one party only. With respect to unilateral blunders, a distinction is drawn between "mechanical miscalculations" which may provide a defense to formation or enforcement, and "errors in business judgment" which never preclude formation of what may prove a disastrous, but perfectly binding obligation.

      a. *Mutual mistake:* Two factors govern judicial reaction to mutual mistake fact patterns: the significance of the mutual error, and the point in time at which it is discovered.

(1) Mutual mistake must negate a basic assumption of both traders, in which case each party may invoke it as a basis of avoiding the obligations of the flawed bargain.

(2) Barriers of relief if the mutual mistake is not unmasked while the bargain is still executory: If the terms of the bargain have been fully performed, courts are most reluctant to entertain a cause of action seeking rescission and restitution.

b. *Unilateral blunders:* If, at the formation stage, only one of the parties is mistaken with respect to material facts, there is no immediate threat to formation. However, depending upon whether the other party has formed a reasonable expectation, the blundering party may be able to invoke a defense to enforcement of the mistaken terms. But before such a defense may be raised, the blunder must survive a vital classification. Unilateral blunders are either mechanical miscalculations or errors in business judgment.

(1) Mechanical miscalculations: If, at the formation stage, a party's intention is deceived by an error in reckoning the terms of the obligation, the bargain that results is not the one which, but for the miscalculation, would have been intended. Unless the nonmistaken party has formed a commercially reasonable expectation, such a miscalculation is a defense to the enforcement of the resulting bargain.

(2) Errors of business judgment: A trader guilty of an error in business judgment formed the bargain he stupidly intended. Even if the other party was subjectively aware of the blunder, the resulting bargain is binding.

2. *Mistakes of third-party intermediaries:* The rules governing the consequences of blunders by third-party intermediaries are identical to those which determine the fate of a trader who made a mechanical miscalculation.

a. *Inaccuracy:* If the recipient knows, or as a reasonable person ought to know, that the message cannot be accurate, he has no reasonable expectation predicated on its content.

b. *Innocence:* If the recipient has formed an innocent and reasonable expectation, the sender is bound by the terms communicated.

CHAPTER 2: THE QUALITIES OF A CONTRACTUAL RELATIONSHIP

I. **VALUABLE CONSIDERATION: The bargained-for incursion of legal detriment.**

A. **Valuable Consideration Defined:** Valuable consideration may be found in the bargained-for promise to do any act, or the doing of any act, which but for this bargain the promisor or the actor was not legally obligated to perform.

CO

B. **The Bargain Element of Valuable Consideration:** The promises (bilateral formation) or promise and act (unilateral formation) must be consciously exchanged by the parties. If a conscious exchange was not intended, the bargain element is missing and there is no "valuable consideration."

1. *While the promises, or promise and act, must be exchanged in order to form a bargain, the motives of the parties in making such a conscious exchange are legally irrelevant.*

2. *Promises rendered nonvaluable because the bargain element is missing*

   a. *Donative transactions*

      (1) Gift with strings attached.

      (2) Bargain favored over gift.

   b. *Past consideration is not valuable:* Again, the bargain element is missing if what prompts the promisor is a service or benefit conferred by the promisee in the past.

   c. *Token consideration:* Not valuable if the bargain is a sham.

   d. *Moral consideration:* Also lacks the element of bargain and, for that reason, is not "valuable."

3. *The concept of legal detriment:* The presence of a conscious exchange or bargain is but one-half of the doctrine of valuable consideration. Unless there is "legal detriment" on both sides of that exchange, there is no contractual relationship.

   a. *Legal detriment defined:* Each party to the exchange must undertake by promise, act, or forbearance to change what had, but for that bargain, been the dimension of her legal rights or liabilities.

   b. *Legal detriment in a bilateral bargain:* Each of the exchanged promises or sets of promises must obligate the respective promisor to undertake some act which **but for** this bargain he was not legally obligated to perform.

   c. *Legal detriment in a unilateral bargain:* If the offeree's act or forbearance alters the existing dimension of his legal rights or obligations, legal detriment is present on his side of the exchange.

   d. *"Economic adequacy" irrelevant:* Bargained-for legal detriment, and not any economic factor, imparts "value" to valuable consideration. So long as any element of bargained-for legal detriment can be identified on both sides of the exchange, courts are disinterested in the distribution of economic gain or advantage resulting from the contract.

e. Limited exception for nonmarketplace transactions arising in the context of a socially protected relationship

(1) Fiduciary relationships defined: A fiduciary relationship is structured by law and devised for the protection of a person or persons targeted for legal concern.

(2) Confidential relationships are not formally established by law but can arise in any human pairing.

f. *Legal benefit:* The concept of "legal benefit" to the promisee is a mirror reflection of a promisor's legal detriment.

4. ***Promises rendered nonvaluable because one of the parties has not incurred legal detriment***

a. *Problems of pre-existing duty:* A promise which merely repledges, or an act which carries out an existing legal duty, is not legally detrimental to the promisor or the actor.

b. *The illusory promise:* If, at the formation stage, one of the parties does not incur legal detriment because he retains an unfettered election to perform or not, his promise is "illusory."

(1) Distinguished from pre-existing duty fact patterns: The defect in a pre-existing duty fact pattern is the repetition of an existing legal obligation. If the problem is one of an "illusory promise," it means that the promisor did not undertake any kind of obligation at all.

(2) Performance as "cure" for missing consideration: Complete performance of a discretionary undertaking cures the want of consideration which had plagued formation.

(3) Part performance of an illusory obligation does not cure the want of consideration.

(4) The implication of a valuable promise: If a court is convinced that a party intended a contractual relationship but expressed his obligation in an inept or incomplete manner, the solution is to imply a valuable promise rather than see the formation effort flounder over the issue of consideration.

(5) U.C.C. in accord.

c. *Phantom problems with consideration*

(1) Promise to forbear the assertion or abandon the prosecution of a legal claim: The modern trend, expressed in § 74 of the *Restatement, Second,* regards as legally valuable a promise to forbear or abandon the prosecution of a legal claim if it is in fact doubtful, *or* the party making the promise held an honest, subjective belief in its merit.

CO

(2) Promises reserving a right of cancellation may be illusory.

(3) Agreements to purchase the "output" of the seller or to supply the buyer's "requirements" are not illusory.

(4) Promise reserving the right of the promisor to elect among alternative performances is illusory if any one of the reserved alternatives does not involve legal detriment.

(5) Voidable promises are not illusory: The contract obligations of a minor or mental defective are voidable but, in the eyes of the law, constitute valuable consideration.

(6) Conditional promises are not illusory if the promisor lacks the power to prevent the satisfaction of the condition.

(7) Unilateral contracts are never wholly executory and therefore are not governed by the rule that the mutual promises of the parties must involve bargained-for legal detriment.

II. SUBSTITUTES FOR VALUABLE CONSIDERATION AS GROUNDS FOR IMPARTING LIABILITY CONSEQUENCES FOR BREACHING A PROMISE

A. Moral Consideration

1. ***The revival of discharged obligations:*** A *new promise* by a promisor repledging performance of a duty discharged in bankruptcy or the running of the statute of limitations, is enforceable without the necessity of any new element of valuable consideration.

   a. Obligation is on the terms of the new promise.

   b. New promise must be in writing.

   c. The impact of federal statutory law: Bankruptcy is a federal remedy, and the provisions of any federal legislation disable the content of any common or state statutory law in the field. In 1978, Congress passed the Bankruptcy Reform Act. One of its objectives was to limit common law contract rules respecting new promises by bankrupt persons. That act, and any subsequent amendments, should be consulted on questions arising in this area.

2. ***Promise to perform a voidable pre-existing duty is enforceable:*** As per the terms of the new promise, without the necessity of any new element of valuable consideration.

B. Promissory Estoppel — the Impact of Detrimental Reliance

1. ***Distinguished from valuable consideration:*** The essence of an estoppel claim is the promisee's detrimental reliance upon the breached promise.

What precludes an action for breach of contract is the fact that there was no bargain supporting the promisor's undertaking.

2. ***Reliance distinguished from a promisee's expectation interest***

 a. *The expectation interest:* If a promise is broken, the most generous remedy would seek to place the aggrieved promisee in the position she would have occupied had there been full and timely performance. If this is accomplished, the law will have vindicated the promisee's expectation interest.

 b. An expectation interest remedy is attainable only if the breached promise was a contract obligation.

 c. *The reliance interest:* If the expectation interest seeks to place the aggrieved party in the position that would have been enjoyed had there been full and timely performance, the reliance interest has the more modest ambition to return the promisee to the prepromise status quo.

 d. *Protected by promissory estoppel:* The goal of a recovery in promissory estoppel is to protect the aggrieved promisee's reliance interest.

3. ***Elements of the doctrine under the* First Restatement:** "A promise which the promisor should reasonably expect to induce action or forbearance of a definite and substantial character on the part of the promisee and which does induce such action or forbearance is binding if injustice can be avoided only by enforcement of the promise."

4. ***The reformulation under § 90 of the* Restatement, Second**

 a. There is no longer a requirement that the action or forbearance by the promisee be of a "definite and substantial character."

 b. Faced with a pattern of detrimental reliance a court is free to limit the remedy "as justice requires."

 c. Significance of these changes.

C. **The Once-upon-a-time Role of Formalisms**

 1. ***The stipulation***

 2. ***The seal***

 a. *Degeneration of the seal*

 b. *Modern status*

 3. ***Promise in writing***

reliance intrst. return to promise prepromise status

promissory Estoppel

CHAPTER 3: THE BARGAIN IN LITIGATION

CO

I.   **DEFECTIVE FORMATION AS A DEFENSE**

A. **Defenses to the Formation of a Bargain:** Begin with the denial of an offer having been extended, include the contention that the offer had been terminated or extended, the contention that the offer had been terminated or expired prior to the attempted acceptance, and conclude with the assertion that the acceptance was defective. [Each of these topics is covered extensively in Chapter 1. What follows is a sketch of the basic formation elements and their potential use as matters of defense.]

1. *Ambiguity as a defense*

   a. Ambiguity must infect an essential term of the attempted bargain.

   b. If an essential term is infected formation is precluded unless fault can be isolated in one of the parties.

      (1) If the parties are either equally at fault or equally blameless, a reviewing court has no choice but to conclude that formation of a bargain was precluded.

      (2) If one of the parties is at fault and the other is innocent, formation takes place giving the ambiguous language the meaning subjectively intended by the innocent trader.

2. *Mistake*

   a. *Mistakes of the parties*

      (1) Mutual mistake: Involves a mistaken assumption of existing fact by both traders at the formation stage.

      (2) Unilateral blunders: If, at the formation stage, only one of the parties is mistaken with respect to material facts concerning the bargain, there is no threat to formation. If the blunder is a mechanical miscalculation, as opposed to an error in business judgment, the blundering party may be able to invoke a personal defense to enforcement of the mistaken terms.

   b. *Mistakes of third-party intermediaries:* May be a defense to enforcement of the terms communicated.

      (1) Reasonable expectation of the recipient of the communication precludes assertion of the defense.

      (2) Defense to enforcement if mistake infects an essential term and the recipient knows or, as a reasonable person, ought to realize its presence.

B. Defense to Status as Contract

1. ***Want of consideration — a defense to formation:*** If, at the formation stage, one of the parties has not incurred legal detriment, the other has a defense to the formation of a contract termed "want of consideration."

2. ***Failure of consideration — a defense to enforcement:*** If the parties exchange promises which have the quality of bargained-for legal detriment, their agreement qualifies for the status of a contractual relationship. If, subsequent to formation, one of the parties materially breaches the terms of his promise, that material breach works a failure of the promised consideration. It may be cited by the aggrieved party as a defense to the enforcement of her own contract duties.

3. ***Inadequacy of consideration — not a defense:*** Unless the bargain was formed within the context of a socially protected relationship, common law courts have long refused to discipline the bargain for any quality of economic fairness.

    a. *Personal defense:* Inadequacy of consideration is a personal defense to the protected party if the context of the bargain was a confidential or fiduciary relationship.

    b. *Economics:* Equity courts as conscience tribunals will examine the economics of a transaction for fairness as one of several factors influencing the grant of discretionary remedies.

II. DEFENSES RELATING TO THE LIFE CAPACITY OF ONE OF THE PARTIES

A. The Contract Promises of Minors are Voidable.

1. ***Election to avoid contract obligations — disaffirmance:*** A contract made during one's legal minority may be disaffirmed at any time before or after the attainment of a legal majority. Unless and until the contract is disaffirmed, it remains binding.

2. ***Disaffirmance may reverse a wholly executed contract:***

    a. *Disaffirmance:* Personal to the minor or his legal representative.

    b. *Right to disaffirm:* Unaffected by promises not to do so or misrepresentation as to age.

    c. *Restitution:* Upon electing to disaffirm, the minor is generally obligated to restore to the other party only those elements of that party's performance that have been retained and are capable of restitution.

        (1) If the other party has conferred services, they cannot be returned, and the minor has no effective obligation to make restitution.

CO

(2) If the subject matter was goods, and they have been damaged or have depreciated, the restitution obligation extends no further than returning them in their present condition.

(3) In many states, if the minor litigates seeking recovery of what she has paid, as opposed to merely defending on the basis of her minority, relief will be conditioned upon her making restitution of what has been received from the other party.

d. *Obligation for necessaries:* If the subject matter of a contract is the provision of necessaries — food, clothing, or medical attention — the minor may still disaffirm but is liable for the reasonable market value of any necessary which cannot be returned in "as received" condition.

e. *Ratification:* Upon the attainment of legal majority, ratification is binding without elements of new consideration.

(1) How accomplished: Ratification may be by words, deeds, or a combination thereof which reasonably signifies the decision of the new adult to abide by the terms of the contract.

(2) Effect of silence by new adult: Courts are divided upon whether silence by the new adult, coupled with retention of the other party's performance, amounts to ratification.

B. **The Contract Promises of Persons Suffering from Mental Infirmity or Disability are Voidable.**

1. ***The test for mental infirmity or disability:*** Though deemed by critics to be unscientific and imprecise, common law courts employ a "cognitive" (understanding) test which, in some jurisdictions, is supplemented by a control or behavior supplement.

a. *Lack of cognition:* If, at the formation stage, one of the parties lacks the ability to appreciate the nature and consequences of the transaction, the resulting bargain is not void, but voidable by that person or his legal representative.

b. *Inability to control behavior:* In a significant number of jurisdictions, an alternative proof of mental disability or infirmity can be mounted on proof that, though able to understand the nature of his action, the afflicted person was unable to control his action.

c. Incapacity need not be permanent.

d. Mental disability may be self-induced.

2. ***State of awareness of the nonimpaired party:*** If the disability or impairment results in lack of understanding, the majority rule is that the awareness or lack of awareness of this factor on the part of the other trader is irrelevant.

a. If the defect is one of lack of control, jurisdictions which recognize this ground for avoidance are divided.

b. If the impairment is both self-induced and of a temporary nature — the consequence of the use of drugs or alcohol — most courts require that the other trader have either had knowledge or at least reasonable grounds to be aware of the condition before avoidance may be claimed.

c. Section 15 of the *Restatement, Second,* approves general use of an understanding test which is free from any necessity that the other party be aware of the problem.

C. **Contracts of Corporate Entities which are *Ultra Vires* — Beyond the Powers — Permitted by Statute or the Articles of Incorporation May be Voidable.**

1. If the contract would oblige the corporation to exceed statutory limitations on its power the defect is fatal, and the attempted formation void.

2. If the contract is merely beyond the powers conferred in the articles of incorporation, the power of the corporate party to disaffirm is severely restricted by statute.

III. **DEFENSES ROOTED IN SOCIAL OBJECTION TO THE CONTENT OF THE BARGAIN**

A. **Illegality:** If the subject matter of the bargain, or the participation of one or both of the parties, is "illegal," there are important distinctions predicated upon the time and nature of the offense.

1. *Time:* Whether illegality will preclude formation, discharge obligations on a theory of excusable nonperformance, or render the attempted bargain void depends upon whether the illegality existed prior to the attempted formation or was an after-arising factor.

a. *If the illegality is after-arising:* If the subject matter or participation of one of the traders is declared illegal at a time when only the offer is outstanding, it is revoked by operation of law. If illegality is established subsequent to formation, but prior to performance, both parties are discharged on a theory of impossibility.

2. *Nature:* The nature of the illegality will govern the willingness of a court to a party in withdrawing from the illegal transaction or claiming relief in quasi-contract.

a. If the illegality is *malum in se,* there will be no judicial involvement for any purpose.

(1) If the subject matter is a penal offense under an existing statute, many common law decisions hold that there will be no judicial

intervention for any purpose, including assisting one party from withdrawing from the venture.

(2) *Locus penitentiae* doctrine — a minority position favoring the party who seeks to withdraw.

b. If the illegality is merely *malum prohibitum,* the attempted bargain is still void, subject to a real defense. However, there is a possibility of judicial intervention to assist an innocent or protected party in recovering in quasi-contract for the market value of any goods or services provided.

c. Malum prohibitum *defined:* Those matters regulated for the convenience of society, and not intrinsically evil, are *malum prohibitum.*

(1) Must not be *in pari delicto:* If, at the formation stage, both parties were aware that the subject matter was *malum prohibitum,* their conscious defiance of the law will preclude any quasi-contractual relief.

(2) Status of member of a protected class: If the bargain is merely *malum prohibitum,* a person for whose protection or benefit the government acted in defining the illegality will be permitted a quasi-contractual recovery of any performance rendered notwithstanding his awareness of the illegality.

(3) If the illegality can be corrected or checked through other means or proceedings, some courts have been reluctant to see it established as a defense to the enforcement of a duty to pay for goods and services already received.

B. Substantive Unconscionability

1. *Distinguished from procedural unconscionability:* When objection is centered on the content of the bargain, as opposed to the tactics of the dominant party, the charge is one of substantive unconscionability. If the content would be permissible, but the tactics of one of the traders have managed to surprise or overbear the resistance of the obviously weaker party, the defense may be termed "procedural unconscionability."

2. *Terms likely to be deemed unconscionable*

a. Stipulated remedies clauses are unconscionable if they seek anything beyond compensation for the aggrieved party's loss or injury.

b. *Limitations on consequential damages:* Under U.C.C. § 2719(3) any attempt to limit the award of consequential damages for breach of contract to sell consumer goods is *prima facie* unconscionable.

c. *The attempted disclaimer of warranties:* U.C.C. §§ 2-314 and 315 create implied warranties that the goods sold shall be merchantable and, if the buyer has permitted the seller to select goods to meet the buyer's disclosed requirements or needs, that they are fit for that purpose. While

CO

the Code permits modification or exclusion of these warranties, many state consumer protection statutes do not.

3. ***Consequences of substantive unconscionability:*** The remedy for substantive unconscionability is to "blue pencil" the offending clause or clauses while enforcing the balance of the bargain.

C. **Public Policy**

1. ***The concept of "public policy":*** Though not "illegal," certain subject matter offends "public policy." In other circumstances, it is the participation by an individual, usually a public official, which is offensive.

   a. *Examples of subject matter held to offend public policy:*

      (1) Covenants in restraint of trade have been held to offend society's interest in the freedom to exploit talent and economic resources.

      (2) Covenants not to compete have been particularly troublesome because they pose a conflict of public policies.

      (3) Covenants which directly encourage or promote tortious interference with a noncontracting party are offensive to public policy.

      (4) Contingent fee agreements for obtaining the passage of special legislation or favorable rulings by government agencies have been held contrary to public policy.

2. ***Consequence of determination that terms of bargain violate public policy:*** A reviewing court may hold the entire agreement voidable or simply "blue pencil" the offensive term or terms while leaving the balance of the agreement to stand.

IV. **DEFENSES CENTERED ON THE DECEPTIVE OR COERCIVE FORMATION TACTICS OF ONE OF THE PARTIES**

A. **Fraud:** The common law distinguishes three types of fraud — fraud in the factum (real fraud), fraud in the inducement, and fraud in the execution.

1. ***Fraud in the factum:*** A real defense rendering the attempted bargain void. It consists of any deceptive strategy which has the consequence of preventing the victim from realizing that a contract is even in contemplation.

2. ***Fraud in the inducement:*** The victim is aware that a contract is in contemplation, but his consent is seduced by lies or deliberate half-truths. Fraud in the inducement is a personal defense rendering the contract obligations of the victim voidable at her election.

CO

    a. *Classical formulation of fraud in the inducement*

        (1) Elements:

            (a) A misrepresentation of a fact material to the bargain at the formation stage;

            (b) The misrepresentation had to be of an existing fact of which the victim was ignorant and which a person of normal sagacity and diligence would not have known;

            (c) The misrepresentation must have been intended to deceive and to induce the victim to enter the contract; and

            (d) Such misrepresentation must have actually induced the victim's consent to the contract.

        (2) Burden of allegation and proof of all four of these elements lies with the person charging fraud in the inducement.

        (3) Difficulties in proving the defendant's evil-intending state of mind — "scienter."

    b. *The liberalized formulation favored by the* Restatement, Second: Scienter is removed as a necessary element if there was a misrepresentation of material fact. If the victim can establish scienter, he need not prove that the fact was material.

  3. *Fraud in the execution:* Here the victim is aware that a contract is being formed, and her consent to its terms is not the product of misrepresentation of material fact. Rather, betrayal takes place when the oral agreement of the parties is committed to writing. The victim trusts the fraudulent party to reduce the agreement to a written expression and, acting on his assurance that he has faithfully done so, signs that writing without reading it.

    a. *Difficult policy choice:* A victim claiming fraud in the execution as a personal defense puts the issue of self-protection and the duty to deploy it as a first line of defense squarely at issue.

        (1) Preference for the fate of a negligent party when the contest is with a dishonest adversary.

        (2) Negligence of victim as a bar to judicial relief: Other courts have sacrificed the immediate victim to demonstrate the general imperative to read documents before signing them.

  4. *Constructive fraud:* Has nothing in common with fraud doctrines other than the term. The doctrine does not involve proof of conscious wrongdoing but was developed by courts to protect the dependent party in a confidential or fiduciary relationship.

a. *Elements*

(1) The presence of a fiduciary or confidential relationship between the parties at the formation stage.

(2) The resulting bargain contains terms that proved significantly disadvantageous to the party for whose protection the relationship existed.

(3) There is no element of moral wrongdoing essential to the doctrine of constructive fraud.

b. *Nature of relief*

(1) If the affected bargain is still executory, a plaintiff able to establish the three elements of constructive fraud has a personal defense to the enforcement of his contract obligations.

B. Duress: Coercive force used or threatened against the victim to induce apparent consent.

1. *Physical duress:* Present whenever physically coercive acts or the threat of such acts are used to induce the victim's apparent consent.

a. Coercive acts or threats of such acts to a third party as physical duress: Such coercive tactics need not be confined to the immediate victim. They are actionable if directed at those near or dear to the victim and their consequence was to "overmaster the will" of the victim.

2. *Consequences of physical duress:* Physical duress is always a personal defense which may be asserted by the victim to avoid the obligations of an executory contract or to gain rescission of an executed transaction.

3. *Economic duress:* Does not exist in a fact pattern where one of the traders is in desperate need of the subject matter and the other takes advantage to drive a harsh, one-sided bargain.

a. *Elements:*

(1) The defendant was guilty of some illicit act or threat of an illicit act, against the victim's property or business interests that created the pressure upon the intended victim.

(2) This illicit pressure must have left the victim with no reasonable alternative but to submit to the terms.

b. Courts are divided on whether the assertion of lawful pressure, or the threat to assert such pressure, can constitute economic duress.

(1) If the parties are roughly matched in terms of bargaining skills and economic strength, neither the blunt assertion of lawful pressure nor the threat to assert it is likely to be viewed as constituting duress.

CO

        (2) However, the abusive or oppressive threat to deploy even lawful pressure has been recognized by some courts as constituting economic duress if the parties were mismatched at the bargaining table and the victim's will was "overmastered."

    c. If the illicit pressure was one which a reasonable person could have withstood, the claim of duress may be rejected.

    d. The repeated assertion of illicit pressures, any one of which might have been reasonably resisted, may create an overmastering quality and, in the aggregate, amount to economic duress.

    e. *Consequences of economic duress:* If the affected bargain is executory, the victim may assert economic duress as a personal defense. If the bargain has been executed, rescission and restitution may be an appropriate remedy.

C. Undue Influence: The deployment of "overpersuasive" bargaining strategies designed to overcome the will without convincing the judgment of a weaker party.

  1. *Elements:*

    a. *Discussing the proposed bargain at an unusual or inappropriate time;*

    b. *Consummation of the transaction at an unusual place;*

    c. *Insistence that the transaction be concluded at once;*

    d. *Extreme emphasis on the risks or disadvantages of delay;*

    e. *The use of multiple persuaders in dealing with the weaker party;*

    f. *The absence of any third-party advisors to assist the weaker party;*

    g. *Statements discouraging the weaker party from acting on an inclination to consult advisors.*

  2. *Consequences of undue influence:* If the bargain is executory, the victim has a personal defense against the enforcement of its terms. If the bargain has been fully executed, some courts have allowed rescission.

D. Procedural Unconscionability: If the dominant social objection is the grotesque imbalance of bargaining strength or sophistication of the parties, *and* the resulting terms can be characterized as oppressive, the victim is likely to claim procedural unconscionability.

  1. *Definition unsettled:* Neither common law decision nor the statutory expression in U.C.C. § 2-302 fix a definition of unconscionability.

2. ***Goal of defense:*** The professed goal of the defense is to prevent oppression or surprise rather than a reallocation of risk.

   a. A contract or clause is not unconscionable in the abstract, but only when measured against the customs and mores of the marketplace at the time and place of attempted formation.

   b. Subsequent developments or events cannot create an unconscionable situation.

   c. Common association with "adhesion contracts":

      (1) Adhesion contracts are not per se unconscionable, but insistence by the party in the dominant position that there is to be no bargaining excludes the resulting "bargain" from the judicial deference normally accorded negotiated agreements.

      (2) "Oppression" consists of terms which are grossly out of line with market expectations or which seek to curtail protections otherwise accorded traders, especially consumers.

      (3) "Unfair surprise" found in terms which depart from expectations created by the customs of the relevant marketplace and which are not clearly disclosed in an understandable manner to the other party at the formation stage.

   d. ***Consequences of unconscionability:*** A reviewing court may (1) refuse to enforce the entire contract; (2) limit the application of the unconscionable clause while enforcing the remainder of the bargain; or (3) condition judgment for the dominant party upon its ability to prove that the weaker party was actually aware of and understood the clause or clauses and subjectively assented to their terms.

V. DEFENSES ARISING FROM THE FORM OF THE BARGAIN

A. The Statute of Frauds: The fact that a contract is oral may be the source of enforcement difficulties only if the subject matter falls within the Statute.

1. ***Subject matter falling within the Statute***

   a. An agreement that by its terms is not to be performed within one year from the date of formation

   b. A promise to answer for the debt or default of another

   c. An agreement made upon consideration of marriage other than the mutual promise to marry

   d. An agreement for the purchase or sale of real property or any fixture permanently attached to the land

CO

      (1) Agreements for the lease of real property for one year or less are normally not within the Statute.

      (2) An agreement authorizing or employing an agent, broker, or any other person to act as a representative in a real estate transaction which would, itself, fall within the Statute must also be in writing.

    e. An agreement which, by its terms, is not to be performed within the lifetime of the promisor.

    f. *Contracts for the sale of goods if the price is $500 or more fall within U.C.C. § 2-201, the Code's special formulation of the statute:* There are, however, three important exceptions:

      (1) If the seller has tendered the goods and the buyer has accepted them, the buyer's oral promise to pay the agreed price is fully enforceable.

      (2) Special order goods: If the subject matter of an oral contract is goods made at the order of the buyer and not suitable for ordinary resale, the buyer's oral promise to pay is enforceable once the seller has made a substantial beginning in their manufacture or procurement.

      (3) If the contract is between merchants, a written confirmation of its terms sent by one party and received by the other who knows, or has reason to know, of its contents satisfies the Statute as to *both* sender and recipient *unless* written notice of objection is given within ten days.

    g. Contracts for the sale of personal property fall within U.C.C. § 1-206 and are not enforceable by way of action or defense beyond $5,000 in amount or value of remedy *unless* there is a written memorandum.

  2. **Requirements of the Statute:** The consequence of a subject matter falling within the Statute is that there must be a written memorandum of essential terms signed by the party to be charged with liability for breach.

    a. *Essential terms:* For purposes of satisfying the Statute, modern legislation focuses upon the parties, subject matter, and price terms.

    b. *Writing need not be formal or prepared with the subjective intention to satisfy the Statute:* The goal of a court asked to grant a damage remedy at law is to gain written evidence traceable to the defendant from which the essential terms may be reconstructed.

    c. *Signature need not be formal:* A printed letterhead or rubber stamp is sufficient.

  3. **Consequences of a failure to satisfy the statute:** May provide the defendant with a personal defense to the enforcement of his oral obligations.

a. *Personal defense precluding a loss-of-bargain damage remedy at law:* Absent an estoppel fact pattern, a plaintiff unable to produce the required memorandum is precluded from maintaining a loss-of-bargain action at law.

(1) Timely assertion: Only the defendant may raise this personal defense, and if it is not raised in a "timely manner" it will be deemed waived.

(2) Third parties may not raise the Statute as a defense.

b. *Estoppel and the Statute of Frauds:* Some courts have applied both promisor and equitable estoppel concepts to preclude a defendant's assertion of the Statute of Frauds.

(1) Promissory estoppel: If the defendant promised to reduce the agreement to a writing and breached that promise as well as the oral contract, some courts have held that reliance on the part of the other party may be used as the basis of an estoppel.

(2) Equitable estoppel: If the consequence of allowing a litigant to assert the Statute would be to leave that party unjustly enriched, fundamental fairness will require that he be estopped from hiding behind the Statute.

4. ***The attitude of equity courts:*** Part performance accepted as an evidentiary substitute for the missing memorandum of essential terms.

a. Performance must point to terms of the alleged contract, not merely the possibility of some agreement.

b. Part performance by the promisee, as well as that by the promisor, may be weighed by an equity court for its tendency to prove the terms of the contract.

5. ***Action at law for restitution interest in quasi-contract not precluded:*** A plaintiff prevented from gaining a loss-of-bargain recovery may still bring an action at law for the market value of any performance which was tendered to the breaching party and which that party has retained.

B. **The Consequences of Adopting a Writing — The Parol Evidence Rule**

1. There are three possible roles for a written instrument in the creation or enforcement of contract obligations:

a. *The last indispensable step on the road to liability:* If this is their attitude, the failure to sign a document containing the terms of the contract means that no contract was ever formed.

b. *A mere memorial of the terms of an already formed oral contract:* Unless the subject matter of the bargain falls within the Statute of Frauds, failure to reduce it to writing does not prevent contract status or preclude a remedy at law for terms.

   c. *The final expression of the terms intended to survive the bargaining process as those of the contract:* If a writing was produced with this mutual intention, the terms there expressed are protected from addition, variation, or contradiction by the Parol Evidence Rule.

2. ***The Rule:*** If the parties to a contract have reduced that agreement to a writing mutually intended as the full and final expression of their bargain, then any evidence — whether written or oral — of prior or contemporaneous promises or understandings is legally irrelevant if it would vary, add to, or contradict the terms of that writing.

3. ***Application of the Rule is by the trial judge:*** A determination of whether the Rule applies and, if so, whether it will operate to exclude from the jury's attention any evidence beyond the terms of the written contract is a matter for the trial judge.

4. ***The Rule:*** Not one of evidence, and is substantive rather than procedural.

5. ***The Rule in litigation:*** The Parol Evidence Rule is a defense to the proof of a term of a contract. It must be raised during the course of litigation by the party seeking to exclude the evidence from the finder of fact or it is waived. Once the Rule is invoked, the trial judge will make the following determinations:

   a. *Integrated writing:* Only written instruments intended by both parties as the final expression of the terms of their contract are protected by the Parol Evidence Rule.

     (1) Integration determined from the written instrument: The most convenient manner to reflect the intention of the parties that the writing is the final expression of those terms they desire to survive as matters of legal obligation is to simply state this intent in the body of the writing. Such a recitation is customarily referred to as an "integration clause."

     (2) Integration determined from extrinsic evidence: Absent an express integration clause, modern trend is to permit any relevant evidence to be introduced to establish the intent of the parties that they regarded the writing as the final and complete embodiment of their contract.

     (3) The U.C.C. position: Section 2-202 appears to guard any terms upon which the confirmatory memoranda of the parties happen to agree.

     (4) If the trial judge is not convinced that the instrument is an integrated writing, it is not protected by the Rule and may be varied or contradicted by any extrinsic evidence which the jury elects to credit.

   b. *Extrinsic evidence must be "parol":* Extrinsic evidence is any oral or written evidence which lies outside the four corners of the written instrument. Whether extrinsic evidence is "parol" is not an issue of form (oral vs. written), but of time.

    (1) It is the fact that the extrinsic evidence would tend to prove a promise or understanding given or arrived at *prior to or contemporaneous with* the formation of the integrated writing that makes it "parol" in nature and thus potentially excludable.

    (2) Evidence of *subsequent* promises or understandings may show rescission or modification of the contract. Such evidence is not disciplined by the Rule.

c. *Forbidden impact:* Parol evidence is precluded only if it would add to, vary, or contradict the content of the integrated writing.

    (1) Parol evidence may be freely used to clarify ambiguity in the terms of the integrated writing.

    (2) Parol evidence may be freely received to prove trade custom or course of dealings as between the parties.

    (3) Parol evidence may not be admitted to clarify a term which is defined within the integrated writing.

d. *The parol evidence must not be admissible under one of the established exceptions to the Rule:* There are both policy and tactical exceptions to the Rule.

    (1) Proof of fraud: Parol evidence may always be received to establish fraud in the factum, inducement, or execution.

    (2) Proof that the entire agreement was subject to an oral or written condition precedent which had to be satisfied before it was to attain the status of a contract.

    (3) Proof of partial integration: Termed an exception, this topic actually revisits the first determination made by the trial judge. Did the parties intend the writing as a final expression of their contract? It is possible that their intent was mixed; that they desired that the writing finally express the content of certain, but not all, the terms of their bargain. If that is the case, the Rule protects only those subjects intended for complete expression.

    (4) Parol evidence may be used to establish the existence of a collateral agreement and its terms. If the bid for admission is mounted on a theory of collateral agreement, the proponent of the parol evidence contends that the parties made two contemporaneous agreements, only one of which was reduced to an integrated writing. If the trial judge accepts this proposition, parol evidence may be used to reconstruct the "collateral" agreement.

CHAPTER 4: THE ALLOCATION OF RISK INHERENT IN THE BARGAIN

I. **THE CLASSIFICATION OF CONDITIONS ACCORDING TO THEIR IM-PACT UPON The MODIFIED PROMISE: Depending upon their nature, a condition has inserted some contingency which: (1) must be satisfied before liability upon the modified promise matures as a matter of present duty, or (2) the happening of which will extinguish what had, until that moment, been a present duty to perform the promise at peril of breach.**

A. **Conditions Precedent:** A condition precedent is any contingency which must be either satisfied or excused before liability on the modified promise becomes a matter of present duty.

B. **Conditions Concurrent:** The impact of a condition concurrent upon the modified promise is identical to that of the condition precedent. It, too, has inserted some contingency which must be either satisfied or excused before liability on the modified promise becomes a matter of present duty. Conditions concurrent are the common law technique for maturing the performance obligations of the parties simultaneously.

C. **Conditions Subsequent:** Extinguish what had, until the condition was triggered, been a present duty of performance.

D. **Distinction Has Major Significance in Civil Procedure:**

1. A complaint does not state a claim upon which relief can be granted unless it alleges that the defendant's promise was either absolute or, if dependent, that all conditions precedent and concurrent have either been satisfied or excused.

2. Conditions subsequent are regarded as matters of affirmative defense.

E. **Position of the *Restatement, Second* — Events Excluded from the Concept of a "Condition"**

1. Events which must occur before an agreement will have the status of a present contract.

2. Events certain to occur are not "conditions;" they merely denominate the passage of time.

3. Events that terminate a contract duty: The *Restatement, Second,* would abandon the term "condition subsequent." There is no suggestion that parties be precluded from inserting terms which treat certain factual developments as terminating the obligation of a promisor.

II. **SOURCES OF CONDITIONS IN A BARGAIN: There are three ways in which a covenant (promise) may be rendered dependent upon a condition. They are inserted by the express language of the bargain, by implication of fact, or by implication of law. Both express and implied-in-fact conditions are derived from the intent of the parties. As such, they are termed "true conditions." Conditions implied-at-law, also termed "constructive condi-**

tions," are creatures of law. They are devised by judges to facilitate application of the loss-of-bargain damage remedy. They function to fix an order for performance of the promises exchanged by the parties in forming a bilateral contract when the express terms of the bargain have failed to address this critical issue.

A. **Express Conditions as Vehicles for Deliberate Risk Allocation:** Used by the parties in framing the nature and content of their performance obligations:

1. *Distinguishing covenants from conditions in a contract:* Covenants (promises) determine *what* must be performed in order to discharge contract duties. Conditions determine *when and if* the duties defined in covenants must be performed at peril of breach.

   a. *Question of the intent of the parties*

      (1) Usually the language used will make it clear to the other trader, and ultimately to a reviewing court, whether it was that of an additional covenant or the insertion of a condition.

      (2) Certain terms or phrases are deemed artful for introducing the presence of conditions. Terms such as "upon condition" are obviously best for alerting the other trader. Others, such as "provided that," "unless," or even "if" have been held to signal the introduction of a condition.

   b. If the phrase is ambiguous as to whether it is that of a covenant or a condition, it will be interpreted as a promise.

   c. Construction leading to forfeiture is disfavored.

   d. *Language which is both a covenant and a condition:* It is possible that a phrase can function in both capacities. this can result from the presence of an implied covenant which modifies the express condition, or the express understanding that performance by one party of her covenant will function as a condition precedent to maturing the liability of the other.

2. *Conditions of satisfaction as examples of express conditions*

   a. Contract calling for the personal satisfaction of the promisee as a condition precedent to maturing her duty to render a counterperformance

      (1) Illusory construction disfavored: If a court construed the terms of such a bargain as obligating one party to pay if, and only if, in his unfettered discretion he expressed satisfaction, it might conclude that such a promisor's obligation was illusory. Such a construction would defeat contract formation.

      (2) Implication of a legally valuable promise to determine satisfaction in good faith: A modern construction would avoid this "no contract" result by simply implying a further promissory obligation on the part of the

individual to be satisfied that he determine his satisfaction "in good faith."

(3) Personal vs. nonpersonal subject matter: In a further effort to prevent the party who was to perform first with payment dependent upon satisfaction of the other trader, common law courts have distinguished between personal and nonpersonal subject matter. If the subject matter is "nonpersonal," dominated by objectively quantifiable attributes of operative fitness, mechanical utility or structural completion, performance which would gratify the expectations of a reasonable person will satisfy the condition and mature the duty of counterperformance even though, in good faith, the promisee declares himself not satisfied.

b. *Contract calling for the satisfaction of a designated third party:*

(1) No distinction drawn between "personal" and "nonpersonal" subject matter. The risk of forfeiture is greatly reduced by committing the judgment of satisfaction to a third party. For this reason, if the bargain calls for the satisfaction of that party a court will not substitute the views of other persons of similar skill and training.

(2) Limitations on the designated third party: The designated third party must function in a strictly neutral fashion, and not as the partisan of either trader. Any "bad faith" exercise of the discretion committed to the third person by the terms of the contract excuses the condition and immediately matures the dependent promise to make payment.

(3) Gross error by designated third party will, in the view of many courts, also excuse the condition and mature the obligation of the other party.

B. **Conditions Implied-in-Fact:** Protects the unexpressed though reasonable expectations of the parties

1. *Implied-in-fact conditions arise by physical or moral inference from what the parties have expressly promised.*

   a. Physical prerequisites or circumstances which a reasonable person would find necessary to render or receive performance must exist as implied conditions to maturing the contract duty of the promisor.

   b. The good-faith cooperation of the promisee in receiving the performance of the promisor is perhaps the most important circumstance made the subject of an implied-in-fact condition.

C. **Conditions Implied-at-Law:** Constructive conditions function to fix the order of performance when the express terms of the bargain have not settled this vital question.

1. *Mutual Tenders:* Where, in the physical order of things, the performance of both buyer and seller are capable of being tendered at the same time and in the same place, then mutual tenders (a manifestation of a present

readiness, willingness, and ability to perform) are required of each as a constructive condition concurrent to maturing the liability of the other party.

2. ***Maturing the liability:*** If the performance of one of the parties will take time, or requires accomplishment in stages, whereas the performance of the other can be accomplished in a moment in time, performance of the party which will take time is a constructive condition precedent to maturing the liability of the party who can perform in an instant.

3. ***Contract date:*** If the terms of the bargain fix a date certain for the performance by one of the parties but say nothing with respect to the time for the other to perform, performance of the promise controlled by the contract date is a constructive condition to maturing the duty of the other party.

III. THE MATURING OF CONTRACT DUTIES — THE SATISFACTION OR EXCUSE OF CONDITIONS: There are two ways in which a condition precedent or concurrent may be removed as a barrier to present liability upon the dependent promise. The happening of the uncertain event satisfies the condition and matures a present liability to perform the dependent promise at peril of breach. Equally effective in removing a condition as a barrier to a state of present liability is one of the numerous doctrines of excuse.

A. **Satisfaction:** The degree to which the contingent event must obtain provides the distinction between what are termed "true conditions" created by the parties and "constructive conditions," which are creatures of law.

1. ***Literal satisfaction of express conditions:*** If the promisor expressly made her duty of performance dependent on a condition precedent, she is entitled to insist upon literal satisfaction of the contingency or event. If it does not occur, her duty never matures and her failure to perform is privileged rather than a breach.

2. ***Substantial performance satisfies implied-at-law (constructive) conditions:***

   a. Substantial performance cannot be precisely quantified, but the concept is that the deviation from full performance must be both trivial and innocent.

   b. Qualitative or quantitative deviations must not deprive the promisee of the function or utility which he reasonably expected as a benefit of his bargain.

      (1) Proof that there has been no such deprivation is most easily found in construction contracts.

      (2) If the deviation from full performance is pervasive, the cumulative effect of individual flaws may be so obnoxious as to fall short of substantial performance.

   c. *Deviation:* Intentional deviation from the terms of a contract promise in

CO

the course of its attempted performance will preclude any claim that the accomplishment was "substantial."

    d. *Effect of substantial performance:* If achieved, substantial performance will mature the liability of the party whose duty of performance is protected by constructive condition. That party will now render his own counterperformance at peril of breach. He will, however, have a cause of action at law for minor breach.

    e. *The U.C.C. position:* The doctrine of substantial performance has no application in the life of a contract for the purchase or sale of goods. Section 2-601 codifies what is termed the "perfect tender doctrine." Faced with a tender of goods by the seller which fails to conform to the terms of the contract "in any respect," the buyer is privileged to:, (1) reject the whole, (2) accept the whole, or (3) accept any commercial unit or units and reject the rest.

B. Excuse of Conditions as an Alternative Means of Maturing Liability on a Dependent Promise: Excuse is every bit as functional as literal satisfaction to remove a condition precedent or concurrent as a barrier to present liability on a dependent promise. Excuse may also disable the operation of an express condition subsequent.

    1. *Prevention:* Any attempt by the party advantaged by a condition to interfere with the unfolding of events so as frustrate satisfaction of the condition excuses it.

    2. *Excuse of condition as a consequence of waiver*

        a. *Waiver:* The voluntary relinquishment of a known and appreciated right.

        b. *Consequence of waiver:* Once a contract right has been waived it cannot be unilaterally reclaimed. It is gone forever.

        c. *Application to conditions:* Waiver can modify both covenants and conditions in a bargain.

        d. *Partial waiver:* In an installment contract a party may limit his waiver to but a single installment of the other trader's performance.

    3. *Estoppel:* If the party who has the protection of a condition precedent or concurrent creates an impression that he will not insist upon its satisfaction in maturing his liability, and acting in reasonable reliance on the impression the other party changes position, the advantaged trader will be estopped from insisting upon satisfaction.

        a. Appearance of noninsistence which later results in estoppel need not have been deliberate and can be the result of accidental or inadvertent behavior.

        b. Condition can be revived if estoppel is lifted.

CO

4. **Decline in a conditional promisor's apparent willingness or ability to perform should the condition be satisfied as a source of excuse**

a. *Excuse of conditions as a consequence of breach by anticipatory repudiation:* If, prior to the satisfaction of conditions precedent or concurrent with the maturing of a contract duty fixed in the future, a promisor communicates to the promisee a definite, defiant, and unyielding renunciation of any intention to be bound by the terms of the exchange, he commits a present, material breach of the contract.

(1) Quality of the communication must impart a definite, unequivocal, and defiant renunciation.

(2) Consequences of such a breach upon the promisee depend upon whether that party has executory duties of her own on the date of the repudiation. If the promisee has such duties she may elect to (1) commence an immediate cause of action for material breach of the repudiated contract, or (2) affirm the contract and await the due date for performance.

b. *Excuse of condition predicated upon a breach of the dependent promise by voluntary disablement:* Any voluntary action taken by the promisor subsequent to formation which places the power of performing the conditional duty beyond her powers is a present breach by voluntary disablement.

(1) Consequences of the voluntary disablement give the aggrieved party an immediate cause of action for present material breach.

(2) Remedial consequences to the aggrieved party: He may elect an immediate cause of action or await the due date to seek a remedy.

(3) Repentance precluded: The majority of American jurisdictions do not permit the breaching party to reinstate the executory terms of the bargain by reacquiring the prospective ability to perform.

c. *Excuse of conditions as a consequence of a failure to give adequate assurance of performance:* At the present time, this doctrine is clearly established only with respect to contracts for the purchase or sale of goods.

(1) The U.C.C. position on "insecurity": Section 2-609(1) declares that a contract of sale imposes an obligation on each party that the other's expectation of receiving due performance will not be impaired. When reasonable grounds for insecurity arise with respect to future performance by the other party, the Code provides a three-stage road to self-help.

(2) The written demand for adequate assurances: A party who is reasonably insecure may make written demand for "... adequate assurance of due performance" by the other party.

(3) Suspension of the insecure party's performance: Having made written demand, he may suspend his own performance pending receipt of a reply.

(4) Failure to provide adequate assurance as repudiation: The insecure party may treat the failure of the other trader to provide adequate assurances within a reasonable time as a present breach of the contract.

(5) Commercial standards determinative: Whether a trader is "reasonably insecure" or the assurances by the party faced with the demand are "adequate" and "timely" is to be determined by commercial standards. Ultimately each presents an issue of fact.

CHAPTER 5: THE RIGHTS AND DUTIES OF NONTRADERS

I. **THE STATUS AND RIGHT OF AN INTENDED BENEFICIARY: If, at the formation of the contract, one of the parties makes a promise, the performance of which will run directly to a designated third person and the other party to the contract consciously intended that result, the designated person is an intended third-party beneficiary.**

   A. **The Elements of Intended Beneficiary Status:** In order to establish the valuable status of intended beneficiary, the third party must establish a quality with respect to the undertaking of the promisor, and a state of mind with respect to the promisee.

      1. *The direct undertaking of the promisor:* The first element of intended beneficiary status is that, at the formation of the bargain, one of the traders has undertaken a promissory duty the performance of which runs directly to a designated third party.

         a. Designation of third party must be either by name or by legal description.

         b. *Test for direct undertaking:* In an intended beneficiary fact pattern, the promise runs to the promisee, but in order to carry out its terms the performance must be bestowed directly upon the designated third party.

      2. *The intention to benefit in the mind of the promisee:* The second element of intended beneficiary status centers on the intention of the promisee, who bargained with the promisor for the undertaking and supported it with valuable consideration.

         a. *Term misleading:* There is no requirement that the promisee evidence a benevolent or altruistic sentiment toward the third party; it is only required that the promisee consciously intend that the promisor's obligation run directly to the beneficiary.

         b. The motives of promisee for harboring this conscious intention are irrelevant.

CO

3. *Exceptional cases:* The *Restatement, Second,* § 302(1) has sought to recast the two elements of intended beneficiary status in a manner which may harmonize some decisions which have departed from the classic formulation.

   a. *Suggested formulation:* An intended beneficiary must show that recognition of a right to performance in the beneficiary status in a manner which may harmonize some decisions which have departed from the classic formulation.

      (1) The performance of the promise will satisfy an obligation of the promisee to pay money to the beneficiary; or

      (2) The circumstances indicate that the promisee intends to give the beneficiary the benefit of the promised performance.

   b. The idea that the "direct undertaking" might be replaced by proof that granting the third party a cause of action for breach of the promisor's undertaking is appropriate to effectuate the intent of the traders may explain certain common law decisions which have allowed third persons to recover against the promisor for breach of an undertaking which did *not* run directly to them.

B. **Legal Consequence of Intended Beneficiary Status:** If the designated third party is able to prove the two elements of intended beneficiary status, the promisor must perform the terms of the direct undertaking at peril of a breach which may be remedied by an action directly maintained by the intended beneficiary.

   1. *Arcane classification of intended beneficiaries as "creditor" and "donee" third parties:* The original *Restatement* promoted a classification of designated third parties predicated on the relationship between the third party and the promisee.

      a. *Creditor third-party beneficiary:* If the third party was an actual or asserted creditor of the promisee, and the performance by the promisor would satisfy that debt, the relationship was that of a creditor third-party beneficiary.

      b. *Donee third-party beneficiary:* If there was no creditor/debtor relationship between the promisee and the third party, or the performance of the promisor would not satisfy that debt, the third party beneficiary is of the donee variety.

      c. *Consequences of the classification*

         (1) The "intention to benefit" in the mind of the promisee was judicially presumed if the resulting relationship was that of a creditor beneficiary.

         (2) The rights of a donee beneficiary vested the moment the contract made for his benefit was formed.

2. ***Classification abandoned in favor of unitary concept of "intended third-party beneficiaries":*** The *Restatement, Second,* § 302, has repudiated the distinction between the two classes of third parties and now urges that they be treated under identical rules in establishing proof of status and vesting of rights.

3. ***Nonvaluable status of incidental beneficiary:*** A third party able to establish pragmatic advantage from performance of a contract, but who is unable to establish either element of intended beneficiary status, has no legally protected rights. He is a mere "incidental beneficiary."

C. **Vesting the Rights of an Intended Beneficiary:** Once the rights of an intended beneficiary have "vested" it is no longer within the legal power of the traders who formed the contract to modify or rescind the direct undertaking of the promisor.

1. ***Vesting:*** How accomplished:

   a. Arcane distinction between creditor and donee beneficiaries under the *First Restatement* extended greater protection to the donee beneficiary.

      (1) A donee beneficiary's rights vested the moment a contract for his benefit was formed.

      (2) A creditor beneficiary, by contrast, could vest her rights only when, having learned of the contract made for her benefit, she changed position in detrimental reliance.

      (3) The rationale for this distinction was that if the contract for the benefit of a donee benificiary was rescinded, he would have nothing. A creditor beneficiary would at least have her original creditor's claim upon the promisee.

   b. *Modern view:* There are three alternative means to vest the rights of an intended beneficiary:

      (1) When having learned of the contract made for his benefit the intended beneficiary changes position in detrimental reliance; or

      (2) The moment the intended beneficiary commences a cause of action against the promisor; or

      (3) When the intended beneficiary expresses consent to receive the performance of the promisor when that consent has been requested by either of the traders.

2. ***The status of an intended beneficiary is dependent upon the vesting of rights:***

   a. *The vulnerable posture of an intended beneficiary who has not vested his rights:* Until he manages to vest his rights, the status of an intended beneficiary is vulnerable to subsequent decisions of the traders who formed the contract that they wish to rescind, modify, or novate their bargain.

(1) If rescission is their decision, the contract created for the intended beneficiary ceases to exist.

(2) Modification alters the nature or dimension of what may be expected.

(3) Novation is a three-cornered agreement wherein the original traders agree upon a substitute promisor who consents to assume the burdens of the original.

b. *Impregnable position of intended beneficiary with vested rights*

(1) Any attempt by the traders to accomplish this agenda is totally ineffective in relieving the promisor of the duty to perform the original terms of his direct undertaking to the third party.

(2) Additional rights of the intended beneficiary with vested rights: If the promisor gives anything of value to the promisee in exchange for the ineffective consent to rescind, modify or novate their bargain, the intended beneficiary may claim that sum. If the promisee seeks to alter the direct undertaking of the promisor, he is liable to the intended beneficiary for tortious interference with contract rights.

D. **The Intended Beneficiary's Cause of Action:** In the event of a failure or refusal to perform on the part of the promisor, or a performance which disappoints the reasonable expectations of the intended beneficiary, the primary cause of action to remedy the breach at law or in equity is that of the intended beneficiary.

1. *Defenses of the promisor:* Faced with an action for material breach by a purported intended beneficiary, the promisor may contest the status of the plaintiff, or, admitting it, may defeat liability by raising any real or personal defense to the formation of the alleged contract or the enforcement of its terms.

a. *Liability of promisor must be fully matured:* If the direct undertaking of the promisor was protected by any express or implied condition precedent or concurrent, it must have been satisfied or excused.

b. *Denial of beneficiary's status:* In order to state a claim upon which relief may be granted, a third party must allege the elements of intended beneficiary status in addition to a matured duty and material breach.

c. *Defenses against a derivative cause of action:* The claim of material breach and prayer for relief at law or in equity by an intended beneficiary is wholly derived from the contract made for her benefit.

(1) Real defenses preclude formation of that contract: Any real defense in the hands of the defendant/promisor precludes formation of the asserted contract and totally defeats the claim.

(2) Personal defenses admit the formation of a contract but render the contract duties of the promisor voidable.

(3) Vicarious defenses may not be raised: The liability of the promisor stands or falls upon the binding nature of his contract with the promisee. Whether the promisee may have defenses to the asserted claims of a creditor beneficiary is irrelevant to the promisor's duty.

2. *Claims of the promisor:* The damage claim of an intended beneficiary may be reduced or extinguished by the amount of any counterclaim which the promisor has against the promisee. It is immune to any setoff.

   a. *Vulnerability to counterclaims:* A counterclaim is any cause of action which the promisor would have against the promisee for breach of the contract containing the direct undertaking to the intended beneficiary.

      (1) Because the intended beneficiary's cause of action is derived from the contract of the traders, any damages claimed in consequence of a breach by the promisor may be reduced by the dimension of any counterclaim which the promisor has against the promisee for breach of that same contract.

      (2) No affirmative recovery against the intended beneficiary.

   b. *Immunity to setoff:* A setoff is any civil claim for damages which the promisor may assert against the promisee arising from any source other than the contract containing the direct undertaking. They are legally irrelevant to the rights of the intended beneficiary.

E. **In the Event of the Promisor's Breach, the Secondary Rights of the Promisee:** The primary cause of action is that of the intended beneficiary. If that cause of action is not pursued, or fails other than on the merits, secondary rights accrue to the promisee.

   1. *An action at law for damages:* Recovery of a loss-of-bargain award of money damages will prove problematic since performance was owed to the third party.

      a. *Loss-of-bargain recovery of damages are precluded if injury to promisee is speculative:*

         (1) If the intended beneficiary was a creditor of the promisee, breach by the promisor may leave the promisee able to establish his damages.

         (2) If the intended beneficiary is not a creditor, proof of consequential damages would be speculative unless the aggrieved promisee formed a replacement contrast obtaining a direct undertaking from another promisor.

      b. *Standing to sue in equity:* A promisee unable to establish a loss of bargain with adequate dollar certainty has no adequate remedy at law. Such circumstances give rise to standing to sue in equity.

  (1) Suit for specific performance: The usual goal of a promisee suing in equity is to obtain a decree compelling the defaulting promisor to carry out the direct undertaking to the intended beneficiary.

  (2) Nature of relief discretionary: As with any prayer for equitable relief, a remedy cannot be claimed as of right but is addressed to the sound discretion of the court.

  c. *Quest for rescission and restitution at law:* If the loss of bargain is speculative, and an equity court proves unwilling to act, an aggrieved promisee who has bestowed anything of value upon the defaulting promisor can reclaim it or its market value in quasi-contract.

II. **THE ASSIGNMENT OF CONTRACT RIGHTS: Faced with a demand for performance by a nontrader who has received a present, operative, and nonrevoked assignment, a promisor must perform the duties assigned or answer for material breach in an action maintained by that assignee.**

  A. **Present Assignment:** In order to achieve a present assignment, the obligee must manifest an intention to make a present assignment, and take steps sufficient to achieve a present transfer, and that intention and those steps must relate to a suitable present subject matter.

   1. ***The intent to make a present assignment:*** Either by words, deeds, or a combination thereof, the obligee must manifest a present intention to act in the present so as to extinguish all right, title and interest in the subject in himself and to transfer the same immediately and exclusively to the designated assignee.

   2. ***Acts of present assignment:*** In addition to manifesting an intent to create the assignment in the present, the assignor must dearly identify the subject matter, the designated assignee, and take such steps as are necessary to transfer the legal interest in the subject matter without further action.

    a. The assignment must amount to a complete transfer of the entire interest of the assignor in the designated subject matter and divest the assignor of all control over the subject matter being assigned.

    b. *No writing is required:* An oral assignment, if it expresses the requisite intention, is effective.

    c. *Partial assignment permissible:* An obligee may assign the right to receive clearly defined portions of the obligor's performance to several non-competing assignees, or retain a portion of the subject matter while assigning the balance.

CO

3. *Present subject matter:* The assignor's intent and actions effecting a present assignment amount to an exercise in futility unless they relate to a suitable present subject matter.

   a. *Future rights under an existing contract are freely assignable in the present.*

   b. *Future rights in a not-yet-existing contract may not be assigned at law.*

   c. *Future rights in future contract potentially assignable in equity:* If the attempted present assignment of rights in a future contract takes place in the context of an expectation predicated upon an established, though informal economic relationship, a present assignment has taken place in the eyes of equity.

      (1) Assignee achieves present transfer of equitable interest.

      (2) In the event of subsequent contract formation, assignor holds the subject matter in trust for assignee.

B. **Unless the Attempted Present Assignment is Operative, the Purported Assignee Achieves No Claim or Standing as Against the Promisor:**

   1. *Common law restraints on the freedom of assignment:* An assignment which would materially alter the nature of the nonconsenting promisor's contract duties or materially enlarge the dimension of his risk is not operative, and the purported assignee acquires no rights.

      a. Assignments which would materially vary the contract duties of the nonconsenting obligor are not operative.

         (1) The right to receive the personal services of another under an existing contract may not be assigned without a material alteration of the nature of the employee's duties.

         (2) Requirement and output if contracts have been held nonassignable for feared alteration of the duties of the buyer or seller.

         (3) Cannot alter material terms: An assignment which would alter a material term of the contract is not operative.

      b. Assignments which do not threaten material alteration of the obligor's duties, but which do materially alter the dimension of the risk which he had assumed in forming the contract are also inoperative.

         (1) Alteration of the risk of having to perform a dependent promise: If the obligor has made the maturing of his performance dependent upon satisfaction or a condition precedent or concurrent, an assignment which would enhance the chance of maturing that promise is inoperative.

(2) Alteration of the risk inherent in attempting performance would render the assignment inoperative.

(3) Alteration of the risk of not receiving the same full measure of counterperformance from the assignor as obligee would also render the assignment inoperative.

2. ***The fate of contract provisions purporting to forbid or restrict the right to create an assignment***

a. There is a positive bias in the common and modern statutory law in favor of freedom of assignment. An initial manifestation of this bias is the presumption that a contract clause prohibiting or restricting a right to assign "the contract" is intended only to preclude the delegation of contract duties, not the assignment of rights.

b. Only the plainest possible language can drive a court to the conclusion that a clause prohibiting assignment means more than a prohibition on delegation.

c. Language as preventing the right to make a licit assignment as opposed to extinguishing the power to make an operative assignment.

(1) If the contract restraint is the form of a covenant not to assign, the legal effect is to prevent an obligee from making a licit assignment.

(2) If the contract restraint takes the form of expressly treating the attempted assignment of rights as an offer to the nonconsenting obligor to rescind the contract or makes such an attempt an express condition subsequent discharging the contract duties of the obligor, it has extinguished the power as well as the right to make a present, operative assignment.

d. *Countervailing values:* To overcome the common law bias in favor of the freedom of assignment, some jurisdictions require proof that the restraint must be reasonably designed to attain and encourage accepted social or economic ends.

e. *Some restraints are void, as being contrary to statutory policy:*

(1) Claim to damages assignable.

(2) Right to receive payment of money assignable.

C. **The Consequences of a Present, Operative Assignment and the Potential for Destruction of the Assignee's Status by Revocation**

1. ***The status of an assignee:*** Assuming that he can prove the elements of a present assignment and defeat any contention by the obligor that it is not operative, all right, title, and interest in the subject matter of the assignment has been extinguished in the assignor and is vested exclusively in the assignee.

a. The obligor must tender performance of the assigned duties to the assignee at peril of material breach.

    (1) An attempt by the obligor to ignore the status of the assignee and tender performance to the original obligee/assignor is totally ineffective in discharging his contract duties.

    (2) If the obligee/assignor accepts a tender of the performance which had been assigned, she exposes herself to an equitable trust and damages at law for conversion.

b. In the event of the obligor's failure, refusal, or defective performance, the primary cause of action to seek recovery of the loss-of-bargain measure of money damages at law belongs to the assignee.

2. ***Revocation — a potential destruction of the assignee's status:*** Before an assignee may be secure in her status, she must consider the possibility that it has been destroyed by the obligee/assignor.

    a. *An oral gratuitous assignment is revocable:* The assignor has a right to change his mind and reacquire legal dominion over the subject matter to the exclusion of the assignee.

        (1) Revocation — how accomplished: If the assignor has a right to revoke he may exercise it by notice given to either the gratuitous assignee or obligor, or the simple act of creating a subsequent, conflicting assignment to a second assignee.

        (2) A gratuitous assignment is irrevocable, meaning that the assignor has no legal right to reacquire legal dominion over the subject matter if (1) the declaration of intent to assign is in writing and the writing is delivered to the assignee; (2) there is a delivery of a token chose to the assignee; (3) the gratuitous assignee changes position in detrimental reliance upon the oral assignment; or (4) the gratuitous assignee obtains performance from the obligor.

        (3) Consequences of wrongful revocation of a gratuitous assignment: If an assignor without legal right achieves the *de facto* revocation of an irrevocable assignment, he is liable to the aggrieved gratuitous assignee in tort for conversion.

    b. *Assignments made for consideration are irrevocable:* Whether oral or written in form, if the assignee has paid value for the assignment, the assignor never has a right to revoke it.

        (1) Power to achieve *de facto* revocation by creation of successor assignee of same subject matter who, depending on the law of the jurisdiction respecting the claims of rival assignees, turns out to have the superior claim to the performance of the obligor.

CO

       (2) Consequences of a wrongful revocation of an assignment made for consideration: The faithless obligor is liable to the aggrieved assignee for breach of an implied warranty which attends every assignment made for consideration. The assignor warrants that he has both the right and power to make a present, operative assignment of the subject matter and that having done so, he will do nothing to interfere with the assignee's quiet enjoyment of the subject matter.

    c. *Priority among conflicting assignees*

       (1) A gratuitous assignee holding a revocable assignment is eliminated from the race. The mere creation of a subsequent rival revokes the earlier assignment.

       (2) As among competitors with irrevocable assignments, the assignee with the superior equity will prevail.

       (3) Conflicting common law positions where rivals have equivalent equities: There are three rival common law rules governing this question. The most widely followed gives preference to the assignee first in time.

D. The Assignee's Claim in Litigation: In the event that the obligor fails, refuses or defectively performs the duty which had been assigned to the sole or prevailing assignee, the remedial consequences all flow from the proposition that the assignee alone has the exclusive right to receive the breached performance.

    1. *No claim against the obligee/assignor:* Unless the assignor is guilty of interfering in the assignee's quiet enjoyment, or his own material breach has discharged the obligor, the assignor has no liability to the assignee.

    2. *Breach:* Breach by obligor is not a violation of the implied warranty attending an assignment for consideration.

    3. *Rights of the aggrieved assignee against the breaching obligor:* A failure or refusal on the part of the obligor to perform a contract duty which has been assigned is a present material breach of the contract. So, too, is a defective attempt to carry out the terms of such a promise. In each instance the primary cause of action to remedy this material breach, at law or in equity, belongs to the assignee.

    4. *Defenses available to the defendant/obligor*

      a. Burden is upon the purported assignor as plaintiff to establish a present assignment and a material breach by the obligor of a fully matured contract duty.

       (1) If the promise of the obligor which was assigned was dependent upon the satisfaction or excuse of a condition precedent or concurrent, the

CO

obligor has no duty to perform and thus no occasion to breach unless those conditions have been removed.

(2) Whether issues of the operative nature of the assignment are treated as part of the plaintiff's case in chief or matters of affirmative defense by an obligor is a matter for civil procedure.

b. *Present assignment:* If the present assignment and its operative nature are either conceded or established, an obligor may raise any real or personal defense to the formation or enforcement of the contract which is the source of the assignee's claim.

(1) Any real defense precludes formation of that contract.

(2) Any personal defense, including failure of consideration, renders the contract duties of the obligor voidable.

(3) Personal defenses of the obligor may be precluded by status of assignee as holder in due course, or waiver by the obligor.

(4) Status of counterclaims and setoffs: Standing in the shoes of the assignor, the assignee's claim against the obligor is vulnerable to any counterclaim, and to any setoff which matured before the effective date of the assignment.

III. THE DELEGATION OF CONTRACT DUTIES: An attempt by an obligor to place primary responsibility for the performance of his executory duties under the terms of contract in a nontrader is termed a "delegation."

A. **The Mechanics of Delegation:** The requirements for an effective delegation are quite simple, and no formality need attend their accomplishment.

1. *No assumption:* If no assumption of the duty on the part of the delegate is desired, an obligor need only clearly identify the intended delegate and manifest consent to permit the delegate to perform contract duties owed by the obligor/delegor to the other trader.

2. *Delegation contract:* If an assumption of duty by the delegate is desired, a contract of delegation must be formed.

a. *Terms explicit:* Usually the promise by the delegate to assume primary legal responsibility for the contract duties of the obligor/delegor will be explicit.

b. *Assumption implied from overall transaction:* Under both the U.C.C. and common law, if a nontrader accepts the assignment of "the contract" without protest, he will be deemed to have impliedly promised to assume legal liability for the duties of the assignor/obligor as well as gaining the status of an assignee of rights.

CO

B. Restraints on Effective Delegation: Like assignment, the power to delegate is a unilateral legal privilege which does not depend upon the prior, contemporaneous, or subsequent consent of the other trader. Yet because delegation poses a far more direct threat to the other trader's interest than does assignment, the terms of the bargain, or the nature of the contract duties may render the attempted assignment ineffective.

1. Contract terms prohibiting or restraining delegation will always be enforced.

2. If the delegation has taken place in the context of a contract for the sale of goods, the U.C.C. § 2-210(5) expressly provides that the obligee may treat it as creating reasonable grounds for insecurity.

   a. The insecure obligee may make written demand upon the delegate for adequate assurance of performance.

   b. A failure on the part of the delegate to provide adequate assurances of both a willingness and capacity to perform the delegated duties of the obligor/delegor is, itself, a material breach of the contract.

3. *Precautions:* If the obligee has not taken the precaution of inserting contract restraints or prohibitions respecting delegation, whether the delegation is effective will depend on the nature of the duties and the impact upon the reasonable expectations of the obligee.

   a. *Contract duties of a "personal character" may not be effectively delegated without the consent of the obligee:* If the commercially reasonable expectations of the obligee founded on the contract include not only what is to be performed, but who is to perform it, those duties are "personal."

   b. If the contract duty is dominated by mechanical or utilitarian qualities or other criteria readily judged for reasonable completion, the subject matter is not personal.

   c. Waiver by obligee of right to object renders delegation effective.

C. The Consequences of an Effective Delegation: The obligee must cooperate in the delegate's attempt to discharge the duties of the obligor/delegor.

1. Failure to cooperate in the face of an effective delegation is a repudiation of the contract by the obligee.

2. If that attempt is successful in gratifying the reasonable expectations which the obligee had in the contract, performance by the delegate discharges the duties of the obligor/delegor.

3. The obligor/delegor is not relieved of her contract duties but recedes to a posture of secondary liability.

CO

D. Remedies Open to an Aggrieved Obligee

1. ***Rights as against the obligor/delegor:*** In the event of material breach by the delegate, the aggrieved obligee may commence an action against the obligor/delegor seeking recovery of the loss of bargain measure of damages at law, or if that remedy is inadequate, may sue in equity.

2. ***Rights as against the delegate***

   a. If the delegate had not assumed the obligor/delegor's contract duties, he is not liable to the aggrieved obligee.

   b. If there had been a contract of delegation between the obligor/delegor and delegate, the obligee is an intended third-party beneficiary of that contract and may commence an action against the delegate in that capacity.

      (1) Faced with such an action, the delegate may raise any real or personal defense arising out of the contract of delegation.

      (2) The delegate may also assert any counterclaim arising from a breach by the obligor/delegor of the contract of delegation.

3. The aggrieved obligee may elect as between the obligor/delegor or the delegate who has assumed duties.

   a. If the aggrieved obligee elects to seek his remedy as against the obligor/delegor the defendant may implead the delegate.

   b. An obligor/delegor who has been forced to perform the contract duties assumed by a delegate to pay damages to the delegate, or to form an alternative contract of delegation to secure their performance, may recover for any loss sustained from the defaulting delegate.

CHAPTER 6: EXCUSABLE NONPERFORMANCE

I. EXCUSABLE NONPERFORMANCE UNDER THE COMMON LAW

A. Impossibility: The promised performance cannot be done. The earliest appeal for excusable nonperformance was mounted upon the contention that, subsequent to formation, physical barriers had arisen which made performance of one of the bargained promises impossible.

1. ***Elements of excusable nonperformance predicated upon a claim of impossibility:*** The party seeking excuse must demonstrate that subsequent to formation, factors neither foreseen by the parties nor reasonably foreseeable have rendered performance of the promised task objectively impossible.

   a. *Role of foreseeability:* In the 1820s the common law was settled that if the factual development cited as a source of claimed impossibility was

CO

foreseeable at the formation stage of the bargain and no provision of the contract had been made to guard against it, the promisor was bound to perform or answer for breach.

b. Consequence of unforeseeable physical barrier must have produced objective impossibility.

(1) Subjective impossibility — this promisor cannot perform — not a source of excuse: If the only consequence of the unforeseen and unforeseeable barrier is to make it personally impossible for the promisor to perform, there is no excuse.

(2) Objective impossibility — the performance cannot be done: By contrast, if the after-arising developments would preclude any person from accomplishing the promised performance, the specific promisor is excused.

2. ***Contract to remodel as example of objective impossibility:*** In contrast to a contract to construct a building, which has rarely been excused on grounds of impossibility, contractors who engage to do repairs or remodeling on existing structures have found it fairly easy to claim excused the building is destroyed without fault.

a. *Supporting rationale:* Failure of an implied-in-fact condition.

b. *Recovery in quasi-contract:* A contractor discharged from duties on grounds of objective impossibility may recover from the owner the reasonable value of any performance bestowed on the project up to the point of destruction.

B. **Impracticability:** After-arising factors have rendered the cost of performing a contract promise grossly in excess of what had been assumed by the parties at the formation of the contract.

1. ***Elements of impracticability:*** While not firmly settled, there is increasing agreement that a party seeking excuse on a theory of impracticability must plead and prove three elements.

a. An unexpected contingency must have arisen subsequent to formation of the contract.

b. The risk of the unexpected occurrence must not have been allocated to the party seeking excuse either by the terms of the bargain or by custom in the marketplace.

c. The consequence of this unexpected and unallocated contingency must have rendered performance commercially impracticable.

2. ***The unexpected after-arising contingency:*** The focus is upon the subjective assumptions of the parties. Did they bargain with a conscious view

toward what has been a subsequent factual development? If they did not, the after-arising contingency was "unexpected."

3. Risk of the unexpected development must not have been allocated to the party seeking excuse either by the terms of the contract or custom of the marketplace.

   a. An implied assumption may be established by proof that risks of the general variety were contemplated by the parties and yet the trader gave an unconditional undertaking.

   b. The customs and mores of the marketplace may cast an assumption of the type of risk later identified as including the after-arising contingency upon one class of traders.

4. Consequence of an unexpected and unallocated after-arising contingency must have rendered performance impracticable.

   a. The test is "objective" in the sense that the cost must have become so distorted that no promisor could seasonably be expected to perform.

   b. *Failure to utilize insurance:* In passing upon a plea of grossly enhanced costs, it is appropriate for the court to consider the potential availability of general or specific insurance. If the party seeking excuse could have protected itself in this manner and failed to do so, the impracticability is subjective and not a source of excuse.

5. ***Rights of the parties in the wake of excuse:*** If impracticability is established, the executory duties of the promisor are excused. So, too, are the rights and duties of the other trader. Their contract is discharged.

   a. *Quasi-contractual adjustments:* A party who has rendered performance prior to the discharge may not recover on the contract but may obtain the market value of such performance on a theory of quasi-contract.

   b. *No protection of the reliance interest:* Any expenses incurred by either trader in preparing for performance may not be recovered.

C. **Frustration of Purpose:** After-arising factors have so depleted the value or utility thought to inhere in the other trader's performance that the contract duties of the party seeking excuse no longer warrant incursion of their original cost.

1. ***Elements of a frustration case:*** A party seeking excuse from the obligation to perform contract duties at peril of breach must establish two elements.

   a. That subsequent to formation some event or contingency neither foreseen nor reasonably foreseeable has occurred,

   b. That the event was not within a class of risk which the parties were tacitly assigning to the promisor by their failure to address them explicitly, and

    c.   That the consequence of this after-arising development is that the value of the other party's performance has been totally or nearly totally destroyed.

  2. *The role of foreseeability:* As noted, a party seeking to establish frustration must allege and prove that the after-arising event was neither foreseen (subjective concept) nor reasonably foreseeable (objective concept) at the formation stage.

    a.   *Risk foreseen:* If it was foreseen, the failure of the trader to guard against the risk by an appropriate condition is fatal.

    b.   *Risk foreseeable:* If the after-arising circumstances could have been foreseen through the exercise of reasonable contracting skills, the same result follows.

    c.   Risks too remote or too obvious as unforeseeable.

  3. *Consequences of frustration:* A party able to establish the two elements of frustration of purpose is excused from all executory duties. The analogy is to failure of consideration.

    a.   *Restitution for any performance to date:* The dominant American view is that a party who has partially performed at the point of frustration may not recover on the contract but may claim in quasi-contract for the reasonable value of any performance bestowed upon and consumed by the other party.

    b.   *Reliance interest not protected:* Any expense by either party incurred in preparing to perform, but which had not been bestowed upon the other trader is lost.

II. **EXCUSABLE NONPERFORMANCE UNDER THE U.C.C.: Article 2 expressly treats three recurrent situations in which a seller may be tempted to seek excusable nonperformance. The first surrounds casualty to the goods intended by the seller as a means of performing contract obligations. The second addresses after-arising conditions which do not affect the goods but substantially prejudice the manner or mode intended to deliver the goods or the means or specie expected from the buyer as payment. Finally, the Code takes over development of the common law concept of commercial impracticability terming its treatment "excuse by failure of presupposed conditions."**

  A. **Casualty to Identified Goods:** Unlike common law cases which usually had the luxury of dealing with the fate of a particular building or talents of a specific individual, the contract for the sale of goods has as its subject matter something that is often "fungible," meaning that any unit of the goods can serve as a replacement for any other.

    1. *Identification:* Though undefined in the Code, if it was the intention of both parties to regard specific, existing goods as the subject matter of their contract, those goods have been "identified" to the contract.

CO ▶

a. *The concept of identification:* Goods which have been identified to the contract are regarded by the Code as the subject matter of a particular bargain.

b. *The techniques for identification of specific goods*

(1) When the contract is made if it is for the sale of goods already existing and designated by the parties as the subject matter;

(2) If the contract is for the sale of future goods, when the goods are shipped, marked or otherwise designated by the seller as goods to which such contract refers; or

(3) When the crops are planted or the young of animals are conceived if the contract is for the sale of crops or the young of animals.

2. ***Excusable nonperformance or modification predicated upon casualty to identified goods:*** Where the contract requires goods identified when the contract was made, casualty without fault of either party before the risk of loss passed to the buyer leaves the issue of discharge or modification to the election of the buyer.

a. *Qualification for excuse:* Under § 2-613, neither party must have been "at fault" in the casualty to identified goods.

(1) If one of the traders is guilty of negligent or willful conduct which produced the casualty, the obligations of that trader are not excused.

(2) If the identification of goods has been by the seller subsequent to contract formation because they were not existing on the date of formation, seller may substitute other goods at any time prior to the date for her performance and in this manner keep the terms of the contract binding.

b. *Consequences of casualty without fault*

(1) If the loss is total, the contract is avoided and the right of the buyer to the goods and the seller to payment are both discharged.

(2) If the loss is partial or the goods have deteriorated so as to no longer conform to contract specifications of quality, the buyer has an election to inspect them and an option to treat the contract as discharged or to accept the goods "as is."

B. **Substituted Performance Rather than Excuse Where Casualty is not to the Goods, but to the Manner or Mode of Delivery or Specie of Payment:** In these circumstances, "avoidance" (destruction) of the affected contract is a last resort. If a commercially acceptable substitute remains both available and practicable, it must be tendered and accepted.

1. ***Substituted manner or mode of delivery:*** Where without fault of either party, the agreed loading, berthing or unloading facilities fail or an agreed

carrier becomes unavailable, or the agreed manner of delivery is otherwise impracticable, if a commercially practicable substitute is available the seller must tender performance in this means and the buyer must accept it as discharging the seller's duties.

2. ***Substituted means or manner of payment:*** If, subsequent to formation, a government in whose jurisdiction the parties must perform interferes to make the manner or means of payment illegal the consequences will depend upon whether the goods have already been tendered by the seller.

   a. If, subsequent to formation, the agreed upon means of payment fails, the seller may withhold or stop delivery unless the buyer arranges for a commercially equivalent manner of payment.

   b. If the goods have already been delivered, the buyer's payment obligation is performed by a tender of the purchase price in a means or manner which remains legal.

C. **Excuse by Failure of Presupposed Conditions:** By its terms, § 2-616 provides for the potential excuse or modification of the contract duties of a seller but not a buyer.

   1. ***Impracticability of performance:*** Subject to having assumed a greater risk and to Code provisions on substituted performance, if the after-arising factors affect the manner of delivery or payment, a seller is excused by subsequent factual developments or governmental intervention.

      a. *After-arising contingency contradicting basic contract assumption:* The after-arising development must have contradicted a basic assumption on which the contract was formed.

      b. *Governmental intervention:* Good-faith compliance by the seller with any foreign or domestic governmental regulation or order may excuse the seller.

      c. Burden of proof is upon seller who would claim excuse.

   2. ***Role of foreseeability:*** The Official Comment to § 2-615 declares that it is directed to circumstances in which the seller's performance ". . .has been rendered commercially impracticable because of unforeseen supervening circumstances not within the contemplation of the parties at the time of contracting."

      a. *Comment 8 further clarifies the point:* If the after-arising factual development or government intervention was forseeable at the formation stage and the contract was silent in making the obligation of the seller dependent upon some protective condition, the foolish seller will be deemed to have impliedly assumed a greater liability and precluded from claiming either partial or total excuse.

      b. *Objective or subjective test of foreseeability:* The parties are held to a standard of reasonable, commercial capacity given the practices, customs and mores of the marketplace.

  c. *Gravity of the disruption*

    (1) Contradiction of "basic assumption of the parties:" While the disruptive factor may affect only the seller, its nonoccurrence must have been a basic assumption of both buyer and seller.

    (2) Increased costs, as well as a rise or collapse of the market in which the contract was formed and is to be performed, are not presumptively a source of excuse.

    (3) By contrast, a severe shortage of raw materials occasioned by war, embargo, crop failure, or an unforeseen shutdown of major sources of supply which result in a market increase in the seller's cost of performance or prevent the seller from obtaining crucial supplies necessary to that performance present the types of failure of presupposed conditions covered by § 615.

    (4) The status of contract for the sale of agricultural produce: The seller who has undertaken the precaution of restricting her liability to the produce of a designated tract or herd is protected by failure without fault of that source. Those who have not must either obtain the goods on the general market or answer for breach.

  d. *Assumption of greater obligation*

    (1) Unless it expressly conditions its liability, a manufacturing seller assumes risk that the most cost-effective means of production may prove unworkable.

    (2) If the contract sees the seller promise the fabrication of innovative products, the seller assumes the risk of achieving the technological breakthroughs.

  e. *Consequences of failure of presupposed conditions may not be total excuse:* The Code rejects the necessity of electing between holding contract duties wholly discharged or fully binding.

    (1) Since parties to a sale of goods contract are bound by the implied covenant to deal in good faith, if the supervening factors do not totally destroy the seller's capacity she must work in good-faith cooperation with the buyer to reschedule or modify the tender.

    (2) Allocation of remaining seller's capacity: A seller faced with a failure of presupposed conditions affecting only a part of her capacity to perform must allocate production and deliveries among her customers.

    (3) Notice of allocation: A seller purporting to modify his contract duties or

seeking total excuse must give seasonable notification to any contract buyer.

(4) Election of the buyer: Assuming that the seller is privileged and has given notice, the election to accept modified performance without further recourse against the seller or treat the contract as discharged is that of the buyer.

f. *Potential application to buyers:* Though unmentioned in the text of the U.C.C., some courts have extended the concepts of excuse to provide relief to buyers.

CHAPTER 7: THE CONSEQUENCES OF BREACH

I. **BREACH — A DISAPPOINTMENT OF THE REASONABLE EXPECTA-TIONS CREATED THE TERMS OF THE EXECUTORY CONTRACT**

A. **Breach of Contract Defined:** If a contract promise is unconditional (it was not dependent on any condition) or all conditions have either been satisfied or excused and no doctrine of excusable nonperformance can be claimed, the promisor's failure or refusal to perform constitutes a "present breach." A defective rendition of the performance attempt called for by the terms of the contract is also a present breach.

B. **Present Breach as Material or Minor:** A failure or refusal to perform is clearly a material breach for it has extinguished the essence of the expectations created in the aggrieved party. But if the promisor attempted performance, a claim of disappointment by the promisee requires that party, and ultimately a court, to determine whether the breach is so serious as to terminate the contract for all purposes other than a remedy, or is merely "minor," impairing the expectations of the aggrieved party but not destroying the relationship.

1. *Material or "total" breach:* If the defect in the promisor's performance seriously disappoints the reasonable expectations of the aggrieved promisee, the breach is "material," or, as the *Restatement, Second,* terms it, "total."

   a. *Question of fact:* Whether or not the defect in the quality, quantity, or timing of the promisor's attempted performance has seriously disappointed the reasonable expectations of the promisee is an issue of fact. The requirement that the impact be serious is a standard of law. The burden of proving the essential quality is that of the promisee who claims the privileges accorded to the victim of a material breach.

   b. *Consequences of a material, total breach:* The promisee may elect to treat a material breach as totally destructive of the contractual relationship for all purposes except a remedy.

      (1) Executory duties of the aggrieved promisee are discharged on a theory of failure of consideration.

(2) **Duty to mitigate:** While abandoning all efforts to carry out the terms of the contract, the aggrieved party will be required to take reasonable self-help steps designed to minimize the damages occasioned by the material breach.

(3) **Litigation to secure the expectation interest of the aggrieved promisee:** The aggrieved party will seek a loss-of-bargain damage remedy at law or, if that proves inadequate, will have standing to sue in equity.

2. ***Minor or "partial" breach:*** Any default or defect in the promisor's performance which does not seriously disappoint the reasonable expectations of the promisee amounts to a present breach, but it is only of a minor or partial quality.

   a. *Consequences of a minor or partial breach:* The contractual relationship is not threatened with destruction.

     (1) **Relationship to the doctrine of substantial performance:** If the defect in the promisor's performance is minor only, there has been substantial performance of that contract duty. If the contract duties of the promisee are protected by constructive conditions, this substantial performance matures the obligation to render that counterperformance.

     (2) The contract duties of the aggrieved party are not discharged. The aggrieved party must now perform her own matured duties or commit a material breach of the contract.

     (3) **Right of aggrieved party to suspend counterperformance:** In an effort to furnish a self-help remedy, some courts have concluded that a partial breach may justify suspension of counterperformance by the aggrieved party in efforts to force the promisor to correct the defect. However, if the defect remains uncorrected, that party must perform at peril of falling into material breach.

   b. *Role of the damage remedy:* The aggrieved party, having performed her own duties, may bring an action for damages sufficient, when added to the substantial performance received, to fully protect her expectation interest.

C. **Distinguishing a Material from a Minor Breach:** The initial determination of the gravity of the breach must be made by the aggrieved promisee in determining her rights and obligations. It is a dangerous assessment, for if the aggrieved party overreacts and treats as material a breach later found by a court to be minor only, her attempt to abandon her own performance will constitute a material breach.

1. Failure of the aggrieved party to treat a breach as material waives the right to subsequently use it as a pretext for terminating the contract.

2. ***Criteria used in making the distinction***

a.   The extent to which the injured party will obtain the substantial benefit which he could have reasonably anticipated;

b.   The extent to which the injured party may be adequately compensated in damages for lack of complete performance;

c.   The extent to which the party failing to perform has already partly performed or made preparations for performance;

d.   The greater or lesser hardship on the party failing to perform in terminating the contract;

e.   The wilful, negligent or innocent behavior of the party failing to perform;

f.   The greater or lesser uncertainty that the party failing to perform will perform the remainder of the contract.

3.   *The added problems of determining the materiality of a breach if the contract calls for one of the parties to perform in installments*

   a.   *Test for determining material impact upon the entire contract:* The aggrieved party must prove that the failure, refusal or defective performance of an installment obligation has defeated her expectations with respect to the entire bargain or severely hampered her ability to carry out her own contract obligations.

   b.   Bias of the law is in favor of isolating the breach to the single installment rather than finding a material breach of the whole contract.

4.   *Installment contracts under the U.C.C.:* The common law bias in favor of contract preservation is intensified under the Code.

   a.   Installment contract defined as one which expressly or by commercial understanding requires or authorizes the delivery of goods in separate lots to be separately accepted by the buyer.

   b.   *Consequence of nonconformity of one or more installments:* Under 2-615 the rights of the aggrieved buyer are presumptively limited to the defective installment(s) rather than the entire contract.

      (1) Right to reject a nonconforming installment: The buyer may reject any installment which fails to meet the perfect tender doctrine and which cannot be cured by the seller. [*See* discussion of the "perfect tender doctrine" and "cure" in Part 11, B].

      (2) If the seller gives adequate assurances that the nonconformity will be cured, the buyer must accept that installment.

   c.   *Right to terminate the entire contract:* If the nonconformity with respect to one or more installments impairs the value of the whole contract, the U.C.C. recognizes a breach of the whole.

CO

(1) Burden of proof that there is substantial impairment to the value of the whole contract must be borne by the party seeking to terminate the entire agreement.

(2) Waiver of right to terminate entire contract: If the aggrieved party accepts a nonconforming installment without notice of cancellation, brings an action with respect to that installment only, or demands further performance from the other trader, the ability to treat the installments to date as a breach of the whole has been waived.

(3) Right to demand adequate assurances: A party who cannot demonstrate a present impairment of the value of the whole contract, but who has been rendered insecure by the nonconformity in an installment with respect to future performance, may make a written demand for adequate assurances of due performance.

II. **THE AFFIRMATIVE OBLIGATIONS OF THE AGGRIEVED PARTY: The classical affirmative obligation of a party faced with a material breach was the simple one of taking reasonable steps to minimize the resulting harm. Recent common law trends, now codified if the contract was for the sale of goods, go far beyond the duty to mitigate damages and impose upon the aggrieved party a duty to cooperate with the other trader in correcting ("curing") the breach. Finally, if the aggrieved party is a buyer in a contract for the sale of goods, the U.C.C. requires a battery of common sense steps to preserve the economic value of any nonconforming goods.**

A. **The Duty to Mitigate**

1. *The duty in general:* At common law, a party faced with a material breach of contract has an affirmative duty to take reasonable steps to avoid any avoidable elements of damage. The duty is enforced by a policy which limits recoverable loss of bargain damages to only those elements of loss which could not have been avoided by the expenditure of such reasonable effort.

2. *Aggrieved employee's duty to mitigate in the face of a breach of a contract for personal services:* A material breach by the employer liberates the time and talent of the aggrieved employee. There is a general duty to turn to the marketplace to resell those assets.

   a. *Special concern for status of employee:* Human talent differs from a liberated chattel or other property. Solicitude for the welfare of those who labor in the marketplace has resulted in three limitations on the dimension of the aggrieved employee's duty to seek out or accept a replacement work opportunity.

      (1) There is no affirmative duty to seek out, or to accept if it is offered, a replacement contract involving work of a different nature than covered by the breached contract.

      (2) The duty to mitigate does not embrace work of the same nature if it is offered at a substantially inferior grade of pay.

CO

(3) Finally, work of comparable nature and pay does not fall within the duty to accept at peril of a reduction in recoverable damages if acceptance would involve relocation to a different locale.

b. Burden of proof rests with the employer to prove that replacement opportunities reasonably within the aggrieved employee's duty to mitigate were available and ignored.

3. ***The duty to mitigate in the face of a breach of a contract for the sale of goods:*** The assumption that the marketplace will serve as a ready source of a substitute supply of fungible goods or an alternative buyer exacts a strong allegiance to the duty to resort to that institution if the aggrieved party's expectation interest is to be protected.

a. *The buyer's duty to mitigate in the event of the seller's breach:* The first remedy provided under the Code is the buyer's right to cover by obtaining conforming goods from a substitute seller and then recovering as consequential damages any difference between the contract price and the cost of the cover contract.

(1) Section 2-712(1) defines a cover as a purchase or contract to purchase substitute goods undertaken by the aggrieved buyer in good faith and without unreasonable delay following the seller's breach.

(2) If the aggrieved buyer has made such a cover, he may be assured of a recovery of loss-of-bargain damages as the difference, if any, between the cost of the cover and the terms of the materially breached contract.

(3) Failure to cover does not preclude the aggrieved buyer from a loss-of-bargain remedy at law, but it will now become his duty to prove the difference between the contract price and market value of the goods at the time and place when the defaulting seller should have performed.

b. *The aggrieved seller's duty to mitigate:* In the event of the buyer's wrongful refusal to accept a tender of the goods, to pay for them, or the failure of the manner of payment, a seller who is still in possession of the goods is free to form a substitute contract for their "resale" in the marketplace.

(1) Effect of a resale contract: A seller who avails himself of this self-help remedy accomplishes the goal of the original contract of converting the goods into a purchase price while fixing the dimension of his consequential damages as the difference, if any, between the terms of the breached contract and the amount realized in the resale.

(2) Danger of abusing the defaulting buyer: There is a danger that the seller will abuse the defaulting buyer by engaging in a collusive resale of the goods. The Code's solution is to require notice of the time, place and manner of any resale which will be other than open and advertised to the public.

B. The Affirmative Duties of the Aggrieved Buyer Faced with a Seller's Tender which is Not Conforming to the Terms of the Contract

1. *Seller's tender of delivery:* Both the rights and obligations of a buyer commence with the seller's effort to deliver the goods, termed by the Code a "tender." The seller is required to put and hold goods conforming to the contract at the buyer's disposition and give any notice reasonably necessary to enable the buyer to take delivery.

   a. The tender must be at a reasonable hour and the goods held available to the buyer for a period reasonably necessary to permit the buyer to take delivery. Unless otherwise agreed, it is the buyer who must furnish any facilities reasonably necessary for receipt of the goods.

   b. Unless otherwise agreed, it is the buyer who must furnish any facilities reasonably necessary for receipt of the goods.

2. *Legal effect of seller's tender:* If the seller has made a tender, a constructive condition to the buyer's duty to make payment is satisfied and that payment obligation matures. The seller is entitled to acceptance of the goods by, and payment at the contract price from, the buyer.

3. *The buyer's right to a perfect tender:* The obligation of the seller is to make a tender of conforming goods. Under § 2-601, the mirrored image of the seller's duty is the buyer's right to insist that the goods and the manner of their delivery conform perfectly to the terms of the contract.

   a. *Buyer's right to inspection of the goods:* In order to protect the buyer's interest, § 2-513 grants the buyer an absolute right to inspect the goods before payment can be demanded or an acceptance decision required.

   b. *If this inspection reveals that either the goods or the tender is "nonconforming"* **in any respect**, *the buyer may*

      (1) Reject the whole;

      (2) Accept the whole; or

      (3) Accept any commercial unit or units and reject the balance.

   c. An acceptance in whole or in part of nonconforming goods by the buyer does *not* preclude the buyer's right to subsequently assert a claim for damages.

   d. Partial acceptance must be in commercial units of the goods.

4. *Manner and consequences of rightful rejection:* A buyer determined to exercise rights under the perfect tender doctrine must reject any nonconformity within a commercially reasonable time following the seller's tender.

   a. *Manner of rejection:* The buyer's rejection is ineffective unless, within a commercially reasonable time following the tender the seller is given specific notice of any claimed nonconformity.

b. Nonseasonable notice of rejection is a *de facto* acceptance of the goods creating an obligation on the part of the buyer to pay the contract price for the goods as tendered.

c. Nonspecific seasonable notice is treated as a waiver of any unmentioned defect which seller could cure.

d. *The meaning of "seasonable":* For all practicable purposes, "seasonable" and "seasonably" are U.C.C. synonyms for "reasonable" and "reasonably."

5. ***The seller's right to cure a nonconforming tender:*** The buyer's duty to make a prompt inspection and, in the case of any nonconformity, to give prompt and specific notice to the seller is now followed by a third affirmative obligation. The buyer must cooperate with the seller in any cure effort aimed at correcting the nonconforming tender.

a. Cure is a matter of the seller's right if the time for the seller's performance has not yet expired.

b. *Time for cure may be extended beyond contract term if seller is surprised by buyer's rejection:* If, in good faith, the seller claims to be surprised by the buyer's rejection he is entitled to a reasonable extension of time to cure the defect unless such extension would prejudice the commercial interests of the buyer.

c. *Effect of a successful cure:* If the seller succeeds in making a conforming replacement tender, it is an academic question whether the earlier nonconforming tender represented a breach. The buyer has now gained his full expectation interest from the seller.

6. ***Disposition of nonconforming goods in a merchant buyer's possession:*** If the seller's tender has left the merchant buyer in possession of goods which have been effectively rejected and there has been no cure effort or that effort has failed, a major complication arises in that the seller is in possession of goods which belong to the seller. While they do not conform to the buyer's contract, such goods do have value and the buyer will be expected to behave in a commercially reasonable manner to preserve that value.

a. A merchant buyer has an affirmative duty to seek and follow reasonable instructions from the defaulting seller in disposing of the nonconforming goods.

b. If the nonconforming goods are threatened and the seller fails or refuses to provide instructions, the merchant buyer has an affirmative duty to act on his own initiative to sell them for the defaulting seller's account.

c. *General buyer's privilege to act in the absence of seller's instructions:* The Code recognizes the rights of both merchant and nonmerchant buyers to dispose of nonconforming goods which are not threatened with imminent destruction or deterioration. The buyer may store them for the seller's account, ship them back to the seller, or resell them for the seller's account.

(1) Any good-faith election by the buyer will be respected.

(2) Buyer is entitled to offset consequential and incidental damages against the proceeds of any good-faith resale.

7. ***The aggrieved buyer's interest in forming a cover contract:*** The final obligation of an aggrieved buyer is to turn to the marketplace to form replacement or cover contract for the goods.

   a. Any difference between the cost of the cover contract and the contract terms may be recovered against the defaulting seller as a certain measure of consequential damages.

   b. The amount of the incidental and consequential damages represents the injury to the buyer's expectation interest.

C. **Revocation of Acceptance in Whole or in Part:** Section 2-608 provides two circumstances in which it is proper for a buyer to revoke acceptance.

   1. Where the nonconformity in the goods escaped detection by a buyer who had made a reasonable preacceptance inspection, the buyer may revoke the acceptance.

      a. Revocation of acceptance must occur within a reasonable time after the buyer discovers or should have discovered the nonconformity.

      b. The buyer's revocation must also take place before any substantial change in the condition of the goods.

   2. If the buyer accepted what were known to be nonconforming goods in reliance upon the seller's express assurance that the defect would be cured, a failure of the seller to cure within a seasonable time entitles the buyer to revoke the acceptance.

   3. ***Means of revocation:*** In either instance, the buyer now determined to revoke acceptance must give notice to the seller.

   4. ***Affirmative duties of the revoking buyer:*** A buyer who revokes has the same duties as if the goods had initially been rejected.

      a. In all circumstances, these duties would include acting in a commercially reasonable manner to preserve the economic value of the seller's tender and mitigate any loss which could be avoided by a timely cover.

      b. If the revocation is occasioned by a discovery of a hidden nonconformity, the affirmative duties of the buyer may extend to cooperating in the seller's effort to cure the defect.

D. The Duty to Mitigate Limits the Election of a Buyer or Seller Faced with Anticipatory Repudiation: The U.C.C. has dramatically limited the option of the aggrieved party to affirm the contract in the face of an anticipatory repudiation and thus postpone the date of breach to the one fixed in the contract for the repudiating party's performance.

1. *The common law election of the aggrieved party:* The early common law granted an aggrieved party who had executory duties on the date of the repudiation, an absolute election between two dramatically different responses.

   a. Treat the anticipatory repudiation as a present breach and bring an immediate cause of action for loss of bargain; or

   b. Affirm the contract and await the original due date for the repudiating party's performance before seeking a loss-of-bargain remedy.

2. *Danger to the breaching party:* If the repudiation was in the face of rising market for the subject matter, the decision of the aggrieved party that to await the due date and to treat the contract as breached on date would increase the dimension of consequential damages.

   a. If the aggrieved party treated the repudiation as accelerating that date, damages were computed as of the date the action was commenced.

   b. If the aggrieved party affirmed the contract, the computation was made as the difference between the market value and contract price on that later date.

3. *Anticipatory repudiation under the U.C.C.:* Section 2-610 provides that when either party repudiates the contract the aggrieved party may:

   a. Resort immediately to any remedy for breach including seeking a loss of bargain recovery, or forming a resale or cover contract; or

   b. Await performance by the repudiating party for a reasonable period of time.

   c. A refusal by the buyer to accept the seller's breach in the face of a rising market, or by the seller to accept the buyer's breach in the face of falling market conditions, would be manifestly unreasonable. Any actual loss sustained beyond what could have been avoided by a timely acceptance of the repudiation would not be recoverable.

E. A resale of the subject matter by a seller with an elastic supply curve need not be counted as mitigation.

1. In the great majority of cases, a material breach by the seller liberates goods which the seller would have otherwise been unable to offer to another buyer.

2. A very different fate awaits a seller who has many standard price goods and few buyers. A breach of contract by Buyer A does not liberate any asset which

CO

the seller needs if she is to deal with Buyer B. Had Buyer B come along, the seller could have accommodated both.

3. Proper measure of damages is loss of the seller's net profit.

III. REMEDIES FOR BREACH OF CONTRACT

A. The Interests of the Aggrieved Party: Whenever a party suffers a material breach of contract, at least three interests are immediately threatened:

1. *The restitution interest:* If, on the date of the breach, the aggrieved party has already wholly or partially performed, a material breach on the part of the other trader leaves the breaching party unjustly enriched by the value of that performance and the aggrieved party unjustly impoverished by its cost.

2. *The reliance interest:* If, on the date of the breach, the aggrieved party has not yet performed but has incurred expenses or foregone other opportunities in reliance upon the expectation that the other would perform, the breaching party is not unjustly enriched, but the out-of-pocket loss to the aggrieved party represents present unjust enrichment.

3. *The expectation interest:* If the aggrieved party has neither performed his own contract obligations nor changed position in detrimental reliance on the date of the breach, there is neither unjust enrichment of the breaching party nor unjust present impoverishment of the aggrieved party. There is, however, a disappointment of expectations of future wealth or advantage which would have been gained had the breaching party performed.

B. Punitive or Exemplary Damages Not Recoverable: The goal of the damage remedy at law is to compensate the aggrieved party, not to inflict a punishment upon the party in breach.

C. The Loss-of-Bargain Measure of Money Damages: The damage remedy at law accepts the fact of a material breach as having destroyed the contract for all purposes save for the computation and award of a sum of money sufficient, insofar as money can approximate it, to place the aggrieved party in the position that would have been occupied had there been full and timely performance.

1. *Presumptive measure of award:* In the absence of special circumstances, the loss of bargain is measured as the difference, if any, between the contract price and market value of the breached performance at the time and place when, under the terms of the contract, it should have been performed.

2. *Loss-of-bargain award is a one-sided approximation of performance*: The aggrieved party is placed in a position akin to that which would have been achieved by performance. The breaching party forfeits all expectation in the bargain and pays what may be a staggering damage award.

3. *Limitations designed to protect the interest of the breaching party:* In recognition of the one-sided nature of the loss-of-bargain award of money

CO

damages, the common law has developed four limiting concepts aimed at reducing the plaintiff's recovery.

a. *Consequential:* In order to be compensable at law, damages must be a consequence of the defendant's breach.

   (1) Unlike a tort recovery, the damage remedy is not subjected to a proximate cause limitation. A similar function is performed by the concept of foresee ability.

   (2) Formation expenses are disallowed. They are regarded as the price of forming a contract, not damages for its breach.

b. *Foreseeable:* Of those damages in fact caused by the breach, plaintiff may recover only for those which were either generally or specially foreseeable at the formation stage.

   (1) Generally foreseeable elements of loss are those which a reasonable person, standing in the shoes of the defendant on the day the contract was formed and aware only of the terms of that bargain, might have foreseen as the probable consequences of breach.

   (2) Specially foreseeable losses are those added elements of injury which a reasonable person might have foreseen if, on the day the contract was formed, he was aware of the special disclosed needs of the other party in addition to the terms of the contract.

   (3) Actual thought not required: Damages are not rendered nonforeseeable because the particular defendant did not contemplate their potential occurrence. Nor must the plaintiff prove that a reasonable person would have actually foreseen them. It is sufficient that had the reasonable person paused to consider the matter, the losses would have been foreseeable.

   (4) Loss need only have been probable; it need not have been foreseen as an inevitable consequence of breach.

c. *Unavoidable:* Of those losses in fact caused by the defendant's breach and either generally or specially foreseeable at the formation of the contract, plaintiff may recover for only those elements of injury which proved unavoidable given an expenditure of reasonable efforts to mitigate damages.

d. *Certain in dollar amount:* Finally, of those losses in fact caused by the defendant's breach, which are either generally or specially foreseeable at the formation of the contract and unavoidable given reasonable efforts to mitigate, the aggrieved party may recover only those damages which can be proved to a certain dollar amount.

   (1) If the marketplace is a ready source of substitution for the breached subject matter, certainty will pose little problem.

CO

(a) If the aggrieved buyer formed a cover contract, his certain damages are the difference, if any, between the cost of the cover contract and the terms of the breached contract.

(b) If the aggrieved party is the seller, a resale contract will fix a certain measure of consequential damages.

(c) If the aggrieved party fails to make a substitute contract, consequential damages may still be established with a requisite certainty by measuring the difference between the terms of the breached contract and the market price of the subject matter at the time and place performance should have been rendered.

(2) Modern trend is to hold plaintiff to proof of consequential damages only to a "reasonable certainty."

(3) The U.C.C. position accords with the modern common law. Damages must be proved with whatever definiteness and accuracy the facts permit, but no more.

D. When Money Fails to Right the Wrong: The potential for equitable intervention

1. *Inadequacy of the damage remedy as a standing prerequisite to sue in equity*

   a. Proof of the inadequacy of the damage remedy to vindicate the expectation interest of the aggrieved party is a standing prerequisite to a plea for equitable intervention.

   b. Where a market exists offering a replacement opportunity to the aggrieved party, the remedy at law is presumptively adequate.

   c. Where no market exists or the subject matter is unique, the presumption is reversed, and the inadequacy of the legal remedy is assumed.

   d. *The U.C.C. view:* The Code's emphasis upon "the commercial feasibility of replacement" requires that courts rethink the definition of "unique" goods. If there is no ready market to which the aggrieved party may turn, specific performance is an appropriate remedy.

2. A plaintiff able to demonstrate standing has no right to relief in equity, merely a prayer addressed to the sound discretion of the court. Some of the factors which may influence the court include:

   a. *Laches:* As a court of conscience, equity tribunals are not bound by the statute of limitations. Instead, the court will require that the complaining party act in a timely manner in asserting "his equity."

   b. *Concern for third parties and public interest:* Equity courts seek to view the exercise of their jurisdiction in the broader context of how a remedy may affect innocent third persons or even the public.

c. *Complaining party must have clean hands:* If the formation tactics or subsequent conduct of the complaining party fails to meet the court's expectations of "conscientious" behavior, relief will be denied.

d. *Equity courts are interested in the pragmatic "adequacy" of consideration:* Equity courts insist that the mere presence of bargained-for legal detriment ("valuable consideration") is insufficient to warrant discretionary relief. Only if the bargain was "fair" in the distribution of benefits and burdens will the court be inclined to intervene.

e. Enforcement difficulties must not overtax the resources of an equity court nor undermine its insistence that its decree be obeyed.

(1) Court must be able to frame a precise decree or it will not act.

(2) Supervision of that decree must not be too burdensome.

3. *Equity courts are not bound by the doctrine of* **stare decisis.**

4. *Nature of equitable relief*

a. *Decree of specific performance:* The defendant will be ordered to literally carry out the terms of the broken bargain.

(1) Imprisonment for equitable contempt: A party who defied an equity court's order to specifically perform may be imprisoned until willing to obey the Chancellor.

(2) Modern preference for fictional performance: Rather than imprison, modern equity practice favors the appointment of a court officer to perform the defendant's obligation.

b. *Injunctive relief:* If enforcement difficulties dissuade the court from ordering specific performance, an effective substitute may be to enjoin the defendant from disposing of the subject matter in any manner other than in compliance with the terms of his contract.

E. **Restitution and Reliance Recoveries:** Consolation prizes at law. An aggrieved party unable to obtain a loss-of-bargain recovery at law and refused equitable relief has failed to protect her expectation interest. Her only recourse is to return to the common law seeking backward-looking measures of damage which aim to restore her to the preagreement status quo.

1. *Recovery in restitution:* A party who has conferred his own performance on the other trader before that party breaches the contract has, at a minimum, a restitution claim.

CO

a. *Defendant in material breach:* Any performance which the aggrieved party had rendered may be recovered in quasi-contract.

   (1) If the defendant can restore performance in the form received (*e.g.,* return the goods or reconvey the real estate) literal restitution may be achieved.

   (2) If the defendant cannot restore the plaintiff's performance as received because it has been consumed, conveyed to an innocent third person, or deteriorated, there will be liability for the "value" of the plaintiff's performance.

b. *Claimant in breach:* A defendant who materially breaches the contract after part performance may be permitted to offset as against the plaintiff's loss of bargain recovery the value of any part performance which the plaintiff has consumed or retained.

2. **Reliance expenses as a measure of damages:** The *Restatement, Second,* recommends that the aggrieved party be allowed to opt for a reliance claim as an alternative to seeking a loss-of-bargain recovery.

F. **Stipulated Remedies Provisions:** The degree to which the terms of the contract may determine the nature and extent of available remedies.

1. **Liquidated damages clause vs. penalty:** The inherent suspicion of common law courts toward stipulated remedies clauses has resulted in their classification under two labels.

   a. *Liquidated damages clauses respected:* If the provision is a "liquidated damages clause," it is valid and will be accepted as the measure of damages without any inquiry into actual loss.

   b. Penalty clause void as an unconscionable affront to public policy.

2. **Criteria for making the distinction**

   a. At the formation stage the parties must have come to the reasonable conclusion that, in the event of breach, a loss of bargain recovery would not be available.

   b. Acting on this reasonable conclusion, the parties must have adopted as a stipulated consequence of breach a term which sought to fairly compensate the aggrieved party, not to penalize the other for failing to perform.

THE AGREEMENT PROCESS

▶ **CHAPTER SUMMARY**

THE AGREEMENT PROCESS

Scope: In this chapter we will review both common law and U.C.C. rules respecting the formation of an agreement. Topics will include offer and acceptance as well as the impact of ambiguity of language or mistakes of the parties as precluding the formation of an agreement. The ability of a private bargain to qualify for contract status will be considered in Chapter 2.

Problems in perspective: The rules reviewed in this chapter wrestle with the following proposition: If contract liability is distinguished from all other legal obligation on the theory that it is created by consent, is it an ironclad defense to any contract action that the defendant did not intend to be bound to the obligation asserted by the plaintiff? If you have ever found hindsight more accurate than foresight in determining the presence or absence of personal advantage, you can immediately see the social problem in allowing an affirmative response to our central question. The thought is aptly captured in the line from "The Fantasticks": "What is scenic in the nighttime may be cynic by the dawn." Substitute the formation stage of the bargain for the nighttime, and the day on which the performance obligation becomes due for the dawn, and you have the picture.

The key solution — the objective theory of contract formation: While the proponents of a subjective theory of contract formation continued to urge that there could be no true contract absent a "meeting of the minds," the needs of rapidly expanding commerce and the increasing instance in which transactions were undertaken between or among comparative strangers assured the triumph of the "objective school" and a negative answer to our central question.

In the narrow sense, the accomplishments of the objective theory are impressive. The legally relevant intent to extend an offer or form an acceptance is gauged from the words and deeds of the parties as they would be interpreted by a reasonable person. Thus if a reasonable person in the position of the party contending that he was in receipt of an offer would have interpreted the outward manifestations of the other trader as extending an offer, an offer had been extended in the eyes of the law. But there was to be more.

As the twentieth century progressed, courts and the drafters of statutes found the objective theory a useful springboard to advance doctrines which frankly favored contract formation. This positive bias in favor of contract formation has reached a contemporary crest with the framing of the Uniform Commercial Code. In § 1-102 this ambition was frankly proclaimed.

Section 1-102. Purposes; Rules of Construction; Variation by Agreement.

(1) This Act shall be liberally construed and applied to promote its underlying purposes and policies.

(2) Underlying purposes and policies of this Act are:

(a) to simplify, clarify, and modernize the law governing commercial transactions;

(b) to permit the continued expansion of commercial practices through custom, usage and agreement of the parties;

(c) to make uniform the law among the various jurisdictions.

A flavor of the Code's determination to facilitate the formation of commercial contracts may be found in § 2-204:

Section 2-204. Formation in General.

(1) A contract for sale of goods may be made in any manner sufficient to show agreement, including conduct by both parties which recognizes the existence of such a contract.

(2) An agreement sufficient to constitute a contract for sale may be found even though the moment of its making is undetermined.

(3) Even though one or more terms are left open, a contract for sale does not fail for indefiniteness if the parties have intended to make a contract and there is a reasonably certain basis for giving an appropriate remedy.

Contrast the positions taken in Section 2-204 with the common law rules respecting formation we now review.

I. **THE PROCESS OF AGREEMENT — THE MANIFESTATION OF MUTUAL CONSENT: Whether by words, deeds, or a combination thereof, the parties must form an agreement by consenting to the same terms at the same time. They accomplish this by the process of offer and acceptance.**

A. **Express and Implied Contracts Distinguished by the Manner of Manifesting Assent.**

1. *Express contracts:* If the offer and acceptance are manifested by oral or written words, the resulting bargain is said to constitute an express contract.

2. *Implied contracts:* If the mutual assent of the parties is manifested by conduct, rather than oral or written words, the resulting bargain is deemed an implied-in-fact contract.

    Example: Smith attends an auction of fine art. The auctioneer holds up a small painting and asks for an opening bid of $10,000. Smith raises her hand. When a call for further bids produces no response the auctioneer lowers his hammer. An implied-in-fact contract has been formed under which Smith has promised to pay the sum of $10,000 and the house to deliver the painting.

B. **Quasi-, or "Implied-at-Law," Contracts:** Both express and implied-in-fact bargains form "true" contracts in that each evidences an objective manifestation of mutual assent to be bound by the terms of the agreement. By contrast, a quasi-contract (also termed an "implied-at-law" contract) is a device created by the common law to avoid the unjust enrichment of a person who has received and retained valuable goods or services of another under circumstances in which it is socially reasonable to expect payment. The simple solution is to imply a promise on the part of the recipient to pay the reasonable value of what has been received and retained.

Example: Rancher Smith notices a break in a fence holding Rancher Jones' cattle in a remote pasture. In order to prevent the escape of the animals, Smith undertakes to repair the break. Jones would be liable to pay Smith the reasonable value of such service as a matter of law. The liability rests on the policy goal of avoiding unjust enrichment of Jones.

THE OFFER

II. **THE OFFER: There are no magic words required to extend an offer, but all offers contain three elements: (1) an expression of intent to enter a present contract, (2) a sufficient articulation of the essential terms of the proposed bargain, and (3) communication of that intent and those terms to another person (the offeree) who is thereby endowed with the capacity to form a contract by a timely and conforming acceptance.**

A. **At Common Law:** Courts insisted upon an express manifestation of the intent to form the present bargain which incorporated an express articulation of the essential terms. Communication to a clearly identified individual or class of persons as "offeree" was also required. A manifestation which failed to satisfy any one of these elements was too indefinite to constitute an offer, irrespective of the intention of the would-be offeror.

B. **Under the U.C.C.:** The Code does not contain a definition of the term "offer." However, provisions of Article 2 make it clear that a less formal or exacting attitude exists respecting the manner in which the three elements of intent, content, and communication may be established.

C. **Elements of an Offer:** Let us now take a look at the three elements which must be present in every offer which can form the basis of a true contract.

   1. *Intent:* As noted, the offeror must utter such words, acts, or a combination of the two, which would convince a reasonable person standing in the shoes of the offeree that an opportunity had been extended to create a present contract. *See Carlill v. Carbolic Smoke Ball Co.,* 1 O.B. 256 (1893).

      a. *Proposed relationship must be formed in the present:* Smith says to Jones "next week I will offer you an opportunity to purchase my car for $15,000." There is no offer, for the intent of Smith is not to form a present bargain with Jones.

      b. *Duties of performance created by present promises may be fixed in the future:* While the intent must be to form a present bargain, the offer can frame an agreement in which the performance of either or both of the parties is fixed at a future date or dates.

Example: On February 5, Smith says to Jones: "If you will promise to pay me $3,000 on the first of June, I will give you the use of my seaside cottage for two months commencing on the first of November." If Jones replies "agreed," a bilateral bargain has been formed on February 5, although the performance obligations of both parties are fixed at dates in the future.

2. ***Fact patterns raising issues of present intent:*** Three fact patterns repeatedly pose the issue of whether the purported offeror has manifested the requisite intent to enter a present contract. The first surrounds statements which cast doubt on the seriousness of the orator's state of mind. The second involves social exchanges. The final category is the most frequently litigated: distinguishing the offer to do business in the present from the discussion of potential business in the future. The key to resolving each is whether a reasonable person, standing in the shoes of the party claiming to have been an "offeree," would have formed the impression that an offer to enter a present contract had been extended.

   a. *State of mind problems:* If the factual setting reveals that the party charged with making an offer spoke or, less frequently, wrote in anger, in jest or in a state of hysteria, the presence of an offer is in serious doubt. The key to resolving this doubt is the impression such words, taken in their total context, would have created in the mind of a reasonable person. If that person would have understood that only an angry statement had been intended, there would be no offer.

      Example: Freda Fox and Paula Pence are taking a weekend pleasure drive when Fox's very expensive automobile breaks down. In obvious frustration Fox declares in a loud voice: "I will sell this piece of junk to the first person who offers me $5!" Should Pence attempt to form a bargain by promising or tendering the sum of $5, the evident frustration, the loud voice, and (perhaps most importantly) the preposterous price will all be factors tending to defeat the claim that an offer existed. *See Chiles v. Good*, 41 S.W.2d 738 *(Tex. Civ. App. 1931)*.

   b. *Social setting:* Sometimes the social relationship or setting which forms the context of a promise or statement can defeat the reasonable expectation that it is an offer of a present contract.

      Example: Sally Jones promises her husband that if he will accompany her to an art exhibit she will purchase two tickets to the local high school basketball game on the following Friday. She does not keep her promise. The family setting, as well as the evidently noncommercial purpose of the exchange, would likely move a court to conclude that no offer to bargain had been extended by Sally Jones.

   c. *Preliminary negotiations:* Cases in which a court is asked to decide whether a statement or promise amounted to an offer of a present contract, or was uttered in the course of yet-to-be-concluded negotiations contemplating potential future business, are both the most common

1

and difficult in litigation. The key remains the one already reviewed. Using the objective theory of formation, the court asks whether, taken in their factual context, the words and actions would have led a reasonable person in the position of the claimed offeree to conclude that an offer of a present contract had been extended. The following factors, no one of which is dispositive, may be considered:

(1) Significance of language: Sometimes the language employed in the controverted statement provides a powerful key to reasonable interpretation. Phrases such as "I am asking. . .," or "I can quote. . .," are suggestive that a present offer has been extended. By contrast, language such as "I am looking for. . ." or "Would you be interested. . ." have often been interpreted as indicative of continuing or even preliminary negotiations.

(2) Significance of the setting: Frequently as important as the words used is the setting of their use. Words which might reasonably be understood as extending an offer of a present contract if employed in a business letter may not have that quality if uttered at a cocktail party.

(3) Offers addressed to the public: It is quite possible for a statement to be reasonably interpreted as an offer of a present contract to a member of the public when the subject matter is suitable for single or limited acceptance, and the party charged with having made an offer has communicated, either orally or in writing, to the public at large.

   (a) An offer of a reward published in a local paper and promising $100 to anyone who locates a lost dog and restores it to the advertiser will be held an offer to contract for the promised sum to anyone who performs the requested act.

   (b) A newspaper advertisement which states that an item of clearly identified sales merchandise will be offered for $5 to the first customer who presents that amount to the store's cashier on Saturday, February 10, will be held an offer to contract. In this case, as well as the offer of a reward, the party charged with making an offer has elected to speak to the general public under circumstances in which there can be but one offeree who is empowered to form the contract. *See Lefkowitz v. Great Minneapolis Surplus Store,* 251 Minn. 188, 86 N.W.2d 689 (1957).

   (c) A mass circular which does not speak of a finite quantity of the subject matter has been held not to constitute a present offer. As in the prior examples, the advertiser has elected to speak to the public in general. However, if this particular mass communication could be treated as an offer by every member of the public, the ability of the offeror to honor resulting "contract" obligations is likely to wither before the number of potentially accepting offerees. *See Lonergan v Scolnick,* 129 Cal. App. 2d 179, 276 P.2d 8 (1954).

   (d) But if the advertiser is a manufacturing seller, as opposed to a retailer, of the same subject matter, there would be a presumptive ability to fabricate a supply responsive to any public demand. Here courts have been less reluctant to conclude that the mass communication could be reasonably understood by potential buyers as a present offer.

  d. *Auctions:* Whether placing an item "on the block" in an auction constitutes an offer to sell or merely an invitation to persons attending the auction to come forward with offers to purchase depends upon whether the auction was "with reserve" or "without reserve."

   (1) Auction with reserve: Neither the advertisement contained in the auction notice, nor the placing of an item on the block by the auctioneer in exhibiting it to the attending audience, is regarded as an offer to sell. Rather it constitutes an invitation to persons in attendance to make offers to buy which may be accepted, rejected, or ignored. When an agreeable bid is received by the auctioneer, acceptance is in the form of "hammering it down."

   (2) Auction without reserve: Once an item is placed on the block and a call is made for bids, it has been offered for sale. It cannot be withdrawn unless no acceptance (in the form of a responsive bid) is made within a reasonable time. *See* U.C.C. § 2-328(3).

3. *Essential terms:* Either by express content or within the realm of permissible implication, the offer must articulate the essential terms of the proposed bargain or else the offeree would have no idea what to accept, and a reviewing court would be unable to fashion an appropriate remedy in the event of breach.

  a. *The common law:* The classical common law insisted that an offer express a definite articulation of the "essential terms." Failure to do so meant that, regardless of the intention of the orator, the proposal was too indefinite as a matter of law to constitute an offer.

   (1) The essential terms amounted to an identification of the parties, a description of the subject matter (including quantity if more than one unit was being offered), the time for performance, and the price.

   (2) Total silence of both parties as a source of implication to trade on a reasonable term: Unyielding application of the classical common law requirement that the offer express the definite content of the essential terms meant that many attempted bargains were doomed by virtue of imprecision. A more modern view seeks to uphold contract formation when that appears to have been the mutual objec-

tive of the parties. The first step in this direction was the common law reform wherein total silence on the part of both traders at the formation stage respecting the content of an essential term prompted the judicial implication that the missing term was intended to be filled by a "reasonable" one. A reasonable term was one consistent with the past dealings of the traders if they had a personal history or, if they did not, then of business customs or practices which they could both be fairly expected to know. *See Cohen & Sons v. Lurie Woolen Co.*, 232 N.Y. 112, 133 N.E 370 (1921).

b. *The U.C.C. reforms:* In a major step designed to facilitate the formation of commercial contracts, the Code has abolished the common law formation rules respecting attempted contracts for the sale of goods. Notwithstanding, there remains an emphasis on both traders having had reasonable opportunity to consent to the same terms, and the ability of a court to form an "appropriate remedy" in the event of breach.

  (1) Under § 2-204(1) there is no emphasis upon the offer as having to impart the content of the essential terms. While it will probably perform that function in the great majority of formation attempts, the Code is satisfied by formation "in any manner sufficient to show agreement, including conduct by both parties which recognizes the existence of such a contract."

  (2) The failure of the parties to identify the content of one or more essential terms by their words or deeds is not fatal under § 2-204(3). ". . .[A] contract for sale does not fail for indefiniteness if the parties have intended to make a contract and there is a reasonably certain basis for giving an appropriate remedy."

c. *The position of the* Restatement, Second: Section 32(2) clearly signals an ambition that the common law evolve in the direction of the U.C.C. reforms. The position of the American Law Institute is that omission by the parties of the content of an essential term need not be fatal ". . if the terms (which can be ascertained from their dealings) provide a basis for determining the existence of a bargain and for giving an appropriate remedy."

d. *Major limitation on the ability of any court to imply a "reasonable term."* Neither the evolving common law nor the U.C.C. is willing to make a better bargain for the parties than they appear to have consciously attempted. Thus a major limitation on the power of a court to imply terms is that, with respect to that subject, the parties must have been entirely silent. If the parties did attempt an overt bargain with respect to that term but did so in a confusing or ambiguous manner, a reasonable term cannot be implied and the bargain fails owing to indefiniteness. *See Goldberg v. City of Santa Clara*, 21 Cal. App. 3d 857, 98 Cal. Rptr. 862 (1971).

(1) Requirement and output contracts are not indefinite. At an early stage of the contact between common law rules and the needs of the business world, courts obtusely refused to find sufficiently definite an agreement which measured the quantity term by the seller's output or the buyer's requirements. The common law has long since abandoned this position and now upholds such bargains, concluding that the quantity term shall be such requirements, if any, as the buyer generates in the. . ."good-faith course of business." If an output term has been selected, the seller does not guarantee any minimum quantity but does pledge all of the output generated in the good-faith course of business.

(2) U.C.C. position: Section 2-306(1) refines the evolved common law view. "A term which measures the quantity by the output of the seller or the requirements of the buyer means such actual output or requirements as may occur in good faith, except that no quantity unreasonably disproportionate to any stated estimate or in the absence of a stated estimate to any normal or otherwise comparable prior output or requirements may be tendered or demanded." In these types of "exclusive dealing" agreements, § 2-306(2) imposes, unless otherwise agreed, an obligation by the seller to use best efforts to supply the goods and by the buyer to use best efforts to promote their sale.

Example: Sperry and Collins enter a written agreement calling upon Collins, a manufacturer whose product line includes natural fiber rope, to supply all of Sperry's requirements for rope until 1994. No express term of this agreement sets an estimate of such requirements, nor does the agreement absolutely pledge Collins to the production of the rope. For the first two years following formation of this bargain, Sperry orders 10,000 feet of rope per month and Collins supplies the goods. In January of the third year, Sperry orders 75,000 feet of rope. Collins refuses to supply this amount and informs Sperry that, owing to the increasing difficulty he is having in locating sources of natural hemp, he will cease production of rope as of June 1. Collins did not breach the agreement by refusing to fill the January order since it was unreasonably disproportionate (exceeding by nearly sevenfold) to the historical dimension of Sperry's pattern of demand. If Collins has made good-faith efforts to sustain production, but a reasonable merchant would no longer continue the effort given the difficulty of acquisition, his determination to cease production is not a breach of the requirements contract with Sperry.

e. *Agreements to agree in the future respecting the content of an essential term:* At common law the attempt by the parties to leave an essential term open but subject to a present promise to agree in the future was too indefinite. No present bargain was formed.

(1) U.C.C. flexibility regarding an "open price" term. As you might suspect, the U.C.C. adopts a more liberal attitude. Under § 2-305 the parties, if they so intend, may form a present contract for sale even though the price is not fixed. They have the following options:

    (a) They may say nothing as to price in which case a court will interpret their mutual silence as consent to trade at a commercially reasonable price.

    (b) They may leave the price to be agreed upon in the future.

    (c) They may assent to have the price fixed by some agreed-upon term setting machinery such as a quotation to appear in the next issue of a designated trade journal.

(2) In the event that the parties opt for the agreement to agree in the future, or to have the term fixed by agreed-upon machinery, a present contract is formed although both traders, and a reviewing court will have to await future events to ascertain the price term.

(3) If the agreed-upon machinery should fail to set the future price, whether formation will be defeated depends upon the earlier intent of the parties. If they intended to form a contract, a court will supply a reasonable price. If they appear not to have intended a contract unless their agreed- upon term setting machinery functioned, there is no contract.

(4) If the original agreement had featured mutual promises to agree on a price term in the future and one of the traders should become disillusioned and seek to frustrate formation by refusing to agree, formation will not be defeated, and a court will imply a reasonable price.

4. **Communication:** The last element of an offer is seldom troublesome. There must be communication of the intention to form a present contract and the essential terms to an intended offeree. Absent communication and knowledge of the offer, the offeree is without power to accept.

Example: Fox dictates the content of a business proposal to her secretary, Tilby. Later that day the typed document is returned for her signature. She signs the document but places it in a hold file on her desk. That evening, Tilby mentions the content of the proposal to Smith, the party named in it as the offeree. Delighted, Smith immediately sends a telegram to Fox accepting the offer. Unfortunately for Smith, there has been no offer, for Fox had taken no steps to place the proposal in a channel of communication.

    a. Performance of an act by one who would otherwise accept an offer to contract in the unilateral mode but is ignorant of the offer cannot form a bargain, for the inadvertent actor is not an offeree.

Example: Hadden advertises in the local newspaper offering a $50 reward for the return of his lost cat, Sgt. Pepper. Barlow, who had not seen the advertisement, finds Sgt. Pepper demanding food at his doorstep. From a name tag he learns the identity of the owner and restores the cat to Hadden. Barlow cannot claim the reward as a matter of contract right. Having no knowledge of the offer, there had been no communication to him. Note that there are two lines of reasoning which are destructive of Barlow's contract status. First that, as to him, there had been no communication and thus no offer by Hadden. The alternative is to admit that an offer was outstanding but to conclude that, without knowledge of its content, Barlow was not an offeree.

b. Indirect, or second tier, communication is effective if the offer was intended for the public. If the offeror had sought to reach the public with her proposal, the fact that a particular member of the public acquired knowledge of the content of the offer by learning of it from one who read or heard the immediate communication does not bar contract formation, should that individual accept the offer.

Example: In the preceding example of the newspaper advertisement by Hadden of a $50 reward for the return of Sgt. Pepper, if Barlow heard of the terms of the proposition from his wife who had read it, and then he discovered and returned the cat, he would be regarded as an "offeree" possessed of knowledge via a second-tier communication of an offer to the public.

D. **Legal Significance of an Offer:** The presence of an offer creates in the offeree the capacity to form a bargain by a timely and effective acceptance.

E. **Duration or Life of an Offer:** The power of the offeree to create a bargain requires that she complete the acceptance before the offer has expired either (1) by its own terms, (2) by operation of law, or (3) by act of the parties.

1. *Expiration or revocation governed by terms of the offer:* An offeror is in complete dominion, not only of the terms upon which he would create contract liability, but also of the time span in which the offeree must act to accept. Thus if he states any expiration date or stipulates any event as revoking the offer, the life of the offer is limited by those terms, no matter how unreasonable. In the absence of some grounds for the doctrine of estoppel, an offeree is powerless to accept an offer subsequent to the term fixed for its expiration or revocation by the offeror.

2. *Duration of an offer which contains no expiration or revocation provision:* If the offeror is silent as to the duration of her offer, it is open for acceptance by the offeree for a reasonable time only.

a. *Computation of a reasonable time:* In any given fact pattern a reasonable time will be determined with reference to the nature of the subject matter and the conditions of the market forming the context of the proposed bargain. The more perishable or seasonable the goods, or the more volatile the market, the shorter will be the reasonable time for the offeree to act.

b. *U.C.C. terminology and concepts:* Section 1-204 of the Code reflects the modern common law view that a reasonable time is a function of the "nature, purpose and circumstances of such action." Subsection (3) introduces and defines the useful term "seasonably." "An action is taken 'seasonably' when it is taken at or within the time agreed or if no time is agreed at or within a reasonable time."

Example #1: On July 10, Purvis offers Oakley a carload of ripe bananas in an unrefrigerated railroad car standing on the Arizona desert. He says nothing concerning the life of his offer. Given the perishable and precarious nature of the goods, Oakley may have a matter of hours only in which to make a "seasonable acceptance."

Example #2: On August 3, Oakley offers Purvis a tray of fifteen one-carat "D flawless" diamonds for $450,000. She says nothing concerning the life of her offer. If we take Ian Fleming seriously, her offer may be open to a seasonable acceptance for a very long time. The goods are imperishable, and the market probably the most stable of any commodity.

3. ***Termination by operation of law:*** An offer which does not provide for its expiration or revocation is open for acceptance during a reasonable time only. This rule is a creation of the common law. In three other circumstances the law also provides for the termination of a previously outstanding offer.

a. *Incapacitation of the offeror:* Death, insanity, or legal incapacity of the offeror revokes any outstanding offer regardless of the offeree's lack of notice or knowledge that any one of these fates has befallen the offeror.

(1) Death, insanity, or legal incapacity of the offeror does not revoke an offer which has been reenforced by an option contract prior to the offeror's loss of capacity.

(2) None of these fates would automatically discharge the obligations of an executory contract formed prior to their occurrence. As will be discussed later, excusable nonperformance would then turn on the question of whether the representatives of the incapacitated trader or his estate could perform the obligations of that contract. They could not if the subject matter was personal.

b. *Destruction of the subject matter prior to an effective acceptance will also revoke the offer by operation of law.*

Example: Baldwin offers to sell his residence to White for $135,000. Before White has acted to accept the offer, Baldwin's house is destroyed by fire. The offer to sell it has been revoked and a postdestruction attempt at acceptance by White would be wholly ineffective.

c. *Supervening illegality of the subject matter:* This is a rather obvious doctrine. If, prior to acceptance, a governmental authority declares dealing in the subject matter illegal, all outstanding offers to accomplish what would now be a violation of the law are revoked.

4. ***Termination by act of the parties:*** At any time prior to acceptance, the offeror is free to revoke the offer. By the same token, if the offeree attempts an acceptance but fails to mirror the terms of the offer, at common law she has blundered into a "rejection/counter-offer" in which case the original offer has been revoked by operation of law and all that remains between the negotiating parties is a dangling counteroffer with respect to the subject matter.

a. *Revocation by the offeror:* Consistent with the proposition that an offeror is in complete control over the terms and circumstances wherein he would expose himself to contract liability, an offer is inherently revocable by the offeror at any time prior to an effective acceptance. And, in what strikes many as a particularly amoral rule, the power of the offeror to revoke by changing his mind and retracting the offer is not disabled by an earlier assurance that the offeree was to have a period of time (i.e.,"ten days") to make up his mind.

(1) Revocation — how accomplished: If, prior to an effective acceptance, the offeror communicates her withdrawal of the offer to the offeree, the offer has been revoked. *See Restatement, Second*, § 42.

(2) Indirect communication effective: Most revocations involve direct communication by the offeror to the offeree. However, there is common law precedent supporting the proposition that if the offeree has acquired reliable information that the offeror has changed his mind and desires to withdraw the offer, there can be no effective acceptance. This result is termed an "indirect revocation." *Dickinson v. Dodds*, 2 Ch. Div. 463 (1876).

(3) Revocation of offers extended to the public: If the offeror has extended an offer to the public at large, a revocation is effective, even to members of the public who do not receive actual notice or indirect knowledge, if the offeror has made reasonable efforts to communicate with the same audience to whom he had extended the original offer. *See Shuey v. United States*, 92 U.S. 73 (1875).

Example #1: On January 29, Peters, a rare book dealer, places an advertisement in the *New York Review of Books* promising to pay $10,000 to anyone who submits a first edition of "The Collected Works of Ibid." On February 5, he places an advertisement of the same type and size in the same publication revoking the offer. On February 7, Harpo, who had read the January 29 advertisement

1

but who had not seen the February 5 issue of the *Review,* sends a first edition by registered mail.

No contract has been formed because the offer has been revoked. The offeror had undertaken reasonable steps to reach the same public audience.

Example #2: Same facts as above except that on February 5, Peters places the notice of revocation in an advertisement in the February issue of *Mechanic's Illustrated.* Harpo, who had not seen the February (or any other) issue of that publication, sends a first edition of "The Collected Works of Ibid" to Peters on February 10. A contract has been formed. There had been no reasonable effort to reach the same audience.

b. *Offers which have been reenforced are not revocable:* As you might expect, there are exceptions to the general rule that an offer is inherently revocable prior to acceptance. Under three circumstances the offer may be "reenforced" and thus irrevocable.

(1) Formation of an option contract: The rationale that an offer may be revoked, notwithstanding the promise or statement by the offeror that the offeree may have time to decide upon an acceptance, is that such a promise is not supported by consideration. Thus a savvy offeree will bargain with the offeror to keep the offer of the potential bargain open for her acceptance.

(a) Option is a distinct contract: The option arrangement takes the form of a distinct, separate contract with its own formation and distinct (though economically nominal) consideration. *See Newberger v. Rifkind,* 29 Cal. App. 3d 1070, 104 Cal. Rptr. 663 (1972).

(b) An offer which has been reenforced by an option contract is irrevocable during the life of the option or, if no time is stated, for a reasonable time. *See Palo Alto Town & Country Village, Inc. v. BBTC Co.,* 11 Cal. 3d 494, 521 P.2d 1097 (1974).

Example: Smith offers to sell her home to Allen for $175,000 stating, "You may have fifteen days to accept this offer." Allen responds: "I will give you $10 if you will promise to hold that offer open for the next fifteen days." Smith accepts the $10 from Allen. Allen has formed an option contract and during the next fifteen days Smith, the homeowner, is without power to revoke the offer of sale on the optioned terms. Note that the option contract contained a separate offer from Allen, an acceptance by Smith and an independent consideration of $10.

(2) An offer which has induced foreseeable reliance on the part of the promisee has become irrevocable. The likelihood that a court will uphold this proposition depends upon the plight of the offeree as

dictated by the terms of the offer, and the opportunity for self-protection by prompt acceptance or formation of an option.

(a) Reenforcement on a theory of reliance where the offer sought performance: If the offer requires formation in what is termed the "unilateral mode," the offeree cannot accept by giving a promise to perform. Only the doing of a requested act or endurance of a stipulated forbearance would constitute acceptance. Yet at common law only the completion of that act or forbearance constitutes acceptance. In the meantime, the offer may be revoked! Section 45 of the *Restatement* seeks to protect the offeree from such revocations by creating an option contract once the offeree tenders or begins the invited pattern of conduct. *Accord Miller v. Dictaphone Corp.*, 334 F.Supp. 840 (D.Or. 1971).

(b) Reenforcement on a reliance theory where the offer sought a promise and not performance: Here there has been a longstanding dispute.

   (i) Many classical common law decisions, while admitting the need to protect an offeree who was attempting to form a unilateral contract by rendering performance, declined to recognize the need to protect an offeree who relied before taking the simple self-protective step of giving the requested promise thus forming the bilateral contract. *See James Baird Co. v. Gimbel Bros, Inc.*, 64 F.2d 344 (2d Cir. 1933).

   (ii) The more recent, and today probably majority, view contends that if it were reasonably foreseeable to the offeror that the offeree would change position in detrimental reliance upon the offer, there is sufficient ground to render the offer irrevocable. *See Drennan v. Star Paving Co.*, 51 Cal.2d 409, 333 P.2d 757 (1958).

   (iii) *Restatement* view: Section 87(2) supports a more modest theory of relief for the offeree. If he has changed position in foreseeable reliance, the *Restatement* would expose the offeror who revoked to such liability as is necessary to avoid injustice. A recovery on this theory may well fall short of vindicating the offeree's expectation interest (placing him in the same position he would have occupied if the contract had been formed and there had been full and timely performance).

(3) Merchant's "firm offer" to buy or sell goods: Under U.C.C. 2-205, a merchant buyer or seller may find her offer irrevocable even though the offeree has not created an option or changed position in foreseeable reliance.

(a) Mechanics of the rule: The terms of the merchant's offer must be firm, meaning that they give express assurance that the offer will be held open. No specific time need be stated. This firm offer must be in writing and signed by the merchant offeror. If the writing containing the firm offer assurance is on a form supplied by the offeree, the firm offer clause must be separately signed by the offeror.

(b) Period of irrevocability: A signed written firm offer by a merchant is irrevocable for the period stated or, if no period is stipulated, for a reasonable time. But in no event may either the stated period of irrevocability or reasonable time exceed three months.

(c) Offeree need not be a merchant: Unlike many of the U.C.C. amendments to the common law which require that both parties to the contract of sale for goods be merchants, under § 2-205, only the offeror need be a merchant trader.

Example: Firo, a dealer in antiques, makes a written offer to Smith to sell her a male puppy from her dog, Rovette's litter. The offer declares that Smith will have ten days to make up her mind. Three days later, Firo telephones Smith and revokes the offer. The revocation is successful. Although all of the requirements of 2-205 appear to have been met, as to puppies Firo is not a "merchant." She deals in antiques, not young canines, and did not represent herself as making a livelihood selling dogs. (U.C.C. § 2-104).

c. *Termination as a consequence of the offeree's response to an outstanding offer:* At common law, an outstanding offer was a fragile legal presence. Rejection by the offeree, or any attempt to vary or add to the terms of the offer in the course of an attempted acceptance, terminated the offer as a matter of law. The U.C.C. has made a major change to the rules respecting attempted acceptances which seek to add terms to the offer, but it has not altered the consequences of a rejection by the offeree.

Example #1: Smith offers to sell her vacation cottage to Hartley for $60,000. Hartley replies with the statement that he is not interested. Fifteen minutes later Hartley sees a picture of Smith's cottage and immediately returns with the news that he "accepts her offer." No bargain is formed. Smith's original offer was terminated as a matter of law the moment it was rejected by Hartley. Thereafter there was nothing for him to accept. His declared desire to purchase the cottage amounts to a counter-offer to buy which the owner, Smith, may accept, reject or ignore.

Example #2: Same facts as above — Smith offers to sell her cottage to Hartley for $60,000. Hartley replies that he will accept the offer provided that Smith will absorb the cost of painting the exterior of the cottage. Clearly, there is no bargain. Hartley's response as offeree did not amount to an acceptance of the terms of Smith's offer.

Of perhaps greater importance, he has triggered the rejection/counter-offer rule [reviewed in the "acceptance" materials]. This means that Smith's original offer to sell has been terminated by operation of law. Should Hartley change his mind and attempt to agree to the precise terms originally offered by Smith, he will not form a bargain. There is no longer any outstanding offer to sell the cottage.

III. **THE ACCEPTANCE: As with the offer, neither common nor statutory law imposes any mandatory words or acts as constituting an acceptance of an offer and formation of a bargain. However, there is a mandatory formula. An acceptance consists of an expression of present, unequivocal, unconditional assent by the offeree to each and every term of the offer. This expression must be communicated to the offeror at a time prior to revocation or termination of the offer. The U.C.C. has made a radical change in the rules respecting the content of an effective assent if the subject matter of the attempted exchange is the sale of goods.**

A. **The Elements of an Effective Acceptance:** The person seeking to accept an offer must be an "offeree"; the content of the offeree's response must express agreement to the terms of the offer within the parameters defined by law; and there must be an effective communication by that person of those terms to the offeror during the life of the offer.

1. *Status as an offeree:* Consistent with the general premise that contract liability is consensual in origin, only a person intended by the offeror may exercise the power inherent in the offer to create a bargain by an effective acceptance. Unlike rights acquired under the terms of an existing contract, the status of offeree may not be assigned.

   a. *Offer extended to the public:* Unless restricted by the terms of the offer, a proposal to form a bargain extended to the public at large may be accepted by any person who has acquired knowledge, directly or indirectly, of the terms of the offer.

   b. *Offer extended to an agent*

   Problems in perspective: In the great majority of cases negotiation takes place between the immediate parties. However, it is not infrequent that individuals seek to expand their negotiating capacity by deputizing others to act in their interest. In legal terminology, such an individual becomes a "principal" and her representative an "agent." If the agent acts within the scope of the instructions laid down by his principal, he is legally invisible. His acts, including the formation of contracts, are those of the absent principal.

   Usually the use of an agent presents no problem, for the agent will disclose his status to the potential offeror and also identity the principal on whose behalf he seeks to contract. Knowing the identity of the principal, the offeror may then decide whether to contract with that absent party. But what if the principal desires to remain unknown? The reasons for such a desire may be many, but a common one is the fear that, should the true identity of the principal be disclosed, the offeror would dramatically increase the cost of doing business! For this reason the late Howard Hughes always sought to deal behind the mask of an agent with an undisclosed principal. Can an offeror who dealt with such an agent complain when she later discovered that she had sold her property to Howard Hughes? It depends.

(1) If the offeror knows that the person to whom she is extending the offer is the agent of another, that agent's principal qualifies as an offeree even though his identity is undisclosed and thus unknown to the offeror.

(a) If the undisclosed principal has used an agent because of subjective knowledge that the offeror would not deal with him were his identity known, some courts have denied the principal the status of an offeree.

(b) Contrary authority recognizes the offeree status of the undisclosed principal, noting that since she knew she was dealing with an agent, the offeror had ample opportunity for self-protection by insisting upon disclosure of the principal's identity or refusing to extend the offer.

(2) Undisclosed agency: If the agency itself is a secret arrangement, as opposed to disclosing the agency but withholding the identity of the principal, the undisclosed principal of an undisclosed agent is not an offeree. The offeror, being unaware of the potential claim by a stranger to offeree status, was deprived of a reasonable opportunity for self-protection.

c. *Offeror's mistake as to identity of offeree*

(1) If the dealing is face to face, an offeror must accept the consequences of his own mistake as to the identity of the offeree. Acceptance by the person to whom the offer was extended forms a bargain unless the other party has subjective knowledge that the offeror has mistaken him for another.

(2) If the dealing was not face to face but conducted through some instrumentality, such as the mails or telecommunications, courts have been more sympathetic to the protest of the offeror that his offer reached the wrong person. If the offeror can demonstrate prejudice should he be held to the bargain and the party erroneously believing herself the offeree has not changed position in reasonable reliance, many courts will permit the offeror to refuse to recognize the acceptance. Here is a clear analogy to the

consequences of a "mechanical miscalculation" reviewed under the topic of unilateral mistake.

2. *Content of the offeree's response:* In order to form a bargain an offeree must express agreement with the terms of the offer within the parameters defined by law.

Problems in perspective: Recall that it is sometimes difficult to determine where an offeror has gone beyond the mere discussion of potential future business to advancing an offer to form a present bargain. Now we make life even more difficult for the offeree, for if an offer has been extended it is a legally fragile route to the offeror's contract liability. If the offeree continues to negotiate for different or additional terms, she risks not only failing to form a bargain but triggering the revocation of the original offer by operation of law. The "mirrored-image" common law rule on an effective acceptance has probably frustrated more attempted bargains than any other. First, let us review its operation and then take note of a major U.C.C. reform if the subject matter of the attempted bargain was the purchase or sale of goods.

3. *The common law's requirement of a mirrored-image acceptance:* At common law the content of an effective acceptance must be a literal mirror-image of the terms of the offer, and only those terms. If the offeree seeks to vary the offer, either by addition, deletion, or substitution of even the most minute change, there was no acceptance. Worse, the attempt is regarded as a "rejection" terminating the outstanding offer and leaving only a counteroffer of the terms as modified by the offeree on the bargaining table. *See Routledge v. Grant*, 4 Bing. 653, 130 Eng. Rep. 920 (1828).

Example: On July 10, Swanson offers to sell an apartment building to Dobbs for $750,000 cash. Dobbs responds, "I will pay $725,000." Dobbs has not only failed to form a bargain, he has triggered the rejection/counteroffer rule. As the original offeree, he no longer has power to create a bargain, for the original offer of a sale at $750,000 has been revoked. If on July 11, Dobbs changes his mind and declares to Swanson, "I accept your offer of July 10, here is $750,000," no contract has been formed. All that exists is a counteroffer to buy the building for that amount.

a. *Rationale for the mirror-image at peril of a rejection/counteroffer rule:* The justification for this extraordinary rule was protection of the offeror. If she made a proposal which was not accepted because the offeree attempted to vary its terms, it was felt that the offeror should be immediately free to propose the transaction to some third person without worry that the original offeree might change his mind and make a mirrored image acceptance. If that had been possible, it would threaten the offeror with having made two contracts respecting the one subject matter!

b. *Common law attempts to limit the application of the rejection/ counteroffer rule:*

(1) Offeree's request that the offeror consider variant terms is not a rejection/counteroffer. If, in response to the offer the offeree makes it clear that he is not rejecting the proposal but, while he contemplates it, requests that the offeror consider variant terms, there has been no acceptance. Such an offeree is in peril of a revocation by the offeror, but if the offeror does not revoke, and the original offer has not been otherwise terminated, it remains open for acceptance on the original terms.

Example: On July 10, Swanson offers to sell an apartment building to Dobbs for $750,000 cash. Dobbs responds: "I will give serious thought to that proposition, but in the meantime would you consider a real estate exchange for the warehouse I own in Biggsville; we could both avoid a substantial amount of federal tax liability."

Dobbs' reply to the offer obviously did not constitute an acceptance. However, because he made it clear to Swanson that he was not rejecting a potential contract on Swanson's terms, there was no rejection/counteroffer. If, twenty-four hours later, Swanson has taken no step to revoke the offer, a statement by Dobbs, "I accept your offer of July 10," is an effective acceptance, being the expression of a present unequivocal, unconditional assent to each and every term of Swanson's original offer.

(2) A response by the offeree which merely makes explicit a term implicit in the offer is not a rejection/counteroffer: The terms of an offer include not only those expressed by the offeror, but also those implied in fact as well as those imposed for policy reasons by operation of law. If, in the course of an attempted acceptance, the offeree makes an explicit articulation of one of these implied terms, she has not varied the terms of the offer and her acceptance forms a bargain.

Example: Primo Car Sales offers to sell a 1980 Corvette to Pam Sparks for $15,000. Sparks replies: "I'll take it. Of course this car is being sold with a warranty of merchantability." Primo refuses her tender of the purchase price, declaring that it no longer is interested in selling the car to her.

Sparks may maintain a cause of action for breach of contract. Not only did her statement not trigger the rejection/counteroffer rule, her response to the offer amounted to an effective acceptance. Her statement merely made explicit a term engrafted by law onto every offer by a merchant seller of goods. *See* U.C.C. 2-314. Unless excluded or modified by explicit language, every offer by a merchant seller of goods carries the implied warranty that the goods are "fit for the ordinary purposes for which such goods are used. . . ."

(3) Revival of the original offer: If, in the wake of a rejection/counteroffer, the offeror remanifests an intention to trade on the terms of the original offer, that offer is once again open to a mirrored image acceptance by the offeree.

Example: In our earlier example of Swanson offering to sell the apartment building to Dobbs, the attempt by Dobbs to vary those terms amounted to a rejection/counteroffer. On July 10, Swanson had offered the building at $750,000 cash. On July 12, Dobbs responded by expressing a willingness to pay $725,000. Now suppose that on July 15, Swanson writes to Dobbs stating: "Cannot reduce my price." Under the objective theory of contract formation, a reasonable person in Dobbs' shoes as offeree would interpret this statement as a remanifestation on the part of the seller, Swanson, of a willingness to sell at $750,000. As such it would "revive" that offer so that a mirrored image, "I accept," statement from Dobbs would form a contract of sale at $750,000. Note that the terms of the sales proposal are now borrowed from the original articulation on July 10.

4. *The offeree's response under the U.C.C.:* The men and women who toil in the marketplace have neither the time nor the inclination to observe the common law expectations respecting the formation of bargains. Indeed, few pay heed to lawyers, who are reckoned an expensive and upsetting step of last resort. Most would rather be stricken with a fatal illness than become a party to litigation. This is the climate for reform in which either people had to change or the law had to be amended. Article 2 amended the law.

Problems in perspective: Most business deals do not evolve in the manner anticipated by the common law. They are handled informally, with writings usually following the fact of agreement and then rarely read. In your contracts class you may spend a good deal of time discussing the "battle of the forms." The invention of printing, followed by photocopying, and most recently of electronic communication has resulted in a society with a capacity to generate writings far greater than its ability to do reading! In this setting, the mirrored image acceptance is probably precluded because the forms sent by both buyer and seller in confirmation of their oral or telephonic agreement contain conflicting fine print neither known nor strongly intended by either party. It is only later, when one of them has become disappointed with the performance of the other, that someone gets the idea to compare these writings and use the discrepancies to deny contract formation. *See McJunkin Corp. v. Mechanicals, Inc.,* 888 F.2d 481, 482 (6th Cir. 1989). Absent reform, the law would then focus on issues which never mattered to the litigants while ignoring the real problems which had defeated their commercial relationship.

The agenda of Article 2 seeks to refocus judicial inquiry from the mechanics of formation familiar to the common law to the question of whether, prior to their disagreement, the merchant parties had — through words, conduct or a combination of both — recognized that they were bound by contract. If they had, it is the task of modern commercial litigation to reconstruct the terms of that bargain and defend the commercially reasonable expectations of the parties who formed it.

a. *The U.C.C. position:* Few provisions of Article 2 have had a more profound impact in altering the common law than § 2-207. And yet it would also be fair to say that no provision of Article 2 has excited more judicial disagreement, nor discordant commentary by text writers and academicians. All agree that the rules stated in § 2-207 are designed to effect important modifications of the common law insistence upon a mirrored image acceptance. In those circumstances in which no bargain would have been formed at common law there will *always* be a bargain. Disagreement surrounds a determination of the terms of that agreement.

(1) Neither the offeror nor the offeree are obliged to assume the risks inherent in formation under 2-207(2): Before we examine the dramatic repeal of the common law rejection/counteroffer rule, let us be clear that neither trader is forced by the U.C.C. to face these brave new possibilities.

(a) Offeree may make an explicit rejection followed by a counteroffer. If the offeree does not wish to be bound by a contract as depicted in the offer but would be willing to deal with the offeror on other terms, she simply responds to the offer by rejecting it and then stating her own proposal. Such a strategy is fully permitted by the Code and is outside the mechanics of 2-207, which are triggered by a "definite and seasonable expression of acceptance. . ."

(b) Offeror may make an "iron-clad offer": An offeror who does not wish to form a contract on any terms other than those of his offer may preempt the ability of the offeree to accept while adding even consistent additional terms (see discussion below). He does this by making an offer which explicitly limits acceptance to the terms of the offer. In the marketplace such proposals are known as "iron-clad" or "take it or leave it" offers. An offeree who attempts acceptance of such an offer while adding different or additional terms is in for a brutal lesson. He forms a contract, but it contains only the terms of the iron clad offer.

(2) Impact of additional or different terms in a purported acceptance of an offer to purchase or sell goods: At common law such a tactic on the part of the offeree would trigger the rejection/counteroffer rule. Under § 2-207(1) this result is repealed by statute. Unless the offeree has clearly conditioned his acceptance upon the offeror's assent to these additional or different terms (in which case the offeror is faced with an explicit rejection and counteroffer) the acceptance creates a bargain! But what are its terms?

(3) Terms of the resulting bargain: Those appear to be governed by the content of § 2-207(2). However, at this point, the drafters have employed what some courts regard as a significant difference in verbal formulation. Section 2-207(1) speaks of "additional or different" terms. Section 2-207(2) refers only to "additional terms." There is a further distinction. Section 2-207 apparently applies to any attempt to form a bargain for the purchase or sale of good. However, the rules on including additional terms contained in 2-207(2) are said to apply only "between merchants."

(4) Fate of additional terms: If the terms contained in the offeree's attempted acceptance vary the offer by seeking to make additions to it, § 2-207(2) decrees that their fate depends upon whether or not they work a "material alteration" in the bargain as framed in the offer.

(a) Consistent additional terms: If the additional terms proposed by the offeree do not work a material alteration of the offer, they are deemed consistent. In such a case, a contract is formed containing the terms of the offer as augmented by the offeree's consistent terms. [U.C.C. § 2-207(2)(b)]

(b) Objection by the offeror: If the offeror objects to the inclusion of consistent additional terms within a "reasonable time," the resulting contract is once again reduced to the terms of the original offer only. [U.C.C. § 2-207(2)(c)]

(c) Inconsistent additional terms are those which work a material alteration in the original offer. Their proposal does not preclude formation of an agreement, but its terms are only those of the original offer. Inconsistent terms proposed by the offeree do *not* enter the bargain unless the offeror expressly assents to their inclusion. [U.C.C. § 2-207 Comment 3.]

(d) Test for consistency: Section 2-207(2) does not define the phrase "materially alter." In practice, courts appear to test the offeree's terms against the content of the offer looking for significant shifts in (1) economic advantage, (2) allocation of the elements of risk inherent in the proposed transaction, or (3) prejudice to remedies which would otherwise apply in the event of breach. If a merchant in the position of the offeror would be surprised or suffer hardship in the event the term or terms added by the offeree were to be included unless she objected, the Comment to § 2-207 suggests that they posed a material alteration.

Example: The Software Link produced a line of multilink software which could be customized by other manufacturers. Step-Saver Data Systems began to purchase copies of a

1

sold to small law and medical offices. The business practice featured Step Saver placing orders on the telephone which were accepted by Software Link. Thereafter the two parties would send confirming memoranda on standard forms. Neither the buyer's nor the seller's confirming forms made any mention of a disclaimer or limitation of warranties. However, the package furnished by Software Link contained what was termed a "box-top license" which declared that the customer had not purchased the software but merely obtained a non-transferrable license. A further provision on the box-top sought to disclaim all express and implied warranties except for a warranty that the disks were free from defects.

Litigation eventually arose over issues of formation and whether the limitation on warranties became a part of the contract. On appeal it was concluded that the tender of the goods in packages which bore the boxtop license and warranty exclusion amounted to an acceptance which had sought to add additional terms. Applying 2-207, the court held that an exclusion of warranties amounted to a material shift in the elements of risk inherent in the transaction and, in the absence of express consent by the offeror, Step-Saver, did not become a term of the resulting contract. *Step-Saver Data Systems, Inc. v. Wyse Technology,* 939 F.2d 91 (3rd Cir. 1991).

(e) Summary: Silence on the part of an offeror faced with a purported acceptance containing consistent additional terms results in a bargain which contains the terms of the offer as augmented by the terms of the acceptance. Silence on the part of an offeror confronted by a purported acceptance containing inconsistent additional terms results in the formation of a bargain containing only the terms of the offer. Note that in either event, the offeror is placed in the dominant position — she will have the contract liability of the offeree on terms which she can dominate!

(5) Fate of "different terms" contained in an attempted expression of acceptance: Here there is major disagreement among those courts which have attempted a judicial implementation of § 2-207.

(a) Equated with additional terms under 2-207(2): Some courts decline to find significance in the language difference between subsections (1) and (2) and, if both parties are merchants, apply the test for "material alteration" in passing on the fate of the offeree's terms. *See In re Marlene Industries Corp. v. Carnac Textiles, Inc.,* 45 N.E.2d 327, 380 N.E.2d 239 (1978).

(b) "Knock-out rule": A rival interpretation of § 2-207 (particularly 2-207(3)) and its official comment have concluded that if the terms of the offer and purported acceptance explicitly contradict one another, they are self-canceling.

Example: In a famous case, the offer specified one performance date while the purported acceptance attempted to change it. The court concluded that neither party's performance date was controlling. The resulting agreement contained no time term, and it was up to the court to salvage the traders' obvious attempt to form a bargain by importing a "commercially reasonable term" to govern the date of performance! This result had been praised and ridiculed in law review comments as the "knock-out rule" or "black-hole theory of contract formation." *See Southern Idaho Pipe & Steel Co. v. Cal-Cut Pipe & Supply, Inc.*, 98 Idaho 495, 567 P.2d 1246 (1977).

(6) Relevance of conduct: Section 2-207(3) may or may not be a persuasive support for the knock-out rule on contradictory terms, but on one major point it seems quite clear. Notwithstanding additions, contradictions or omissions in the writings otherwise relied upon to reconstruct the offer and acceptance, if the conduct of the parties recognizes the existence of a contract, and if a reviewing court can somehow reconstruct the essential terms, then there is contract status.

Example: On August 4, Smith, a wholesaler of oranges, sends the following written proposal to Kraley, the owner of a chain of supermarkets: "Offer you 10,000 crates navel oranges, USDA inspected and graded fruit, price $40,000 f.o.b. Fresno, California." Kraley responds by telegram: "We have a deal; see details in confirmation mailed today." Two days later a written confirmation arrives which agrees with the quantity and price terms but adds an arbitration in lieu of litigation clause in the event of disagreement between the traders. Smith makes no response to this writing. On August 10, Smith places 10,000 crates of oranges at the disposal of an interstate trucking firm with instructions to transport them to Kraley's warehouse in Reno, Nevada. Kraley, disappointed with the quality of the goods, refuses to accept them. When Smith seeks to litigate the dispute, Kraley moves to dismiss the litigation and submit the matter to binding arbitration in Nevada.

The first question to be determined is whether Smith and Kraley have formed a bargain. If the common law governed the issue, the answer would be clearly "no." Kraley's purported acceptance did not mirror the content of Smith's offer. Under U.C.C. 2-207(1), however, it would appear that an acceptance did occur. The test would be whether, viewed reasonably, Kraley's response to the offer amounted to a "definite and seasonable" (timely) expression of acceptance.

The next issue would be the content of that bargain. It is clear that both Kraley and Smith are merchants, as each appears to make his livelihood dealing in the type of goods covered by their bargain. Under 2-207(2) the additional term providing for arbitration as a complete alternative to litigation became part of the contract part of that bargain unless it materially altered the

1

terms of Smith's offer. Note that Smith might have protected himself from this potential consequence by: (1) making an iron-clad, take it or leave it offer, or (2) notifying Kraley that he objected to the arbitration term within a reasonable time after receiving Kraley's confirmation.

Whether an arbitration in lieu of litigation term poses a material alteration is the subject of disagreement among recently decided cases. Clearly, it does not pose a reallocation of the economic advantage envisioned in Smith's offer, nor does it redistribute the elements of risk inherent in the transaction. However, it does clearly affect a remedy which would otherwise be available in the event of breach. The better view appears to be the one articulated in New York, that it *is* "material." If this view were upheld in the Smith/Kraley dispute, the term would not have become part of the resulting contract, and Kraley's application to dismiss the litigation commenced by Smith would have been refused.

Any attempt by either party to deny the formation of a contract predicated upon the disparity in terms between the original offer and purported acceptance would have been twice doomed. First, § 2-207(1) repeals the mirrored image acceptance rule. Second, under § 2-207(3) the conduct of both parties subsequent to the exchange of written communications indicated that they had recognized the existence of a contract. Smith shipped 10,000 crates of navel oranges from California to Nevada. Kraley took delivery, inspected the goods, and objected to their claimed nonconformity. Such conduct is clear evidence that, as merchants, both thought they had "done business."

b. **Reform of § 2-207:** In 1994 drafters of the Uniform Commercial Code proposed a reformed content for Section 2-207. If enacted by a state legislature, the new provision would curtail the reforms worked by the original formulation. Gone is the language about additional or different terms contained in an attempted acceptance. Instead, the new section speaks of "varying terms" contained in a standard form writing and provides that they do not become part of a contract unless the party claiming inclusion proves that the party against whom they operate expressly agreed to the terms or assented to and had notice of the terms from trade usage, previous course of dealing, or course of performance.

B. **Determining the Moment of Formation:** Classical contract analysis envisioned two distinct formation patterns. If the offer and acceptance each contained a promise of performance, the exchange of such promises formed a bargain in the bilateral mode. However, if the offer contained a promise but also specified that the acceptance was to take the form of the offeree's doing of a designated act or enduring a stipulated pattern of forbearance, formation was said to be in the *unilateral mode.* In each instance both decisional law and a volume of commentary have debated the moment of formation. The issue has been the appropriate allocation of the risk that the other party has changed his mind and is attempting to withdraw from the formation process.

1. ***Formation in the bilateral mode:*** A promise standing against a responsive promise creates a bargain in the bilateral mode. We are already familiar with the rule that an offer is inherently revocable at any time prior to acceptance. And, we have just completed a review of the rules which impose a requirement that the terms of the purported acceptance agree with those of the offer. Only the third element remains: the communication of the offeree's assent. This is not a problem if the offeror and offeree deal face to face. But if they deal at a distance, the time consumed by the instrumentalities of communication raises interesting questions of logistics, if not morality.

   a. *The deposited acceptance rule:* In the nineteenth century, persons began to use the mails to conclude bargains. The logistical problem facing the offeree is that once she posts her acceptance she has no way of knowing whether it obtained routine delivery or was the subject of some inordinate delay or loss by the postal authorities. How was this risk to be allocated?

      (1) The common law began from its classical premise that the offeror was in complete control not only of the terms but also of the circumstances in which he would expose himself to contract liability. Thus if he restricted the offeree to a selected channel of communication, and did not take the trouble to make it clear that he would be bound only upon receipt of the acceptance, the rule was announced that the acceptance was effective (meaning the bargain was formed) the moment the offeree entrusted the terms of a mirrored image acceptance to that *authorized* channel of communication. Naturally, it had to be properly addressed with any delivery fees prepaid.

      (2) Concept of implied authorization: In further efforts to render the use of the mails routine and opportune, common law cases recognized that, in the absence of explicit directions or restrictions, the offeree was always impliedly authorized to use, for the purposes of communicating her acceptance, the channel of communication utilized by the offeror in extending the offer. *See Adams v. Lindsell*, 1 B. & Ald 681, 106 Eng. Rep. 250 (K.B. 1818).

      (3) The "mail box rule": In the era when the alternatives were hand delivery or the use of the mails, the rule for facilitating acceptance by the offeree was termed the "mail box rule." Such a rule imposed all risk of delay and loss upon the offeror. If the bargain was formed effective upon mailing the offeree's acceptance, it existed at a time when the offeror did not, and could not, know of this fact!

      (4) Today's "deposited acceptance rule": Modern expansion of the principle of implied authorization has been forced to recognize an

1

increasing array of communication alternatives. If the offer has been extended by the use of a channel of remote communication, the offeree is impliedly authorized to use any *reasonable channel* for communicating her acceptance. If she does, the acceptance is effective upon dispatch.

(a) A "reasonable" channel or mode is judged by criteria of speed and dependability. To be reasonable, the offeree must select a channel which is at least as fast and dependable as the one employed by the offeror.

Example: Jackson extends an offer of Able by telegram. Able uses a fax machine to transmit her acceptance. It is likely that Able has attained the advantage of the deposited acceptance rule, so that her acceptance was effective the moment she initiated the process of transmitting her fax message.

(b) U.C.C. rule: Section 2-206(1) expands the modern concept of implied authorization. "Unless otherwise unambiguously indicated by the language or circumstances an offer to make a contract shall be construed as inviting acceptance in any manner and by any medium reasonable in the circumstances."

Example: Barton uses e-mail to offer to sell Trott one ton of coal for $100. Later that day, Trott sends a fax message accepting the offer. Under 2-206(1) it would appear that the acceptance is effective upon dispatch. The language of the Code does not explicitly declare that the acceptance is effective upon dispatch, but the weight of academic commentary favors that construction.

(c) Rule not available where the offer has been reenforced by an option contract. A majority common law view, supported by the *Restatement*, takes the position that the exercise of an option requires receipt by the option giver of the notice of acceptance within the time optioned.

(5) If the offeree did not use an authorized channel of communication, a bargain may still be formed. However, formation is now delayed until the offeror receives the acceptance. In the meantime, the offer remains revocable.

(6) Self-protective strategies for the offeror: The easiest way for the offeror to protect himself is to stipulate in the offer that he must receive the acceptance by a certain date or else it is not effective. If such a step is taken an acceptance communicated through a reasonable medium which arrives after that date will not form a bargain.

(a) If the offeror explicitly restricts the acceptance to a single mode of communication, use by the offeree of any other medium triggers the common law rejection/counteroffer rule.

(b) Whether this result would obtain in a fact pattern governed by Article 2 of the U.C.C. is unclear. The language of § 2-206(1), "Unless otherwise unambiguously indicated by the language [of the offer]" would suggest that a no-bargain result would be proper.

b. *Silence as acceptance:* Under neither the common law nor the U.C.C. may an offeror impose upon an offeree the risk that her silence in the face of an offer may be treated as an acceptance. But there are exceptions to this rule when, to use the terminology of older cases, the offeree was under a "duty to speak." *See Laredo Natl. Bank v. Gordon,* 61 F.2d 906 (5th Cir. 1932). A modern formulation of the exception would treat the offeree's silence as communicating acceptance when the offeror has a commercially reasonable basis for that conclusion. The "duty to speak" or source of those reasonable expectations may be briefly summarized.

(1) Previous dealings: If the offeror and offeree have a recent history of prior transactions in which the offeree has allowed his silence to be treated as an acceptance, a repetition of the identical offer greeted by the offeree's silence will create a bargain.

(2) Conduct of the offeree in retaining the goods: If an offeree consciously retains goods which were tendered under the terms of an explicit offer, his conduct, coupled with a failure to express any objection to the offer, may be treated as an effective acceptance. *See Austin v. Burge,* 156 Mo. App. 286, 137 S.W. 618 (1911).

(a) Distinguished from quasi-contractual liability: If the offeree's conduct plus a failure to object to the terms of an explicit offer is treated as an effective acceptance, the measure of the offeree's liability is to be found in the terms of the offer. By contrast, if the offeree was not aware of the terms but retained the goods or services of another under circumstances where no gift could be reasonably implied, the liability is in quasi-contract to pay the reasonable value of those goods or services.

(b) Unsolicited goods — a statutory exception: Federal law [39 U.S.C. § 3009] and the statutory law of several of the states contain provisions to the effect that any unsolicited merchandise mailed with a request for payment or a charitable contribution may be treated by the recipient as a gift. In such circumstances, the recipient has no liability to the sender in either contract or quasi-contract.

1

c. *Crossed communications*

(1) Crossed acceptance and revocation: Under the majority view, a revocation by the offeror is only effective upon receipt by the offeree. Thus, if subsequent to the posting of the notice of revocation but prior to its receipt, an offeree who has the benefit of the deposited acceptance rule dispatches his acceptance, a bargain is formed. If the offeree cannot claim the benefit of the deposited acceptance rule, the formation will be achieved or defeated depending upon which communication — the revocation or the acceptance — is first received.

(2) Rejection followed by acceptance: If the offeree's first reaction to an offer is to dispatch a notice of rejection, there is no deposited acceptance rule. Thus if the offeree changes his mind and manages to send an overtaking acceptance which is the first communication received by the offeror, a bargain is formed. However, if the rejection arrives first, a belated acceptance is too late. The offer has been revoked by the received rejection.

(3) Acceptance followed by retraction or repudiation: In these fact patterns the offeree's initial response to the offer is to dispatch a notice of acceptance. Later she changes her mind and attempts to retract or repudiate her acceptance.

(a) If the offeree's acceptance was effective upon dispatch by virtue of the deposited acceptance rule, a bargain is formed. The rationale is that if dispatch has formed the contract, it is too late for either party to unilaterally withdraw.

(b) If the offeree's acceptance would be effective only upon receipt, whether a bargain is formed will again depend upon which communication by the offeree arrives first. If it is the acceptance, a contract is formed and both parties are bound. If the repudiation overtakes the acceptance, formation is avoided.

2. *Formation in the unilateral mode:* Where the offer specifies that acceptance, is to take the form of the performance of some specified act or endurance of some prescribed forbearance, formation is in the unilateral mode. Thus a promise for an responsive act or forbearance creates a bargain in the unilateral mode.

a. *Moment of formation:* The common law rule is that an offer to contract in the unilateral mode, has not been accepted until the designated pattern of behavior or forbearance has been totally completed. The moment the offeree completes performance of the designated act she has accepted the offer, so that only the offeror will now have the duty to carry out the terms of his promise.

b. *Peculiar risks faced by the offeree:* Until the offeree has completed his attempted acceptance he faces the peril that the offer may be revoked at any time prior to acceptance!

Example: In one of the more stunning conjunctions of these rules, a New York court upheld the right of an offeror who had pledged a sum of money if the offeree would walk across the Brooklyn Bridge to revoke the offer when the offeree was half-way across the span!

c. *Rules designed to protect the offeree*

(1) Positive bias of the law in favor of bilateral formation: Unless the offeror is very explicit that acceptance must take the form of an act or forbearance rather than a promise to so act or forbear, a reviewing court will construe the offer as inviting acceptance in the bilateral mode. Under this construction a promise by the offeree that mirrors the offer is an effective acceptance creating the bargain. *See Davis v. Jacoby*, 1 Cal.2d 370, 34 P.2d 1026 (1934).

(2) U.C.C. solution: If the offer is one to buy goods, § 2-206(l)(b) declares that it" shall be construed as inviting acceptance either by a prompt promise to ship or by the prompt or current shipment" of the subject matter. Comment 2 does not state that the U.C.C. abolishes the offeror's election to bargain only in the unilateral mode but comes close to reaching that result.

(3) Offer rendered irrevocable once offeree begins to perform: If the offer clearly contemplates formation in the unilateral mode, an effective means of protecting the interest of the offeree is found in the modern common law rule that once the offeree begins to perform (as opposed to merely preparing to begin performance) the contract is not formed, but the power of the offeror to revoke is suspended so as to afford the offeree a reasonable opportunity to complete the performance and form the bargain. Two theoretical lines of reasoning support this result.

(a) Equitable estoppel: The most concise explanation for prohibiting the offeror from revoking in the face of the offeree's attempted performance is that the hardship imposed on the offeree would make such a result inequitable.

(b) Implied promise not to revoke: The view of the *Restatement, Second,* reflecting what may be the majority of cases, is that the undertaking of performance by the offeree creates an implied option. There is an implied offer not to revoke for a reasonable time which is accepted by the offeree's commencement of performance.

d. *Risks to the offeror who elects to bargain in the unilateral mode:* While most of the attention is focused upon the offeree's risk that the offer will be revoked, election of this formation strategy also imposes peril upon the offeror.

    (1) Offeree who commences performance is not bound to complete it: A consequence of the cardinal rule that formation takes place only upon completion of the offeree's performance is that an offeree who begins the act or forbearance necessary to accept is not legally bound to persist. If he undergoes a change of heart he may abandon the effort and the offeror may not complain. If the offeror desired to have the parties bound at the promise stage, she should have elected to bargain in the bilateral mode.

    (2) The "unilateral contract trick": What if an offeree appears to complete the requested act only to have it discovered that his goods or services were defective, failing to meet the reasonable expectations of the offeror? Is such an offeree in breach? At common law there are cases which reach a negative answer, contending that in such circumstances there was merely a defective acceptance which defeated formation of the bargain!

  e. *Notice to the offeror:* In theory, formation of a contract in the unilateral mode was accomplished with the completion by the offeree of the specified act or pattern of forbearance. As a consequence, notice to the offeror of this accomplishment was unnecessary.

    (1) Power of offeror to protect self: An offeror who desired notification as well as performance was deemed able to protect herself by either contracting in the bilateral mode or by making the giving of notice a part of the offeree's act of acceptance.

    (2) Notice of completed performance at peril of discharging the offeror's promissory obligation under an implied condition subsequent: This rather baroque doctrine preserved the major premises of unilateral formation, but placed the giving of notice to the offeror in the self-interest of the offeree. If the offeror was unlikely to be in a position to acquire independent knowledge of the offeree's acceptance and the offeree as a reasonable person should have realized this, then the failure to give such notice triggered an implied in-fact- condition subsequent. A contract had been formed, but the promissory obligations of the offeror would be discharged.

  f. *U.C.C. solutions:* The ability of the offeree to disappoint the expectations of the offeror and then avoid liability by claiming defective formation and the issue of when notice of performance is required are both addressed in § 2-206.

    (1) If the seller reacts to the buyer's offer to purchase goods by sending goods which fail to meet the buyer's reasonable expectations, the seller has both accepted the offer and breached the resulting bargain. [U.C.C. § 2-206(1)(b)]

(2) This result can be avoided by the seller if at the time he ships nonconforming goods, he notifies the seller that the shipment does not conform to the terms of the offer but is being offered merely as an accommodation to the buyer. The buyer is under no obligation to accept such goods, but if he does not the seller is not in breach.

(3) An offeree who elects to begin performance as a mode of acceptance must notify the offeror within a "reasonable time" of such commenced effort, or else the offeror may treat her offer as having lapsed before acceptance.

IV. THE IMPACT OF AMBIGUITY AND MISTAKE AS POTENTIALLY PRECLUDING THE FORMATION OF A BARGAIN: Assuming the presence of an offer and an effective and timely acceptance, it would appear that the parties have formed a bargain. If that bargain contains elements of legal detriment on both sides of the exchange, qualification for contract status would appear assured. It may not be so. There are two important doctrines which, if established, may defeat the contention that a bargain has been formed. If there was no bargain, there could be no contract.

1

THE IMPACT OF AMBIGUITY AND MISTAKE AS POTENTIALLY PRECLUDING THE FORMATION OF A BARGAIN

The doctrines are: (1) ambiguity of the language employed in framing the terms of the apparent bargain, and (2) a mistake by either or both of the traders in giving what appears to be assent to formation. There is also potential danger from the mistakes of third-party intermediaries who have undertaken communication tasks for the parties in attempting to form the bargain. Note that the presence of these factors *may* defeat formation. As you will soon see, it is not every instance of ambiguity of language or mistake which, given the modern pro-formation bias of statutory and common law, can defeat the expectations growing out of a bargain.

A. **Ambiguity — When Language Betrays:** If a word or phrase used by the parties to identify a term of their bargain is susceptible to more than one reasonable meaning or interpretation and the parties subjectively attached divergent meanings, their bargain is plagued by misunderstanding occasioned by ambiguity.

Problems in perspective: John Steinbeck put a relatively less serious aspect of the problem neatly in *The Grapes of Wrath:*

"I knowed you wasn't Oklahomy folks. You talk queer kinda—That ain't no blame, you understan'.

Ever'body says words different," said Ivy, "Arkansas folks says 'em different, and Oklahomy folks says 'em different. And we seen a lady from Massachusetts, an' she said 'em differentest of all. Couldn't hardly make out what she was sayin."

More vexing, even among "Oklahomy folks", is that the words they use have multiple meanings. It is said that the English language contains the largest vocabulary of any system of communication devised by humankind. Thus between or among English speakers, meaning is shaded more by the selection of words rather than the tone of voice or accompanying facial or hand gestures. These traits are of substantial advantage to persons desiring to conduct business at a distance — employing the written word. But they also contain a pitfall. In addition to problems of pronunciation or accents, local usage may emphasize one definition for a word in Boston which is not commonly associated with that word in Baton Rouge.

Even within Boston, persons who toil in a given trade or market may give artful meaning to words which would elude the understanding of a local who lacked such exposure or experience. Consider that the word "dry" may have one dominant meaning to a bartender, another to a cleaner, and yet another to a person who follows neither trade or calling.

1. *Impact of ambiguity in the language of the bargain:* The modern rule is both simply stated and understood. It is derived from the need of the court to be able to reconstruct the essential terms of the bargain and the goal of that tribunal to protect the commercially reasonable expectations of the parties. Thus if the ambiguity goes to an essential term of the exchange, and each party — having attached a different meaning — had developed equally reasonable expectations, the resulting misunderstanding is fatal to formation.

    a. *Irreconcilable and equally reasonable expectations of the parties defeat formation of a bargain because an essential term is now missing.*

    b. *Court forbidden to overcome omission by implication of a reasonable term:* One might anticipate that a modern court would seek to overcome this barrier to formation by the implication of some commercially reasonable term. The reason it will not is that to do so would make a bargain for the parties other than the one which they had attempted. Total silence of the parties is regarded as evidence of consent to trade on a commercially reasonable term. Here, however, the parties have spoken and, with evidence of their divergent interpretations now before us, we recognize that each attempted a tailored content of the disputed term.

2. *Ambiguity classified as "latent" or "patent":* The classical common law developed a potentially useful classification of ambiguity problems depending upon whether the potential of more than one reasonable meaning or interpretation was hidden from the parties at the time of formation or obvious at that crucial juncture.

    a. *Latent ambiguity:* If, at the formation stage of offer and acceptance, the parties employ a term unaware that it is susceptible to more than one reasonable meaning and each attaches a different meaning in developing personal expectations, the bargain is flawed by latent — hidden — ambiguity. If the two are equally blameless in falling into this trap, the latent ambiguity is fatal to formation. By definition a reviewing court would have no rational basis for preferring the expectations of the innocent buyer to those of the equally innocent seller.

b. *Patent ambiguity:* Here the application of more than one reasonable meaning to a term employed in the bargain is obvious to both parties. If each has attached a different subjective interpretation in forming personal expectations, the flaw is again fatal, but for a very different reason. Here a reviewing court is without a rational basis to uphold the personal expectation of the careless buyer over those of the equally slovenly seller.

c. *One party at fault:* If, at the formation stage, one of the parties (let us say, the offeror) is aware that one of the terms of her offer has more than one reasonable meaning, while the offeree is innocent of such appreciation, the ambiguity is not fatal.

   (1) If the knowing offeror is subjectively aware that the offeree's innocent interpretation differs from the one she intends, formation is accomplished. It is achieved by giving the ambiguous word or term that meaning which the innocent party attached and which the knowing party knew he attached. *Restatement, Second*, § 20.

   (2) If the knowing offeror employs without definition a term or word which has more than one reasonable meaning, and makes no inquiry of the intention or state of mind of the offeree, the "fault" of the offeror is less dramatically present. It consists in failing to act upon a recognized opportunity to preclude confusion. A court intent upon the formulation of rules which would make it in the self-interest of parties to clear up such realized opportunities would hold the offeror bound to the interpretation given by the nonalerted and thus innocent offeree. The notion that, as between the two, it is the party who deliberately or negligently failed to prevent the harm who should bear the consequences is cardinal to the civil law.

d. *Role of the "reasonable person":* A party who subjectively selects a term known to have more than one reasonable meaning and then declines to specify a definition is obviously "at fault." But what if the offeror did not know, but a reasonable person in her circumstances would have appreciated, the presence of multiple restorable interpretations of the words selected in framing the bargain? Modern courts regard this as an actionable specie of negligence and will impute the knowledge and skill of that restorable person to the party who should have known. Such a view is supported by § 20 of the *Restatement, Second*.

e. *The status of the novice trader:* The application of the skill and knowledge of a "reasonable person" is a neutral principle of modern contract interpretation. Both parties in a contract dispute are expected to bring their level of performance up to this standard. Thus a word or term with a common meaning in society may take on a very special and artful meaning within a certain trade, market, or profession. What is the fair expectation of the novice trader who is attempting his first deal? If he employs the common understanding while apparently assenting to a term with an artful, and very different, meaning to nonnovice traders, is he "at fault?"

(1) **Disclosed or undisclosed status:** The answer to this question has been held by some courts to turn upon the disclosed or undisclosed novice status of the uninformed party.

(a) If he has informed the other trader, or that party has knowledge, of the novice status prior to or contemporaneous with the formation of the bargain, the ability of the experienced trader to reasonably assume knowledge and skill has been undermined.

(b) But if that factor is unknown to and hidden from the experienced trader, then it would appear that she is reasonable in assuming the competence of the other party to avoid misunderstanding. An after-the-fact disclosure that "this was my very first deal" is too late to influence the formation process.

(2) **Notorious or nonnotorious usage:** A means of dividing the risk of novice status is to hold that on the day he enters the marketplace a novice is charged with knowledge of those terms, customs, or usages which are notorious. But, if his status is known or disclosed, the novice may be forgiven ignorance of nonnotorious factors which may produce misunderstanding.

f. *Burden of proof:* One key to understanding many of the cases which confront misunderstanding generated by the ambiguity of language is that a party seeking to recover for breach of contract has the burden of proof in establishing both formation and breach. Faced with a defense of a claimed different understanding, the plaintiff must prove that: (1) there was no subjective misunderstanding; or (2) if there was, the defendant was at fault because his claimed understanding was not "reasonable," there being only one reasonable meaning to the disputed term; or (3) the defendant was responsible for failing to preclude the misunderstanding which subsequently developed while plaintiff had no such opportunity. If the traders are equally innocent, or equally at fault, neither can sustain this burden.

g. *U.C.C. provisions:* No provision of Article 1 on general terms, nor of Article 2 on sales, directly addresses the topic of misunderstanding resulting from ambiguous language. However, § 1-205 (Course of Dealing and Usage of Trade) and § 2-208 (Course of Performance or Practical Construction) would be used by a court to determine the scope of reasonable behavior if the attempted bargain involved the sale of goods.

(1) These Code sections emphasize that previous conduct between the parties may be used as a common basis of understanding in interpreting the words of the parties.

(2) Usage of trade must be proven as with any other fact. The litigant advancing a trade custom must prove that a practice of method of dealing had achieved such regularity of observance in a place, vocation, or trade as to justify the expectation that, in the absence of an expression of contrary intent, it would be observed.

(3) If there is conflict between course of dealing and usage of trade, the course of dealing — representing the specific history of these parties — governs. Express terms of the bargain control either.

(4) Finally, under § 2-208(3), a course of performance may be used to show that subsequent to formation, one party became aware of the misunderstanding and the interpretation being given by the other and acted in such a manner as to acquiesce. Such behavior would be taken as a *waiver* or *modification* of the term or a dispute as to its meaning.

> **Example #1:** In June, Jones, an importer of cotton, enters a written contract with Farlow, a wholesaler of the same product. The subject matter of their agreement is described as: "40,000 bales No. 1 grade Surat cotton, *'ex Peerless.'*" Unknown to either Jones or Farlow, there are two vessels plying the cotton trade between India and Liverpool, each bearing the registration "*Peerless.*" When he assented to the written text, Jones intended the only *Peerless* within his knowledge, a vessel anticipated sailing from India in December. By the same token, Farlow, also ignorant of the double registry problem, intended the only *Peerless* known to him — a transport vessel departing from India in October.
>
> Their misunderstanding becomes evident months later when the *Peerless* anticipated by Farlow, the buyer, arrived bearing in its cargo manifest Surat cotton. The seller, Jones, refused to tender that cotton contending that it was not the cargo he had intended to sell. The buyer then commenced an action for a loss of bargain recovery of money damages only to be met by the seller's claim that the buyer had, in the meantime, refused to take delivery of the cotton tendered from the cargo of the December *Peerless*. In *Raffles v. Wichelhaus,* 159 Eng. Rep. 375 (Ex. 1864), the court accepted these facts as establishing fatal latent, hidden, ambiguity. It was obvious that at the time they attempted to form the bargain, neither trader had actual knowledge of the dual registration and consequent potential for misunderstanding resulting from their use of the term *"ex Peerless."*
>
> In 1864 the concept of the imputed knowledge of a reasonable trader had not yet been deployed in the effort to salvage attempted bargains and was not addressed by the court. Were that problem to recur in modern litigation, the result would be the same unless the

1

buyer could convince the court that the seller's interpretation was unreasonable.

Example #2: A Swiss buyer, acting for an ultimate purchaser on the wrong side of the Iron Curtain during the depth of the Cold War, sought to purchase an apt subject matter from a New York seller: frozen chickens. The deal, encompassing two sales, was to be the seller's first venture into the frozen poultry market. The two sales were each reflected in written agreements which described the goods as: "US Fresh Frozen Chicken, Grade A, Government Inspected, Eviscerated." Quantity, price, and shipment terms were then specified.

The dispute arose when the buyer objected that a large quantity of the chickens tendered by the seller consisted of stewing hens. The buyer asserted that when it consented to the use of the word "chicken" it intended that only birds suitable for broiling or frying would conform to the contract description. The seller replied that it understood a "chicken" to include stewing chickens. When the plaintiff commenced an action for breach of the contract, defendant produced witnesses who testified that a "chicken is everything except a goose, a duck, and a turkey."

In *Frigaliment Importing Co. v. B.N.S. International Sales Corp.*, 190 F. Supp. 116 (S.D.N.Y. 1960), the court rejected the buyer's claim of breach, concluding that it had failed to sustain the burden of proof that when the parties employed the term "chicken" they did so in the narrower sense. Among the points deemed important was the fact that each contract called for a selection of birds weighing under two pounds as well as those in a two-to-three pound range. It was proven to have been commercially impossible for the seller to have obtained younger birds in the larger weight range at a price which permitted it to break even, let alone realize a profit, given the contract's price terms. Only elderly matriarchs — the stewing hens submitted by the seller — could meet both the contract language and the economic realities. In a case ultimately turning on commercially reasonable expectations, the court found it manifestly unreasonable for the buyer to expect the seller to absorb a loss on each sale!

The court admitted the relevance of trade custom and usage but noted that the seller's neophyte status was well known to the buyer at the formation stage, and the narrower meaning of the term "chicken" within the relevant market had not been proven notorious.

In the final analysis, whether deemed latent or patent, the plaintiff buyer had failed to convince the court that it had the only commercially reasonable expectation in the transaction. The nature of the litigation did not force the court to sustain the seller's interpretation of "chicken," only to turn aside the buyer's contention that it was, in the total context of the transaction, unreasonable.

B. Mistake: In mistake fact patterns the problem is not that the words used by the parties are ambiguous, but rather that they do not convey the subjective intent which would have been entertained but for a mistake by either or both of the traders. In another variation, the mistake is committed by some third party who has attempted communication services that ought to have facilitated rather than sabotaged the process of formation. Do such mistakes preclude the formation of a bargain? The law's answer is an unequivocal "perhaps."

1. ***Mistakes of the parties:*** The common law has long distinguished between those fact patterns in which both traders are mistaken and those that feature the blunder of one party only. With respect to unilateral blunders, a distinction is drawn between "mechanical miscalculations" which may provide a defense to formation or enforcement of the terms of the resulting bargain, and "errors in business judgment" which never preclude the formation of what may prove a disastrous but perfectly binding obligation.

   a. *Mutual mistake:* While these fact patterns are relatively rare, they generally involve a mistaken assumption of fact by both traders at the formation stage. Two factors govern judicial reaction to such fact patterns: the significance of the mutual error, and the point in time at which it is discovered.

      (1) Mutual mistake must negate a basic assumption of both traders: If the erroneously assumed fact is basic, going to the " very heart of their exchange," each party may invoke it as a basis for avoiding the obligations of the fatally flawed bargain. *Restatement, Second,* § 152.

         (a) Mistake can only relate to an existing fact, not future or unknowable conditions or events: Mistakes of fact are committed at the formation stage; they may not be created by subsequent developments. A party may mistake a present fact, but she can only predict the future. A blunder in guessing at the future is never ground for relief.

         (b) Earlier decisions attempted to convey the same idea by insisting that the mutual mistake had to go to the "essence of the subject matter," as opposed to some "collateral quality." Supplanting this formulation with the term "basic assumption" has permitted courts to also grant relief in fact patterns in which the mutual mistake did not regard the nature of the subject but rather the use to which it might be put by the owner.

         Example #1: Buyer and seller form a bargain for the sale of a cow assumed to be sterile for a price which reflected a slaughter value only. Unknown to either, the cow was fertile and, given distinguished bovine lineage, had a true market value some ten times more than the agreed-upon price. If the cow's fertility is

1 ▶

detected while the bargain is still executory (meaning that neither party has performed on the mutual promises to surrender the animal and pay the purchase price), either can avoid its obligations by invoking the doctrine of mutual mistake. Here is the classical case of a mutual mistake going to the very essence of the subject matter. The cow which both parties thought was involved in the sale — a sterile animal — did not exist. *See Sherwood v. Walker*, 66 Mich. 568, 33 N. W. 919 (1887).

Example #2: Fox, a New York art dealer, forms a bargain with Catron, an art collector known to reside in Canada for the sale and purchase of *Olympos and Marsyas,* a work of the seveneenth-century French master Nicolas Poussin. On the date this bargain is formed, the canvas is located in Paris, where Fox had purchased it from a French owner. Unknown to either Fox or Catron, on the very day they conclude their bargain the French Minister of Culture forbids the export of any work of art created in France prior to 1900. The goal of the government action is to protect the patrimony of France.

Such a development while the contract is still wholly executory (Catron has not paid the purchase price, nor has Fox surrendered possession of the Poussin) contravenes a basic assumption of fact by both traders: that the owner would be able to remove the subject matter from France. Unlike the example of the nonsterile cow, the mutual mistake did not go to the subject matter per se, but rather to a basic assumption which motivated the parties to deal in the subject matter. Under the modern formulation of the mutual mistake doctrine, either trader could avoid the obligations of their bargain.

(c) One party must not have assumed the risk: If, at the formation stage, the parties entertained doubt as to the fertility of the cow, or the ability to remove an old master from France, the doctrine of mutual mistake would not apply. In such circumstances the risk factor was appreciated. Failure to provide for the bearing of an anticipated risk amounts to its assumption by the party adversely affected. *Restatement, Second*, § 154.

(d) Mutual mistakes of minor consequence are legally irrelevant: If the mutual mistake of assumed fact does not violate a fundamental assumption of both parties regarding either the subject matter or rights of the owner, it is not a threat to the bargain which continues to bind both traders.

(2) Barriers to relief if the mutual mistake is not unmasked while the bargain is still executory: If the terms of the bargain predicated upon a mutual mistake have been fully performed, courts are most reluctant to entertain a cause of action seeking rescission and

restitution. In such circumstances, relief can no longer be claimed as a matter of right, but lies within the discretion of equity.

(a) Equity of rescission: In addition to having to prove the elements of an actionable mutual mistake, a party seeking to overturn an executed contract must be prepared to prove that the mistake was discovered within a reasonable time following execution of the contract and that both traders can now be returned to the preagreement status quo.

Example: Smedly, a collector of art deco pottery, enters into an agreement with Fox, the owner of what both suppose to be a tea service by the famous English potter, Shelly. The year is 1985, the height of the art deco craze among pottery collectors. Five years after payment of the purchase price and delivery of the tea service, Smedly discovers that the set is not an original, but a clever copy done in the 1950s.

If Smedly seeks an equity of rescission he will have little difficulty demonstrating that the original bargain was infected with a mutual mistake which went to the essence of their exchange. But since that agreement has long been executed, he will have to demonstrate that he discovered the true nature of the tea service within a "reasonable time" (a period during which a reasonable person would have discovered the true facts), and be able to return the innocent seller, Fox, to the preagreement status quo. If the tea service had been exposed to wear and tear, this would no longer be possible. More problematic, if the intervening five years had witnessed a substantial decline in the public fancy for art deco objects, even the return of the tea service in its precise former condition would not restore Fox to the position he held in 1985. *See Leaf v. International Galleries*, 1 All Eng. Rep. 693 (Court of Appeal, 1950).

b. *Unilateral blunders:* If, at the formation stage, only one of the parties is mistaken with respect to material facts concerning the bargain, there is no immediate threat to formation. However, depending upon whether the other party has formed a reasonable expectation, the blundering party may be able to invoke a defense to enforcement of the mistaken terms. But before he can get to the threshold of this relief doctrine, his blunder must survive a vital classification. Unilateral blunders are either ***mechanical miscalculations*** or ***errors of judgment***.

(1) Mechanical miscalculations: If, at the formation stage, a party's intention is deceived by an error in reckoning the terms of the obligation, the bargain that results is not the one which, but for the miscalculation, would have been intended. Typical examples involve a bidder who makes an error in math, misreads plans or specifications, or fails to carry a decimal point. Does such a

1

miscalculation preclude formation or provide a defense to enforcing the terms of the resulting bargain? It depends upon the state of mind of the other, the nonmistaken party.

(a) If the nonmistaken party has formed a commercially reasonable expectation upon the terms to which the blundering party apparently consented, the blundering party is bound. Remember that a cardinal principle of modern contract law aims to protect the commercially reasonable expectations of the parties. *Panco v. Rogers,* 19 N.J. Super. 12, 87 A.2d 770 (1952). But this principle does not require that the law sanction the behavior of a party who would leap on what he knows, or as a reasonable person ought to know, was the miscalculation of another.

(b) Test for commercially reasonable expectation is objective: In order to qualify as possessing such an expectation, the nonmistaken party must have been subjectively unaware that the bargain with the other trader was too good to be true. But there is more — a reasonable person, standing in the shoes of the non mistaken party, must also have been unaware of the presence of a miscalculation infecting the assent of the blundering party.

(c) More demanding standard of nonawareness demanded of government in public sector bargains: If the bargain is formed between a governmental entity and a private party, numerous decisions have recognized that the government is precluded from claiming the benefits of a bargain predicated upon a mechanical miscalculation of the private party if: (1) the agent of the government had subjective awareness of the presence of such a blunder; (2) a reasonable person standing in the shoes of the government agent would have recognized the presence of the blunder; or (3) though unable to detect *the* blunder, a reasonable person acting for the government would have suspected the presence of *some* blunder. In the last instance — which does not seem to be an element of private sector mistake cases — the government is said to have a duty to inquire of the private party, seeking confirmation of the terms. If they are repeated, a contract may be formed. *See Alabama Shirt & Trouser Co. v. United States*, 121 Ct. Cl. 313 (1952).

(d) Where the nonmistaken trader does not have a commercially reasonable expectation, the party guilty of the mechanical miscalculation may avoid liability on the mistaken terms. Some courts term a mechanical miscalculation known or discoverable by a reasonable person a "palpable mistake." The label suggests a mechanical miscalculation made in circumstances in which the blundering party may claim relief.

(i) Where the mechanical miscalculation is discovered while the bargain is still wholly executory, some courts treat it as a bar to formation.

(ii) Other courts admit formation but then give the blundering party a personal defense (discussed in greater detail under the topic of "defenses") to the enforcement of the mistaken obligation.

(iii) If the contract is no longer wholly executory, meaning that there has been performance of some or all of its obligations, the ability of the mechanically blundering party to claim relief at the hands of the trader who knew or should have known depends upon the aptitude of the court in devising an appropriate remedy. As the Court of Claims put it, ". . .can the eggs be unscrambled?" *Chernick v. United States,* 372 F.2d 492 (Ct. Cl. 1967).

(iv) If the non-mistaken party is guilty of attempting to prevent the blundering trader from discovering the miscalculation, the blundering party may have equitable reformation of the resulting bargain even if it has been fully executed. *Stare v. Tate,* 21 Cal. App. 3d 432, 98 Cal. Rptr. 264 (1971).

(e) Limited hardship relief in equity even when the other party has formed a commercially reasonable expectation: If the consequences of the mechanical miscalculation threaten the blundering party with disastrous economic consequences, some equity courts have permitted an equity of rescission provided that the blundering party can establish all of the following elements:

(i) The miscalculation must have been the product of ordinary, as opposed to gross negligence;

(ii) It must have been discovered within a reasonable time following commission and thereafter promptly communicated to the other party;

(iii) It must threaten the blundering party with very serious adverse consequences; and

(iv) Notice to the nonmistaken party must be given before she has changed position in good-faith reliance on the stated terms.

(2) Errors of business judgment: A trader guilty of an error in business judgment will encounter courts deaf to any plea for relief.

Problems in perspective: If you think about it, the reason many persons get up on cold mornings, slip on their socks and venture into the marketplace is the hope of catching some booby making an error in business judgment. If, in the exercise of hindsight, every stupid deal could be recalled, the economic system upon which we have come to depend would cease to function.

(a) **Distinguished from mechanical miscalculation:** The Supreme Court of California justified the distinction between, and differing judicial treatment of the two species of, unilateral mistake, as follows. "Where a person is denied relief because of an error in judgment, the agreement which is enforced is the one he [stupidly] intended to make, whereas, if he is denied relief from a clerical error, he is forced to perform an agreement he had no intention of making." *M.F. Kemper Construction Co. v. City of Los Angeles*, 37 Cal. 2d 696, 235 P.2d 7 (1951).

(b) Knowledge of the nonmistaken party that the other trader has made an error in business judgment is no barrier to the binding nature of the resulting bargain.

Example: Stimpson, an art dealer, enters an executory bargain to purchase a painting from the inventory of another art dealer, Samuels. Samuels asks $50,000 for the painting. Stimpson immediately accepts, promising to pay that sum. As he is forming the bargain, Stimpson is aware that the painting has a market value of $200,000.

Samuels is bound. The bargain he made is the one he stupidly intended. He is guilty of an error in reckoning value — the classical business judgment.

2. ***Mistakes of third-party intermediaries:*** If, at the formation stage, one party employs some intermediary to handle communication of the offer or acceptance, the potential for mistake is broadened to include those of the intermediary. The rules governing the consequences of such blunders are identical to those which determined the fate of a party who had made a mechanical miscalculation. Whether it provides a bar to formation or defense to enforcement of the terms actually communicated will turn upon whether the recipient of such a message has developed a reasonable expectation.

a. *If the recipient knows, or as a reasonable person ought to know, that the message cannot be accurate, he has no reasonable expectation predicated on its content:* In such circumstances, the sender may avoid liability on the terms communicated by either denying that a bargain was objectively formed, or by claiming a personal defense against its obligations.

b. *If the recipient has formed an innocent and reasonable expectation, the sender is bound by the terms communicated.*

(1) The rationales for this liability conclusion range from the notion that the intermediary is an agent of the sender to the more satisfactory explanation that, as between the two innocent parties, the sender should bear the loss since he selected the intermediary, had the only real opportunity to take steps to minimize the likelihood of error, and was in a position to take out insurance against such a blunder. The recipient, lacking any of these advantages or opportunities, is to be protected if she has developed a reasonable expectation.

(2) Sender to have cause of action against intermediary for breach of the implied or express terms of the contract of transmission: In theory, the liability of a blundering intermediary should hold the sender harmless in the event he is exposed to a contract with the recipient of his communication on the terms communicated. In reality, if the intermediary is a common carrier, such as a telegraph company, there is probably a limitation on the liability of the firm. The reason such limitations pass public policy muster is solicitude for the huge volume of transmissions which the needs of society impose and the necessity to keep costs to a minimum. If the intermediary was exposed to consequential damages one court has speculated that it would become a reader rather than a transmitter of other people's business! *Kerr S.S. Co. v. Radio Corporation of America*, 245 N. Y. 284, 157 N.E. 140 (1927).

THE QUALITIES OF A
CONTRACTUAL RELATIONSHIP

▶ **CHAPTER SUMMARY**

THE QUALITIES OF A CONTRACTUAL RELATIONSHIP

Scope: Private individuals may form agreements (bargains), but a contract is a legal status. Whether that status has been achieved is dependent upon two factors: the presence of bargained-for legal detriment on both sides of the exchange, and the absence of any real defenses which would preclude formation. In this chapter we deal with the first of these qualities: bargained-for legal detriment, better known by the less revealing label "valuable consideration."

Problems in perspective: As we shall shortly discover, a contract is a promise or set of promises which the law will enforce, sometimes specifically, but usually by an award of money damages. Naturally, before either remedy may be pursued, the promise must have been breached — broken. Personal experience suggests that many, if not most, broken promises do not attract such remedies. The reason is that they were either not given by a promisor bound to a contractual relationship, or the aggrieved party lacked the motive or resources to litigate. In this chapter we will first distinguish those promises destined for contract status from those which are not. We will then explore some of the major misconceptions about bargains in our society. Most troubling will be the persistent expectation that courts are interested in promoting some concept of "fairness" in the economic consequences of the exchange. If you have encountered the "peppercorn theory of consideration," you have been warned that it is not so. Not only is there no general requirement for a "square deal," but the parties need not be bound to the same legal extent. Is there anything objectionable to a bargain which obligates the seller to perform for a year but allows the buyer to cancel the entire arrangement on five days' written notice? Maximum freedom in the marketplace requires negative answers to such questions, but there is a boundary, and promises beyond that point are meaningless to the law.

Key terminology: Most opportunities for confusion in this area can be precluded by mastery of three terms which recur in both judicial opinions and commentary.

Want of consideration: A defense to the formation of a contract. If, at the formation stage, one of the parties does not incur any element of bargained-for legal detriment, the other trader may point to this fatal flaw as precluding contract formation. A synonym used in older cases is "want of mutuality of obligation."

Failure of consideration: A personal defense available to a party who has suffered a present material breach at the hands of the other trader. A failure of consideration fact pattern thus admits the formation of a contract but is centered on the subsequent material breach by the other party of a promise which had the quality of bargained-for legal detriment.

Inadequacy of consideration: Involves the belated recognition that a promisor made a stupid deal. Aside from the unusual context of a bargain formed by parties within a fiduciary or confidential relationship, inadequacy of consideration is no defense at all.

I. **VALUABLE CONSIDERATION: THE BARGAINED-FOR INCURSION OF LEGAL DETRIMENT**

Scope: Simply stated, this rather mysterious doctrine has survived as the answer of English-speaking peoples to the question: "What promises should be enforced?" Only those supported by valuable consideration are regarded as enforceable from the moment they are made. The two crucial elements of this doctrine are immediately evident from its standard definition. As we shall see, they may be found in the context of a bilateral bargain wherein the parties have exchanged promises. These same elements are equally possible in a unilateral bargain wherein the acceptance of the promise contained in the offer was the performance of a stipulated act or endurance of a prescribed forbearance.

A. **Valuable Consideration Defined:** Valuable consideration may be found in the bargained-for promise to do any act, or the doing of any act, which but for this bargain the promisor or the actor was not legally obligated to perform. Valuable consideration may also be found in the bargained-for promise to forbear or the actual forbearance of any course of conduct which, but for this bargain, the promisor or abstainer was legally free to pursue.

B. **The Bargain Element of Valuable Consideration:** What is required is that the promises (bilateral formation) or promise and act (unilateral formation) have been consciously exchanged by the parties. If this element of conscious exchange is missing, the element of bargain is absent, and there is no "valuable" consideration. *See McGovern v. City of New York*, 234 N.Y. 377, 138 N.E. 26 (1923).

Example: Susan Foley promises to lend a valuable book to her friend, Jack Thompson. One month later, before Susan has acted on her promise, Thompson promises to help her in moving some bulky personal effects. Neither promise is supported by valuable consideration and thus there is no contract. While each promise might obligate the promisor to do something beyond the existing state of liability, the promises were not bargained. They were not consciously exchanged for one another.

1. *While the promises, or promise and act, must be exchanged in order to form a bargain, the motives of the parties in making such a conscious exchange are legally irrelevant.*

   Example: Smith, who is highly allergic to pollen, promises Bentley $50 if Bentley will promise not to plant ragweed in her "back-to-nature garden." Bentley agrees and makes the requested promise. Bentley's promise was consciously exchanged for that of Smith and thus was bargained. The fact that Bentley had previously decided not to plant a garden at all the following spring is irrelevant. Her motive in accepting Smith's offer is not a component of the bargained-for element of valuable consideration.

2. *Promises rendered nonvaluable because the bargain element is missing*

a. *Donative transactions:* If one party bestows a gift on another, an item of substantial economic value may change ownership. But the change has nothing to do with the law of contracts because the bargain element is missing.

(1) Gift with strings attached: Problems arise if the donor attaches stipulations which must be satisfied before the donee can collect the bounty or prohibitions concerning the rights of the donee to enjoy or disposed of the subject matter.

(a) Distinguishing the gift on condition from a bargain

(i) In the instance of a condition imposed upon the donee's qualification for the promised subject matter, the test is whether the act or forbearance which forms the qualification benefits the promisor in **any** manner. If it does, the offer was of a bargain.

Example: Diaz says to Conklin: "My friend, you look cold. If you will go to Harrod's Department Store you may select a coat and pair of gloves and charge them to my account." Conklin walks five blocks to Harrod's. The effort expended by Conklin was an attempt to qualify for receipt of a gift from Diaz. But because it did not benefit the promisor, Diaz, in any way, it failed as bargained-for legal detriment.

(ii) If the promisor imposed a restriction upon the use or disposition of the subject matter, the promise remains donative in nature. It is a maxim of the common law that an offeror cannot supply his own consideration.

Example: Parson says to her nephew, Chance: "I will give you my late father's watch, but you must promise that you will never sell or pawn it." Chance makes the desired promise. The reason no contract is formed here is best explained by the "legal detriment" element of valuable consideration. Since the moment before making the promise Chance had no rights of any nature with respect to the watch, a promise to restrict his use as a condition to receiving it as a gift is not "valuable." *See Walton Water v. Village of Walton,* 238 N.Y. 46, 143 N.E. 786 (1924).

(2) Bargain favored over gift: The distinction just articulated is not always easy to apply. As noted, the "benefit" to the promisor need not be economic. In doubtful cases, the objective theory of contract formation favors the finding of a bargain if the promise has induced the promisee to change position in a way that was both foreseeable to the promisor and detrimental to the promisee. *See DeCicco v. Schweizer,* 221 N.Y. 431, 117 N.E. 807 (1917).

b. *Past consideration is not valuable:* Again, the crucial element of bargain is missing if what prompts the promisor is a service or benefit conferred by the promisee in the past. The bargain element requires a conscious exchange at the time the promise is given.

Example: Barron, a theatrical producer, says to her secretary, Story, "In view of your years of faithful service, I promise that tomorrow morning I will buy you a ticket for a week's holiday in Bermuda." Unfortunately for Story, Barron's promise is not supported by bargained-for legal detriment. Rather, it is based on past services.

c. *Token consideration is not valuable if the bargain is a sham.* If parties attempt to disguise a gift in the form of a bargain by reciting the receipt or promise of a token consideration, the law will look to the substance and deny contract formation.

Example: A father wishing to make provision for a retarded adult child hands her a piece of paper declaring that it is a deed to land and promising to remove the encumbrances. Another member of the family suggests that the recipient hand her father $1 in exchange for the deed and promise.

In *Fischer v. Union Trust Co.*, 138 Mich. 612, 101 N.W. 852 (1904), the Supreme Court of Michigan declared that looking beyond this form the absence of a bargain in what was really a donative transaction was apparent. For this reason, no valuable consideration supported the father's promise to remove the encumbrances. The bank representing his estate, was allowed the defense of "want of consideration" when a guardian of the retarded child sought to enforce the promise out of estate assets. *Accord Restatement, Second § 87.*

d. *Moral consideration also lacks the element of bargain and, for that reason, is not "valuable":* A promise motivated by a sense of honor or moral obligation is not "valuable" because the bargain element is missing.

Example: The promise by a father to reimburse a good Samaritan for expenses incurred in treating the final illness of an adult child and burying him is not a contract obligation. Since the services were not requested, and a parent is without legal responsibility for the status or affairs of an adult offspring, the element of conscious or implied bargain is missing. *See Mills v. Wyman,* 20 Mass. (3 Pick.) 207 (1825). [For a discussion of the limited utility of moral consideration, see Part II, Substitutes for Valuable Consideration, *infra.*]

3. ***The concept of legal detriment:*** The presence of a conscious exchange or bargain is but one half of the doctrine of valuable consideration. Unless there is "legal detriment" on both sides of an exchange there is no contractual relationship.

a. *Legal detriment defined:* The concept of legal detriment is so simple that many students attempt to make it more difficult or complex! It comes down to this: Each party to the exchange must undertake by promise, act, or forbearance to change what had, but for that bargain, been the dimension of her legal rights or liabilities.

b. *Legal detriment in a bilateral bargain:* Each of the exchanged promises or sets of promises must obligate the respective promisor to undertake some act which **but for** this bargain he was not legally obligated to perform. If the subject matter of the exchange features a promise to forbear some act or course of conduct, it must be an act which **but for** this bargain the promisor was legally at liberty to pursue.

Example: On Tuesday morning, Steinberg promises to repair Smedley's sports car by Friday if Smedley will promise to pay for any necessary parts and compensate Steinberg for his time at $40 per hour. Smedley gives that promise. An executory bilateral contract has been formed between the mechanic and the auto owner. Their respective promises were consciously exchanged, one for the other. Further, each promised to do an act which, but for this bargain, neither was legally obligated to perform.

c. *Legal detriment in a unilateral bargain:* As reviewed in Chapter 1, "The Agreement Process," unilateral formation features a promise on the part of the offeror exchanged for an act or pattern of forbearance conforming to the terms of the offer by the accepting offeree. So long as that act or forbearance alters the existing dimension of the offeree's legal rights or obligations, legal detriment is present on his side of the bargain.

Example #1: Clinton offers Fetters $20 if he will rake Clinton's yard. Fetters responds by performing the requested act. Fetters has formed a contract in the unilateral mode. Clinton's promise of $20 must now be performed at peril of material breach.

Example #2: On October 30, Fetters promises Clinton, a resident of Oregon, $100 if Clinton will not vote in the California election for governor of that state scheduled one week later. Clinton does not cast a ballot. Fetters has no contractual obligation to pay the promised $100. True, Clinton forbore an act, but there was no legal detriment since, but for the bargain with Fetters, Clinton — an Oregonian — had no legal right to participate in a California election.

d. *"Economic adequacy" irrelevant:* The single most vital lesson to absorb is that bargained-for legal detriment, and not any economic factor, imparts "value" to valuable consideration. As long as any element of bargained-for legal detriment can be identified on both sides of the exchange, courts are totally disinterested in the distribution of economic gain or advantage resulting from the contract. Two reasons support the disinterest in economics.

2

(1) From a philosophical perspective, the right to be "wrong," or even "stupid," is fundamental in a free society. If courts were to impose some paternalistic insistence that only provident, reasonably equivalent bargains would be tolerated, a great deal of the personal freedom essential to a capitalistic, market-driven society would vanish.

    (a) Meaning of the "peppercorn theory": In the nineteenth century, American courts began to emphasize their disinterest in economics by borrowing from an illustration of Blackstone that even a trifling economic element could support the promise by another to part with things or elements of great worth that was the intended bargain. In *Whitney v. Steams,* 16 Me. 394, 397 (1839), the court declared that "a cent or a pepper corn. . .would constitute a valuable consideration."

    (b) "Adequacy" left to the judgment of the parties, not the courts: By 1891, the Supreme Court of Ohio could state the concept with confidence even as it felt compelled to cite English authority.

        It is an elementary principle that the law will not enter into an inquiry as to the adequacy of consideration, but will leave the parties to judge of that for themselves. The reason for the rule is succinctly expressed by Anderson, B., in *Pilkington v. Scott,* 15 Mees. & W. 657, 'Before the decision in *Hitchcock v. Coker.. .*a notion prevailed that the consideration must be adequate to the restraint. That was, in truth, the law making the bargain, instead of leaving the parties to make it. . . .'

        Judy v. Louderman, 48 Ohio St. 562, 29 N.E. 181 (1891).

(2) From the vantage point of pragmatics, courts have come to appreciate that economic values are highly subjective and thus very hard to second guess. Judges have declared that if they cannot accurately reconstruct the elements of value in use or value in exchange which attended the formation of the bargain, they have no business guessing. *See Walton Water v. Village of Walton,* 238 N.Y. 46, 143 N.E. 786 (1924), and *Schumm v. Berg,* 37 Cal.2d 174, 231 P.2d 39 (1951).

(3) Equitable remedies may depend upon the adequacy of consideration. The rule that economic adequacy is irrelevant is firmly established in actions seeking money damages at law. But if the aggrieved party seeks the extraordinary intervention of equity, she will find herself before a "court of conscience" which will examine the fairness of the terms of an exchange it is asked to enforce with a specific performance decree or injunctive relief.

e. *Limited exception for nonmarketplace transactions arising in the context of a socially protected relationship:* The major premise that value is left to the parties and its "adequacy" beyond judicial concern is the rule for the vast majority of transactions. But there are exceptions, and they arise in the context of two socially protected settings: where the parties are bound by a fiduciary or confidential relationship, a court will scrutinize the resulting bargain for economic fairness to the dependent or weaker party.

(1) Fiduciary relationships defined: A fiduciary relationship is structured by law and devised for the protection of a person or persons targeted for legal concern. Examples would include a lawyer and her client, a guardian and his ward, a trustee and the trust beneficiary. Bargains between persons bound by such ties are looked upon with judicial suspicion and will be scrutinized for a "consideration" that is not only legally valuable, but is also fair and advantageous to the needs of the dependent party. If found wanting in terms of such advantage, the dependent party may raise a personal defense termed "inadequacy of consideration."

(2) Confidential relationships are not formally established by law but can arise in any human pairing featuring trust and dependence on the one side and the assumption of dominion on the other.

(a) How formed: Blood relationships do not mandate such relationships, but they are a frequent setting. Friendship is another. If the needs of the dependent party are particularly obvious or glaring, a confidential relationship can quickly characterize a human association. *See Wagbo v. Smiseth,* 227 Mich. 313, 198 N.W. 913 (1924).

(b) How disciplined: However formed, bargains forged in the context of a confidential relationship are disciplined by the same judicial rules developed to protect the dependent party in a fiduciary setting. He may avoid the obligations of the disadvantageous bargain by invoking the personal defense of "inadequacy of consideration."

f. *The concept of "legal benefit":* Persons fond of debating propositions such as the number of angels able to stand on the head of a pin have caused needless confusion by speculating about the existence of "legal benefit" and whether it could substitute for "legal detriment" in imparting value.

(1) As a mirrored reflection of legal detriment: If Gonzales gives Greene a bargained promise to do an act which, but for that bargain, he had no obligation to perform, Gonzales had clearly incurred "legal detriment." Equally certain, Greene has obtained a "legal benefit" in that he now has an action for breach of contract (assuming that he, too, has exchanged legal detriment on his side of the bargain) should Gonzales refuse to perform, or render a performance which disappoints Greene's reasonable expectations. Seen as a mirrored reflection of legal detriment, the notion of legal benefit adds no important analytical tool to contract law.

(2) As a substitute for legal detriment in pre-existing duty cases: If Gonzales was already legally obligated to do the act which he promised Greene, repeating the tenor of an existing legal duty is not valuable consideration. Failing in this vital quality, the promise of Gonzales would not bind Greene to the performance of his own bargained obligation. However, a minority of courts ask whether, absent the promise made to Greene, Gonzales would have been exposed to an action by Greene in the event he had failed, refused, or defectively performed the pre-existing duty. If the answer is "no, he would have been liable to Able, the promisee of that earlier bargain," these decisions recognize that the subsequent bargain with Greene conferred a legal benefit on Greene. This benefit (Greene's right to maintain an action in the event of breach by Gonzales) is then recognized as imparting valuable consideration to the second bargain. The purpose of this exercise is to bind Greene to the terms of his promise to Gonzales.

4. ***Promises rendered nonvaluable because one of the parties has not incurred legal detriment in the course of the bargained-for exchange***

Problems in perspective: In the following materials we will review recurrent fact patterns in which the formation of a contract is denied because it is alleged that one of the parties has failed to incur legal detriment. Though promoted as "want of consideration" fact patterns, most are really claiming an inadequacy of consideration and seek to resurrect the error that the law will look for some pragmatic equivalency or economic adequacy in the terms of the exchange. Where that is the true nature of the problem, expect modern courts to conclude that a contract has been formed.

More difficult will be the fact patterns in which the express terms of the bargain do not clearly implicate legal detriment on one side of the exchange. If it is evident that the parties were attempting to form a contract, a modern court will rely upon an "implied promise" to preclude the denial that valuable consideration was present. In both classes of controversies, you will note the modern pro-formation bias of courts following the objective theory of contract formation. If the attempted transaction was between merchants and the subject matter was goods, look for provisions of the U.C.C. to preclude attacks premised upon alleged problems with consideration.

a. *Problems of pre-existing duty:* This is a textbook denial of contract formation using the defense "want of consideration." The claim is that the promise of one of the traders did not involve legal detriment because it merely repeated the tenor of an existing legal duty rather than adding to the legal obligations of the promisor. In the marketplace the identical legal problem can arise in two apparently opposite settings: (1) where a buyer of goods or services agrees to pay more for them than the original contract price, (2) where a debtor agrees to pay less than the amount of a contract indebtedness on condition that the creditor forgive the balance. Let's sort them out one at a time.

(1) Modification of an existing contract: In the yesterdecades of commerce, as well as today, parties who have formed contractual arrangements may desire to change their terms. So long as the changes modify the legal obligations of *both parties*, there will be no difficulty with the doctrine of valuable consideration. Their mutual concessions provide new elements of bargained-for legal detriment resulting in the discharge of the original obligations and substitution of the new. The problem of pre-existing duty arises when only one of the parties changes the dimension of his existing legal obligation.

Example: Assume that Smith has formed a contract with Kong to sell him 5,000 tons of coal at $20 per ton. Before he has performed his duty to deliver the coal, Smith sustains a major business loss owing to employee negligence, desperate to recoup his financial stability, Smith informs Kong that he will not deliver the coal unless Kong will promise to increase the price to $25 per ton. If Kong gives the demanded promise, is he contractually bound to pay the additional $5 per ton?

(a) Traditional common law: No, Kong's promise of an additional $5 per ton is not supported by any legal detriment incurred by Smith. Smith is merely seeking to rebargain what is an existing legal obligation under the original contract — to deliver the goods. Kong may assert the defense "want of consideration." In early British and American cases, this result was mandated by the rule of *Foakes v. Beer,* L.R. 9 A.C. 605 (H.L. 1884). *See Restatement, Second,* § 73.

(b) Weakness of the common law as a restraint on overreaching traders: Smith can avoid Kong's want of consideration defense by making a modification in the terms of his pre-existing duty. Thus if he makes his demand for an additional $5 per ton but adds a promise to deliver the coal one hour earlier than the term of his original contract obligation, Smith would have honored the letter of the law by proposing a change in the existing legal duties of both parties. If, faced with his urgent need for the coal, Kong capitulates to this artful extortion, he will find himself trapped by the rule that common law courts do not examine the adequacy of consideration.

(c) Equitable modifications binding: Not all parties who demand concessions from the other party to a contract are scoundrels. Following the merger between law and equity, the common law began to enforce concessions (which could include the promise of additional compensation, a relaxation of original performance standards, or extensions of time) if the party making the request had made a good faith attempt to perform his contract duty only to meet unforeseen and unforeseeable difficulties which threatened substantial hardship unless an adjustment was made. If these factors were all present, a concession by the other party would be binding, and he would be equitably estopped from later seeking to avoid honoring it by a claim of want of consideration.

(d) U.C.C. solution: Takes the danger out of modifications sought under legitimate circumstances and the advantage out of those which are not.

   (i) Modification sought in good faith: Under § 2-209(1), parties to an existing contract are free to modify its terms, and such modifications do not require any further consideration to be binding. However, the modification demand must have been asserted in "good faith" defined by the Code as the morality of the marketplace. Unlike the earlier equity doctrine, the reason prompting the demand need not have been unforeseeable at the formation of the original contract.

   (ii) The other party is **not** obligated to make concessions in the face of such a demand. She may elect to stand upon her contract claim. But if she does consent, the modification is binding by dent of the statute. *See Fasolino Foods Co. v. Banca Nazionale del Lavoro*, 961 F.2d 1052 (2nd Cir. 1992): "[Y]ou are not obliged to become an altruist toward the other party and relax the terms if he gets into trouble in performing his side of the bargain."

   (iii) A modification extorted in bad faith (premised on grounds which traders in the marketplace would not regard as reasonable) is not binding under the U.C.C. even if supported by some technical element of valuable consideration supplied by the over-reaching trader.

(e) Pre-existing duty owed to third person: Astro Construction enters into a bilateral contract with Susan Warren to construct a commercial building on Warren's vacant lot in Smallsville. Terry Trott, owner of the adjacent parcel, now promises Astro $5,000 if it will be certain that the commercial building on Warren's land is finished by the date promised in the Astro/Warren contract. Astro makes a timely completion of the construction project. Does it have a contract claim for $5,000 against Trott?

   (i) Traditional common law view: No, Astro was already under an existing legal duty to complete construction, a duty arising out of its contract with owner, Warren. Its promise to complete the building by that date made to Trott involved no further element of legal detriment. *De Cicco v Schweizer*, 221 N.Y. 431, 117 N.E 807 (1917).

2

(ii) Astro's promise to Trott as "legal benefit": Some courts would uphold Astro's claim against Trott concluding that it conferred a legal benefit on Trott even if there was no additional legal detriment assumed by Astro. The reasoning is that but for the promise made to Trott, a breach of the construction deadline in the Astro/Warren contract would not have been actionable by Trott. In a flaw shared with many legal arguments, this reasoning meets itself in a perfect circle.

(iii) All courts agree that a promise by Trott made to Astro and Warren seeking their promise not to modify the completion date in their contract is supported by bargained legal detriment. But for their promise to Trott, Astro and Warren had a legal right to modify that date. *De Cicco v. Schweizer, supra.*

(2) Debtors with ambitions to rebargain

Problems in perspective: Another recurrent problem is posed by the debtor who suddenly realizes that he is in a position of strength with respect to the need of his creditor for repayment. What is to prevent him from holding the payment hostage to a demand that the creditor accept less, and that on the condition that he promise to forgive the balance of the obligation? But not all debtors are grasping. There are those with a genuine grievance which prompts their desire to pay less. As with the party who was demanding modifications to a contract, the trick for the common law has been to devise doctrines which make moral distinctions facilitating the ambitions of the "good debtor" while thwarting the bad.

(a) The overreaching debtor thwarted by a pre-existing duty in efforts to coerce modification of a liquidated debt: It is obvious that if promising to do an act which the promisor is already legally obligated to perform is not legal detriment, then promising to do only a portion of that pre-existing obligation could never qualify as valuable consideration! But this is precisely the bold gambit of a debtor who, freely admitting that his liquidated (undisputed) debt is due, offers only a portion of that sum and then on condition that the creditor promise to forgive the balance. A desperate creditor can make such a promise, but it is not binding. Having received the part payment, the creditor could then commence an action for the balance using the defense "want of consideration" to defeat the promise to forgive. *Gitre v. Kessler Products Co.,* 387 Mich. 619, 198 N.W.2d 405 (1972).

(b) The aggrieved debtor's safe strategy: discharging an unliquidated debt by an accord and satisfaction. If a creditor asserts a payment obligation which the debtor contests in good faith, the creditor's claim is unliquidated. The parties can either litigate or work out their honest differences. In the nineteenth century, judges had ceased to be paid by the case. They reacted by favoring out-of-court settlements.

(c) The machinery of accord and satisfaction

    (i) The accord: The first element is the presence of a good-faith dispute between debtor and creditor. This dispute may involve the binding nature of the debt, the amount owed, the time of payment or the specie (whether in money or something else of economic value) of the alleged obligation. The debtor's position need not be a certain winner in litigation. It is sufficient if he held it in good faith, and a reasonable person would have considered it debatable. If such a dispute exists, the creditor's claim is unliquidated. The second element is an agreement whereby the debtor promises to make a payment and the creditor promises to modify the original claim. At this point debtor and creditor have bargained their dispute and formed an *executory accord.*

    (ii) The satisfaction: Arises if the parties now carry out the terms of the executory accord (the debtor makes the promised payment and the creditor executes a written release of the original claim), and the original debt is discharged by accord and satisfaction. *See Restatement, Second,* § 281.

    (iii) Status of the original creditor's claim pending satisfaction: Once the disputed debt has been reduced to an accord, the original claim is suspended. If satisfaction is accomplished, it is discharged. If the debtor breaches the accord by refusing to honor its terms, the aggrieved creditor may elect between causes of action. She may assert the original claim which is now revived (and take her chances of prevailing on the debtor's ground of dispute); or, she may commence an action for breach of the accord seeking to enforce the debtor's modified promise. The latter cause of action will usually be worth less, but it is free of the dispute surrounding the original claim.

    (iv) Accord on debtor's terms: One vexing problem is an accord in which the debtor has refused to budge beyond the terms of what he contends was originally owed. If the creditor grees to accept this sum and forgive the balance, may she raise the objection "want of consideration" since the debtor did not promise or do anything beyond what he admitted to be the tenor of his existing duty? Logically, the answer would be "yes," but preference for out-of-court settlements has prompted the majority of courts to say "no." Again, the dispute must have been in good faith.

b. *The illusory promise:* If, at the formation stage, one of the parties does not incur legal detriment because he retains an unfettered election to perform or not, his promise is illusory. The other party to such a one-sided bargain may claim the defense "want of consideration" and deny formation of a contract.

Problems in perspective: Often, bargains assaulted as containing illusory promises were seriously intended by the parties, who then gave imperfect or incomplete expression to the exchange of obligations. In yet another illustration of the pro-formation bias of modern courts, the attempt to salvage these bargains has taken two forms. The first is to regard total performance by the party who gave the illusory promise of its terms as "curing" the want of consideration and forming a contract. The second is even more dramatic. It involves judicial implication of a promise which clearly involves legal detriment so as to regard the contract as formed on the day the parties framed their bargain. As you might suspect, the U.C.C. is heavily involved in promoting this second strategy.

(1) **Distinguished from pre-existing duty fact patterns:** Although both involve a want of consideration, the defect in a pre-existing duty is the repetition of an existing legal obligation. If the problem is described as an "illusory promise," it means that the promisor did not undertake any kind of obligation at all.

Example #1: Smith offers to tend Farley's garden for $30 per week. Farley responds: "We have a deal, I'll pay you if I want to." Obviously, there is no deal. Farley did not accept Smith's offer. However, if Smith were to agree to Farley's counterproposition, there still would be no executory bilateral contract because Farley has retained unfettered control over whether he will choose to pay Smith. Put in the language of the law, Smith gave an illusory promise. Farley can cite this defect as grounds for refusing to perform on his promise to tend the garden. Older cases would term this "want of consideration" a "want of mutuality of obligation."

Example #2: In May, Langford Building Company negotiates with Copley Steel for the purchase of prefabricated steel girders. The written agreement calls upon Copley to sell such products at $800 per unit for so many units as Langford elects to order during the months of June and July. Again, the terms of the written agreement fail as an executory bilateral contract. Langford Building Company has not incurred any express legal detriment. It would appear that Copley could renounce its own promise or refuse any and all orders submitted by Langford claiming want of consideration.

(2) **Performance as "cure" for missing consideration:** If a party who retained complete discretion over whether she would perform on the terms of her promise in fact elects to do so, her complete performance cures the want of consideration which had plagued formation. At the moment the discretionary performance has been ten-

dered, the other party is contractually bound to carry out the terms of his own promise.

Example: On July 6, Aero Aviation Service, operator of the civil aviation fuel concession at the local metropolitan air field makes the following written proposal to Hi-Test Petroleum, a local refiner of aviation fuel: If we decide to place an order for 100,000 gallons regular grade aviation fuel, you will promise to fill it within forty-eight hours and grant us a 10% discount off of your then-lowest wholesale price. Hi-Test replies in writing promising to accept, fill and discount such an order.

As an executory bargain, the writings do not create a contract. Aero has given only an illusion of detriment. The moment before it communicated with Hi-Test it had complete control over whether it would elect to purchase products from Hi-Test. The moment after Hi-Test received that communication, Aero had the same full measure of freedom. If Aero is not bound to purchase the fuel, Hi-Test is not bound to sell it.

But now suppose that on July 20, Aero sends an unconditional order to Hi-Test for 100,000 gallons of aviation fuel. Such a step would amount to complete performance of the illusory obligation. Faced with a tender of complete performance, it would be foolish to allow Hi-Test to refuse performance on its promises to accept that order, fill it within forty-eight hours, and discount the goods. The full performance by Aero has cured the want of consideration and formed a contract with Hi-Test on July 20.

(3) Part performance of an illusory obligation does not cure the want of consideration and the other trader remains at liberty to ignore it while refusing its own performance.

Example: Assume the facts stated above with respect to the July 6 exchangeof writings between Aero Aviation Service and Hi-Test Petroleum. On July 20, Aero submits an order to Hi-Test for 20,000 gallons of aviation fuel. Hi-Test refuses to accept or fill that order. Should Aero commence a cause of action Hi-Test will prevail. Since Aero's July 6 undertaking was illusory there was no executory contract formed when Hi-Test accepted the proposition. Part performance is not a "cure" for this want of consideration because that would hold Hi-Test to a bargain it did not contemplate. Its expectation was that it would be bound to accept, fill, and discount only in the face of a 100,000-gallon order.

(4) The implication of a valuable promise: If a court is convinced that a party intended a contractual relationship but expressed his obligation in an inept or incomplete manner, the solution is to imply a valuable promise rather than see the formation effort flounder over the issue of consideration.

Example: Duff-Gordon, an English fashion designer, enters into a written agreement with Wood, a American distributor of women's clothing. By the terms of the agreement, Duff-Gordon grants Wood an exclusive right to market her seal of fashion approval in the United States for the period of one year. Wood makes express promises to account quarterly for any sales he might make and to split any profits from such sales 50/50. Shortly thereafter, Duff-Gordon breaches her express promise to regard Wood as her exclusive agent. She markets her seal of approval directly on the West Coast. Wood commences soft for a declaratory judgment and an accounting. Duff-Gordon raises "want of consideration," claiming that by his express language Wood never promised to sell anything. If he had no legal obligation to make a sale, the express promises to account for any sales he might make and to split the profits on those sales were illusory. If he sold nothing there would be no occasion to account and no profits to divide.

Having raised what she considered a fatal flaw defending an action brought by a petty bourgeois, and a Colonial to boot, Lady Duff-Gordon sailed for the United Kingdom. She survived the German U-boat attack on the *Lusitania* but did not survive her battle with the New York judiciary. Declaring that the agreement with Wood was "instinct with obligation imperfectly expressed," the Court of Appeals noted that at the formation stage both Wood and Duff-Gordon had a business purpose. All the court had to do was to imply that Wood had pledged best efforts toward the attainment of their business purpose and the claimed want of consideration never existed. *See Wood v Lucy, Lady Duff-Gordon,* 222 N.Y. 88, 118 N. E. 214 (1917).

(5) U.C.C. in accord: Section 2-306(2) codifies the rule of Lady Duff-Gordon's case in any transaction by either the seller or the buyer for exclusive dealing in the subject matter. Unless otherwise specifically agreed, the Code simply imposes an obligation on the seller to use best efforts to supply the goods and the buyer to use best efforts to promote their sale.

(a) Section 1-203's obligation to deal in good faith may go even further in precluding "want of consideration" when combined with § 2-103 of the sales article. Read together, these sections require of merchant traders not only honesty in fact, but also the observance of reasonable commercial standards of fair dealing in the trade.

(b) Recent common law cases (which articulate rules governing all transactions other than the purchase or sale of goods) also seem to be extending the rationale of Lady Duff-Gordon's case and imposing good-faith dealing obligations as a means of precluding claimed want of consideration when it appears that, at the formation stage, the parties intended a binding agreement. *See Tanglewood Land Co. Inc. v. Byrd,* 299 N.C. 260, 261 S.E.2d 655 (1980).

c. *Phantom problems with consideration:* The following fact patterns are a staple in many casebooks. Some raise fact patterns rarely encountered in the "real world." Others are confronted by some court, somewhere every day. In each, modern common and statutory law has overcome initial doubts respecting the consideration.

(1) Promise to forbear the assertion or abandon the prosecution of a legal claim: Courts have long recognized that the threat or initiation of groundless litigation can be an effective terror tactic which has frequently prompted the victim to buy his peace. Opposed to the suspicion engendered by such danger is the policy of favoring out-of-court settlements. Where is the line to be drawn?

(a) Early rule: Such a promise was valuable consideration if the party making it had a subjective good-faith belief in the merit of the claim *and* it was at least legally colorable (meaning that a reasonable person could believe in its validity).

(b) Modern rule: Section 74 of the *Restatement, Second*, reflects a modern trend even more tolerant of bargains that preclude or dispose of litigation. Under this rule the promise to forbear or abandon the prosecution of a legal claim is valuable consideration if it is in fact doubtful because of uncertainty as to the facts or the law, *or* the party making the promise holds an honest, subjective belief in its merit.

(2) Promises reserving a right of cancellation may be illusory.

(a) If one of the parties reserves an unqualified right to cancel her obligation without notice to the other party, her promise is illusory and wanting in consideration.

(b) If the right of cancellation is conditioned in any way so that the party reserving it is bound under any circumstance, the other trader may have made a foolish bargain, but there is no problem with consideration.

Example: A maker of soft drink syrup concentrate enters a written agreement with a regional bottler granting the bottler a limited territorial exclusive. The bottler promises to prepare and market the product for a minimum period of five years. The syrup manufacturer reserves the right to cancel the arrangement at any time upon ten days written notice.

The promise of the syrup manufacturer is *not* illusory. During the ten-day period before such notice would be effective, it is bound by the terms of its promise. The bottler may have made a stupid business arrangement, but his complaint is really with the adequacy of the consideration, a matter of no concern to a common law court.

(c) U.C.C. position: Section 2-309(3) may preclude consideration problems in the instances of reserved rights of termination. It provides that termination of a contract by one party, except on the happening of an agreed event, requires that reasonable notification be received by the other party. An agreement which appears to give a party to a sale of goods transaction an unqualified right to terminate would not have that content when read in light of § 2-309.

(3) Agreements to purchase the "output" of the seller or to supply the buyer's "requirements" are not illusory.

(a) Early common law decisions had problems with bargains which measured the quantity term in this manner. Since no specific minimum was mandatory, some reached the conclusion that the bargain was wanting in consideration.

(b) Modern common law rules recognize that both requirement and output contracts are types of exclusive dealing agreements. There is legal detriment to a buyer in a requirements contract even if he never generates a requirement for the subject matter. Having promised to satisfy that want from the seller, he is no longer free to obtain the subject matter from any other source. This is bargained-for legal detriment. Identical reasons support the finding of consideration in a seller's promise to sell its output of a certain product to one buyer. At a minimum, its legal freedom has been altered because it may no longer manufacture or produce the item and sell to any other buyer.

(c) The U.C.C. position: Section 2-306 is more precise in protecting the reasonable expectations of parties to output or requirement contracts.

(i) A term which measures the quantity by the output of the seller or requirements of the buyer means such actual output or requirements as may occur in **good faith.**

(ii) To protect the other trader who has consented to this elastic quantity term, § 2-306(1) provides that no quantity unreasonably disproportionate to any stated estimate, or in the absence of a stated estimate, to any normal pattern of prior output or requirements may be tendered or demanded.

(4) Promise reserving the right to the promisor to elect among alternative performances is illusory if any one of the reserved alternatives does not involve legal detriment.

Example: Bonnie Berrier, age fifteen, makes the following proposal to her uncle, Frederick Goodlife: "Uncle, if you will promise to pay me $5,000 on my twenty-first birthday, I promise to straighten out my life in one of these areas: either (1) I will not consume alcoholic beverages; or (2) I will not smoke; or (3) I will not date boys who do up their hair in spikes." Delighted with the proposal of his niece, Goodlife makes the requested promise. The two have **not** formed an executory bilateral contract. Since Bonnie reserved the right to elect among these three courses of reform, her executory promise is illusory if any of the reserved alternatives does not involve legal detriment. Unfortunately for her, the promise by a minor not to consume alcoholic beverages during the balance of her minority is not a promise to forbear a course of conduct otherwise legally privileged. It does not involve legal detriment.

(a) If the party making the promise vests the right of selection in a third party, her promise is legally detrimental and valuable consideration even if one of the reserved alternatives is illusory. Merely taking a chance that the designated third person will select a nonillusory alternative is, itself, legal detriment.

Example: In our bargain between Bonnie Berrier and her uncle, if Bonnie had promised to allow her mother, Bettie Berrier, to make the selection, her proposal would not have been illusory. If her uncle agrees, an executory bilateral contract is formed. Note that if Bettie Berrier then selects abstinence from alcohol for her minor daughter, the bargain would still be binding on the uncle. Bonnie had taken the chance that her mother would select the swearing off of spiked-haired boys. Minors do have a legal right to freedom of association.

(b) If the right of selection is reserved to the promisor, her selection of a legally valuable alternative cures the want of consideration and creates a bargain.

Example: If Bonnie had reserved the selection to herself, the initial promise would be illusory. But if she thereafter elected to circumscribe her freedom to date, she would have elected a legally detrimental alternative and cured the want of consideration.

(5) Voidable promises are not illusory: The contract obligations of a minor or mental defective are voidable because the law extends the protective privilege. Notwithstanding, the promises of such persons do constitute valuable consideration supporting the obligations of the other trader. Why? Because common law decisions have decreed that they have this quality!

(6) Conditional promises are not illusory if the promisor lacks the power to prevent the satisfaction of the condition. Such promises carry with them the elements of valuable consideration even if the odds of the conditional liability ever maturing as a matter of present duty are quite long.

2

Example: Willow promises to purchase Twilby's antique book collection for $15,000 "provided a black cat wearing purple socks and white booties crosses my front lawn in the next ten minutes." Twilby (for unknown reasons) agrees. The parties have a perfectly valid executory bilateral contract although the obligation of Willow is subject to an express condition precedent which is rather unlikely to be satisfied. But the fact that it might be, and that such a factor is beyond Willow's control, imparts "bargained-for legal detriment."

(7) Unilateral contracts are never wholly executory and therefore are not governed by the rule that the mutual promises of the parties must involve bargained-for legal detriment. If the formation of the contract is in the unilateral mode, there is no acceptance of the offer until the offeree has totally completed the requested act or stipulated forbearance. At that point, the consideration supplied by the offeree has been received by the offeror who alone now has executory duties. If the performance by the offeree involved the incursion of legal detriment — he did an act which but for the attempted bargain with the offeror he was not legally obligated to perform — the offeror must now perform on her promise at peril of breaching the contract.

II. SUBSTITUTES FOR VALUABLE CONSIDERATION AS GROUNDS FOR IMPARTING LIABILITY CONSEQUENCES FOR BREACHING A PROMISE

Scope: Only valuable consideration can transform an executory bilateral agreement into a contractual relationship. This short statement is more profound than might at first appear. If the mere bargained-for exchange of promises carrying the quality of legal detriment can create a contract at that moment, it means that either party will be able to claim remedies aimed at protecting expectation interests in the event of breach. In Chapter 7, "The Consequences of Breach," we will see that the normal defense of this expectation interest is a loss-of-bargain award of money damages at law. If that remedy proves inadequate to protect the aggrieved party's expectation interest, he has standing to seek equitable remedies such as specific performance decree or injunctions. But in law, as in life, things are rarely all or nothing. There is a middle ground, encompassing several doctrines, but mainly promissory estoppel, which offer limited remedies for breach of promises which were not supported by valuable consideration.

A. **Moral Consideration:** As noted in the discussion of valuable consideration, it is the absence of the bargain element which relegates moral consideration to a relatively minor role in upholding promissory obligations.

Problems in perspective: There are three areas in which moral consideration is regarded by decisional law as sufficient to expose the promisor to contract remedies should he breach his promise. The first deals with what is termed "the revival of discharged obligations." The second is a new promise given by one whose original bargain was voidable due to some defect in his capacity to contract. The third is far more rare; the enforcement of a promise supported by a "perfect moral obligation."

1. *The revival of discharged obligations:* Obligations previously supported by valuable consideration but have become unenforceable due to either a discharge of the promisor in bankruptcy or the running of the applicable statute of limitations on its breach litter the marketplace. Common law courts have long held that a *new promise* by the promisor of that discharged obligation is enforceable without the necessity of any new element of valuable consideration. *Accord Restatement, Second,* § 82.

   a. *Obligation is on the terms of the new promise:* Thus, if Fox owed Sibley $1,000 on outstanding contract debts at the time Fox was discharged in bankruptcy, his subsequent promise to pay Sibley $300 would be enforceable only to that extent. The balance of the original debt, $700, would be beyond Sibley's reach.

   b. *New promise must be in writing:* In some states, statutes or judicial decisions have required that the new promise by the discharged party be in writing. This is especially true if the discharge arose through bankruptcy since federal law limits the number of times that debtors can claim a "new start" by gaining release from the obligation to pay their creditors.

   c. *The impact of federal statutory law:* Bankruptcy is a federal remedy, and the provisions of any federal legislation disable the content of any common or state statutory law in the field. In 1978, Congress passed the Bankruptcy Reform Act. One of its objectives was to limit common law contract rules respecting new promises by bankrupt persons. That act, and any subsequent amendments, should be consulted on questions arising in this area.

2. *Promise to perform a voidable pre-existing duty:* Our review of the formation materials in Chapter 1 revealed that the promises of minors and mentally impaired persons are "voidable," meaning that such promisors may assert their status as a personal defense against enforcement of the terms of their contracts. If such a defense is raised, only to be followed by a *new promise* by the promisor subsequent to having attained her legal majority or recovered from the mental impairment, the voidable obligation is said to have been "ratified." As such it is enforceable as per the terms of the new promise without further requirement of valuable consideration. *See Restatement, Second,* § 85.

3. *Enforcement of the "perfect moral obligation"*

   a. *Actions against the estate of the promisor:* Some courts have held an estate liable to continue payments made pursuant to a promise supported by moral consideration when all of the following criteria have been satisfied: (1) the promisor had received a material benefit during his lifetime which motivated the subsequent promise; (2) the promisor thereafter commenced performance according to the terms of his promise; (3) the promisor died without ever evidencing an intention to repudiate the promise; and (4) there were no superior moral claimants to the benefits of his estate. *See Webb v. McGowan,* 27 Ala. App. 82, 168 So. 196 (1935), and *Homefinders v. Lawrence,* 80 Idaho 543, 335 P.2d 893 (1959).

b. *Restatement position:* Section 86 of the *Restatement, Second,* advocates a rather cautious approach toward enforcing promises grounded on moral consideration. The basic requirement is that the promisor have acted in recognition of the receipt of some prior benefit from the promisee. However, liability is generated only to the extent "necessary to prevent injustice," which may fall far short of the dimension of the promise. Subsection (2) adds a further qualification. The promise is *not* binding if the promisee conferred the benefit as a gift or, for other reasons, the promisor has not been unjustly enriched.

B. Promissory Estoppel — The Impact of Detrimental Reliance

Problems in perspective: If an unbargained promise causes the promisee to change position in reliance upon the assumption that the promisor would keep his word, the breach of that promise will leave the promisee worse off than before the promise was ever given. If his detrimental reliance was reasonably foreseeable to the promisor, it has long been thought unjust that the promisee bear the whole burden of disappointment. An action with the limited ambition of shifting to the breaching promisor the reliance expenses or losses of the promisee can succeed notwithstanding the absence of valuable consideration.

The legal vehicle for protecting what we may term the promisee's *reliance interest* is termed promissory estoppel. Today, its dimension generally mirrors the formulation found in the *Restatement of Contracts.* Both the *First and Second Restatements* have treated this subject in § 90. So famous is that section that it has become a synonym for the term. Originally, the doctrine operated only in the area of donative promises. Modern courts have been extending its application into the world of commerce despite the efforts of such giants as Cardozo and L. Hand to restrict it to the world of gifts. Whatever the merits of that controversy, as a student of contract law it is important that you recognize that in the eyes of most courts and commentators, promissory estoppel — § 90 — is an alternative civil law theory for breach of promise. Thus it is *not* a doctrine of contract law. Many rules which discipline remedies for breach of contract — for instance, the Statute of Frauds — have no application if the plaintiff seeks only reliance damages predicated on promissory estoppel.

1. *Distinguished from valuable consideration:* In a promissory estoppel fact pattern, the element of bargain is missing. The promisor has made a promise for whatever reason he deems sufficient. While most such promises are donative in nature, the promisor may have acted with business motives. What prevents contract formation is the absence of the bargained-for exchange of legal detriment on the part of the promisee. *See Holman v. Omaha & C B. Railway & Bridge Co.,* 117 Iowa 268, 90 N.W. 833 (1902).

2. ***Reliance distinguished from a promisee's expectation interest:***
Much of the early and continuing controversy about promissory estoppel has centered on its ambition as a protective device.

a. *The expectation interest:* If a promise is broken, the most generous remedy which the law can devise would seek to place the aggrieved promisee in the position she would have occupied had there been full and timely performance. If this is accomplished, the law will have vindicated her "expectation interest." As will be explained in Chapter 7, "The Consequences of Breach," this is the goal of both the loss-of-bargain recovery of money damages and specific performance decrees.

b. *An expectation interest remedy is attainable only if the breached promise was a contract obligation:* Traditional decisional law has reserved expectation loss remedies only for those plaintiffs able to prove the formation and breach of a contract. This remains the overwhelming tendency of modern decisions.

c. *The reliance interest:* If the expectation interest seeks to place the aggrieved party in the position she would have occupied had there been full and timely performance, the reliance interest has the far more modest ambition of returning her to the prepromise status quo. Such a recovery is important if, in reliance uponthe promise and before it was broken, the promisee changed position by either taking actions or forbearing actions which would have been beneficial or protective.

d. *Protected by promissory estoppel:* Many have advocated the use of promissory estoppel as an apt guardian of the reliance interest. In those jurisdictions where estoppel theories have been limited to this role, there has been no tension between the emergence of this doctrine and traditional contract law.

3. ***Elements of the doctrine under the* First Restatement:*** Section 90 defined both the nature of the legal injury and dimension of the legal right as follows:

A promise which the promisor should reasonably expect to induce action or forbearance of a definite and substantial character on the part of the promisee and which does induce such action or forbearance is binding if injustice can be avoided only by enforcement of the promise.

a. *Potential protection of promisee's expectation interest:* Under the formulation in the *First Restatement,* the doctrine of promissory estoppel had the potential of protecting the expectation interest of the promisee if his reliance was so definite and substantial that "injustice" could only be avoided by enforcement of the promise.

b. *Circumstances in which there is no pragmatic difference between a measure of damages predicated upon reliance and one based on expectation interests:* If the gratuitous or otherwise unbargained promise had been to procure insurance coverage and the promisee relied upon the promise by failing to take further steps to protect her person or property, an award of damages for breach of that promise will equal the fruits of the missing coverage under either theory. *Lusk-Harbison-Jones, Inc. v. Universal Credit Co.*, 164 Miss. 693, 145 So. 623 (1933).

4. **The reformulation under the Restatement, Second:** Section 90 has been recast in two important particulars in the 1981 revision.

    a. *There is no longer a requirement that the action or forbearance by the promisee be of a "definite and substantial character."*

    b. *Faced with a pattern of detrimental reliance a court is free to limit the remedy "as justice requires."*

    c. *Significance of these changes:* Taken together, the revised elements of § 90 respond to critics who disputed the wisdom of its potential use as an alternative to traditional contract status in protecting the expectation interest. Permitting a court to limit the dimension of the recovery to the extent of the reliance should refocus the remedy as a consolation prize for the breach of unbargained promises.

C. **The Once-upon-a-time Role of Formalisms.** One of the factors which makes the study of promises so interesting is the deep history of societal efforts to make productive use of this tool for arranging the future. I have previously suggested that "valuable consideration" is currently the answer of English-speaking peoples to the question, "What promises should be enforced?" But the question had been posed and had received very different answers long before the doctrine of bargained-for legal detriment was invented or accidentally discovered. If you are interested in developing an historical perspective on promises within the context of the evolving social, economic and governmental history of the English, *see* Jenks, *History of the Doctrine of Consideration in English Law.*

1. **The stipulation:** One of the earliest means of imparting enforceability to a promise was for the promisor to utter its terms before a representative of his feudal overlord or, more commonly, a member of the clergy. Usually this very formal exercise took place in a church. With both an official witness and a very impressive setting, promises given in the early Middle Ages would be taken very seriously.

2. **The seal:** With the passage of time, two things of importance began to influence the attitude toward promises. First, although most important persons could neither read nor write, their affairs were increasingly being committed to writing by scriveners. Second, the civil government began a long campaign to reduce the influence of the church on things that were seen as belonging to Caesar. As a result, the seal, a wax impression of a distinctive signet began to grow in popularity. Most of us are vaguely aware of the phrase "signed, sealed, and delivered." If these formalisms

had been observed, a promise contained in the sealed writing was enforceable by the common law action of covenant.

a. *Degeneration of the seal:* The growing presence of a middle class which was particularly needful of promises — for they were the merchants of their time — put tremendous strain on the seal. Too many people needed them for the design to be distinctive! The invention of the printing press and growing literacy of the populace reduced the seal to what was often a meaningless formality or afterthought. When some courts began to recognize that the printed initials "L.S." *(locus sigilli* for you Latin speakers) after a signature were magic, the affront to common sense doomed the seal at common law.

b. *Modern status:* In 1500, the status of the seal was that it was *the* means of lending enforceability to a promise. By 1850, it was being spoken of as "imparting consideration," a sure sign that valuable consideration was the doctrine with a future. By the time the Civil War ended in the United States, common law decisions were reducing the significance of the seal to merely raising a "presumption of consideration." By 1900, legislation in most states had abolished all legal significance of the seal. *See* § 1626 of the California Civil Code.

3. *Promise in writing:* If the growing literacy of the populace had contributed to the demise of the seal, there were those who argued that any written promise should be enforceable. Indeed, there was even proposed a Uniform Written Obligations Act. It was a notable flop, adopted only in Pennsylvania! Today, in certain limited contexts, statutory law may provide that a written promise is binding without the necessity of valuable consideration or reliance. The most common are debtor's relief acts passed during periods of depression. In the 1930s many states enacted bills to the effect that a written release given by a creditor in exchange for part payment by the debtor was binding.

NOTES

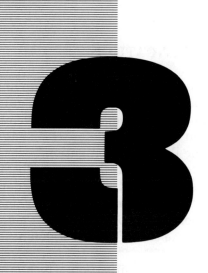

THE BARGAIN IN LITIGATION

▶ **CHAPTER SUMMARY**

THE BARGAIN IN LITIGATION

Scope: In Chapter 1 we explored the formation of a private bargain and, in Chapter 2, determined whether that private bargain could qualify for the legal status of a contractual relationship. In reality, we merely established a presumptive qualification for contract status, for we have yet to focus on the topic of defenses. That unfinished study will now be completed in Chapter 3, "The Bargain in Litigation."

This chapter reviews "real defenses," also known as defenses to formation. If a real defense exists, the attempted contract is void. Fortunately for traders, such defenses are relatively rare. Far more abundant are "personal defenses" which admit the formation of a contract but render the obligations of one of the traders voidable. There are important civil procedure implications to the classification of defenses as real or merely personal.

There is one other important topic. In the event of litigation, which are the legally relevant terms of the bargain? A natural answer would be "all of them." It may not be so. If the parties have reduced their bargain to a formal written expression, and come to regard that writing as containing the entirety of their agreement, then any evidence — written or oral — which would add to, vary, or contradict the bargain as reflected in that writing will encounter difficulty with the Parol Evidence Rule.

Problems in perspective: May I suggest that you conceptualize defenses under five broad headings. The first relates to **defective formation**. The second group will question the **capacity** of one of the traders to participate in contractual relationships in general, or (more rarely) this particular bargain. The third will involve some serious social objection to the **content** of the bargain. In other words, the ends which the parties have sought to achieve are objectionable. The fourth will have no difficulty with content, but will be centered on deceptive or coercive **tactics** employed by one of the parties in seeking to form the bargain. The fifth deals with the consequences of **form**.

Defenses rooted in form only appear mysterious. They come down to two of the more frequently encountered defenses in litigation: one centered on the absence of a written expression, and the other on the consequences of the bargain having been reduced to writing. The Statute of Frauds is a personal defense to enforcement of an oral bargain the subject matter of which has triggered a disciplinary requirement that there be a written memorandum of essential terms. If the parties have reduced their agreement to an "integrated writing," any attempt to go outside of that written instrument in efforts to prove a term of the bargain, or the understanding of the parties, is likely to trigger an encounter with the Parol Evidence Rule.

Some basic terminology: A discussion of defenses frequently is an occasion for stumbling over both concepts and language. Not all of the confusion is artificial. If a contract is defined as a promise or set of promises which the law will enforce, or in some sense regard as the source of obligation, then any factor which precludes enforcement could logically be said to prevent the creation — formation — of a contract. It turns out that the distinction between real and personal defenses is based on the degree of society's concern or objection.

Real defense: Any defense which, if established, would render the attempted contract void is a defense to formation. Put simply, there never was a contract. Though few in number, these are the most powerful defensive weapons. They are so significant that, from the vantage point of civil procedure, a court may **notice** their presence independently of the suggestion of either litigant. It is this capacity of a court to raise the issue ***sua sponte*** which truly distinguishes the real from the personal defense. An obvious example would be an attempted bargain involving an intrinsically evil subject matter. The offeror has dialed "M" for murder. There is another important consequence of classification as a "real defense." In the interest of promoting commerce, a purchase of a contract right or claim by an innocent third party will cut off the right of an original party to assert a personal defense to the enforcement of her obligations. By contrast, real defenses may be freely asserted. They preclude formation of the contract to which the innocent third party would claim a right of succession.

Personal defenses: Do not preclude the formation of a contract. However, if asserted in a timely manner, they render the obligations of the party possessed of the personal defense "voidable." Personal defenses do not arise unless they are asserted by the party possessed of the defense. Third persons may not raise them, and a court will not take independent notice of their existence. Personal defenses may not be asserted against an assignee of the contract obligation who paid value for the assignment and had neither notice nor knowledge of the defect.

I. **DEFECTIVE FORMATION AS A DEFENSE: Though normally studied before the materials which emphasize defenses, any defect in the formation of a bargain or the qualification of that bargain as a contract may be used in litigation to avoid liability on a contract theory.**

DEFECTIVE FORMATION AS A DEFENSE

  A. **Defenses to the Formation of a Bargain:** Begin with the denial of an offer having been extended, include the contention that the offer had been terminated or expired prior to the attempted acceptance, and conclude with the assertion that the acceptance was defective. [Each of these topics is covered extensively in Chapter 1, "The Agreement Process." What follows is an outline of the basic formation elements and their potential use as matters of defense. Detailed explanations and examples may be found in Chapter 1.]

  Example: Pat Wiley, a resident of Smallsville, drives his new car to Metropolis. Finding the traffic fierce, he pulls into "Park & Save," a multistory parking facility. The attendant hands Wiley a cardboard claim check. On the face is a number and the time of entry. There is a notation to "see back." On the reverse in rather small type is a statement that the claim check constitutes a contract, and that by parking the car and accepting the ticket the owner promises to absolve the parking facility of all liability for theft or accidental damage whether inflicted by a third party or the parking staff.
  Wiley puts the ticket into his pocket without bothering to read it. Three hours later, he claims his car only to find that the parking attendant had backed another vehicle into Wiley's car inflicting $1,000 worth of damage. When Wiley demands compensation the company cites the ticket and claims to have been "exculpated" by a term of that contract.
  Wiley will prevail. His defense to Park & Save's contract theory is that no contract was ever formed. If the ticket was intended as an "offer," it was never communicated. There can be no "acceptance" by a person unaware that he is an offeree! *See Parkrite Auto Park v. Badgett*, 242 S.W.2d 630 (Ky. 1951), and § 211 of the *Restatement, Second.*

1. **Ambiguity as a defense:** As noted in Chapter 1, if in their formation effort the parties have used a word or phrase which has more than one reasonable meaning and each has attached a different meaning, their attempted bargain is plagued by ambiguity of language. Whether this factor will preclude formation of a contract will depend upon whether the ambiguity infected an essential term of the attempted exchange and, if so, whether primary fault can be attributed to one of the parties.

   a. *Ambiguity must infect an essential term of the attempted bargain:* If the ambiguity does not extend to an essential term, formation is not defeated because it does not threaten the commercially reasonable expectations of the parties.

   b. If an essential term is infected, formation is precluded unless fault can be isolated in one of the parties.

      (1) If the parties are either equally at fault or equally blameless in using without definition a word or phrase with more than one reasonable meaning, a reviewing court has no choice but to conclude that formation of a bargain was precluded.

      (2) If one of the parties is at fault and the other is innocent, formation takes place giving the ambiguous language the meaning subjectively intended by the innocent trader.

2. **Mistake:** In mistake fact patterns the problem is not that the words used by the parties are ambiguous, but rather that they do not convey the subjective intent which would have been entertained but for a mistake by either or both of the traders. In another variation, the mistake is committed by some third party who has attempted communication services which ought to have served rather than sabotaged the process of formation.

   a. *Mistakes of the parties:* The common law distinguishes those fact patterns in which both traders are mistaken from those which feature the blunder of one party only. With respect to unilateral blunders, a distinction is drawn between "mechanical miscalculations" which may provide a defense to formation or enforcement of the terms of the resulting bargain, and "errors in business judgment," which never preclude the formation of what may prove a disastrous but perfectly binding obligation.

      (1) Mutual mistake: Involves a mistaken assumption of existing fact by both traders at the formation stage. Two factors govern judicial reaction to such fact patterns: the significance of the mutual error, and the point in time at which it is discovered.

         (a) Must negate a basic assumption of both traders: If the erroneously assumed fact is basic, going to the "very heart of their exchange," each party may invoke it as a basis for avoiding the obligations of the fatally flawed bargain.

(b) Mutual mistakes of minor consequence are legally irrelevant: If the mutual mistake of assumed fact does not violate a fundamentalassumption of both parties regarding either the subject matter or rights of the owner, the bargain continues to bind both traders.

(c) As defense to enforcement: If the mutual mistake of basic fact is discovered while the bargain is still executory, either trader may prove it as a defense to the enforcement of the terms of the flawed bargain. If the bargain has been fully executed, performed on both sides, courts are very reluctant to disturb the status quo.

(2) Unilateral blunders: If, at the formation stage, only one of the parties is mistaken with respect to material facts concerning the bargain, there is no threat to formation. If the blunder is a mechanical miscalculation, as opposed to an error in business judgment, the blundering party may be able to invoke a personal defense to enforcement of the mistaken terms.

(a) Mechanical miscalculations may be a defense to enforcement: If, at the formation stage, a party's intention is deceived by an error in reckoning the terms of the obligation, the bargain that results is not the one which, but for the miscalculation, would have been intended.

(i) If the nonmistaken party has formed a commercially reasonable expectation upon the terms to which the blundering party apparently consented, the blundering party is bound.

(ii) Test for commercially reasonable expectation is objective: To prevail, the other trader must not only be innocent of subjective appreciation of the mistake, but a reasonable person, standing in her shoes, must also have been innocent of such knowledge.

(b) Errors of business judgment no defense: If, at the formation stage, a party makes an error in business judgment in assenting to the agreement, the bargain formed is the one stupidly intended. Such a party is bound to the terms of what may be a disastrous but perfectly binding bargain.

b. *Mistakes of third-party intermediaries may be a defense to enforcement of the terms communicated:* If, at the formation stage, one party employs some intermediary to handle communication of the offer or acceptance, the potential for mistake is broadened to include those of the intermediary.

(1) **Reasonable expectation of the recipient of the communication precludes assertion of defense:** If the recipient of the communication forms a commercially reasonable expectation — meaning that he neither knows, nor as a reasonable person ought to know — of the mistake made by the intermediary, a bargain is formed.

(2) **Defense to enforcement if mistake infects an essential term** and the recipient knows or, as a reasonable person, ought to realize its presence.

B. **Defense to Status as Contract:** As reviewed in Chapter 2, "The Qualities of a Contractual Relationship", private parties may form an agreement, but a contract is alegal status and its existence depends upon the presence of valuable consideration — bargained-for legal detriment — on both sides of the exchange. [Chapter 2 should be consulted for a detailed discussion of the following doctrines along with examples of their use.]

1. *Want of consideration — a defense to formation:* If, at the formation stage, one of the parties has not incurred legal detriment, the other has a defense to the formation of a contract termed "want of consideration." This real defense arises where one party:

   a. Merely rebargains a pre-existing legal duty; or

   b. Gives an illusory promise.

2. *Failure of consideration — a defense to enforcement:* If the parties exchange promises which have the quality of bargained-for legal detriment, their agreement qualifies for the status of a contractual relationship. If, subsequent to formation, one of the parties materially breaches the terms of his promise, that material breach works a failure of the promised consideration. It may be cited by the aggrieved party as a defense to the enforcement of her own contract duties.

3. *Inadequacy of consideration — not a defense:* Common law courts have long refused to discipline the bargain for any quality of economic fairness. Such matters are left to determination by the parties.

   a. Personal defense: Inadequacy of consideration is a personal defense to the protected party if the context of the bargain was a confidential or fiduciary relationship. In these settings only, common law courts are willing to examine the adequacy of the exchange. Unless the bargain is fair in its terms and shown to be in the pragmatic interest of the protected party, that individual may invoke the inadequacy of the consideration as a personal defense to enforcement of the terms of the bargain.

   b. Economics: Equity courts as conscience tribunals will examine the economics of transaction for fairness as one of several factors influencing the grant of discretionary remedies.

II. DEFENSES RELATING TO THE CAPACITY OF ONE OF THE PARTIES

Problems in perspective: A defect in the capacity of one of the traders does not preclude formation of a contract but results in that person having an election to avoid his obligations by raising the defense of lack of capacity. There are two classes of protected persons recognized by decisional law as generally having an impaired capacity to contract: minors and those suffering from mental incompetency. Corporate persons have a general capacity to contract, but in certain circumstances particular transactions may be beyond their powers.

Because these doctrines have been devised to protect the party with the impaired capacity, and not the other trader, the promises of persons who have a legal election to avoid liability do constitute valuable consideration! The technical term for an exercise of the option to avoid liability is to "disaffirm" the contract.

A. The Contract Promises of Minors Are Voidable: Minors may form contracts, but their obligations are voidable. The common law age of majority is 21. In some states it has been lowered by statute to 18.

1. *Election to avoid contract obligations — disaffirmance:* A contract made during one's legal minority may be disaffirmed at any time before or after the attainment of a legal majority. Unless and until the contract is disaffirmed, it remains binding. Disaffirmance is accomplished by words or deeds which objectively signify the election to avoid liability.

2. *Disaffirmance may reverse a wholly executed contract.* While most instances of disaffirmance occur prior to performance, the legal election is not limited to executory contracts. Subject to an obligation to restore any goods or benefits still in the possession of the disaffirming party, she is able to reverse a completely performed contract and demand the restitution of her consideration.

   a. *Disaffirmance is personal to the minor or his legal representative:* The right may not be exercised by third parties.

   b. *Right to disaffirm unaffected by promises not to do so or misrepresentation as to age:* During the period of minority, a promise by the minor not to disaffirm is, itself, voidable! The fact that a minor misrepresents his age to the other party, who is thus deprived of an appreciation of the potential danger of disaffirmance, does not result in the surrender of the legal right. However, in some states an affirmative misrepresentation of age is considered a tort exposing the liar to a damage claim by the deceived party. *See Byers v. LeMay Bank & Trust*, 365 Mo. 341, 282 S.W. 2d 512 (1955).

   c. *Restitution:* Upon electing to disaffirm, the minor is generally obligated to restore to the other party only those elements of that party's performance that have been retained and are capable of restitution.

If the other party has conferred services, they cannot be returned and the minor has no effective obligation to make restitution.

(2) If the subject matter was goods, and they have been damaged or have depreciated, the restitution obligation extends no further than returning them "as now."

(3) Exception for the minor as plaintiff: In many states, if the minor litigates seeking recovery of what she has paid, as opposed to merely defending on the basis of her minority, relief will be conditioned upon her making restitution of what has been received from the other party. The effect of such a rule is to make a minor who has paid cash and seeks to regain it fully accountable. If she made the same purchase by credit she is not, for she need only defend on the basis of her minority!

d. *Obligation for necessaries:* If the subject matter of a contract between a minor andan adult is the provision of necessaries — food, clothing, shelter or medical attention — the minor may still disaffirm but is liable for the reasonable market value of any necessary which cannot be returned in "as received" condition.

Example: Sean Riley, age 17, purchases a used 1980 Corvette from Byer's Motors. The agreed price is $11,000. Riley makes a $2,000 down payment and agrees to make monthly payments of $300 to Byer's. Ten days after taking delivery Riley is involved in an accident with the car. As a result of a misrepresentation which Riley made in his application for insurance, there is no coverage on the car on the date of the accident.

As a minor, Sean Riley may disaffirm his contract with Byer's Motors. To do so he need only make an affirmative manifestation of his election and return the twisted remains of what had once been a proud automobile!

If the car had been a "necessary" (which it was not), he would have been liable for its reasonable market value, though not the contract price upon electing to disaffirm. If Riley had paid cash for the car and now sought as the plaintiff to recover it, in some states he would be faced with a liability to make restitution as a price tag for relief. This would be to Riley's advantage only if the reasonable market value of the car at the time of sale was less than the contract price.

e. *Ratification binding without elements of new consideration:* After attaining her legal majority, a person making a new promise to assume the liabilities of a contract formed during infancy is bound without the necessity of any further element of valuable consideration.

(1) How accomplished: Ratification may be by words, deeds, or a combination thereof which reasonably signifies the decision of the new adult to abide by the terms of the contract.

(2) **Effect of silence by new adult:** Courts are divided on the issue of whether mere silence on the part of a person who has attained his majority, coupled with retention of the other party's performance, amounts to ratification.

B. The Contract Promises of Persons Suffering from Mental Infirmity or Disability Are Voidable

1. ***The test for mental infirmity or disability:*** As in the case of legal criteria for a defense of "insanity" in criminal law, the test for infirmity or disability in this area has been criticized as unscientific and imprecise. Notwithstanding, common law courts seem to unite on a "cognitive" (understanding) test, to which many add a control-of-behavior supplement.

   a. *Lack of cognition:* If, at the formation stage, one of the parties lacks the ability to appreciate the nature and consequences of the transaction, the resulting bargain is not void, but voidable by that person or his legal representative on grounds of mental disability.

   b. *Inability to control behavior:* In a significant number of jurisdictions, an alternative proof of mental disability or infirmity can be mounted on proof that, though able to understand the nature of his actions, the afflicted person was unable to control his actions.

   c. *Incapacity need not be permanent:* The state or condition which will provide a personal defense need only have existed at the formation of the bargain.

   d. *Mental disability may be self-induced:* Early judicial decisions were very hostile to the claims of a person who sought to avoid the obligations of a contract made during a state of intoxication. More recent decisions have placed a greater condemnation on the other trader if she was aware of the state of intoxication and took advantage of it. Cases dealing with the disabling effects of drug use have tended to follow the more modern rule. If one party was aware of a debilitation which deprived the afflicted person of an ability to understand the nature of his actions or control his behavior, the impaired person may avoid the obligations of the bargain.

2. ***State of awareness of the nonimpaired party:*** If the disability or impairment results in lack of understanding, the majority rule in the United States is that the awareness or lack of awareness of this factor on the part of the other party is irrelevant. He may be innocent of either knowledge or reason to know, and the impaired party may still avoid the contract obligations.

   a. If the defect is one of lack of control, jurisdictions which recognize this ground for avoidance are divided. Many hold that it may be claimed only if the nonimpaired party knew or, as a reasonable person, ought to have realized the inability of the afflicted trader to control his actions or responses.

b. If the impairment is both self-induced and of a temporary nature — the consequence of the use of drugs or alcohol — most courts require that the other trader have either had knowledge or at least reasonable grounds to be aware of the condition before avoidance may be claimed.

c. *Restatement position:* Section 15 of the *Restatement, Second*, approves general use of an understanding test which is free from any necessity that the other party be aware of the problem. If the problem is one of lack of control, it may be cited as grounds for avoidance only if the other party knows or has "reason to know of his condition." Election to disaffirm is personal to the afflicted party or her legal representative. The rules for disaffirmance mirror those for minors, *supra*. Obligation to make restitution upon disaffirming: Courts have historically been less generous to persons claiming mental disability or infirmity than to minors. While a minor is under a duty to make restitution of any benefit retained only to the extent that it is possible on the date of disaffirmance, persons disaffirming on grounds of mental incompetency have generally been obliged to make restitution of any performance received from the other party. If that cannot be done in specie, then the reasonable value of what has been consumed must be paid. Obligation with respect to necessaries: As in the case of minors, if the subject matter of the contract being disaffirmed was a necessary — food, clothing, shelter or medical attention — there is no liability to pay the contract price, but the provider may enforce an obligation to pay the market value.

C. **The Contracts of Corporate Entities Which Are *Ultra Vires* — Beyond the Powers — Permitted by Statute or the Articles of Incorporation May Be Voidable:** In the eyes of the law a corporate entity is a "person" with the same powers to contract as those enjoyed by natural persons. But the useful myth of a corporate person standing apart from the legal rights and duties of its beneficial owners has always had limits.

1. If the contract would oblige the corporation to exceed **statutory** limitations on its power, the defect is fatal, and the attempted formation void. This doctrine was important in the nineteenth century, when corporations were formed by specific permission from a state legislature which articulated specific restrictions on the nature or dimension of corporate activities. If a particular contract was *ultra vires* in this sense, it was void. If the third party was innocent of this knowledge, some states permitted him to recover against the corporate officers or agents in their personal capacities.

2. If the contract is merely beyond the powers conferred in the articles of incorporation, the power of the corporate party to disaffirm is severely restricted by statute. Here, the effort is to protect the reasonable expecta-

tions of a third party. Unless that person was aware of the contract being ultra vires the articles, her expectations will prevail.

Example: The articles of incorporation of Impala Corporation expressly forbid the entity to purchase real property. Notwithstanding, Alice Franz, president of Impala, enters into a contract with Sam Keller to purchase a small apartment complex in Biggsville. Keller is unaware of the content of Impala's articles. Fred Martin, a shareholder of Impala, learns of the purchase and immediately consults a lawyer asking whether Impala can disaffirm.

The answer will almost certainly be dictated by statute. If the contract has been fully executed — performed on both sides — and the seller, Sam Keller, was innocent it is virtually certain that there can be no disaffirmance. If the agreement is wholly executory — the bargain has been formed but there has been no performance by either buyer or seller — some statutes would allow a shareholder to bring a derivative soft seeking to enjoin performance.

III. DEFENSES ROOTED IN SOCIAL OBJECTION TO THE CONTENT OF THE BARGAIN

DEFENSES ROOTED IN SOCIAL OBJECTION TO THE CONTENT OF THE BARGAIN

Problems in perspective: The distinction between defenses rooted in an objection to the content of the bargain, as opposed to the tactics used by one of the parties in gaining formation, is useful but not airtight. The modern defense which manages to straddle the fence is unconscionability. Society may condemn the content of a bargain as objectionable if, for instance, it calls for a debtor to pay a 40% rate of interest. On the other hand, the content may be less of a problem than the tactics used by a party with dominant bargaining power who has succeeded in manipulating a trader with considerably fewer bargaining weapons or skills.

A. Illegality: If the subject matter of the bargain, or the participation of one or both of the parties, is "illegal," there are important distinctions predicated upon the time and nature of the offense.

1. *Time:* Whether illegality will preclude formation, discharge obligations on a theory of excusable nonperformance, or render the attempted bargain void depends upon whether the illegality existed prior to the attempted formation or was an after-arising factor.

   a. *If the illegality is after-arising:* If the subject matter or participation of one of the traders is declared illegal at a time when only the offer is outstanding, it is revoked by operation of law. If illegality is established subsequent to formation but prior to performance, both parties are discharged on a theory of impossibility.

   Example #1: The local parish makes an offer to Jane Collins under the terms of which it will pay her $5 per hour for three hours of employment per week as a bingo caller at Saturday night gaming sessions. While that offer is still outstanding, but before Collins has accepted, the municipal government enacts an ordinance prohibiting "religious gambling or gaming." The offer has been revoked by operation of law.

Example #2: Collins has accepted the offer and has functioned as a caller on two successive weekends. On the third Monday, the municipal government enacts its ordinance giving it an immediate effective date. The obligations of both parties, the parish and Ms. Collins, are discharged by operation of law. The excusable nonperformance is rationalized on a theory of objective impossibility. *See* discussion, *infra*. U.C.C. policy on substituted performance: Under § 2-614(2), if an agreed means or manner of payment fails because of domestic or foreign governmental regulation, the seller may withdraw unless the buyer can provide a commercially equivalent and legal substitute payment. Such policy is consistent with the Code's desire to promote the formation and performance of commercial agreements. If the illegality existed prior to the attempted formation, the bargain is subject to a real defense. It is void. Neither party need see it as a source of legal obligation, and neither can claim it as a source of any legal right. *See Singer Sewing Machine Co. v. Escoe*, 179 Okl. 100, 64 P.2d 855 (1937).

Example #3: Fred Barnes, an employee of Signer Sewing Machine Co., is discovered by that firm to have been guilty of embezzlement. Upon learning of this, Barnes' uncle approaches Signer with the promise that he will make up the loss by giving them a promissory note if they will promise to conceal the crime from the public authorities. Signer accepts this offer and makes the requested promise. The agreement between Barnes' uncle and his employer is void. The subject matter, concealment of a crime, is, itself, an offense to criminal law and public morals. Signer is not bound by its promise to conceal. The uncle may repudiate his promissory note, and Signer can have no remedy.

2. The nature of the illegality will govern the willingness of a court to assist a party in withdrawing from the illegal transaction or claiming relief in quasi-contract.

   a. If the illegality is *malum in se* there will be no judicial involvement for any purpose. Illegality is *malum in se* if the subject matter is intrinsically evil. Thetest is whether any person, having reached the age of reason, could detect the intrinsic wrongfulness by merely consulting personal conscience.

      (1) If the subject matter is a penal offense under an existing statute, many common law decisions hold that there will be no judicial intervention for any purpose, including assisting one party from withdrawing from the venture. In effect, the subject is treated as if it was *malum in se*. *See Schenck v. Hirshfeld*, 22 Cal. App. 709, 136 P. 725 (1913).

      (2) *"Locus penitentiae"* doctrine — a minority position favoring the party who seeks to withdraw. Under the majority rule, if the sub-

ject matter is *malum in se*, there can be no use of the courts for ***any*** purpose. This includes assisting one party who seeks to withdraw from the venture before any part of it has been performed and desires to use the courts solely for the purpose of recovering what he had given in part-performance. The minority rule would grant this limited assistance to the repenting party.

Example: Charlie Windsor, owner of a restaurant increasingly avoided because of the quality of its food, enters an agreement to hire Fred Flicker, a "torch" who specializes in committing arson for persons who then seek to collect insurance. Flicker's fee is $15,000 with $5,000 down and the balance due after the incendiary event. Windsor pays Flicker $5,000 and then decides to "pull out of the deal." Windsor will find the courts in most jurisdictions deaf to his bid for assistance in recovering the $5,000 paid to Flicker. If he happens to reside in a jurisdiction which follows the minority *locus penitentiae* doctrine, he may litigate to recover the $5,000.

b. If the illegality is merely *malum prohibitum*, the attempted bargain is still void, subject to a real defense. However, there is a possibility of judicial intervention to assist an innocent or protected party in recovering in quasi-contract for the market value of any goods or services provided.

c. Malum prohibitum *defined:* Those matters regulated for the convenience of society, and not intrinsically evil, are *malum prohibitum*. In this area personal conscience cannot be relied upon to provide a warning of the potential transgression. One would know of the illegality only if one were aware of the terms of a statute or governmental regulation.

(1) Must not be *in pari delicto*: If, at the formation stage, both parties were aware that the subject matter was *malum prohibitum*, their conscious defiance of the law will preclude any quasi-contractual relief. However, if one of the parties was innocent of such knowledge, he may recover in quasi-contract for the market value of any consideration bestowed upon the other under what he supposed to be a binding bargain. *See Early Detection Center, Inc. v. Wilson*, 811 P.2d 860 (Kan. 1991).

(2) Status of member a protected class: If the bargain is merely *malum prohibitum*, a person for whose protection or benefit the government acted in defining the illegality will be permitted a quasi-contractual recovery of any performance rendered, notwithstanding his awareness of the illegality.

Example: Paul White, age 14, takes a job with a local laundry. Under the terms of his bargain with the owner, White, a school dropout, is to be paid $2.00 per hour for a forty-hour work week. This bargain is a clear violation of the child labor laws of the state in which both parties reside. The laundry owner later fires Paul, owing him for one week's work.

Paul White is a member of a protected class. As a minor, it was for his protection that legislative restrictions on child labor were created. Thus, notwithstanding his being "in pari delicto" with his adult employer, White may recover. He cannot obtain a loss of bargain recovery of money damages because the contract is void. However, he will be permitted to recover the fair market value of his services. In some states if that value exceeds the contract amount (let us say that the fair value of the service young White provided was $4.50 per hour), the relief in quasi-contract may exceed that which could have been gained had the contract been enforceable.

3. If the illegality can be corrected or checked through other means or proceedings, some courts have been reluctant to see it established as a defense to the enforcement of a duty to pay for goods and services already received. Their fear has been one of unjust enrichment of the party asserting the defense of illegality to the payment obligation.

   a. The most frequent circumstance in which this clash of policy is confronted deals with contracts said to offend the antitrust laws. *See X.L.O. Concrete Corp. v. Rivergate Corp.*, 83 N.Y. 2d 513, 634 N.E. 2d 158 (1994). The defendant, the owner of a large newly constructed office building raised an antitrust defense to a claim by the concrete subcontractor. The defendant alleged that he had been forced to do business with an entity termed "the Club" which featured as its members the Cosa Nostra in the form of four of the City's five crime families, seven concrete construction firms operating in New York City, and the District Council of Cement and Concrete Workers, Laborers International Union. The Club was alleged to restrict entrance into the concrete business in New York City by exacting protection money from the small number of firms allowed to bid and perform on such contracts. The second set of victims were persons or entities who desired to contract for such construction. Rivergate Corporation, the defendant, claimed to be such a victim and to have faced a rigged bidding scheme.

   The New York Court of Appeals rejected Rivergate's bid to set up the rigged bidding aspect of its contract with X.L.O. as an illegality under the state's antitrust statute capable of rendering unenforceable Rivergate's promise to pay for the concrete work. The court cited both state and United States Supreme Court cases for the generation proposition that "[t]he interposition of antitrust defenses in contract actions is not favored....The concern is that successful interposition of antitrust defense is too likely to enrich parties who reap the benefits of a contract and then seek to avoid the corresponding burdens."

   b. Perhaps more startling was the court's refusal to allow Rivergate to rely on the illegality of the "Club" and its stranglehold on this line of commerce in New York City. It appears to have taken the view that use of a private contract dispute was at best an indirect means to attack this institution. It suggested that the danger posed by the Club was "reduced where statutory remedies exist and the State Attorney General can directly attack the alleged antitrust violations."

B. Substantive Unconscionability: Closely related to the defense that the content of a bargain is contrary to public policy, *infra*, is the rather recent line of cases promoting the idea that the content of a bargain may be so unfair and grossly one-sided as to threaten important social values.

1. *Distinguished from procedural unconscionability:* When objection is centered on the content of the bargain, as opposed to the tactics of the dominant party, the charge is one of substantive unconscionability. If the content would be permissible but the tactics of one of the traders have managed to surprise or overbear the resistance of an obviously weaker party, the defense may be termed "procedural unconscionability." It will be discussed in Part IV of this chapter.

2. *Terms likely to be deemed unconscionable:* Usually, freedom of the marketplace allows traders great latitude in fixing the content of their bargain. However, several decisions as well as provisions of the U.C.C. conclude that certain important protections are not to be diminished or eliminated in the context of a bargain.

    a. *Stipulated remedies clauses:* A social decision has been made that the object of contract remedies is compensation of the aggrieved party, not punishment of the party in breach. If, at the formation stage, the parties include a stipulated remedy which goes beyond compensation, the clause is unconscionable. *See* U.C.C. § 2-718(1).

    b. *Limitations on consequential damages:* Penalty clauses are repugnant because they seek to go beyond compensation to provide the contract equivalent of a nuclear deterrent to breach. But the opposite goal may be equally objectionable. What if a seller insists on a clause limiting the buyer's right to be compensated for loss of bargain in the event of seller's breach? U.C.C. § 2-719(3) declares that any attempt to limit the award of consequential damages for breach of a contract to sell consumer goods is prima facie unconscionable. Such limitations in other contracts for the sale of goods may be unconscionable, but there is no presumption that this is so.

    c. *The attempted disclaimer of warranties:* U.C.C. §§ 2-314 and 315 create implied warranties that the goods sold shall be merchantable and, if the buyer has permitted the seller to select goods to meet the buyer's disclosed requirements or needs, that they are fit for that purpose. Section 2-316 permits modification or exclusion of these implied warranties even as it regulates how this may be accomplished. Consumer protection legislation in many states has gone much further and made the attempted elimination of such implied warranties unconscionable.

3. *Consequences of substantive unconscionability:* Unlike most defenses which either preclude formation or render the obligations of a contract voidable, the remedy for substantive unconscionability is to "blue pencil" the offending clause or clauses while enforcing the balance of the bargain. *See* U.C.C. § 2-302(1).

C. **Public Policy:** Though not "illegal" in the sense that it is contrary to statutes which either reflect a *malum in se* or define a *malum prohibitum*, certain subject matter offends "public policy." In other circumstances, it is the participation by an individual, usually a public official, which is offensive.

Problems in perspective: In the United States there is no common law of crimes. They are purely a creature of statute. But the moral convictions of common law judges have found other means of expression. One is a rather significant lump under the judicial carpet termed "public policy."

Problems begin with the term "public policy." It is not possessed of a settled definition, nor is there political comfort with making common law judges the arbiters of its content. Reading many cases one gets the impression that judicial motives range from protection of certain social institutions such as the family, to felt vindication of widely held economic opinions. An example of the latter may be found in common law hostility toward the restraint of trade. Adding to the muddle, the question of providing a legal remedy for a broken bargain is beset with competing interests. On the one hand are notions of public decency or morals which may have been offended. On the other is the public's interest in individual freedom, the freedom of the marketplace to test the validity of ideas and projects, and the possibility that one of the parties may be relatively innocent.

1. *The concept of "public policy":* If, at the formation stage, one of the parties seeks to gain an objective which threatens the values or institutions of society, a court will declare an offense to public policy.

   a. *Examples of subject matter held to offend public policy:* The elastic formula for recognizing offenses to public policy precludes any exhaustive list. Some of the more common and longstanding include:

      (1) Covenants in restraint of trade have been held to offend society's interest in the freedom to exploit talent and economic resources. Today, much of this field is taken up by statutes regulating unfair competition or antitrust offenses.

      (2) Covenants not to compete have been particularly troublesome because they pose a conflict of public policies. On the one hand there is the freedom to contract, which requires respect for freely negotiated and clearly understood promises. Yet there is also a primal interest in the freedom to work and the convenience to society that it enjoy a choice of providers of what are frequently professional services.

The *Second Restatement* §§ 186-87 suggest a balancing test termed a "rule of reason" which asserts that a "restraint is reasonable only if it (1) is no greater than is required for protection of the employer, (2) does not impose undue hardship on the employee, and (3) is not injurious to the public."

Example: Recently the Supreme Court of Wyoming was faced with a suit for injunctive relief to enforce a covenant not to compete formed by two veterinarians. Dr. Glenna Hooper had been hired on the staff of the All Pet Animal Clinic in Laramie shortly after her graduation. At the time she was a stranger to Laramie. An express provision in her contract of employment declared that the agreement might be terminated by either party on thirty days notice. Hooper then agreed that in the event of termination she wouldnot practice small animal medicine for a period of three years within five miles of Laramie. Hooper voluntarily left the employ of All Pet and purchased an interest in a rival practice in Laramie. The trial court granted the injunction.

On appeal the decision was affirmed using the Restatement's rule of reason. However, the majority concluded that a three-year prohibition was unreasonable imposing too great a hardship on Hooper and exceeded the protection needed by All Pet. *Hooper v. All Pet Animal Clinic*, 861 P.2d 531 (Wyo. 1993).

(3) Covenants which directly encourage or promote tortious interference with a noncontracting party are offensive to public policy.

    (a) If the encouragement is not direct and was not intended by an innocent trader, the contract will be enforced.

        Example #1: If Smith enters a bargain to sell explosives to Franklin, who later uses them in such a manner as to create a nuisance affecting Sato, the connection between the Smith/Franklin bargain and the Franklin/Sato tort is too remote to occasion public policy difficulties with the enforcement of its terms.

        Example #2: If Smith was consulted by Franklin and asked to select explosives capable of causing injury to Sato's property, a contract between Smith and Franklin would, given Smith's complicity, be against public policy.

(4) Contingent fee agreements for obtaining the passage of special legislation or favorable rulings by government agencies have been held contrary to public policy in that they tend to promote the corruption of the political process if not the personnel of government. *See Ewing v. National Airport Corp.*, 115 F.2d 859 (4th Cir. 1940).

2. ***Consequence of determination that terms of bargain violate public policy:*** Just as courts have remained flexible in their formulation of the

offense, they have remained pragmatic as to the nature of an appropriate response. Faced with a proven offense to public policy, a reviewing court may hold the entire agreement voidable or simply "blue pencil" the offensive term or terms while leaving the balance of the agreement to stand. *See Loescher v. Policky*, 84 S.D. 477, 173 N.W.2d 50 (1969), and §§ 183 and 184 of the *Restatement (Second)*.

IV. DEFENSES CENTERED ON THE DECEPTIVE OR COERCIVE FORMATION TACTICS OF ONE OF THE PARTIES

Problems in perspective: The idea that the free market is the best testing ground for both ideas and products has inhibited English speaking courts from developing long lists of defenses predicated upon the content of the bargain. In concert with the general refusal to police the economic terms of the bargain, such matters are left to the judgment of the parties. But when it comes to tactics which may be employed to gain such bargains, courts have been far less reticent about articulating grounds of "fair play" and then enforcing them by permitting avoidance by a person victimized. Yet even in this area there are tensions. On the one hand we wish to discourage coercive or misleading formation tactics. Yet on the other we recognize that the best line of defense against these strategies is self-defense on the part of the intended victim. We have no long-term interest in developing a market populated by persons who make no effort at self-protection and then clog courts with a docket full of cases seeking to avoid the consequences of passive indifference.

A. **Fraud:** The common law distinguishes three types of fraud — fraud in the factum (also termed real fraud), fraud in the inducement, and fraud in the execution.

   Problems in perspective: It is a natural tendency of many first-year law students to lump any case of deception under the generic label "fraud." This is a major oversimplification of what tends to be a rather subtle doctrine with at least three different manifestations. One reason that explains the tendency to make excessive use of the label is that common law judges stubbornly refused to give a precise definition of fraud. Their reasoning was as follows: The moment a court provided a definition of fraud, the fallen nature of humanity would devise schemes which stopped just short of that line but which still managed to victimize others! But if the courts refused to define fraud, persons with base instincts would be forced to err on the side of caution (lessening the incidence of fraudulent behavior) and courts would be free to meet inventive schemes with equally inventive retribution. Adding to the potential confusion is that "fraud" may also be a tort. In the following materials, be alert to the three different types or manifestations of fraud, the elements of each and the degree to which they differ from the intentional tort.

   1. ***Fraud in the factum is a real defense rendering the attempted bargain void:*** It consists of any deceptive strategy which has the consequence of preventing the victim from realizing that a contract is even in contemplation.

Example: Barton hands a blank piece of paper to Polous and asks her to autograph it. Polous obliges with her signature and returns the paper to Barton. Later, Barton fills in text above the signature of Polous which appears to be the terms of a contract selling her farm. Polous has been the victim of fraud in the factum — real fraud. In the circumstances she could not protect herself because neither she, nor a reasonable person in her circumstances, would have been aware that a contract concerning the disposition of her farm or any other subject matter was even in contemplation. The alleged bargain is void.

2. ***Fraud in the inducement:*** Here the victim is aware that a contract is in contemplation, but his consent to the bargain is seduced by lies or deliberate half-truths. Fraud in the inducement is a personal defense rendering the contract obligations of the victim voidable at her election.

   a. *Classical formulation of fraud in the inducement:*

   (1) Elements: While there is some disagreement respecting the elements which must be proven in order to establish a case of fraud in the inducement, a classical formulation would come quite close to the one employed in tort analysis.

      (a) A misrepresentation of a fact material to the bargain at the formation stage;

      (b) The misrepresentation had to be of an existing fact of which the victim was ignorant and which a person of normal sagacity and diligence would not have known;

      (c) The misrepresentation must have been intended to deceive and to induce the victim to enter the contract; and

      (d) Such misrepresentation must have actually induced the victim's consent to the contract. *See James Talcott, Inc. v Finley*, 389 P.2d 988 (Okl. 1964).

   (2) Burden of allegation and proof of all four of these elements lies with the person charging fraud in the inducement. Of the four, element number three, involving proof that the misrepresentation was intended to deceive and to induce the victim to enter the contract, has been most difficult.

   (3) Difficulties in proving the defendant's evil-intending state of mind — "scienter": Proving that Kane made a representation of fact to Able which proved to be untrue, and that this representation was material in Able's decision to enter the contract is rather easy. Proof that Able was ignorant of the truth and that a reasonable person also would not have known the true fact is possible and vindicates the law's expectation that the victim had taken reasonable steps to establish the material facts. But

proving that Kane knowingly devised the deception and intended it to cause formation asks Able to prove Kane's state of mind. As you might imagine, few defendants will play the role of a cooperative witness.

b. *The liberalized formulation favored by the* Restatement, Second: There is a tendency among recent decisions to relax the elements of fraud in the inducement if it is being used by the alleged victim to avoid the obligations of a contract rather than recover damages in tort. This trend is encouraged by the formulation of the doctrine suggested in Chapter 7 of the *Restatement, Second*.

(1) Elements: The major difference between the liberalized and classical formulations deals with the elements of scienter and the victim's duty to engage in self-protection.

(a) Under the *Restatement*, scienter is removed as a necessary element if there was a misrepresentation of a material fact. It would suffice if the misrepresentation were the result of negligence, or even innocent mistake.

(b) If the victim can establish scienter, that the misrepresentation was deliberate, then she need not prove that the fact was material.

(c) The misrepresentation must be of a present fact, not a prediction of future facts or statement of opinion. *See* §§ 168 and 169 of the *Restatement, Second*.

(d) Half truth as misrepresentation: As a general rule, silence has not been regarded as misrepresentation, since there is no general duty to make disclosure to the adversary in the course of forming the bargain. Telling half of the truth, however, may constitute misrepresentation of a material fact if the overall effect is a misleading impression. *See* § 159, *Restatement, Second*.

(e) Reliance must be justifiable: The *Restatement* would not abandon the classical insistence that the potential victim engage in self-protective steps to learn the truth about material facts. The difference is one of degree. *See Kannavos v. Annino*, 356 Mass. 42, 247 N.E.2d 708 (1969).

3. *Fraud in the execution:* Here the victim is aware that a contract is being formed, and her consent to its terms is not the product of misrepresentation of material facts. Rather, betrayal takes place as the oral agreement of the parties is committed to writing. The victim trusts the fraudulent party to reduce the agreement to a written expression and, acting on his

assurance that he has faithfully done so, signs that writing without reading it. Later the writing is found to be the product of a selective or inventive memory.

a. *Difficult policy choice:* A victim claiming fraud in the execution as a personal defense puts the issue of self-protection and the duty to use it as a line of first defense squarely at issue. The entire scheme could have been unmasked had the victim merely taken the precaution to read the documents before affixing her signature.

   (1) Preference for the fate of a negligent party when the contest is with a dishonest adversary: Some courts simply overlook the fact that the victim had easy access to self-protection. *See Rood v. Midwest Matrix Mart, Inc.*, 350 Mich. 559, 87 N.W.2d 186 (1957).

   (2) Negligence of victim as a bar to judicial relief: Other courts have sacrificed the immediate victim to demonstrate the general imperative to read documents before signing them. *See Lewis v. Foy*, 189 Ga. 596, 6 S.E.2d 788 (1940).

4. *Constructive fraud:* Has nothing in common with the fraud doctrines reviewed above except the term. It is a doctrine developed by equity courts before the merger of equity and common law jurisdictions became common in the United States. The purpose was to protect the dependent party in a confidential or fiduciary relationship. [For a full explanation of these relationships and their significance see Chapter 2, "The Qualities of a Contractual Relationship."]

   a. *Elements*

      (1) The presence of a fiduciary or confidential relationship between the parties at the formation stage.

      (2) The resulting bargain contains terms that proved significantly disadvantageous to the party for whose protection the relationship existed. This doctrine involves a deliberate exception to the general rule that courts donot measure the adequacy of consideration.

      (3) There is no element of moral wrongdoing essential to the doctrine of constructive fraud. The inadequacy need not have been deliberately caused by the defendant and may have been quite accidental.

   b. *Nature of relief:* Traditionally, relief was available only in an equity court. With the merger of law and equity, the requirements for equitable relief seem to have been maintained.

      (1) If the affected bargain is still executory, a plaintiff able to establish the three elements of constructive fraud has a personal defense to the enforcement of his contract obligations. If the bargain has been executed (fully performed on both sides), a plaintiff able to estab-

lish constructive fraud may obtain a decree of rescission conditioned upon his ability to restore the consideration received from the defendant.

3

> **Example:** Lucy Jackson approached her brother Benjamin with the request that he purchase a parcel of land which lay in a remote area between their respective farms. Lucy was a widow, and for several years prior to making this suggestion, she had relied upon Benjamin to rent out her farm, oversee the work of the tenant and settle the cash accounts. Five years after she had surrendered a deed and been paid the agreed amount for the land, she discovered that Benjamin had harvested timber from the land and sold it for more than ten times the amount paid to her. She brought suit praying for rescission of the five-year-old deed.
>
> Lucy was successful. The existence of the brother/sister relationship did not create a confidential relationship, but when one added the recent history of trusting the brother to manage her agricultural affairs, she was deemed to be the protected party in such a relationship. The fact that the brother later realized a tenfold gain in dealing with the subject matter of their executed contract shows that, as things turned out, the bargain was significantly disadvantageous from Lucy's perspective. No element of actual wrongdoing need be proved. Her remedy may be had even if the court believes the brother's claim that, at the formation stage, he had not been on the parcel and thought it to have only a marginal value as pasture land.
>
> The decree of rescission was conditioned upon Lucy's returning the purchase price with interest and reimbursing her brother for any taxes paid on the land. Once this was done she was to receive a reconveyance of the deeded interest plus the monies realized by the brother in the sale of the timber together with interest on that money. *See Jackson v. Seymour*, 193 Va. 735, 71 S.E.2d 181 (1952).

B. Duress: A coercive force used or threatened against the victim to induce apparent consent. There are two types of duress recognized at common law: physical and economic duress (sometimes termed "duress of goods"). The first is quite brutal and always a defense available to the victim. Economic duress is far more subtle.

1. *Physical duress:* Present whenever physically coercive acts or the threat of such acts are used to induce the victim's apparent consent.

   a. Coercive acts or threats of such acts to a third party are physical duress. Such coercive tactics need not be confined to the immediate victim. They are actionable if directed at those near or dear to the victim and their consequence was to "overmaster the will of the victim."

2. *Consequences of physical duress:* Physical duress is always a personal defense that may be asserted by the victim to avoid the obligations of an

executory contract or to gain rescission of an executed transaction. *See Barton v. Armstrong*, 2 All Eng. Rep. 465 (P.C. 1973).

3. ***Economic duress:*** Economic duress does not exist in a fact pattern where one of the traders is in desperate need of the subject matter and the other takes advantage of that need to drive a harsh, one-sided bargain. The claim of duress becomes tenable only when the victim can prove some illicit act by the aggressor which created this desperate situation or actively intermeddled in it to make it worse. *See Chouinard v. Chouinard*, 568 F.2d 430 (5th Cir. 1978).

   a. *Elements:* Economic duress is established only if each of the following elements can be established by the victim.

      (1) The defendant was guilty of some illicit act or threat of an illicit act against the victim's property or business interests that created the pressure upon the intended victim.

      (2) This illicit pressure must have left the victim with no reasonable alternative but to submit to the terms insisted upon by the aggressor.

   b. *The assertion of lawful pressure, or the threat to assert such pressure, as potential economic duress:* Courts are divided on this issue.

      (1) If the parties are roughly matched in terms of bargaining skills and economic strength, neither the blunt assertion of lawful pressure nor the threat to assert it is likely to be viewed as constituting duress.

         Example: A joint venture composed of three experienced and well-financed construction companies had formed a contract with the Department of Defense to do runway modifications on defense installations in Greenland. As the date fixed for completion of the work by the terms of the contract neared, a government inspection found the contractors far behind schedule. When this was reported to the Corps of Engineers, the plaintiffs and their lawyers found themselves summoned to a performance review with representatives of the Department. At that meeting, the government spokesperson bluntly threatened to terminate the plaintiffs "for cause" if they did not consent to modify the contract on terms advantageous to the government and promise to refrain from seeking government work in Greenland in the following year. Claiming that they were fearful of the loss of government contracts should they be terminated for cause, plaintiffs complied. Later they sought to overturn the release which they had signed claiming economic duress.

         Their claim was rejected. Hard, honest bargaining between experienced parties is to be encouraged, not inhibited by fear of claims of duress. The government lawyers honestly believed in the position they were asserting, and it was clearly a plausible alternative given the facts. *See Johnson, Drake & Piper, Inc. v. United States*, 531 F.2d 1037 (Ct. Cl. 1976).

    (2) However, the abusive or oppressive threat to deploy even lawful pressure has been recognized by some courts as constituting economic duress if the parties were mismatched at the bargaining table and victim's will was "overmastered." *See Laemmar v. J. Walter Thompson Co.*, 435 F.2d 680 (7th Cir. 1970).

c. If the illicit pressure was one which a reasonable person could have withstood, the claim of duress may be rejected.

    Example: Plaintiff brought suit seeking to set aside terms of a marriage settlement agreement with his former wife on grounds of both physical and economic duress. He claimed that his consent had been induced by her threats to ensnare him in litigation for years, see to it that he went to prison, and lie about him to their minor children. His petition in equity was dismissed. The court held that any reasonable person should put faith in the ability of courts to dispose of groundless litigation; that any adult should recognize that private citizens lack the capacity in our society to send others to prison; and that if she told lies he could reply with the truth! *See Raezer v. Raezer*, 428 Pa. 163, 236 A.2d 513 (1963).

d. The repeated assertion of illicit pressures, any one of which might have been reasonably resisted, may create an overmastering quality and, in the aggregate, amount to economic duress. *See Scheinberg v. Scheinberg*, 249 N.Y. 277, 164 N.E. 98 (1928).

e. *Consequences of economic duress:* If the affected bargain is executory, the victim may assert economic duress as a personal defense against the obligations apparently assumed. If the bargain has been fully executed, rescission and restitution has been deemed an appropriate remedy. *See Leeper v. Beltrami*, 53 Cal. 2d 195, 347 P.2d 12 (1959).

C. Undue Influence: This is the deployment of "overpersuasive" bargaining strategies designed to overcome the will without convincing the judgment of a weaker party. Bargains are forged in the crucible of negotiation, but some recent decisions have begun to suggest limitations on the mix of strategies one party may use in order to gain the consent of another.

Problems in perspective: We now review two defenses which have gained recognition only recently. Neither benefits from a set definition followed routinely by courts. Each illustrates the law in transition. The doctrines are "undue influence" and "unconscionability." Each represents an attempt by common law to cope with the fact that not all parties approach the bargaining table with relative equality of skill, needs, or resiliency.

    If the mismatch is glaring and the resulting bargain is improvident from the vantage point of the obviously weaker party, the law is faced with difficult choices. On the one hand, judges have no magic wand to remedy the disparity in wealth, education or circumstances. Then, too, there is the long venerated goal of promoting freedom in the marketplace and leaving the computation of value and advantage to the traders. But when individual cases present clear evidence that one of the parties had no real choice, freedom to bargain begins to sound rather hollow. So, too, does the expectation that the best line of defense is self-defense. I can't prove it, but I suspect that judges are more tempted to recognize defenses when the weaker party suffered from some temporary infirmity which, if he can be rescued from this particular bargain, may permit him to regain function in the marketplace. Where the condition is chronic and a defense in this transaction is, at best, a temporary reprieve from a near inevitable fate, some judges have resisted remedies on the grounds that they would instill a hope for change beyond the power of courts to achieve.

1. *Elements:* The defense of undue influence is established when a victim is able to convince a court that he has been subjected to "overpersuasive pressure" by the other party. Of necessity, the formula for such a result is not set but may vary. A common scenario in some of the more widely noted cases has been a recent event which greatly distressed the victim and the appearance on this scene of persons who, if not supposed friends, would not be perceived as enemies. If these persons then exhibit any of the following strategies in dealing with the weaker or distressed party, they invite the assertion of a personal defense. Not all of these elements need be present in any given fact pattern, and the list is not exhaustive.

   a. *Discussing the proposed bargain at an unusual or inappropriate time;*

   b. *Consummation of the transaction at an unusual place;*

   c. *Insistence that the transaction be concluded at once;*

   d. *Extreme emphasis on the risks or disadvantages of delay;*

   e. *The use of multiple persuaders in dealing with the weaker party;*

   f. *The absence of any third-party advisors to assist the weaker party;*

   g. *Statements discouraging the weaker party from acting on an inclination to consult advisors.*

2. *Consequences of undue influence:* If the bargain which resulted from the assertion of overpersuasive tactics is executory — yet to be performed — the victim has a personal defense to the enforcement of his contract obligations. If the bargain has been fully performed, and yet the evidence of undue influence can be established by clear and convincing proof, some courts have allowed rescission.

   Example: Plaintiff, a primary grade teacher in the public schools, was arrested and charged with homosexual action in a jurisdiction where the par-

3

ticular act was deemed a felony. After a twenty-four-hour experience of arrest, booking, detention and being bailed, the plaintiff had retreated to his home. He had been without sleep for most of this time. It was then that the superintendent of his district and principal of his school visited him. They told him that, unless he was willing to resign immediately, they were without any alternative but to commence public proceedings to suspend his teaching privileges. They emphasized that such proceedings would attract media attention which would probably destroy the accused's ability to teach in the public schools in any district. By contrast, if he resigned, they suggested that the grounds need never emerge. He could find employment elsewhere. Plaintiff resigned. Six months later the charges against him were dropped in an act of prosecutorial discretion.

Plaintiff then sued to rescind his resignation, charging undue influence. Plaintiff's complaint, dismissed by the trial court, was reinstated on appeal. The appeals court noted that there was neither duress nor fraud. The school representatives honestly believed that their conduct was in the best interest of both the district and plaintiff. Nor, given the topic of resignation, was the court prepared to recognize any confidential relationship surrounding that particular negotiation. However, the representatives were generally aware of plaintiff's trauma and his lack of sleep. These factors, combined with their visit to his home in the early morning hours with an agenda that urged haste raised the triable issue of potential undue influence. *See Odorizzi v. Bloomfield School District*, 246 Cal. App. 2d 123, 54 Cal. Rptr. 533 (1966).

D. **Procedural Unconscionability:** If the dominant social objection is the grotesque imbalance of bargaining strength or sophistication of the parties, and the resulting terms can be characterized as oppressive, the victim is likely to claim the defense of procedural unconscionability.

1. *Definition unsettled:* Neither common law decisions nor the statutory expression in U.C.C. § 2-302 fix a definition of unconscionability. This has led to complaints by some commentators that it is to the law of contracts what obscenity is to the law of freedom of expression. Apparently, judges know it when they see it.

2. *Goal of defense:* According to the Official Comment to § 2-302, the goal of the doctrine is to "prevent oppression and unfair surprise ... and not of disturbance of allocation of risks because of superior bargaining power."

   a. A contract or clause is not unconscionable in the abstract, but only when measured against the customs and mores of the marketplace at the time and place of attempted formation.

   b. Subsequent developments or events cannot create an unconscionable situation. The defense exists at the formation stage or it does not exist at all.

c. *Common association with "adhesion contracts":* In an adhesion contract, formation is not marked by bargaining over terms but rather by a take-it-or-leave-it proposition extended by a party in a superior bargaining position to a weaker party who is generally in need of the subject matter.

(1) Adhesion contracts are not per se unconscionable, but insistence by the party in the dominant position that there is to be no bargaining excludes the resulting "bargain" from the judicial deference normally accorded negotiated agreements.

(2) "Oppression" consists of terms which are grossly out of line with market expectations or which seek to curtail protections otherwise accorded traders, especially consumers.

(a) Commonly deemed "unconscionable" are price or credit terms that greatly exceed general market expectations or statutory ceilings.

Example: Defendant purchased certain household goods on credit from the plaintiff. A New Hampshire statute required that a credit-extending seller furnish the customer with a clearly written statement of the finance charges, expressed both in dollars and a rate of interest. Plaintiff clearly disclosed the total dollar cost of credit but did not stipulate the rate of interest. At trial it was conceded that this was a result of negligence and not a deliberate violation of the statute. After making several payments the consumer defaulted. The seller commenced suit. A personal defense of unconscionability was mounted with the proof of the omission of the disclosure of the rate of interest and evidence that the goods cost the seller (excluding sales, commission and other items of overhead) approximately $1,000 while their deferred credit price was nearly $2,600. The Supreme Court of New Hampshire reversed a judgment for the plaintiff-seller. It held that the combination of factors — failure to follow the statute in disclosing the interest rate at the time of formation, and the disparity between the wholesale cost and deferred sales price of the goods — rendered the contract "unconscionable" both at common law and under U.C.C. 2-302. *American Home Improvement, Inc. v. MacIver,* 105 N.H. 435, 201 A.2d 886 (1964).

(b) A dominant credit-seller's insistence upon brutal self-help remedies in the event of consumer default which are intended to be undisciplined by government is oppressive, especially if the consumer is unsophisticated.

Example: Plaintiff operated a furniture and appliance sales store in a ghetto neighborhood. The vast percentage of its sales were to recipients of Aid to Families with Dependent Children.

Nearly all of its sales were on credit to persons known to the seller to have no resources other than these government subsistence grants for food, clothing, and shelter.

Defendant was the recipient of such a grant and the sole head of a household including a number of minor children. She had dealt with the seller before. This time she arranged to purchase a stereo on credit. The written credit application contained an elaborate battery of protections for the seller set forth on a printed form. Without making any effort to call attention to these terms or to explain their import to consumers who would not have a lawyer or legal education, the seller purported to "add on" the latest credit purchase to all historical purchases. The intent was to create a security interest in all items historically purchased even though total payments to date had long since exceeded their cost. In the event of default, the seller was to have self-help repossession not only of the latest purchase, but of everything.

Defendant defaulted on her purchase, and plaintiff sought to exercise its "rights" under the "contract of purchase." The defense responded with the contention that both the manner of formation and terms were unconscionable. On appeal this was sustained. The court noted that "unconscionability has generally been recognized to include an absence of meaningful choice on the part of one of the parties together with contract terms which are unreasonably favorable to the other party. Whether a meaningful choice is present in a particular case can only be determined by consideration of all the circumstances surrounding the transaction. In many cases the meaningfulness of the choice is negated by a gross inequality of bargaining power." It then looked to relative education and deceptive sales practices such as a "maze of fine print." *Williams v. Walter-Thomas Furniture Co.*, 350 F.2d 445 (1965).

(3) "Unfair surprise" found in terms which depart from expectations created by the customs of the relevant marketplace and which are not clearly disclosed in an understandable manner to the other party at the formation stage.

Example #1: In the *Williams* case, *supra*, the court placed emphasis upon the fact that the store's adhesion contract buried the key terms in fine print while expressing them in highly technical language.

Example #2: Defendant was the lessee of a service station from plaintiff. He was possessed of an eighth-grade education and little experience with the art of contracting. A lengthy, printed standard form contract was placed before him by a representative of the petroleum company and he was invited to "sign." No effort was made to explain the content of the document, nor was he urged to consult any advisor before "consenting." Defendant signed and repeated this ritual each year for six years.

In fact, paragraphs placed in the middle of this long document, devoid of any captions or headings which would attract attention, purported to: (1) exculpate lessor from the consequences of its negligence or that of its employees in the delivery or handling of flammable substances, (2) obligate the lessee to hold the lessor harmless against any personal or property injury claims by the lessee or any third-party, and (3) indemnify the lessor in the event of any adverse judgment!

Defendant and one of his employees were severely burned when gasoline was negligently sprayed on them by one of the lessor's delivery agents. The leased premises were also extensively damaged. Plaintiff sued to obtain a declaratory judgment that the three clauses bound the defendant who answered by asserting that the contract clauses were unconscionable.

A divided Supreme Court of Indiana upheld the defense. Emphasis was placed on the disparity of bargaining strength and sophistication of the parties (including their relative access to legal advice), as well as the social importance of the responsibility for negligence which was overthrown by the terms of the "bargain." *See Weaver v. American Oil Co.*, 257 Ind. 458, 276 N.E.2d 144 (1971).

A strong dissenting opinion stressed defendant's total disinterest in ever reading or seeking knowledge of the content of a document always as close as his desk drawer and mindlessly renewed annually.

d. *Consequences of unconscionability:* Courts have reacted to proof of unconscionability by electing among three courses. They can (1) refuse to enforce the entire contract, (2) limit the application of the unconscionable clause or clauses while enforcing the remainder of the bargain, or (3) condition judgment for the dominant party upon its ability to prove that the weaker party was actually aware of and understood the clause or clauses and subjectively assented to their terms. *See* U.C.C. § 2-302(1), and *Restatement, Second,* § 178.

V. **DEFENSES ARISING FROM THE FORM OF THE BARGAIN: The fact that the parties have or have not reduced their agreement to a written expression is significant in the two items we now address. If the subject matter of their bargain fell within the categories for which the Statute of Frauds has commanded that there be at least a memorandum of essential terms signed by the defendant, the absence of such a writing may preclude any remedy at law. It is a personal defense in the hands of a defendant who must assert it in a timely manner. At the opposite extreme, if the parties have reduced their bargain to a written expression which both regard as final and complete, any attempt in litigation by one of them to introduce evidence of a promise, understanding, or representation not found in that writing is likely to trigger trouble with the Parol Evidence Rule.**

A. The Statute of Frauds: The fact that a contract is oral may create enforcement difficulties only if the subject matter is covered by an ancient piece of legislation termed the Statute of Frauds. Originally enacted by Parliament in 1677 during the reign of Charles II, the Statute is reflected in more or less its classical form in the statutory laws of nearly all English-speaking jurisdictions. While early judicial construction treated an oral contract covering an included subject matter as void, today the overwhelming view is that the terms of the oral agreement may be voidable. In other words, subject to some interesting limitations in the interest of fairness, the Statute provides a personal defense.

1. *Subject matter falling within the Statute:* The Statute of Frauds is entirely subject-matter sensitive. Only if the subject matter of the bargain falls within one of the covered categories is the loss-of-bargain damage remedy at law conditioned upon the proof of a written memorandum of essential terms signed by the defendant. Today, the important subjects covered include:

   a. *An agreement that by its terms is not to be performed within one year from the date of formation:* However, if there is any possibility, no matter how statistically remote, that performance obligations could be performed within a year the subject matter is not within the Statute, even if performance actually takes a year, a decade, or a century.

      Example: Provident Insurance Company enters into an oral contract to pay $1,000 per month "for life" to Clarice Cliff, then age six. Such an oral promise is not within the Statute of Frauds. Though the mortality tables suggest that Clarice will live into her late sixties, there is a remote possibility that she might die before attaining her seventh birthday. If that were to happen, the obligations of Provident could be performed within one year. When Clarice is fifty, the insurance company will still be unable to raise the Statute.

   b. *A promise to answer for the debt or default of another:* Promises of both suretyship and guarantee obligate the promisor to assume the liability for the debts of another. Their essential terms must be in a writing signed by the promisor, or she may raise the Statute as a personal defense.

   c. *An agreement made upon consideration of marriage other than the mutual promise to marry:* Such promises are seldom of importance today, but in the past, "marriage settlements" were vital in the redistribution of family wealth. Again, their essential terms had to be in writing and signed by the promisor at peril of his ability to raise the Statute as a personal defense.

   d. *An agreement for the purchase or sale of real property or any fixture permanently attached to the land:* This remains a vital subject and perhaps the most frequent modern experience with the Statute.

(1) Agreements for the lease of real property for one year or less are normally not within the Statute.

(2) An agreement authorizing or employing an agent, broker, or any other person to act as a representative in a real estate transaction which would, itself, fall within the Statute must also be in writing.

e. *An agreement which, by its terms, is not to be performed within the lifetime of the promisor:* The target of this provision is a promise to make a will or testamentary devise or bequest of property.

f. *Contracts for the sale of goods if the price is $500 or more fall within U.C.C. § 2-201, the Code's special formulation of the statute:* There are, however, three important exceptions. Two deal with subjects which do not require a writing, the third with a unique means of satisfying the statute.

(1) If the seller has tendered the goods and the buyer has accepted them, the buyer's oral promise to pay the agreed price is fully enforceable. So, too, is the seller's oral promise to deliver goods if the buyer has submitted payment and the seller has retained it. *See* U.C.C. § 2-201(3)(c).

(2) Special order goods: If the subject matter of an oral contract is goods made at the order of the buyer and not suitable for ordinary resale, the buyer's oral promise to pay for them is enforceable once the seller has made a substantial beginning in their manufacture or commitments for their procurement. *See* U.C.C. § 2-201(3)(a).

(3) If the contract is between merchants, a written confirmation of its terms sentby one party and received by the other who knows, or has reason to. know, of its contents satisfies the Statute as to both sender and recipient unless written notice of objection is given within ten days. *See* U.C.C. § 2-201(2).

g. Contracts for the sale of personal property fall within U.C.C. § 1-206 and are not enforceable by way of action or defense beyond $5,000 in amount or value of remedy unless there is a written memorandum signed by the party against whom enforcement is sought which identifies the subject matter and the price.

2. **Requirements of the Statute:** The consequence of a subject matter failing within the Statute is that there must be a written memorandum of essential terms signed by the party to be charged with liability for breach.

a. *Essential terms:* As noted in Chapter 1, the essential terms are the parties, the subject matter, the time for performance and the price. For purpose of satisfying the Statute, most legislation focuses upon the parties, subject matter and price.

3

b. *Writing need not be formal or prepared with the subjective intention to satisfy the Statute:* The goal of a court asked to grant a damage remedy at law is to gain written evidence traceable to the defendant from which the essential terms of the bargain may be reconstructed. No more is required. The writing or writings can be quite informal; notes and letters are readily accepted. Even a series of writings may be used if they are physically attached or refer to the writing bearing the defendant's signature. *See Leach v. Crucible Center Co.*, 388 F.2d 176 (1st Cir. 1968).

c. *Signature need not be formal:* Modern cases regard a printed letter-head or rubber stamp as sufficient. Doubtless, future cases will sanction the use of a fax message.

3. ***Consequences of a failure to satisfy the statute may provide the defendant with a personal defense to the enforcement of his oral obligations***

Problems in perspective: The Statute of Frauds represents legislative interference with the agenda of the judiciary. It has never enjoyed a warm judicial reception. From the time of its creation to the present date, the Statute has been regarded as a technical defense frequently at odds with a moral or just disposition of the plaintiff's ability to enforce the contract at law. As we shall see, equity courts never regarded themselves as bound by the Statute, and in recent years there has been a disposition to estop a defendant from asserting the Statute if its use would affront the court's sense of justice.

a. *Personal defense precluding a loss of bargain damage remedy at law:* Subject to the possibility of estoppel, *infra*, a plaintiff unable to produce a memorandum of essential terms of the contract alleged to have been breached bearing the signature of the defendant is precluded from maintaining a loss-of-bargain action at law.

(1) Timely assertion: Only the defendant, as the party to be charged, may raise this personal defense, and if it is not raised in a "timely manner" it will be deemed waived. Assertion is timely if it is contained in a responsive pleading. In the case of a defendant, this generally requires assertion in the answer.

(2) Third parties may not raise the Statute as a defense: Because the defense is personal in nature, it may not be raised or relied upon by third parties.

b. *Estoppel and the Statute of Frauds:* While there is substantial discord within the body of decided cases, some courts have applied both promissory and equitable estoppel concepts to preclude a defendant's assertion of the Statute of Frauds.

(1) Promissory estoppel: If the defendant specifically promised to reduce the contract to writing and breached that promise as well as the oral contract, some courts have held that reliance on the part of the other party can be used as the basis of an estoppel. *See Alaska Airlines v. Stephenson*, 217 F.2d 295 (9th Cir. 1954). Other courts have refused to defy what they see as a legislative decision that contracts are not to be enforced at law. *See Tanenbaum v. Biscayne Osteopathic Hospital, Inc.*, 173 So.2d 492 (Fla. 1966).

(2) Equitable estoppel: If the consequence of allowing a litigant to assert the Statute of Frauds would be to leave that party unjustly enriched, fundamental fairness will require that she be estopped from hiding behind the Statute. Other courts have even extended this doctrine to cases in which there was no enrichment of the defendant but obvious impoverishment of a plaintiff who had relied on the oral contract though there had been no promise to reduce it to writing. *See McIntosh v. Murphy*, 52 Hawaii 29, 469 P.2d 177 (1970).

(3) *Restatement* position: Section 139 of the *Restatement, Second*, adopts a middle course. It sanctions enforcement of the oral promise if the promisor should have expected the promise to induce reliance on the part of the promisee or a third person, there has been reliance, and injustice cannot be avoided except by enforcement of the promise. However, a court may stop short of full enforcement.

4. ***The attitude of equity courts:*** Part performance was accepted as an evidentiary substitute for the missing memorandum of essential terms: The original language of the Statute of Frauds forbade any "action" to enforce an oral promise dealing in one of the covered subject matters. No mention was made of "suits in equity." This omission, plus the attitude that equity courts were conscience tribunals, promoted limited defiance of the Statute.

a. Performance must point to terms of the alleged contract, not merely the possibility of some agreement. If the plaintiff sues for specific performance or injunctive relief in equity, the court may accept proof of part performance by the defendant of the terms of his oral promise as an evidentiary substitute for a signed memorandum of those terms. However, the performance must "unequivocally" refer to the contract and not merely the possibility of some understanding between the parties. *See Burns v. McCormick*, 233 N.Y. 230, 135 N.E. 273 (1922), and *Chevron U.S.A., Inc. v. Schirmer*, 11 F.3d 1473 (9th Cir. 1993).

b. Part performance by the promisee, as well as that by the promisor, may be weighed by an equity court for its tendency to prove the terms of the contract. *See Walter v. Hoffman*, 267 N.Y. 365, 196 N.E. 291 (1935).

5. ***Action at law for restitution interest in quasi-contract not precluded:*** A plaintiff prevented from gaining a loss of bargain measure of damages for breach of contract may still bring an action for the market value of any performance which she has tendered to the breaching party and which that party has retained. The Statute of Frauds is no barrier here because the action is not for the loss of an expectation created by the promise, but for the value of the plaintiff's performance under the terms of that bargain.

B. **The Consequences of Adopting a Writing — The Parol Evidence Rule:** Except in those instances in which the Statute of Frauds requires a memorandum of essential terms signed by the party to be charged, the use of a writing is optional with the parties to a contract.

1. ***Three possible roles:*** There are three possible roles for a written instrument in the creation or enforcement of contract obligations. Depending upon their attitude, a writing may be:

   a. *The last indispensable step on the road to liability:* If this is their attitude, the failure to sign a document containing the terms of the contract means that no contract was ever formed. *See Mississippi & Dominion Steamship Co. v. Swift,* 86 Me. 248, 29 A. 1063 (1894).

   b. *A mere memorial of the terms of an already formed oral contract:* In these circumstances the failure of the parties to generate a written expression is without legal significance unless the subject falls within the Statute of Frauds. *See Lambert Corp. v. Evans,* 575 F.2d 132 (7th Cir. 1978).

   c. *The final expression of the terms intended to survive the bargaining process as those of the contract:* If a writing was produced with this mutual intention, the terms there expressed are protected from addition, variation, or contradiction by the Parol Evidence Rule. *See The Countess of Rutland's Case,* 5 Coke Rep. 25, 26a-b, 77 Eng. Rep. 89 (K.B. 1605).

   Problems in perspective: Few areas of the common law have produced more misunderstanding or been the occasion for more evident stupidity than the policy respecting the utility of a writing. While many contracts are the end product of rapid and straightforward agreement, others are not. They come into existence only after protracted negotiation in which the parties move haltingly from incompatible positions to the final terms of a bargain. During the course of this bargaining many tentative positions or promises may have been put forth either orally or in writing. One would think that it would then be the essence of common sense to have some procedure whereby the parties could literally erase all of the discarded or modified premises and walk away from the table with but a single authoritative expression of those terms which they have intended survive as their contract.

Such a step would have at least three immediate beneficial consequences, each relating to a different constituency. First, the parties would have a final occasion on which to harmonize their expectations of both the benefits and burdens of their bargain. Thereafter they could live out the terms of their contract free from fear that tentative promises or understandings, finally discarded, could be dredged up by an adversary who suddenly finds them advantageous. Second, third parties would be able to consult a neutral and conclusive source for determining the terms of a bargain which may well affect their own lives or fortunes. Third, in the event of dispute and litigation, a trial court — as finder of fact — would find its task of determining the issues of breach and an appropriate remedy much simpler and certain. What human invention could better serve each of these important interests than the use of a writing?

Each of these benefits was a conscious goal of the Court of King's Bench on the day it invented what we now term the Parol Evidence Rule. It was the summer of 1605, Elizabeth I was dead, a "foreign" monarch had been imported from Scotland, society had been divided by the Reformation, the New World was being exploited for its minerals and other riches, and the demands of commerce were increasingly met by the use of writings. If you keep the goals of the traders, third parties, and trial courts in mind, you will avoid the confusion which has beset many lawyers and not a few judges.

2. ***The Rule:*** If the parties to a contract have reduced that agreement to a writing mutually intended as the full and final expression of their bargain, then any evidence — whether written or oral — of prior or contemporaneous promises or understandings is legally irrelevant if it would vary, add to, or contradict the terms of that writing.

3. ***Application of the Rule is by the trial judge:*** A determination of whether the Rule applies, and if so, whether it will operate to exclude from the jury's attention any evidence beyond the terms of a written contract is a matter for the trial judge. If she determines that the Rule applies and requires exclusion, it is not upon that predicate that the judge finds the evidence lacking in credibility. Rather, it is on the premise that, believable or not, it is legally irrelevant. If the trial judge concludes that the evidence is not barred by the Rule, it is for the jury to weigh its credibility.

4. ***Rule is not one of evidence and is substantive rather than procedural:*** In light of terms invented in subsequent centuries, the Parol Evidence Rule is saddled with a highly misleading label. Because it has nothing to do with the credibility of evidence, it is not "evidentiary" in nature. Because it has nothing to do with the manner whereby a proposition is proven, but rather with whether the proposition has any legal significance, the Parol Evidence Rule is "substantive" for purposes of choice of law and the Erie doctrine.

5. ***The Rule in litigation:*** The Parol Evidence Rule is a defense to the proof of a term of a contract. It must be raised during the course of litigation by the party seeking to exclude the evidence from the finder of fact or it is waived. Once the Rule is invoked, the trial judge will make the following determinations:

    a. *Integrated writing:* Only written instruments intended by both parties as the final expression of the terms of their contract are protected by the Parol Evidence Rule. The burden is on the party seeking to invoke the Rule to convince the trial judge that the writing was created with that mutual intention.

        (1) Integration determined from the written instrument: The most convenient manner to reflect the intention of the parties that the writing is intended as the final expression of those terms which they desire to survive as matters of legal obligation is to simply state this intent in the body of the writing. Such a recitation is customarily referred to as an "integration clause."

        (2) Integration determined from extrinsic evidence: Although early decisions tended to insist that the intent to integrate be expressed in the instrument itself, the prevailing current view is that any relevant evidence may be introduced to establish the intent of the parties that they regarded the written instrument as the final and complete embodiment of their contract. *See Salyer Grain & Milling Co. v. Henson*, 13 Cal. App. 3d 493, 91 Cal. Rptr. 847 (1970); and, *Restatement, Second,* § 209.

        (3) The U.C.C. position: Section 2-202 contains a formulation of the Rule for contracts for the purchase or sale of goods. Its meaning is not totally clear. On the one hand, it may be easier for the protections of the Rule to attach to a writing. On the other, the resulting protection is of a diminished scope.

            (a) Section 2-202 appears to guard any terms upon which the confirmatory memoranda of the parties happen to agree without further evidence of integration. For other terms, proof of integration may be found within the instrument or in extrinsic evidence.

            (b) If the Rule does attach, it merely protects the writing from being "contradicted by evidence of any prior agreement or of a contemporaneous oral agreement. . . ."

        (4) If the trial judge is not convinced that the instrument is an integrated writing, it is not protected by the Rule and may be varied or contradicted by any extrinsic evidence which the jury elects to credit.

b. *Extrinsic evidence must be "parol"*: Extrinsic evidence is any oral or written evidence which lies outside the four corners of the written instrument. But the rule only excludes "parol" evidence. Again, the choice of labels is not a happy one, for it suggests that only "oral" evidence may be challenged. Nothing could be further from the truth. Evidence of a promise or understanding chiseled in stone may be parol and thus excludable. The issue is not one of form, but of *time*.

(1) It is the fact that the extrinsic evidence would tend to prove a promise or understanding given or arrived at *prior to* or *contemporaneous with* the formation of the integrated writing that makes it "parol" in nature and thus potentially excludable.

(2) Evidence of *subsequent* promises or understandings may show rescission or modification of the contract. It is not disciplined by the Parol Evidence Rule.

(a) Subsequent extrinsic evidence may be disciplined by the Doctrine of Equal Dignity: The rule that written instruments should only be modified by evidence of equal dignity appears to also have been born in the *Countess of Rutland's Case*. During the time in which the seal was important, a sealed writing could only be modified by a subsequent sealed instrument.

(b) Modern status of the Doctrine of Equal Dignity: Common law judges have proven far less protective of the Doctrine than of the Rule. They have insisted that the Doctrine be specifically invoked in the original writing before it will be observed. Even then, an estoppel has frequently been raised against a party who sought an oral modification of a written contract and then attempted to resist payment by pointing to the failure to get the modification in writing. *See Wagner v Graziano Construction Co.*, 390 Pa. 445, 136 A.2d 82 (1957).

(c) U.C.C. position: To the surprise of many, the Code gives significant new lie to the Doctrine. Section 2-209(2) provides that a signed writing which excludes modification or rescission except by a signed writing cannot be otherwise modified or rescinded. But subsequent conduct inconsistent with this provision may be held to have "waived" that written restriction. Section 2-209(4), (5).

c. *Forbidden impact*: Parol evidence is precluded only if it would add to, vary or contradict the content of the integrated writing. Again, it is the trial judge who determines if a proffer of parol evidence would have one of these forbidden impacts.

(1) Parol evidence may be freely used to clarify ambiguity in the terms of the integrated writing.

3

(a) Ambiguity need not be evident on the face of the instrument. In a leading opinion praised by some and condemned by others, the Supreme Court of California held that: "The test of admissibility of extrinsic evidence to explain the meaning of a written instrument is not whether it appears to the court to be plain and unambiguous on its face, but whether the offered evidence is relevant to prove a meaning to which the language of the instrument is reasonably susceptible." *Pacific Gas & Electric Co. v. Thomas Drayage Co.*, 69 Cal. 2d 33, 442 P.2d 641 (1968).

(b) Parol evidence may be used to clarify an ambiguity, not to create one. Courts more protective of the content of integrated writings than the Supreme Court of California have recognized that ambiguity may be latent (hidden). Yet they caution against permitting a litigant to employ parol evidence to create an ambiguity and then to resolve it. *See Patti v. Western Machine Co.*, 72 Wis. 2d 348, 241 N.W.2d 158 (1976).

(2) Parol evidence may be freely received to prove trade custom or course of dealings as between the parties. *See* U.C.C. § 2-202(a).

(3) Parol evidence may not be admitted to clarify a term which is defined within the integrated writing.

Example: An author and publishing firm entered a written contract which contained royalty and bonus clauses on titles published by "Western Publishing Co.," a term which was defined in the writing. Later a dispute broke out concerning the publication of certain titles by an affiliate company. The author brought suit seeking an accounting. His proof was to be the testimony of his attorney, who had conducted the contract negotiations, that the term "Western" embraced affiliates and subsidiaries. The defendant immediately invoked the Parol Evidence Rule. It contended that the term "Western" was defined in the agreement. The author countered with the proposition that the term was ambiguous. The parol evidence was excluded by the trial court, a result affirmed on appeal. Where the parties have taken the trouble to define the term the meaning of which is now contested, parol evidence is to be excluded. *See Zim v. Western Publishing Co.*, 573 F.2d 1318 (5th Cir. 1978).

d. The parol evidence must not be admissible under one of the established exceptions to the Rule. There are both policy and tactical exceptions to the Rule. Again, it is the trial judge who determines whether one of the exceptions is apt and renders the evidence admissible for evaluation by the jury.

(1) Proof of fraud: Here is a moral trump card. Interested as courts are in the relative convenience of establishing the terms of a bargain from an integrated writing, they are more concerned with fer-

reting out a party guilty of fraud in the factum, inducement, or execution.

(2) Proof that the entire agreement was subject to an oral or written condition precedent which had to be satisfied before it was to attain the status of a contract: *See Hicks v. Bush*, 10 N.2d 488 180 N.E.2d 425 (1962). However, proof that a promise within an existing contract was subject to some condition not expressed in the integrated writing would be forbidden. In the former case the parol evidence proves there was no contract. In the second instance, it contradicts the apparent obligations of a contract.

(3) Proof of partial integration: In reality, this so-called exception merely revisits the initial determination by the trial judge. Did the parties intend the writing as a final expression of their contract? It turns out that the answer may be "yes" and "no." They may have intended it as complete with respect to certain, but not all terms of the bargain. If that is the case, the Rule protects only those subjects intended for complete expression. The balance of the agreement may be freely contested by extrinsic evidence.

   (a) Traditional four corners test: Courts disposed to favor the Rule have required that the integrated writing appear to be incomplete within its "four corners." The trial judge was to make this determination, and in doing so he was not even to know the content of the parol evidence!

   (b) Liberal plausible explanation for omission test: Other courts have reasoned that the trial judge cannot know whether a writing appears incomplete unless first advised of what might have been covered. Such jurisdictions leave the determination to the trial judge but only after she has reviewed the offered parol evidence and listened to an attemptedplausible explanation as to why parties in a writing frame of mind would not have included coverage of that subject.

      Example: A leading precedent which adopted the liberal test concerned a written contract for the purchase and sale of a hotel. Later a dispute broke out between the buyer and seller as to whether furnishings were to have been included. They were not mentioned in a writing which appeared exclusively devoted to the real estate conveyance. The Supreme Court of Kansas concluded that the buyer's offer of testimony by a scrivener that he had heard no mention of the inclusion or exclusion of the furnishings was properly admitted. The issue was one of intent of the parties, and the trial judge could not know it until he had heard the buyer's version of what had been intended. *See Brown v. Oliver*, 123 Kan. 711, 256 P. 1008 (1927).

(c) The U.C.C. position: Section 2-202 follows the more liberal of the common law rules. The official comment declares that the Code rejects the "assumption that because a writing has been worked out which is final on some matters, it is to be taken as including all the matters agreed upon."

(4) Parol evidence may be used to establish the existence of a collateral agreement and its terms: In a partial integration fact pattern, the proffer of parol evidence is based on the theory that while the parties made but a single agreement, they intended that only certain of its terms appear in the integrated writing. If the bid for admission is mounted on a theory of collateral agreement, the proponent of the parol evidence contends that the parties made two contemporaneous agreements only one of which was reduced to an integrated writing. The other was left to "rest in parol."

(a) Limitations on the use of a collateral agreement exception: A moment of reflection will alert you that this theory threatens to swallow the entire Rule in the guise of an exception. Courts tend to agree that the proponent of parol evidence put forward on a theory of collateral agreement must clear three hurdles:

(i) The evidence must prove the existence of a second agreement which is "collateral in form," meaning that it has a subject matter of lesser importance than the subject matter of the contract reflected in the integrated writing.

(ii) No term of the alleged collateral agreement may contradict any provision of the integrated writing.

(iii)The subject of the alleged collateral agreement must be sufficiently distinct from that of the integrated writing that it would be natural that persons in a writing frame of mind would not have included it as "part and parcel of a single bargain."

Example: In what is perhaps the leading case on collateral agreements, the litigation was between a buyer and seller of a country manor in upstate New York. Following the conveyance, the buyer commenced suit to force the sellers to remove an ice house from an adjacent parcel which they had not sold and which obstructed the new owner's view. The defendants immediately invoked the Parol Evidence Rule noting that the formal instrument of sale declared that it contained all of the duties of the seller and made no mention of the ice house. Plaintiff answered that the removal of the ice house was the subject of a contemporaneous collateral agreement which, by mutual consent, the parties had not reduced to writing. The trial judge admitted the evidence, and this was affirmed in the intermediate appellate court.

A divided New York Court of Appeals reversed. The majority concluded that while the alleged parol agreement affecting the ice house was collateral in form (being of a significantly less important subject matter than the written sale of the estate), the offer of parol evidence probably flunked the second test. It contradicted the term in the integrated writing which declared that it reflected all of the duties of the seller. The holding was that it definitely flunked the third test. In the eyes of the majority the subject matter of the sale of the estate and clearing of the view from its mansion house were simply too close to admit that, had it been intended to survive the negotiations, it would have escaped mention in the writing. *See Mitchill v. Lath,* 247 N. Y. 377, 160 N.E. 646 (1928).

(b) Collateral agreement, to be binding, must have all of the elements of an independent contract including separate consideration. In yet another sharp limitation on the utility of this strategy for evading the Rule, the New York Court of Appeals concluded that to stand as a source of further obligation, the collateral agreement must have all of the elements of an independent contract. *Halloran v. N. & C. Contracting Co.,* 249 N.Y. 381, 164 N.E. 324 (1928). This would have been fatal in the dispute over the fate of the ice house because Mrs. Mitchell did not allege that she had provided any independent consideration for Lath's alleged collateral agreement to remove the offending ice house.

NOTES

THE ALLOCATION OF RISK
INHERENT IN THE BARGAIN

▶ **CHAPTER SUMMARY**

4

THE ALLOCATION OF RISK
INHERENT IN THE BARGAIN

Conditions in perspective: The material on conditions is, to many, the most mysterious aspect of their study of contracts. Perhaps only the topic of future interests in the property course can rival it as a source of frustration and misery. It need not be so. Conditions were developed at a rather early stage in the evolution of contract doctrines to serve two critical functions. Each relates to fixing a time and order for the performance of the promises which the parties have exchanged in the formation of an executory bilateral contract. Once you understand the reasons which demand the existence of conditions, you will not find them difficult to grasp in theory or to observe in practice.

Here is a point so elementary that your professor will probably not mention it. Yet it may be the key to understanding. **Every condition modifies a promise. There is no such thing as a condition standing in the abstract.** The concept of modification is not mysterious. The modification will either set up or extinguish a state of present liability on the promise that it modifies. If the condition inserts a contingency which must either be satisfied or excused before liability on the modified promise becomes a matter of present duty, you have found a "condition precedent" or a "condition concurrent." By contrast, if the condition inserts some contingency the happening of which will discharge what had, until that moment, been a state of present liability on the modified promise, you have encountered a "condition subsequent."

There is a second way in which the law classifies conditions and that has to do with their origin, the manner in which they enter the bargain. Viewed from this perspective, conditions are express, implied-in-fact, and implied-at-law. Conditions implied-at-law are also termed "constructive conditions."

The final topic in this chapter will be the means to remove a condition precedent or concurrent as a barrier to present liability on the modified promise. There are but two. The condition is either "satisfied," meaning that the specified contingency has occurred, or it is "excused." Excuse can also disable a condition subsequent with the consequence that a factual development which would otherwise trigger its operation will not result in discharging the promisor.

The first utility of conditions arises at the formation stage: Conditions provide the parties with the machinery for allocating the risks inherent in their proposed contract. Every contract is a mechanism for legalized gambling. The gamble is that I will be able to keep the promise or promises I am making to you in the course of the exchanged offer and acceptance. The longer the time gap between the making of the promise and the time set for performance, the greater the degree of assumed risk. I can chart an uncompromising path into the unknown future by giving you an unconditional promise. As a more prudent alternative, I may reflect upon those risks which I am able to foresee and then make deliberate choices whether to assume or shift them to you, the "other party." The technique for shifting risk is to make a conditional promise. If my promise is subject to an express condition precedent, then the risk which I have specified is born by the promisee. Until that danger has passed, I am not liable to perform. If the feared factor is not avoided, my liability will never have become a matter of present duty, and my nonperformance is not a breach.

Example: In February, before he has even planted seed, Bill Franker, a Nebraska farmer, desires to make a contract to sell his wheat crop to Ben Quick, operator of a local grain elevator. Neither Franker nor Quick can do more than guess about weather conditions and market forces which may affect whether a crop can be realized from Franker's efforts and, if so, how large it will be. Many of the dangers are readily identified: too much or too little rain, too hot or too cold temperatures, diseases like "rust" which frequently infect wheat fields, etc. Others cannot be easily called to mind either because they have never been experienced or they are freakish in nature. There is such a thing as a Mongolian wheat bore, but it has never been detected in North America. Meteors fall to the earth daily, but what are the chances of a large one obliterating 200 acres of Franklin's farm?

Looking at this host of worries, Franker must make choices. He can say nothing and give an unconditional promise to deliver 40,000 bushels of #1 Grade Durham Wheat on July 10. That would be rather silly. And yet, dependent on the price which Quick is willing to pay, Franker may agree to make a promise which sees him assume all or only some of these risks. Let us suppose that $2.40 per bushel is a very attractive price given the conditions of last year's summer wheat market. Quick offers to pay that price. Franker is willing to assume the risks of general market conditions but is most concerned about drought threats to his dry land wheat farming. He counters with a promise to deliver 40,000 bushels of #1 Grade Durham Wheat on July 10 at $2.40 per bushel "provided that at least eight inches of precipitation are recorded at the nearby Montrose weather station between March 1 and June 15." Quick accepts this counteroffer.

If fewer than eight inches of precipitation are recorded at the designated weather station between the stipulated dates, Franker's duty to sell the designated quantity and quality of wheat to Quick will never mature. He protected himself by inserting an express condition precedent and, in this manner, shifted the risk of drought to Quick. When the minimum moisture was not received, the condition precedent to Franker's duty to sell was not satisfied. His refusal to sell in these circumstances is expressly privileged. It is not a breach.

The second utility of conditions is that they permit common law courts to isolate the party in breach of a bilateral contract which has been broken and which will be remedied by an award of "loss-of-bargain damages" to one of the parties: The nature of the damage remedy at law is that it is totally one-sided. In the event of breach, it aims to put one party, insofar as money can approximate it, in the position which would have been enjoyed had there been full and timely performance. By definition, the other party receives nothing other than the legal mandate to pay this compensation. Given these severe and one-sided consequences, courts at law were, and remain, very anxious to isolate the party whose refusal, failure or disappointing efforts to perform occasioned the breakdown. Conditions are used to fix a time and order for performance of the promises which the parties have exchanged at the formation of the bilateral contract. Thereafter, a court can look to this schedule to isolate the party who, at a given point in time, had a present duty of performance which was breached.

Example: Returning to the contract between Frankel and Quick, let us suppose that the express condition precedent to Frankel's liability was satisfied. In fact, nine inches of moisture was recorded at Montrose between the specified dates. It is now July 10. On that day Frankel makes no effort to deliver 40,000 bushels of wheat, and Quick makes no effort to pay for the goods.

Can a court award a loss-of-bargain recovery to either party? Quick will explain that he did not tender the funds because Frankel did not deliver the wheat. Frankel will seek to excuse the fact that he did not tender the wheat by pointing to Quick's failure to tender the money. What is a judge to do? Unless one of these traders had a duty to "go first," the court cannot be certain that either was ever ready, willing and able to perform. Yet the parties do not appear to have fixed a schedule for their respective performances in the express terms of their bargain. Unless a court can impose a schedule which operates in default of an express agreement, the ability to remedy this bargain at law would appear doomed.

The distinction between "dependent" and "independent" covenants: Let me again remind you of a critical point and some useful terminology about conditions which you must understand. *Every condition modifies a promise, or, if you prefer the fancy legal synonym, "a covenant."* There is no such thing as a condition in the abstract. Conditions are to promises what moons are to planets. If a promise is not hedged by any condition, it is *independent*. However, if the promise is conditional in nature, we term it *dependent*. A contract duty has matured if the promise was independent, or all conditions which had rendered it dependent have been eliminated through satisfaction or excuse. Breach of contact arises when a party refuses or fails to perform the duties defined in a matured promise, or defectively carries out that task.

The critical function of conditions in contracts formed in the bilateral mode: Why do conditions seem to relate only to bilateral contracts? The reason is so simple as to be nonobvious. If formation is in the unilateral mode we already know which party must perform first. It is the offeree, for only by completing the requested act or forbearance can she accept the offer. Once acceptance has taken place the offeree no longer has any duties on the unilateral contract. She does, however, have a right to receive the performance promised in the offer. So the order of performance is always determined in the unilateral contract. But the promise contained in the offer may have been expressly conditioned. If there is a condition precedent, then in addition to acceptance some stipulated contingency must also be either satisfied or excused before the offeror will be in peril of breach if he does not perform. Far less frequently, there will be some express condition subsequent which, if triggered, would discharge what had, at the moment the offeree accepted, become a present duty on the part of the offeror to perform.

Do not be distressed if you do not fully understand each of these comments at this point. They merely paint the "big picture." After you review the materials in this chapter these statements should appear as self-evident propositions.

CLASSIFICA-
TION OF
CONDITIONS
ACCORDING
TO THEIR
IMPACT UPON
THE MODIFIED
PROMISE

I. **THE CLASSIFICATION OF CONDITIONS ACCORDING TO THEIR IMPACT UPON THE MODIFIED PROMISE: Depending upon their nature, a condition has inserted some contingency which: (1) must be satisfied before liability upon the modified promise matures as a matter of present duty, or (2) the happening of which will extinguish what had, until that moment, been a present duty to perform the promise at peril of breach. The terms long applied by the common law are a clear indication of these essential, and very different, natures.**

A. **Conditions Precedent:** A condition precedent is any contingency which must be either satisfied or excused before liability on the modified promise becomes a matter of present duty. No matter how it may be worded, the litmus test for a condition precedent is this: One of the parties has said to the other, "I am not liable to perform this promise *unless* (here insert the stipulated contingency)."

Example: Gene Sutton purchases a policy of automobile insurance from Fidelity National Insurance. Under the terms of policy, Fidelity promises to indemnify Sutton or his estate in an amount up to $250,000 for any liability he may sustain in an accident involving bodily injury or property destruction to a third party. The liability of the insurance carrier is subject to four conditions: (1) that the insured suffer a casualty loss within the coverage of the policy; (2) that in the event of such a loss the insured gives written notice to the carrier within 24 hours; (3) that full particulars establishing the dimension and circumstances of the loss be made to the carrier within six months; and (4) that in the event of a dispute between the carrier and insured over the existence or amount of coverage litigation be initiated within one year.

The first and second of these express conditions are regarded as precedent in nature. Unless a casualty loss occurs within the coverage of the policy and notice of the claim is given, the carrier has no matured obligation to make payment. The third condition, respecting proof of loss within six months, has been debated. Some courts have treated it as a condition subsequent, *infra*. The majority, including the Connecticut judiciary which has the greatest influence over the insurance industry, treat it as a third condition precedent.

B. **Conditions Concurrent:** The impact of a condition concurrent upon the modified promise is identical to that of the condition precedent. It, too, has inserted some contingency which must either be satisfied or excused *before* liability on the modified promise becomes a matter of present duty. The distinction between conditions precedent and concurrent has to do with scheduling the respective performances of the two parties. Satisfaction of a condition precedent will remove it as a barrier to the present liability of one of the parties. It has no impact upon maturing the duty of the other. By contrast, conditions concurrent are the common law technique for maturing the performance duties of the parties simultaneously. While it is possible to create express conditions concurrent, they are almost always constructive (implied-at-law) in their origin.

Example: Tony Marini enters into an agreement with Pam Klein to sell her his 1987 BMW for $20,000. One week passes, and Marini has made no effort to deliver the car. When Klein telephones, he explains that she has not sent the money. Klein tells Marini that she will send him the money after he surrenders the car, the keys, and a clean title. Marini responds that he is not parting with the car until her check clears the bank.

It is evident that the parties are at an impasse. At this point, can either obtain a damage remedy at law for loss of bargain? Not without establishing that the other party is in present material breach. Since the terms of their agreement failed to fix a schedule for the performance of the mutual promises to deliver the car and pay for it, neither can prove that the obligation of the other ever matured. But there is an alternative to allowing this attempted contract to fail as a source of obligation. A court could furnish a default schedule for performance of the respective promises. Looking to the nature of the performances it might ask, "Are they physically capable of being tendered at the same time and in the same place?" They clearly are. This being the case, mutual tenders (a manifestation that I am ready, willing, and able to perform right here right now) will be required of both buyer and seller as constructive conditions concurrent to maturing the liability of the other party.

To place Marini in peril of breach, Klein will have to tender the $20,000 purchase price. If she does this and Marini does not tender the BMW, the keys, and the title, he will be in material breach. A common law court can grant the damage remedy to Klein with certitude that but for Marini's refusal the contract would have been performed. The genius of this solution is that by making the promises mutually dependent upon concurrent conditions, both Klein and Marini have been given a motive for manifesting their ability and willingness to perform. It is the only way to place the other party in breach. Faced with such a tender, the anxiety of the other trader will normally evaporate, and he will perform.

C. **Conditions Subsequent Extinguish What Had, until the Condition Was Triggered, Been a Present Duty of Performance:** If the terms of the bargain specify that a factual development will extinguish what had, until that moment, been a state of current liability to perform a promise, the condition is subsequent in nature. Conditions subsequent are relatively rare, but their presence in a bargain can be unearthed with the following test. Translated from the terminology of the bargain, one of the parties has declared to the other: "I am liable to perform this promise *until* (here insert the contingent factual development)." *See Gray v. Gardner,* 17 Mass. 188 (1821).

Example: The typical insurance policy's provision on the necessity of commencing litigation within a stipulated period following a claimed casualty loss is the most widely recognized use of a condition precedent. As noted in the example following the description of a condition precedent, a policy of insurance usually hedges the carrier's liability to disburse funds upon the insured's suffering a casualty loss within the terms of the policy, giving notice of the claim within a prescribed period, and making proof of the loss. These matters are regarded as conditions precedent. Assuming that the insured satisfied each of these conditions, the liability of the carrier on its promise to disburse funds matures.

At this point, the fourth condition will become critical. In the event of a dispute between the carrier and the insured over either the fact of liability or its amount, the typical policy will declare that the carrier's liability is discharged and the insured's claim extinguished if litigation is not commenced within a speedier time. The effect of this condition is clearly subsequent in nature. It operates to discharge what had, until that moment, been a matured obligation to perform on the promise to pay.

D. **Distinction Has Major Significance in Civil Procedure:** The classification of conditions as other precedent/concurrent or subsequent in nature has its greatest significance in trial litigation.

1. A complaint does not state a claim upon which relief can be granted unless it alleges that the defendant's promise was either absolute or, if dependent, that all conditions precedent and concurrent have either been satisfied or

excused. At trial, it is the plaintiff who has the burden of proof and risks nonpersuasion of the trier of fact concerning the satisfaction or excuse of all conditions contested in the defendant's answer. *See* Fed. R. Civ. P. 9(c).

2. ***Conditions subsequent are regarded as matters of affirmative defense:*** It is the defendant's burden to allege that a condition subsequent modified the promise asserted by the plaintiff, and that it was factually triggered with the legal consequence that liability to perform at peril of breach had been extinguished. The burden of proof and risk of nonpersuasion of the trier of fact, both as to the existence of the condition subsequent and its having been triggered, are those of the defendant.

E. **Position of the *Restatement, Second,* Events Excluded from the Concept of a "Condition":** The framers of the *Restatement* have sought to narrow the use and alter the terminology of traditional contract doctrine relating to conditions. Three events or contingencies would not be treated as conditions under the *Restatement. See* § 224.

1. ***Events which must occur before an agreement will have the status of a present contract***

   a. If both agree that some contingency must be satisfied before their set of promises has the status of a present contract, some courts have treated this as a condition precedent. *See Burns v. Board of Public Instruction of Okaloosa County,* 212 So. 2d 654 (Fla. App. 1968).

   b. The *Restatement* would not quarrel with the "no contract" conclusion but does not regard it as resulting from the failure to satisfy an express condition precedent. In the eyes of the *Restatement,* a condition modifies a contractual promise of the one of the parties. Factors which preclude formation of a contract are not "conditions."

2. ***Events certain to occur are not "conditions," they merely denominate the passage of time:*** In the view of the *Restatement,* a condition is a contingency or "event" not certain to occur. A statement that the promisor is not bound to perform until the passage of six months from the date of signing is not regarded as a condition by the *Restatement.* Indulging an optimistic assessment with respect to a nuclear holocaust and a terminal decision by the Creator, passage of time is deemed certain to occur.

3. ***Events that terminate a contract duty:*** Here is the most significant departure in concept and terminology from traditional contract usage. The *Restatement, Second,* would abandon the term "condition subsequent." The change is conceptual and cosmetic. The *Restatement* does not suggest that parties be precluded from inserting terms which treat certain factual developments as terminating the obligation of a promisor. It urges that such terms be viewed as an alternative means of discharging a contract obligation. *See* § 230. A condition precedent is simply termed a "condition."

II. **SOURCES OF CONDITIONS IN A BARGAIN:** There are three ways in which a covenant (promise) may be rendered dependent upon a condition. They are inserted by the express language of the bargain, by implication of fact, or by implication of law. Both express and implied-in-fact conditions are derived from the intent of the parties. As such they are termed "true conditions." Conditions implied-at-law, also termed "constructive conditions," are creatures of law. They are devised by judges to facilitate application of the loss-of-bargain damage remedy. They function to fix an order for the performance of the promises exchanged by the parties in forming a bilateral contract when the express terms of the bargain have failed to address this critical issue. The distinction between conditions as "true" and "constructive" will be important with respect to the question of satisfaction.

A. **Express Conditions as Vehicles for Deliberate Risk Allocation:** At the formation stage of a bilateral contract, the parties are presented with an opportunity to define the nature of their performance obligations. Of equal importance, they may hedge the duty to perform their promises given a conscious appreciation of risk factors inherent in the transaction or its setting. The machinery for the allocation of risk is that of express conditions.

Example: Steve Smith is a house painter by trade. He approaches Tom Tang, the owner of a large mansion in Biggsville, with the proposition that Tang's house is in need of exterior painting. Tang agrees that this should be done but indicates that he wants the work performed while he is at home. This presents a problem given Tang's plans to visit China for the months of May through August. Smith would like the job, but Tang's availability effectively eliminates those months in which, given the climate in Biggsville, conditions are most ideal for exterior painting. The question is whether Smith should obligate himself to do the job in April, a month in which it frequently rains heavily and the temperatures may be too cold for the paint to set properly. Knowing of these risks, Smith may either elect to bear them or attempt to shift the incidence to Tang.

Smith decides to adopt a negotiation strategy designed to shift certain elements of these foreseeable risks to Tang. He makes the following offer: "For $2,000 I will paint the exterior of your house and detached garage to match the existing colonial white color. I will begin this work no later than the fifth of April provided that it has not rained more than one inch in the preceding 72 hours, is not raining on that day, and the temperature is at least 60 degrees. If these conditions do not obtain, I will have no obligation to you, and you will have no obligation to me. If the weather cooperates, you will pay me either by cash or check upon my completion of the work." Tang responds, "I accept your offer."

Tang's unconditional, unequivocal acceptance of the terms of Smith's offer expressly created a bargain. Although it is clearly not absolute, Smith's promise to paint is not illusory. It is dependent upon explicitly articulated express conditions the satisfaction of which lie beyond Smith's control. Thus, he has incurred bargained-for legal detriment in the exchange with Tang. The risk which the express conditions shift to Tang are those of temperature and precipitation during the critical time period fixed for starting Smith's work. If the conditions are not satisfied by the absence of moisture and the presence of warmth on April 5, Smith's obligation to paint at peril of breaching his contract with Tang will not mature. But there are major elements of risk which have not been shifted. What if the rains come on April 7, when only part of the work has been accomplished and the project is most vulnerable? Apparently, painter Smith will bear all risk of both temperature and precipitation if work begins on April 5. Any delays or additional costs incurred in dealing with these problems will be born by Smith. There is no provision in the contract obligating Tang to make additional payment tied to Smith's cost of performance.

1. ***Distinguishing covenants from conditions in a contract:*** The distinction between covenants and conditions is critical. Covenants — promises — determine *what* must be performed in order to discharge contract duties. Conditions determine *when* and *if* the duties defined in covenants must be performed at peril of breach. Thus, the failure of a promisor to perform the duties created by a covenant which was either unconditional or which has fully matured (all conditions either satisfied or excused) is a present breach of contract. But if circumstances eventuate to leave conditions unsatisfied, the legal consequence is that the dependent promise does not become a matter of matured (present) duty. So, failure to satisfy a condition is never a breach of contract.

   a. *Question of the intent of the parties:* At the formation stage, a party is perfectly free to attach any conditions to her contract duties. There will be no problem with consideration so long as a possibility, no matter how statistically remote, exists that the conditional duty could become a matter of present obligation. The real check upon the nature and extent of conditions is not the law but the other party. He will quickly recognize that every express condition affords security to the promisor purchased at the expense of making him insecure!

      (1) Usually the language used will make it clear to the other trader, and ultimately to a reviewing court, whether it was that of an additional covenant or the insertion of a condition rendering one of the existing covenants dependent.

         (a) Significance of second mention of subject: A second mention of a subject previously addressed in the clear terms of a promise is probably that of a condition.

         (b) Role of business customs or mores: Under the objective theory of contract formation, courts are urged to seek the understanding which the terms of the bargain would have imparted to a reasonable person. If the bargain is between merchants, the customs, uses, and mores of the relevant market are useful in deciding whether a reasonable person would have appreciated the presence of a condition.

      (2) Certain terms or phrases are deemed artful for introducing the presence of conditions. Terms such as "upon condition" are obvi-

ously best at alerting the other trader. Others, such as "provided that," "unless," or even "if" have been held to signal the introduction of a condition.

b. *If the phrase is ambiguous as to whether it is that of a covenant or a condition, it will be interpreted as a promise:* This basic rule of construction vindicates fundamental notions of fairness. At the formation stage, the reallocation of risk should present the other trader with a reasonable opportunity to appreciate the nature and dimension of the insecurity she is being asked to accept. Conditions cannot be introduced by stealth, and whether deliberate or intended, doubtful language will never be construed as that of a condition. *See Southern Surety Co. v. MacMillan Co.,* 58 F.2d 541 (10th Cir. 1932).

c. *Construction leading to forfeiture disfavored:* It is possible for the terms of a bargain to impose upon one of the parties the risk of having to perform and then not being paid. Such a situation involves a forfeiture of such performance and before a court will tolerate it, the language must have plainly called for that result.

Example: At 10:00 a.m., Sue Barlow telephones Fleet Feet Deliveries and makes the following proposition: "I will pay you $100 if your agent leaves in the next five minutes and delivers this parcel to 33 Tie Street, Biggsville, by noon today." The delivery agent is delayed in departing for ten minutes but still manages to deliver Barlow's parcel to the stipulated address by noon. Unless Barlow can demonstrate some obvious advantage in the time of departure, as opposed to the time of delivery, it is doubtful that a court would permit her to refuse payment on the grounds that leaving within five minutes was an express condition precedent to her duty to pay for the service.

d. *Language which is both a covenant and a condition:* It is possible that a phrase can function in both capacities. This can result from the presence of an implied covenant which modifies the condition, or the express understanding that performance by one party of her covenant will function as a condition precedent to maturing the liability of the other.

(1) Promissory condition: This term is used to describe a condition, the satisfaction of which is within the control of the promisor. In order to save such an arrangement from being illusory, a court will imply a best efforts promise on the part of such a promisor to achieve the objective of the bargain and thus satisfy the condition.

Example: In real estate purchases it is common for the buyer to condition his liability to go forward with the transaction upon securing "satisfactory financing." Obviously, this will require effort to seek and evaluate the propositions of a variety of lenders. Yet modern courts do not regard such arrangements as illusory on the part of the buyer, for he is under the duty of an implied covenant to seek and evaluate financing packages "in good faith."

(2) Equally common is the situation in which the parties clearly settle the order of performance by making one party complete his promise as an express condition precedent to maturing the liability of the second trader.

2. ***Conditions of satisfaction as examples of express conditions:*** Not infrequently, the terms of a bargain will condition the duty of one party to pay for the performance of the other upon the satisfactory nature of that performance. The determination of satisfaction may be left to the adversary or to some designated third party.

Problems in perspective: A major risk inherent in the formation of a bilateral contract is that the other party will fail or refuse to perform. When this happens, the issue of breach is clear, and although litigation costs dearly in terms of time and treasure, courts can be expected to make an effort to protect the expectation interest of the aggrieved party. But what if the other party attempts performance but fails to gratify the expectations of the promisee? In these circumstances both the issue of breach and the nature of an appropriate remedy are far less clear. Can a trader take self-help steps to avoid this uncertainty by placing a condition on her own duty to make payment that the performance of the other party prove satisfactory, either to herself or to some designated third party? The response of the common law to these efforts teaches a good deal about the use of, and restrictions upon, conditions.

a. *Contract calling for the personal satisfaction of the promisee as a condition precedent to maturing her duty to render a counterperformance*

Example: In an earlier example we reconstructed a conditional bargain between Steve Smith, the house painter, and Tom Tang, the owner of a large dwelling in need of such service. Suppose that at a time when climatic conditions could not be a problem, Smith were to approach Tang with the following proposition: "For $2,000 I will paint your house, giving it two coats of premium paint matching the colonial white." Tang responds, "I agree, and promise to pay you $2,000 provided I am satisfied with the paint job."

In fact Tang did not "agree"; his response changed the terms of Smith's offer and was, by operation of law, a rejection counteroffer. But, confident of his ability, Smith responds by saying, "Fine, we have a bargain." It is clear that a bargain has been formed on the terms of Smith's acceptance of the counteroffer. But does that bargain qualify for contract status?

(1) Illusory construction disfavored: If a court were to construe the terms of this bargain as obligating Tang to pay if, and only if, in his unfettered discretion he expressed satisfaction, it might conclude that Tang's promise was illusory. He really said no more than "I will pay you if I want to." Such a construction would defeat contract formation. If, acting under the illusion that he had a contract,

Smith were to render painting services he could recover only in quasi-contract.

(2) **Implication of a legally valuable promise to determine satisfaction in good faith:** A modern court, following the objective theory of contract formation, could avoid a "no contract" result by simply implying a further promissory obligation on the part of Tang to determine his satisfaction "in good faith."

(3) **Personal vs. nonpersonal subject matter:** Even if construed as nonillusory, a bargain which makes the obligation to pay $2,000 dependent upon Tang's satisfaction with the painting performance of Smith has operated to shift all elements of risk in that transaction to Smith. It has also clearly settled the order of performance. Smith is to paint first. His duty is apparently unconditional. Tang is to pay second, following Smith's performance and then only if he is satisfied. A distinction developed by the common law has sought to minimize the instances in which such conditions can lead to forfeiture. It is drawn on the nature of the performance which is to be judged for satisfaction.

   (a) If the subject matter made the object of a judgment of satisfaction is "nonpersonal," being dominated by objectively quantifiable attributes of operative fitness, mechanical utility or structural completion, a level of performance which would gratify the expectations of a reasonable person will satisfy the condition and mature the duty of counterperformance even though, in good faith, the promisee declares himself not satisfied.

   (b) If the subject matter is "personal," being marked by qualities of taste and aesthetics and the express condition of personal satisfaction is aptly drawn to warn of its content, it will be literally construed. The duty of the promisee will not mature if, in good faith, he declares himself not to be satisfied.

   Example #1: The contract between Steve Smith and Tom Tang, which had as its subject matter the painting of the exterior of a residence, would be deemed "nonpersonal" so that a level of painting by Smith which would gratify the expectations of a reasonable homeowner in Biggsville would satisfy the condition precedent to Tang's duty to pay $2,000. *See Haymore v. Levinson,* 8 Utah 2d 66, 328 P.2d 307 (1958).

   Example #2: A written contract between a soft drink manufacturer and a regional bottler contained numerous performance standards with respect to quality and taste of the finished product, sanitation of the bottling premises, and efforts of the bottler to develop and work the exclusive territory being conceded. The duty of the manufacturer to maintain the franchise and bottling license was explicitly conditioned on good-faith determinations by the manufacturer that the bottler's performance satisfied the contract standards. It declared: "The judgment and determination of Dr. Pepper Company when made in good faith as to the failure of Grantee to comply with any of the terms of this license shall be, and is hereby, made conclusive and final."

Ten years after forming this agreement, the manufacturer claimed the right to cancel the bottler's license and cited detailed objections to the bottler's performance respecting sanitation, promotion and advertising.

Both the trial and appellate courts concluded that the manufacturer was entitled to the subjective standard in exercising its determination of satisfaction. The court of appeals stressed that the contract had been aptly drafted to warn of this quality; the bargain was clearly for the determination by Dr. Pepper and "not some imaginary reasonable person." The manufacturer had acted in evident good faith, was in a position to sustain severe business loss if an inferior product bearing its label were marketed, and the cancellation left it without any regional representative. *See Dr. Pepper Bottling Co. v. Dr. Pepper Co.,* 202 F.2d 372 (1953).

b. *Contract calling for the satisfaction of a designated third party:* The most common encounter with this type of bargain is in the construction industry, in which the owner's duty to make payment is conditioned upon a designated architect's certification that the builder's work is in compliance with plans and specifications.

   (1) No distinction drawn between "personal" and "nonpersonal" subject matter: The risk of forfeiture in these circumstances is greatly reduced by committing the judgment of satisfaction to a third party. Subject to the limitations listed below, the bargain having called for the satisfaction of that party, a court will not substitute the views of other persons of similar skill and training. *See Terminal Construction Corp. v. Bergen County,* 18 N.J. 294, 113 A.2d 787 (1955).

   (2) Limitations on the designated third party: Courts are clear that such a third party must function in a strictly neutral fashion and not as the partisan of either trader.

      (a) Any "bad faith" exercise of the discretion committed to the third person by the terms of the contract excuses the condition and immediately matures the dependent promise to make payment.

      (b) "Bad faith" defined: The type of conduct or refusal which can prompt an excuse of the condition of satisfaction need not be malevolent. Any attempt by the designated third party to exercise a decision as to satisfaction on grounds other than those committed by the terms of the contract is bad faith.

Example: In *Southwest Engineering Co. v. Reorganized School District R-9,* 434 S.W.2d 743 (Mo. App. 1968), an architect attempted to construe the language of the contract, rather than the performance of the contractor. Predicating his judgment on such a premise was beyond the bounds conceded to his determination. The condition was excused.

(3) Gross error by designated third party: While all courts seem prepared to excuse the condition if the third party acts in bad faith, others have concluded that excuse is also proper if the designated third party acts with gross disregard for the facts committed to her judgment. *See Macomber v. California,* 250 Cal. App. 2d 391, 58 Cal. Rptr. 393 (1967).

B. Conditions Implied-in-fact: Conditions implied-in-fact protect the unexpressed through reasonable expectations of the parties.

Example: Rarely will express conditions address all of the hazards inherent in a bilateral contract. Some will be omitted because the parties were incapable of foreseeing their threat. Recall the introductory example of the wheat farmer and grain merchant. There was nothing in the express terms of their bargain relieving the seller in the event the Mongolian wheat bore made its first appearance in North America. Other hazards, such as the falling of a giant meteor, might pass through the minds of the traders but are quickly dismissed as too improbable to burden the bargain. Neither of these contingencies will be directly addressed by the common law doctrine of conditions implied-in-fact. Rather, this vital concept speaks to a third type of risk, one which is so obvious that its nonoccurrence may be rationally taken for granted lest we create a market populated by paranoids. One of the primary goals of the doctrine of implied-in-fact conditions is to achieve cooperation between the parties in seeking the goals of their relationship.

1. *Implied-in-fact conditions arise by physical or moral inference from what the parties have expressly promised:* Though unexpressed in the language of the bargain, every promise is made against a backdrop of reasonable assumptions. They are the stuff of implied-in-fact conditions.

   a. Physical prerequisites or circumstances which a reasonable person would find necessary to render or receive performance must exist as implied conditions to maturing the contract duty of the promisor.

   Example: In our hypothetical of house painter Steve Smith and homeowner Tom Tang, no mention was made in their agreement of Tang's residence being in physical existence on the date conditionally designated for Smith's performance, April 5. If on that day the express conditions of temperature and moisture have been satisfied, Smith faces an apparently matured obligation to paint Tang's house. If he arrives ready and willing to do the work only to find that an earthquake has substantially damaged the premises and made them unsafe to approach, an implied-in-fact condition — that the house would exist and be available — would not be satisfied. Smith's failure to perform under such circumstances is not a breach.

b. The good-faith cooperation of the promisee in receiving the performance of the promisor is perhaps the most important circumstance made the subject of an implied-in-fact condition. In Chapter 2, "The Qualities of a Contractual Relationship," we discovered that the U.C.C. and modern common law are quick to imply mutual covenants to cooperate in good faith to attain the commercial objective of a bargain. We now find that same goal pursued in the common law recognition of an implied-in-fact condition of good-faith cooperation which must be satisfied before the obligation of the promisor matures. Working together, the implied covenant and implied condition can produce some startling results to one who is familiar only with the express terms of a bargain.

Example: On August 1, Piney Forest Products enters into a written contract to supply one million board feet of white pine logs to the Ellington Pulp Mill. The terms of the contract obligate Piney to deliver the goods on or before September 15 by floating them some forty miles down the Paxton River to Sandy Hook Point, where Ellington maintains massive log-harvesting equipment. It is a custom in the timber-harvesting business that buyers extend the use of such facilities to sellers who operate the equipment with their own crews.

On September 13, Piney begins the downriver movement of the goods. On the morning of September 15, with a strong current running in the river, the logs arrive off of Sandy Hook Point. Ellington deliberately refuses to make available the log-harvesting equipment to the Piney Forest Products crew. Without such equipment, Piney is helpless as the logs are swept beyond Sandy Hook Point. Piney Forest's failure to accomplish delivery of the goods is not a breach. The conduct of Ellington Pulp Mill failed to satisfy the implied-in-fact condition of good-faith cooperation. Though the use of the harvesting equipment had not been expressly promised, it was a legitimate physical and moral expectation of the seller. The failure to satisfy an implied-in-fact condition means that the seller's duty never matured.

Ellington Pulp Mill is likely in material breach of this contract. It has breached the implied covenant to cooperate in good faith. U.C.C. § 1-203 flatly mandates: "Every contract or duty within this Act imposes an obligation of good faith in its performance or enforcement." Implied terms prevented the maturing of the seller's duties, thus saving him from a charge of breach. They also added to the dimension of the buyer's obligation and placed Ellington in peril of material breach and a loss-of-bargain recovery of money damages. *See* Chapter 7, *infra*.

C. Conditions implied-at-law (constructive conditions) function to fix the order of performance when the express terms of the bargain have not settled this vital question.

Problems in perspective: In the formation of an executory bilateral bargain, the parties merely exchange promises which have about them the quality of legal detriment. But in moving from promise to performance there must be some order or schedule for carrying out the terms of the exchange. There are only three possibilities: (1) either A must perform before B; (2) B must perform before A; or (3) A and B are to render their performances simultaneously.

Usually the order or schedule of performance will have been expressly settled by the parties. But if they have failed to speak to this vital matter and neither is willing to "go first" in rendering performance, a court must chose among three alternatives. First, it could allow both parties to maintain an action for material breach without regard to their own state of performance. Second, it could refuse to permit either party to seek a damage remedy since there is no proof that the plaintiff was ever ready, willing, and able to perform. Third, the court could supply a default schedule so as to fix a time and order which, if not observed, would isolate the party in breach and pave the way for an award of loss-of-bargain damages to the aggrieved party.

From 1615 until 1773 the common law utilized the first solution. For judges paid by the case, allowing each party to bring an action against the other had a certain financial attraction. This may also explain why the second solution (prohibiting either from maintaining an action) was not favored. Yet at about the time of the American Revolution, English judges were converted to a system of fixed judicial salaries. Their newfound disinterest in handling two cases when one would suffice soon promoted the third solution. Devised by Lord Mansfield in *Kingston v. Preston,* 2 Doug. 689, 99 Eng. Rep. 437 (K.B. 1773), three constructive conditions were deployed to structure the performance obligations of traders who had failed to do so in the express terms of their bargain.

There are two vital points you must remember about the origin and selection of constructive condition. First, they only function in default of the parties having spoken to the question of an order for performance. Second, selection of the appropriate implied-at-law condition is totally dependent upon the physical order in which the performances of the parties are physically capable of being tendered.

1. *Mutual tenders:* Where, in the physical order of things, the performance of both buyer and seller are capable of being tendered at the same time and in the same place, then mutual tenders (a manifestation of a present readiness, willingness, and ability to perform) are required of each as a constructive condition concurrent to maturing the liability of the other party.

   Example: Farmer Nichols and Farmer Raynbred agree on the purchase and sale of a cow. Nothing is said fixing an order for the buyer to tender the money or the seller to tender the cow. In 1615, the King's Bench held that either could maintain an action at law for damages without having to show that he had tendered his own performance! *Nichols v. Raynbred,* Hobb. 88, 80 Eng. Rep. 238 (K.B. 1615).

   With the invention of the first of the constructive conditions, that result was forever precluded. Henceforth, if Nichols wanted to have a loss-of-bargain action against Raynbred he would first have to tender the cow. Then, if Raynbred failed to tender the agreed-upon purchase price, the seller was free to approach a court which could be confident that it had isolated the seller as being in breach. But for buyer Raynbred's refusal to tender the funds, the presence of the cow meant that the bargain would have been performed. *See Morton v. Lamb,* 7 T.R. 125, 101 Eng. Rep. 890 (K.B. 1797).

2. *Maturing the liability:* If the performance of one of the parties will take time or requires accomplishment in stages, whereas the performance of the other can be accomplished in a moment in time, performance of the party which will take time is a constructive condition precedent to maturing the liability of the party who can perform in an instant.

    Example: In our earlier hypotheticals concerning agreements between the house painter, Steve Smith, and the homeowner, Tom Tang, if the contract obligated Smith to paint Tang's house in exchange for $2,000, Smith would have to perform on his promise to paint as a constructive condition precedent maturing Tang's duty to pay. So, Smith goes first. If he does not like this arrangement, he is free to bargain with Tang for an express specification of the time and order of performance.

3. *Performance of the promise:* If the terms of the bargain fix a date certain for the performance by one of the parties but say nothing with respect to the time for the other to perform, performance of the promise controlled by the contract date is a constructive condition to maturing the duty of the other party.

    Example: The contract between Piney Forest Products and Ellington Pulp Mill had fixed September 15 as the date for Piney to accomplish the delivery of the logs. It said nothing about the timing of Ellington's payment obligation. Under the third constructive condition, Piney would have to accomplish delivery of the logs as a constructive condition precedent to maturing Ellington's duty to pay. If Piney fails or refuses to perform, or materially breaches in its attempt to do so, Ellington may recover a loss-of-bargain award of money damages without ever having to show that it was in a position to pay for the logs. This is because its duty to make payment will never mature.

III. **THE MATURING OF CONTRACT DUTIES — THE SATISFACTION OR EXCUSE OF CONDITIONS: There are two ways in which a condition precedent or concurrent may be removed as a barrier to present liability upon the dependent promise. The happening of the uncertain event which was the subject matter of the condition satisfies it and matures a present liability to perform the dependent promise at peril of breach. Equally effective in removing a condition as a barrier to a state of present liability is one of the numerous doctrines of excuse.** THE MATURING OF CONTRACT DUTIES: THE SATISFACTION OR EXCUSE OF CONDITIONS

A. **Satisfaction:** The degree to which the contingent event must obtain provides the distinction between what are termed "true conditions" created by the parties and "constructive conditions" which are creatures of the law.

1. *Literal satisfaction of express conditions:* If the promisor expressly made her duty of performance dependent on a condition precedent, she is

entitled to insist upon literal satisfaction of the contingency or event. If it does not occur, her duty never matures and her failure to perform is privileged rather than a breach. *Kammert Brothers Enterprises, Inc. v. Tanque Verde Plaza Co.,* 4 Ariz. App. 349, 420 P.2d 592 (1966).

Example: A written contract between an oil drill rig operator and his employer required that, in the event of dispute, the employee give written notice within thirty days of his claim to the employer as a condition precedent to the employer's liability. When a dispute did arise, the employee left the work site and returned to the city which contained the employer's headquarters. He immediately commenced an action, serving process upon the employer.

The employer defended on the grounds that, irrespective of the potential merit of the grievance, it could not be liable, for under the terms of the contract such liability could not be established until the employee had given the written notice. The employee countered with the argument that service of process amounted to substantially equivalent notification.

Summary judgment for the employer was upheld. To sustain the employee's claim that service of the complaint was a substantial equivalent would be to permit him to alter an express and unequivocal term of the contract. *See Inman v. Clyde Hall Drilling Co.,* 369 P.2d 498 (Alaska, 1962).

2. ***Substantial performance satisfies implied-at-law (constructive) conditions:*** If the condition was one of the default arrangements supplied by law in the absence of express provisions in the bargain, performance of the promise tendered first satisfies the constructive condition precedent or concurrent and matures the liability of the other party, if the performance is "substantial."

Problems in perspective: As you might anticipate, modern contract doctrines which aim to protect the commercially reasonable expectations of the parties are uncomfortable with a result which leaves one party under no obligation to pay for the performance of the other on grounds that a condition to the payment obligation has not been satisfied. This will be particularly objectionable when the party seeking to avoid liability has received, from the standpoint of objective utility or function, virtually everything he sought to gain from the other party's performance. If the parties have unequivocally contracted for such a result in terms which clearly warn the party who must perform first of her perilous posture, their bargain must be respected. As usual, Benjamin Cardozo put it best:

> From the conclusion that promises may not be treated as dependent to the extent of their uttermost minutiae without a sacrifice of justice, the progress is a short one to the conclusion that they may not be so treated without a perversion of intention. Intention not otherwise revealed may be presumed to hold in contemplation the reasonable and probable. If something else is in view, it must not be left to implication. There will be no assumption of a purpose to visit venial faults with oppressive retribution.

Jacob & Youngs, Inc. v. Kent, 230 N.Y. 239, 129 N.E. 889 (1921).

You immediately recognize that Cardozo has stated in general terms a policy reflected in the maxim that the common law abhors a forfeiture. The major difficulty in working from these general concepts to results in specific cases is to define "substantial performance" and to determine how important the role of intentional deviation may be in disabling a trader from claiming the protection of the doctrine.

a. *Substantial performance cannot be precisely quantified:* Perhaps the best shorthand attempt is again found in *Jacob & Youngs, Inc. v. Kent.* The duty of the party resisting performance must not have been protected by an express condition, and the deviation from full performance found in the efforts of the first party must be "both trivial and innocent."

b. Qualitative or quantitative deviations must not deprive the promisee of the function or utility which he reasonably expected as a benefit of his bargain.

   (1) Proof that there has been no such deprivation is most easily found in construction contracts where the owner has occupied the structure and is putting it to its intended use.

   (2) If the deviation from full performance is pervasive, the cumulative effect of individual flaws may be so obnoxious as to fall short of substantial performance. *See Tolstoy Construction Co. v. Minter,* 78 Cal. App. 3d 665, 143 Cal. Rptr. 570 (1978).

c. *Intentional deviation:* Intentional deviation from the terms of a contract promise in the course of its attempted performance will preclude any claim that the accomplishment was "substantial." Courts are divided on the issue of whether gross negligence in deviation should be equated with intentional behavior. *See McLaughlin, J.,* dissenting for three in *Jacob & Youngs, Inc. v. Kent, supra.*

d. *Effect of substantial performance:* If achieved, substantial performance will mature the liability of the party whose duty of performance is protected by a constructive condition only. That party must now render her own counterperformance at peril of breach. She will, however, have a cause of action at law for minor breach (*see* discussion in Chapter 7, *infra)* for any damages which she can establish.

e. *The U.C.C. position:* The doctrine of substantial performance has no application in the life of a contract for the purchase or sale of goods under Article 2. Section 2-601 codifies what is termed the "perfect tender doctrine." Faced with a tender of goods by the seller which fails to conform to the terms of the contract "in any respect," the buyer is privileged to: (1) reject the whole, (2) accept the whole, or (3) accept any commercial unit or units and reject the rest. [For an explanation of the affirmative duties of an aggrieved buyer under the U.C.C, *see,* Chapter 7, "The Consequences of Breach."]

B. Excuse of Conditions as an Alternative Means of Maturing Liability on a Dependent Promise: Excuse is every bit as functional as literal satisfaction to remove a condition precedent or concurrent as a barrier to present liability on a dependent promise. Excuse may also disable the operation of an express condition subsequent so that the happening of the event which would have discharged liability does not have that effect.

Problems in perspective: Though sometimes treated in an obscure or incomplete manner in casebooks, the doctrines of excuse are well established in the law. Is there a common thread which runs through their formulation and application? I believe that there is, though at times it is rather subtle. If the contract sees one of the parties hedge her promises by express conditions, she has shifted to the other party risk which she otherwise would have borne. So long as the terms are sufficiently clear to give the other trader fair warning of this reallocation, public policy is not offended. But if, subsequent to this formation, the words or deeds of the advantaged party suggest any retreat from this abnormally high ground, or she seeks to interfere in the unfolding of future events so as to frustrate the satisfaction of the condition, she runs the risk of attracting application of an excuse doctrine. Finally, if notwithstanding her conditional promise to perform, her words or deeds evidence a repudiation of that potential obligation, the doctrine of excuse will also surely follow.

1. *Prevention:* Here is a rather obvious doctrine. Any attempt by the party advantaged by a condition to interfere with the unfolding of events so as to frustrate the satisfaction of the condition is totally self-defeating. The other party had assumed the risk of nonsatisfaction of the condition. He had not assumed the risk of manipulation of events by the promisor. The condition is excused, and the dependent promise immediately ripens. If it is not performed, the promisor is in breach.

   Example: In *Casale v. Carrigan and Boland, Inc.*, 288 So. 2d 299 (Fla. App. 1974), a real estate firm was obligated to pay a commission only if the agent produced a prospect and thereafter a signed copy of a contract of purchase. Casale located a prospect and made his identity known to Carrigan and Boland. He then departed for a scheduled vacation. While he was gone, Carrigan and Boland went behind his back and negotiated the sale directly with the prospect located by Casale. When Casale learned of this he sued for payment of his commission. The defendants cited the fact that Casale had not satisfied the condition precedent. He had not produced a signed copy of a contract of sale.
   The court held that the conduct of Carrigan and Boland in attempting to prevent Casale from taking the steps necessary to satisfy the condition excused it. The condition having thus been excused, the liability to pay the commission matured and was absolute.

2. *Excuse of condition as a consequence of waiver:* There is an evident vindication of moral expectation in the law's treatment of prevention as a source of excuse. Waiver, by contrast, has its dramatic power because of a conviction that it was intended by the advantaged party.

a. *Nature of waiver:* Waiver is the voluntary relinquishment of a known and appreciated right. There can be no such thing as an accidental or inadvertent waiver.

b. *Consequence of waiver:* Because it has this conscious and deliberate quality, the common law has concluded that once a contract right has been waived it cannot be unilaterally reclaimed. It is gone forever.

c. *Application to conditions:* Waiver can modify both covenants and conditions in a bargain. If a promisee knowingly accepts without protest a flawed tender of performance by the promisor, the content of the promisor's obligation has been modified. In a proper factual setting, waiver can also excuse conditions precedent and concurrent and disable the consequences of having triggered a condition subsequent.

> **Example:** A famous publisher of legal materials and a distinguished law professor desired to enter an executory bilateral contract under the terms of which the professor would author a short treatise on the law of corporations. A major element of risk known to both parties inhered in the fact that the professor was a brilliant but only quasi-reformed alcoholic. The publisher sought to shift the risk of incapacitation resulting from this disease in two ways. It made its obligation to publish the book subject to an express condition precedent of satisfaction with the quality of the manuscript which was to be produced in chapter installments. The consideration supporting the professor's obligation to write was a promise by the publisher to pay $6 per page of acceptable manuscript unless the author was to partake of "intoxicating liquors during the continuance of this contract." If the author did not remain abstemious, he was to receive only $2 per page.
>
> Having signed this contract, the professor wrote and sent off for evaluation the text of Chapter 1. The reaction of the publisher was one of expressed delight. When the professor read this congratulatory message, he had a small, very private celebration! The publisher did not learn of this fall from the wagon. Shortly thereafter, the professor dispatched the text of Chapter 2. This time a representative of the publisher encountered the professor at an academic convention and there conveyed the congratulations and delight of the editorial staff. Such words of public praise proved the undoing of the author. He became very intoxicated and was seen in this condition by the publisher's representative.
>
> Shortly after this episode the author mailed off Chapter 3, which the publisher accepted without a word of protest. Further installments followed, as did bouts with the bottle. These falls were known to the publisher which continued to accept the manuscript until it was completed. Thereafter, the publisher remitted only $2 per page. The author immediately commenced an action alleging that he was entitled to the full contract price of $6. The publisher defended on the basis of the condition. It argued that the condition that the author remain free of drink was either a condition precedent, in which case its duty to pay the additional $4 never matured, or a condition subsequent in which

case his drinking discharged the duty to pay the additional compensation. The author relied on a theory of waiver.

The author prevailed. The court held that there could be no waiver in the publisher's acceptance of Chapter 2 since it was then not aware of the author's consumption of liquor. But, when with conscious knowledge of his public display of intoxication it accepted Chapter 3 without a word of protest, the condition respecting drink had been waived. *See Clark v. West,* 193 N.Y. 349, 86 N.E. 1 (1908).

   d. *Partial waiver:* In an installment contract, it is quite possible for a party to limit his waiver to but a single installment of the other's performance. In *Clark v. West,* the court was at pains to point out that the publisher could have accepted Chapter 3 with the express statement that it would overlook the single drinking episode but no others. This would have been a limited waiver and, if Professor Clark thereafter drank intoxicants, it would be at peril of failing to satisfy the express condition or triggering the condition subsequent.

3. *Estoppel:* If the party who has the protection of a condition precedent or concurrent creates an impression that he will not insist upon its satisfaction in maturing his liability on a dependent promise and, acting in reasonable reliance on this impression the other party changes position, the advantaged trader will be estopped to thereafter insist upon satisfaction. *See Fritts v. Cloud Oak Flooring Co.,* 478 S.W.2d 8 (Mo. App. 1972).

   a. Appearance of noninsistence which later results in estoppel need not have been deliberate and can be the result of accidental or inadvertent behavior. Unlike waiver, which is the conscious choice of a deliberate mind, estoppel is rooted in the impression of noninsistence coupled with reasonable detrimental reliance on the part of the trader disadvantaged by the condition.

   Example: In the immediately preceding hypotheticals based on *Clark v. West,* imagine that when the publisher's representative met Professor Clark at the academic convention he declared as a matter of social reflex: "Professor, let me buy you a drink." If Professor Clark accepted that invitation and consumed a gin and tonic, West would have been estopped from claiming that episode as having reduced its obligation to pay from the promised $6 to a mere $2 per page.

   b. *Condition can be revived if estoppel is lifted:* Because it is not the consequence of intentional and informed behavior, if the impression of noninsistence is dispelled before the other party has changed position in detrimental reliance, the bar of estoppel is lifted and the condition is once again fully operative. Further, if the estoppel affected one installment, a clear indication that with respect to future installments that the condition must be observed will revive it as to those future installments.

   Example #1: Assume that as they were heading from the hotel lobby to the bar it suddenly dawned on the representative of West Publishing that he was about to buy a drink for a man with a serious medical problem. Acting upon that realization, the man from West declared: "Professor, surely you would like to have something nonalcoholic such as a Shirley Temple." If, in response, Clark insisted on ordering a martini, he would consume it at peril of dramatically reducing his compensation under the terms of his contract. The appearance of noninsistence had been lifted before he changed position.

Example #2: Assume instead that Professor Clark had consumed a martini at the invitation of the West representative. West could clearly be estopped from claiming the advantage of the condition with respect to the next chapter of the manuscript. However, if upon accepting that chapter West wrote to Clark stating that it regretted the episode and forcefully reminding Clark of the terms of their bargain, noting that from that point on it would demand abstinence as per the contract, that condition would have been revived as to future installments.

4. *Decline in a conditional promisor's apparent willingness or ability to perform should the condition be satisfied as a source of excuse:*

Problems in perspective: It sometimes happens that a party who has the advantage of a condition precedent or concurrent communicates either by word or deed to the other party that, irrespective of whether the condition is satisfied, he either will not or cannot perform the duties of his promise. In either circumstance, the plight of the other party is quite desperate, for under the terms of the original bargain she had the obligation to perform first. Must she still do so knowing that the only thing her expense and effort will mature is disappointment, rather than the performance of the trader who had the luxury of performing second in point of time? Common sense and common decency suggest that the answer should be "no."

Two common law doctrines have been devised to produce a negative answer. If the party with the advantage of a condition is guilty of either *anticipatory repudiation* or *voluntary disablement,* all conditions which have heretofore buffered his duty of performance are excused. The conditional performance is accelerated in time to the date of the repudiation or disablement and, on that date, regarded as present and unconditional. The resulting material breach works a failure of consideration and thus excuses the contract duties of the aggrieved party, who may elect to bring an immediate cause of action for loss of bargain. This may be as close as the common law comes to high drama.

What if the advantaged party's actions fall short of repudiation or disability but manage to implant reasonable insecurity in the mind of the party who has the duty to perform first that the other trader will eventually prove willing or able to abide by the terms of her promise? At common law, the anxious promisor must bite his nails and march forward with his own performance. Only then will he mature the obligation of the other party which, if not then tendered, will amount to a breach. Under the U.C.C., if the transaction involves the purchase or sale of goods, there is a far more agreeable response. The party who is "insecure" may make a written demand for what are termed "adequate assurances of performance." If the party who has aroused the insecurity fails or refuses to provide such adequate assurance of both an ability and willingness to perform should that duty mature, the absence of assurance works a present material breach of the contract. The conditions which had protected the advantaged party are excused. The covenants of the insecure party are discharged on a theory of failure of consideration.

a. *Excuse of conditions as a consequence of breach by anticipatory repudiation:* If, prior to the satisfaction of conditions precedent or concurrent with the maturing of a contract duty fixed in the future, a promisor communicates to the promisee a definite, defiant and unyielding renunciation of any intention to be bound by the terms of the exchange, he commits a present, material breach of the contract.

(1) Quality of the communication must impart a definite, unequivocal, and defiant renunciation. If the tenor of the communication falls short of this it does not amount to a present breach by anticipatory repudiation. *See Regional Enterprises v. Teachers Insurance & Annuity Association,* 352 F.2d 768 (9th Cir. 1965).

(a) A party who mistakenly concludes that the other trader is guilty of a breach by anticipatory repudiation and elects to regard her own contract duties as having been discharged is in for the rudest of shocks. She will find that there is, indeed, a party in present material breach. If a court later concludes that the communication lacked the qualities of a clear and unequivocal renunciation of a willingness or ability to perform, the party who deemed herself aggrieved will be the party in breach. *See John Kubinski & Sons, Inc. v. Dockside Development Corp.,* 33 Ill. App. 3d 1015, 339 N.E.2d 529 (1975).

(2) Consequences of such a breach upon the promisee depend upon whether that party has executory duties of her own on the date of the repudiation

(a) If the other party has such duties, she has a common law election of responses to an anticipatory repudiation. She may either commence an immediate cause of action for material breach of the repudiated contract, or affirm the contract and await the due date of performance.

i) The immediate cause of action for present material breach: The aggrieved party with executory duties of her own may bring an immediate cause of action for present material breach. The defendant's breach will have had the following impact upon the terms of the bargain:

a) All conditions which had protected the repudiated duty of the breaching party are excused. His performance, originally fixed at a future, dependent date, is accelerated in time to the date of the repudiation and on that date regarded as fully matured and unconditional.

b) The executory covenants of the aggrieved party are discharged on a theory of failure of consideration. This failure is occasioned by the breach by anticipatory repudiation.

c) The aggrieved party is entitled to a loss of bargain recovery of money damages or, if the damage remedy is inadequate to put her in the position she would have occupied had there been full and timely performance, she has standing to sue in equity. [For a full discussion of these contract remedies *see* Chapter 7, "The Consequences of Breach."]

ii) As an alternative, the aggrieved party may affirm the repudiated contract. Such a response is an open invitation to the repudiating party to reconsider the matter, repent, and repledge allegiance to the terms of the bargain.

a) Status of the terms of the bargain pending repentance by the repudiating party: The covenants of the aggrieved party and conditions of the contract are suspended. If they mature prior to repentance, the covenants are discharged and the conditions excused.

b) Consequences of repentance: A subsequent communication by the repudiating to the aggrieved party which clearly retracts the announced unwillingness or inability to perform reinstates all executory terms of the bargain. The covenants of the formerly aggrieved party which are due subsequent to that date are revived as are any express conditions which again must be satisfied before the obligation of the formerly repudiating party will mature. *See Salot v. Wershow,* 157 Cal. App. 2d 353, 320 P.2d 926 (1958).

c) Any performance on the part of the formerly aggrieved party which had matured at a point following repudiation and before the date of repentance must now be performed as a constructive condition concurrent to maturing the liability of the repenting party.

(d) Repentance is precluded if aggrieved party has changed position in detrimental reliance upon appearance that the breach would not be retracted. The aggrieved party need not communicate further with the repudiator warning of this pending change. *See Helsley v. Anderson,* 519 S.W.2d 130 (Tex. Civ. App. 1975).

e) U.C.C. position: Under § 2-611, the repudiating party may retract the repudiation at any time before his performance would be due unless the aggrieved party has materially changed position in detrimental reliance or indicated that he accepted the repudiation as final.

Example: On June 1, Julie Vendee and Alex Vendor enter into an executory bilateral contract for the purchase of Vendor's Doublecross Farm outside Biggsville. The contract price is $450,000. Express terms of the written contract provide that the buyer is to pay that price in four installments: On July 1, Vendee is to tender a $100,000 cash downpayment to Vendor; on August 1, Vendee is to make an installment payment of $100,000; on September 1, Vendee is to tender $100,000 as the third installment payment; and, on November 1, Vendee is to tender the balance of the purchase price, $150,000. The contract then declares that "provided Vendee shall have faithfully observed these four covenants, it shall become the duty of Alex Vendor to convey Doublecross Farm by warranty deed."

Having signed this written agreement, Ms. Vendee has returned to her home in another city. It is the 25th of June. She receives the following telegram: "Forget payment next week as our deal is off. I have a far more attractive offer from Millie Fergus and have decided to sell Doublecross Farm to her. /s/ Alex Vendor."

It is evident that on the date she receives this telegram, Vendee still has executory duties of her own under the terms of the contract. Her first step is to determine whether Vendor is guilty of a present breach by anticipatory repudiation. It would appear that Vendor has directly communicated a definite, defiant, and unyielding renunciation of any intention to abide by the terms of the bargain and honor his promise in the event it is matured. He is guilty of a present breach.

Vendee's next step is to make her election. If she desires, she may commence an immediate cause of action on June 25. Her own payment covenants are discharged on a theory of failure of consideration. The fact that their faithful performance had been the subject of four express conditions precedent to maturing Vendor's obligation to convey the farm by warranty deed is no barrier. The conditions are excused. If Vendee seeks a loss-of-bargain award of damages at law she may recover without ever being forced to demonstrate that she could have paid any of the $450,000 purchase price. If, however, she sues for specific performance she will be forced to tender the purchase price as a condition of the decree.

4

She who seeks equity must do equity. [*See* Chapter 7, "The Consequences of Breach."]

Let us assume that instead of electing the immediate cause of action, Ms. Vendee affirms. She dispatches a wire to Vendor telling him, "I cannot accept your view that the deal is off given the terms of our binding contract. I trust, that upon reflection, you will see that the offer of Ms. Fergus, however attractive it may be, simply came too late. You have sold Doublecross Farm to me." The immediate consequence of this affirmation is to open the door to Vendor's repentance. In the meantime, Vendee is facing a covenant to make the first installment payment of $100,000 on July 1. That term is suspended both as a covenant on her part and as a condition to maturing Vendor's liability. Assume that on July 15, a telegram arrives from Vendor in which he announces that, after consulting a lawyer and his mother, he has decided to do the honorable thing and abide by the terms of the Vendor/Vendee contract. The consequence of this communicated repentance is to revive all terms of the contract from July 15 on. They include the three covenants on the part of Vendee to make the installment and final payments. Each is also revived as a condition precedent to Vendor's dependent promise to convey the farm.

Vendee must now make the payments on August 1, September 1, and November 1. Her failure to do any of these things would be a present material breach and also mean that Vendor's conditional duty to convey would never mature. If she makes all three payments for a total of $350,000, does it mean that she is now entitled to conveyance of the Doublecross Farm? No, the contract price is still $450,000, but the original covenant to make a $100,000 payment on July 1 matured before the repentance of Vendor. It was excused as a condition but must now be observed as a covenant. Its relationship to the performance by Vendor is governed by the constructive conditions. Since the payment of the $100,000 residual of the contract price is capable of being tendered at the same time and same place as Vendor's tender of the warranty deed, Vendee must tender this sum as a constructive condition concurrent maturing Vendor's liability.

(b) Restriction on the freedom to elect response: As in the case of any other material breach, the aggrieved party is under a general duty to mitigate her damages. [*See* Chapter 7, "The Consequences of Breach."]

(i) Repudiation in the face of a rising market: Because consequential damages are measured as the difference between the contract price and the market value of performance, if the cost of the breached performance is rising in the market-place, a decision by the aggrieved party not to bring an immediate action and to await the due date before litigating may be inconsistent with the duty to mitigate.

(ii) U.C.C. position: Under § 2-610 an innocent party may await the repudiated performance for a "commercially reasonable time" only. If he delays beyond this before bringing a loss-of-bargain action, the consequential damages will be limited to those which could not have been avoided by timely acceptance of the fact of the breach. *See Oloffson v. Coomer,* 11 Ill. App. 3d 918, 296 N.E.2d 871 (1973).

a) If, on the date of the anticipatory repudiation, the aggrieved party has no executory duties of his own, he must await the due date fixed in the contract to commence an action for loss of bargain. *See Dodson v. Phagen,* 122 Ga. App. 752, 178 S.E.2d 748 (1970).

b. *Excuse of condition predicated upon a breach of the dependent promise by voluntary disablement:* Any voluntary action taken by the promisor subsequent to formation which places the power of performing the conditional duty beyond her powers is a present breach by voluntary disablement.

(1) Consequences of the voluntary disablement give the aggrieved party an immediate cause of action for present material breach. All covenants of the aggrieved party are discharged, and all conditions which heretofore hedged the obligations of the disabled party are excused. The dependent promise is immediately accelerated from the point fixed in the bargain to the date of the voluntary disablement and, on that date, regarded as fully matured and materially breached. *See Zogarts v. Smith,* 86 Cal. App. 2d 165, 194 P.2d 143 (1948).

(2) Remedial consequences to the aggrieved party: He may elect an immediate cause of action or await the due date to seek a remedy.

(3) Repentance precluded: Acting on the maxim that actions speak louder than words, if the breach is by voluntary disablement rather than anticipatory repudiation, the majority of American jurisdictions would not permit the breaching party to reinstate the executory terms of the bargain by reacquiring the prospective ability to perform.

Example: Assume the identical contract between Alex Vendor and Julie Vendee on June 1. By its terms Vendee promises to pay $450,000 in exchange for Vendor's promise to convey the Doublecross Farm by warranty deed. The express terms of the bargain obligate the buyer to pay the purchase price in four installments. The full performance of those covenants is then made an express condition precedent to maturing liability of the seller to convey the farm by warranty deed on November 1.

Assume that it is June 20, less than two weeks before Vendee is to make her $100,000 downpayment on the purchase price. She is reading the *Biggsville Gazette* of that date when her eye is drawn to a legal notice. The County Recorder is publishing the fact of a conveyance in which Alex Vendoris listed as the grantor and Millie Fergus the grantee. The legal description of the property is unquestionably that of the Doublecross Farm. Such a notice cannot constitute a breach by anticipatory repudiation since there has been no communication by Vendor to Vendee. However, it would appear that Vendee has gained authoritative information that three days earlier Vendor has taken a voluntary step which placed his ability to perform the dependent promise to convey the farm on November 1 beyond his power.

The act of conveyance to Fergus breached the contract with Vendee by voluntary disablement. Vendee may commence an immediate cause of action for present material breach. If she elects to seek the loss-of-bargain remedy at law she can recover the difference between the contract price and market value of the Doublecross Farm without ever having to demonstrate her own ability to make any of her payment obligations. Her covenants have all been discharged on a theory of failure of consideration. Their performance as conditions has been excused.

c. Excuse of conditions as a consequence of a failure to give adequate assurance of performance:

Problems in perspective: A major problem presented by a communication which *might* be deemed an anticipatory repudiation or an act which *might* amount to a voluntary disablement is the judgment by the aggrieved party as to whether to treat the communication or event as discharging his own duties of performance. If he elects to treat the contract as having been materially breached and, in the cold light of hindsight, a court were to disagree, his refusal to perform his own contract obligations would have been the material breach. Such fears are not fanciful. *See Cook v. Nordstrand,* 83 Cal. App. 2d 188, 188 P.2d 282 (1948). A buyer in a real estate contract treated the seller's statement as a breach by anticipatory repudiation. Accordingly, he did not perform his own contract duties, deeming them discharged on a theory of failure of consideration. In subsequent litigation, the court decided that the seller's statement did not have the definite, unyielding, and unequivocal quality of renunciation needed to establish breach. The unfortunate buyer learned that there was, indeed, a party in material breach. It was the vendee!

As you might anticipate, the Uniform Commercial Code has adopted a better strategy than the lie or death decision respecting the future of a contract if one the parties has developed insecurity respecting the apparent willingness or ability of the other to eventually perform.

(1) The U.C.C. position on "insecurity": Section 2-609(1) declares that a contract of sale imposes an obligation on each party that the other's expectation of receiving due performance will not be impaired. When reasonable grounds for insecurity arise with respect to the future performance of the other party, the Code provides a three-stage road to self-help.

(2) The written demand for adequate assurances: A party who is reasonably insecure may make written demand for "adequate assurance of due performance" by the other party.

(3) Suspension of the insecure party's performance: Having made written demand, he may suspend his own performance pending receipt of a reply. During this period of suspension, the terms of his own performance, both as covenants and conditions, are suspended.

(4) Failure to provide adequate assurance as repudiation: The insecure party may treat the failure of the other party to provide adequate assurances within a reasonable time (not exceeding thirty days) as a present breach of the contract by repudiation. Such a breach would discharge any executory covenants of the aggrieved party on a theory of failure of consideration and excuse all conditions which had heretofore protected the nonresponsive trader.

(5) Commercial standards determinative: Whether a trader is "reasonably insecure" or the assurances by the party faced with the demand are "adequate" and "timely" is to be determined by commercial standards if both traders are merchants. Ultimately each presents an issue of fact.

   (a) A cumulative impact of factors, not one of which would provoke reasonable insecurity, may in the aggregate justify the demand for adequate assurance.

   (b) So, too, may a repeated instance of the source of insecurity or the apparent ineffectiveness of corrective efforts. *See AMF, Inc. v. McDonald's Corp.*, 536 F.2d 1167 (7th Cir. 1976) (establishing the above points and also reaching the debatable conclusion that despite the Code's requirement of a written demand, proof that the other party was aware of the insecure trader's oral demand was sufficient to trigger the duty to give assurance or fall into material breach).

THE RIGHTS AND DUTIES OF NONTRADERS

▶ **CHAPTER SUMMARY**

RIGHTS AND DUTIES OF NONTRADERS

Scope: It is regrettable that nontrader status is, in virtually every casebook including my own, presented in the final chapter. The flight of time frequently requires that it be given rushed, if not spotty, attention. The placement is more the dictate of an assumed logic than relevance. Indeed, the sale of the right to receive the performance of an executory contract is, save only for labor, probably the largest item in our gross national product. There could be neither market nor commodity without the concept of assignment.

In this chapter we will review the status of two species of nontraders who may have rights with respect to contracts formed by others. The rights of an intended beneficiary are created in the very terms of the original bargain. By contrast, the assignee of rights is a total stranger to the formation of the contract. She arrives only later, owing to the unilateral acts of one of the traders who has sought to extinguish the right to receive the performance of the other trader in himself, and to set that right up exclusively in his stranger of choice — the assignee. But not all nontraders relate to the contracts of others merely for the good times. A delegate of duties is to the world of executory contracts what Hessian soldiers were to George III during the American Revolution.

Article 2 of the U.C.C. will play a rather modest role in this chapter. It is not that the Code is disinterested in the subject of assignment and delegation. Indeed, quite the opposite is the case. Secured Transactions, Sales of Accounts, and Chattel Paper are gathered together and codified in Article 9. Coverage of these topics is not found in the contemporary contracts course but rather in a second- or third-year elective.

THE STATUS AND RIGHT OF AN INTENDED BENEFICIARY

I. THE STATUS AND RIGHT OF AN INTENDED BENEFICIARY: If, at the formation of a contract, one of the parties makes a promise the performance of which will run directly to a designated third person, and the other party to the contract consciously intended that result, the designated person is an intended third-party beneficiary.

Problems in perspective: There is a single key to third-party beneficiary status, the mastery of which will forever preclude confusion with the rights of an assignee. A third-party beneficiary status must be established at the formation of the contract or it cannot exist. Thus, like the late Dean Acheson, a third-party beneficiary is always present at the creation. By contrast, an assignee is a stranger, an individual who arrives on the scene subsequent to formation owing to the unilateral decision of one of the parties to transfer the right to receive all or a designated portion of the performance owing from the other party to the stranger.

Basic terminology: Up to this point our concern has been with the immediate parties to the contract. We now introduce a third person who may turn out to have important legal rights respecting the performance of one of those parties. In order to avoid confusion, may I suggest that you adopt the following terms. Let us call the offeror and offeree who formed the contract the "traders." This will avoid difficulty with the common law's insistence upon referring to the third person as a "party." With respect to the traders, we label the one who assumes the promissory duty which runs to the third party as the "promisor." The other trader, who bargained for that promise and supported it with valuable consideration, is the "promisee." If the nontrader is able to establish the elements of valuable status, we term her an "intended beneficiary." If she fails to establish either of the elements of intended beneficiary status, she is relegated to the non-status of an "incidental beneficiary."

A. The Elements of Intended Beneficiary Status: In order to establish the valuable status of intended beneficiary, the third party must establish a quality with respect to the undertaking of the promisor and a state of mind with respect to the promisee.

    1. *The direct undertaking of the promisor:* The first element of intended beneficiary status is that, at the formation of the bargain, one of the traders has undertaken a promissory duty the performance of which runs directly to a designated third party. Such a promise is termed the "direct undertaking of the promisor."

        a. *Designation of third party must be either by name or by legal description:* While most intended beneficiaries are identified by name as the recipients of the promisor's performance, a legal description which is later proven to identify a specific individual is sufficient.

        Example: A contract between Western Automobile Club and Ray's Automotive, a regional service station operator, identifies the road assistance obligations of Ray's Automotive as running to any member of the Club requesting help within Goshen County. John Smith, a member, experiences mechanical difficulty within the county. Smith will be able to establish his identity as an intended beneficiary of the contract between the Club as promisee, and Ray's Automotive as promisor.

        b. *Test for direct undertaking:* In order to determine if the promisor has made the requisite direct promissory undertaking, simply look to the terms of his promise. In a garden variety two-party transaction, both the promise and its performance run directly to the other trader. In an intended beneficiary fact pattern, the promise runs to the promisee, but in order to carry out its terms the performance must be bestowed directly upon the designated third party. *See H.P. Moch Co. v. Pensselaer Water Co.,* 247 N.Y. 160, 159 N.E. 896 (1928).

        Example: In the above example, Ray's Automotive made its promise to the Western Automotive Club as promisee. However, it cannot carry out the terms of that promise by rendering assistance to a corporate entity or to its officers. Rather, that promise can only be redeemed by a performance rendered to a member or members requesting aid within the designated area.

    2. *The intention to benefit in the mind of the promisee:* The second element of intended beneficiary status centers on the intention of the promisee, who bargained with the promisor for the undertaking and supported it with valuable consideration.

a. *Term misleading:* The term "intention to benefit" is potentially confusing, for it suggests that the promisee must have some altruistic or benevolent sentiment regarding the third party. If such sentiments exist, they may promote human happiness but add no crucial element to the legal equation. All that is required is that the promisee consciously intend that the undertaking of the promisor run directly to the designated nontrader, the "beneficiary."

b. *Motives of promisee irrelevant:* Under the modern formulation of the doctrine, the motive prompting the promisee to contract for an undertaking running directly to the third party is irrelevant. It is sufficient that she had such a conscious desire.

Example: Rob Smith has been attempting to sell an office building in downtown Biggsville for several months. In April he conducted serious negotiations with Ernesto Chavez, an Oregon investor. Chavez made a $10,000 earnest money deposit on the building. Two weeks later he indicated to Smith that he wanted to withdraw the offer. A dispute then erupted as to whether Chavez had a right to withdraw and receive a refund of his deposit.

While that dispute remained unsettled, Smith was approached by Ann Schneider, a Denver investor. When Schneider discovered the history of Smith's dealings with Chavez she made it plain that she would offer Smith his asking price upon condition that he promise to return the earnest money deposit to Ernesto Chavez. Smith made such a promise, and Schneider purchased the building.

Chavez now asserts his status as an intended beneficiary of the Smith/Schneider contract. Smith does not deny that he made a promise to Schneider, the discharge of which would require payment to Chavez. He does deny that Schneider had any "intention to benefit" Chavez. His lawyer informs the trial court that Smith is prepared to call Schneider who will testify that she exacted the promise from Smith in her own selfish interest. She did not want any cloud on the title to the land she was purchasing. Chavez has never met Schneider.

The testimony is legally irrelevant. It would not refute the allegation that Schneider consciously intended Smith's promise to obligate him to pay Chavez. No more is required. Her motive for such a conscious desire is not an element of Chavez's status as an intended beneficiary. *See Vikingstad v. Baggott,* 46 Wash. 2d 494, 282 P.2d 824 (1955).

3. *Exceptional cases:* The *Restatement, Second,* § 302(1) has sought to recast the two elements of intended beneficiary status in a manner which may harmonize some decisions which have departed from the classic formulation.

a. *Suggested formulation:* An intended beneficiary must show that "recognition of a right to performance in the beneficiary is appropriate to effectuate the intention of the parties" and that either:

(1) The performance of the promise will satisfy an obligation of the promisee to pay money to the beneficiary; or

(2) The circumstances indicate that the promisee intends to give the beneficiary the benefit of the promised performance.

b. The idea that the "direct undertaking" might be replaced by proof that granting the third party a cause of action for breach of the promisor's undertaking is appropriate to effectuate the intent of the traders may explain certain common law decisions which have allowed third persons to recover against the promisor for breach of an undertaking which did *not* run directly to them.

Example: The Supreme Court of California has recognized the status of a third party intended by a decedent as the beneficiary of a term in his will to recover for malpractice when the lawyer neglected to include the provision. Drafting the will was a contractual service bestowed directly upon the testator, not the beneficiary. *See Lucas v. Hamm,* 56 Cal. 2d 583, 364 P.2d 685 (1961).

B. Legal Consequence of Intended Beneficiary Status: If the designated third party is able to prove the two elements of intended beneficiary status, the promisor must perform the terms of the direct undertaking at peril of a breach which may be remedied by an action directly maintained by the intended beneficiary. *See Restatement, Second,* § 304.

1. ***Arcane classification of intended beneficiaries as "creditor" and "donee" third parties:*** The original *Restatement* promoted a classification of designated third parties predicated on the relationship between the third party and the promisee.

   a. *Creditor third-party beneficiary:* If the third party was an "actual, supposed, or asserted" creditor of the promisee and the performance of the direct undertaking of the promisor would satisfy that debt, in whole or in part, the relationship was that of a creditor third-party beneficiary. *See Restatement, First,* § 133(b).

   b. *Donee third-party beneficiary:* If there was no creditor/debtor relationship between the promisee and the third party, or the direct undertaking of the promisor would not satisfy that debt, the third-party beneficiary was of the donee variety. *See Restatement, First,* § 133(a).

   c. *Consequences of the classification:* Courts influenced to accept the classification scheme used it to work two important distinctions.

      (1) The "intention to benefit" in the mind of the promisee was judicially presumed if the resulting relationship was that of a creditor beneficiary. A donee beneficiary was required to allege and prove this element.

      (2) The rights of a donee beneficiary vested the moment the contract made for his benefit was formed. He did not even have to know of its existence. By contrast, the rights of a creditor beneficiary

vested only when, having learned of the contract made for his benefit, he has changed position in detrimental reliance. [*See discussion of vesting, infra.*]

2. ***Classification abandoned in favor of unitary concept of "intended third-party beneficiaries":*** The *Restatement, Second,* § 302, has repudiated the distinction between the two classes of third parties and now urges that they be treated under identical rules in establishing proof of status and vesting of rights.

3. ***Nonvaluable status of incidental beneficiary:*** It frequently happens that a nontrader can make a convincing demonstration that the faithful performance of promises contained in the contracts of others would result in economic or emotional advantage. Such a demonstration, no matter how compelling, is legally unavailing unless the two elements of intended beneficiary status can be established. Failing this, the third person is a mere "incidental beneficiary," which is to say that he has no legally protected interest in the performance of the contract duties.

Examples: Tim Moch is a resident of Biggsville. The City of Biggsville has entered into a contract with the Lusk Water Company under the terms of which the company is to supply water for sewer flushing, street cleaning, consumption in public buildings and fire hydrants. Moch's home catches fire. An alarm is sounded, and the Biggsville Fire Department responds. However, pressure in the fire hydrant is inadequate to operate the equipment. Moch seeks to bring an direct action against the Lusk Water Company asserting that he is an intended beneficiary.

Although not free from doubt, the majority view in decided cases is that Moch is a mere incidental beneficiary. Assuming that faithful execution of the contract duty of the Lusk Water Company to supply adequate pressure for Biggsville fire hydrants would have saved his home from destruction, the duty ran to the city and not to individual residents. Thus the direct undertaking of the promisor was missing, a fatal flaw in Moch's contention that he was an intended beneficiary. *See Moch v. Rensselaer Water Co.,* 247 N.Y. 160, 159 N.E. 896 (1928). *Accord Justice v. CSX Transp., Inc.,* 908 F.2d 119, 124 (7th Cir. 1990).

In *Martinez v. Socoma Companies, Inc.,* 11 Cal. 3d 394, 521 P.2d 841 (1974), plaintiffs sought to assert standing in a class action as intended beneficiaries under terms of a contract between the defendant and the United States Department of Labor. Defendant had promised the Department to create jobs in East Los Angeles in return for a grant of more than $1 million in antipoverty funds. Alleging that as "hard core unemployed residents of East Los Angeles" they would have earned more than $9 million in wages had the defendant not failed miserably in efforts to keep its promise, the plaintiffs sought to recover this amount as expectation damages.

By a vote of four to three, the Supreme Court of California concluded that the plaintiffs were mere incidental beneficiaries. In the eyes of the majority, the flaw in plaintiffs' case was proof of an intention to benefit them in the mind of the Department of Labor as promisee. It concluded that the apparent purpose of the government was not to benefit these particular citizens directly, but to improve general social conditions.

More recently, a federal appeal court rejected the claim by the sellers that the attorneys who represented the buyer of their business owed the sellers a duty to disclose that there were misrepresentations in the buyer's financial statements. While agreeing that the lawyers were under an ethical duty to make disclosure or withdraw from representing the buyer, the court refused to recognize the asserted third-party beneficiary status advanced by the seller's. Put simply, there had been no direct undertaking by the lawyers their contract with their client the buyer of a duty in to the sellers. The court refused to engraft on an ethical obligation an imputed contractual promise. *Schatz v. Rosenberg*, 943 F.2d 485 (4th Cir. 1991).

C. Vesting the Rights of an Intended Beneficiary: Vesting the rights of an intended beneficiary puts the modification or rescission of the direct undertaking of the promisor beyond the power of the traders who formed the contract.

Problems in perspective: Before an intended beneficiary may be secure in the expectation interest created by the contract made for his benefit, he must vest his rights. The danger comes from the very parties who created the contract. What if they now seek to rescind, modify, or novate the contract made for his benefit? Unless his rights have "vested," the beneficiary is totally vulnerable to any one of these possibilities. But if his rights to the performance of the promisor have vested, the intended beneficiary becomes the legal equivalent of a pit bull, an animal not known to relax its grip.

1. *Vesting, how accomplished:* The most significant difference between the first and second *Restatements* with respect to the treatment of third-party beneficiaries concerned the circumstances under which the rights of the beneficiary would vest.

   a. *Arcane distinction between creditor and donee beneficiaries under the first* Restatement: A donee beneficiary was given far more protection with respect to the vesting of rights.

      (1) A donee beneficiary's rights vested the moment a contract for his benefit was formed. He did not even have to know of its existence.

      (2) A creditor beneficiary, by contrast, could vest her rights only when, having learned of the contract made for her benefit, she changed position in detrimental reliance.

      (3) The rationale for this distinction was that if the contract for the benefit of a donee beneficiary was rescinded, he would have nothing. A creditor beneficiary would at least have her original creditor's claim upon the promisee.

b. *Modern view:* There are three alternative means to vest the rights of an intended beneficiary. The *Restatement, Second,* urges that courts recognize any of three alternative developments as vesting the rights of an intended beneficiary.

(1) When having learned of the contract made for his benefit the intended beneficiary changes position in detrimental reliance; or

(2) The moment the intended beneficiary commences a cause of action against the promisor for any refusal, failure, or defective performance of the terms of the direct undertaking; or

(3) When the intended beneficiary expresses consent to receive the performance of the promisor when that consent has been requested by either of the traders and not merely volunteered. *See Restatement, Second,* § 311.

2. ***Status of an intended beneficiary dependent upon the vesting of rights***

a. *The vulnerable posture of an intended beneficiary who has not vested his rights:* Until he manages to vest his rights, the status of an intended beneficiary is vulnerable to subsequent decisions of the traders who formed the contract that they wish to rescind, modify, or novate their bargain.

(1) If rescission is their decision, the contract created for the intended beneficiary ceases to exist and with it any expectation interest he may have had.

(2) Modification alters the nature or dimension of what may be expected.

(3) Novation is a three-cornered agreement wherein the original traders agree upon a substitute promisor who consents to assume the burdens of the original. If this is accomplished, the alternation in the expectation of the intended beneficiary is not with respect to the nature or dimension of the promised performance, but from whom that performance is to be received and against whom an action for breach may be maintained. *See Copeland v. Beard,* 217 Ala. 216, 115 So. 389 (1928).

b. *Impregnable position of intended beneficiary with vested rights:* Once the rights of the beneficiary have vested, the traders no longer have it within their legal power to rescind or alter the terms of the promisor's direct undertaking or to novate the contract made for her benefit.

(1) Any attempt by the traders to accomplish this agenda is totally ineffective in relieving the promisor of the duty to perform the origi-

nal terms of his direct undertaking to the third party at peril of an exposure to the beneficiary's right to commence an action for material breach.

    (2) Additional rights of the intended beneficiary with vested rights: In addition to the right to demand the original performance of the promisor at peril of a cause of action for material breach, the aggrieved intended beneficiary may pursue the following remedies.

        (a) If the promisor gives anything of value to the promisee in exchange for her wholly ineffective consent to rescind, modify or novate the terms of the promisor's undertaking, the intended beneficiary may commence an action against the promisee to recover that consideration on grounds that it represented an attempted sale of her property. *See Restatement, Second,* § 311(4).

        (b) If the promisee actively seeks to entice the promisor into refusing to perform or altering the terms of his direct undertaking, the aggrieved intended beneficiary may maintain a cause of action against the promisee for tortious interference with her contract rights.

D. The Intended Beneficiary's Cause of Action: In the event of a failure or refusal to perform on the part of the promisor, or a performance which disappoints the reasonable expectations of the intended beneficiary, the primary cause of action to remedy the breach at law or in equity is that of the intended beneficiary.

Problems in perspective: The potential complication presented by the promisor's breach is that the broken promise had been given to the promisee while its pledge of performance ran to the intended beneficiary. Recollection of two key points will preclude confusion in working out the remedial consequences of such a breach or the nature of the defenses which the promisor may raise in an attempt to defeat the claim.

    First, the primary cause of action is that of the intended beneficiary, not the promisee. The reason lies in the nature of the loss-of-bargain measure of money damages. As reviewed in Chapter 7, the goal of common law courts presented with a material breach is to place the aggrieved party, insofar as a sum of money can approximate it, in the position he would have enjoyed had there been full and timely performance. We term this the expectation interest. If the contract featured an undertaking by the promisor of a duty of performance which ran directly to the intended beneficiary, she alone had the expectation interest. In the event of breach, the intended beneficiary could establish the dollar dimension of the disappointment of that expectation. By contrast, the promisee would frequently have to speculate as to the appropriate dollar dimension of his expectation since, under the terms of the contract, he was not to receive the performance.

    The second vital point to recollect is that the claim of the intended beneficiary is *wholly derived from the contract made for her benefit.* Absent that contract, the intended beneficiary would have no right against the promisor at all.

For this reason, any real or personal defense which the promisor may establish respecting either the formation or enforcement of that contract may be used to defeat liability to the intended beneficiary. Any counterclaim arising out of the promisee's breach of that contract may be used to defeat or diminish the claim of the intended beneficiary, who may have no right greater than could have been enjoyed by the promisee in a simple two-party bargain.

1. ***Defenses of the promisor:*** Faced with an action for material breach by a purported intended beneficiary, the promisor may contest the status of the plaintiff, or, admitting it, may defeat liability by raising any real or personal defense to the formation of the alleged contract or the enforcement of its terms.

   a. *Liability of promisor must be fully matured:* If the direct undertaking of the promisor was protected by any express or implied condition precedent or concurrent, it must have been either satisfied or excused before the duty of performance had fully matured. Until that time, the promisor is legally privileged to withhold his performance. *See Camelot Excavating Co. v. St. Paul Fire & Marine Ins. Co.,* 410 Mich. 118, 301 N.W. 2d 275 (1981). [For a general discussion of the utility and law of conditions *see* Chapter 4, "The Allocation of Risk Inherent the Bargain," *supra.*]

   b. *Denial of beneficiary's status:* In order to state a claim upon which relief can be granted, a third party must allege the elements of intended beneficiary status in addition to a matured duty and material breach. At trial, the plaintiff has the burden of proof with respect to her status and risks nonpersuasion of the trier of fact. The defendant is free to contest the status of the purported beneficiary by general or specific denials and proofs. Failure to establish the elements of intended beneficiary status by a preponderance of the evidence is fatal to the plaintiff's claim.

   c. *Defenses against a derivative cause of action:* The claim of material breach and prayer for relief at law or in equity by an intended beneficiary is wholly derived from the contract made for her benefit.

      (1) Real defenses preclude formation of that contract: Any real defense in the hands of the defendant/promisor precludes formation of the asserted contract and totally defeats the claim of the purported intended beneficiary. The defenses include want of consideration as well as those serious moral infractions which generate the short list of real defenses. [*See* Chapter 3, "Barriers to Contractual Status," *supra.*]

      (2) Personal defenses admit the formation of a contract but render the contract duties of the promisor voidable. Among the duties which may be avoided by a timely assertion of a personal defense is an undertaking running directly to a designated third party.

(a) Failure of consideration: If the promise of the defendant was dependent upon the prior or contemporaneous performance of the promisee, a material breach on the part of the promisee works a failure of the valuable consideration supporting the promisor's undertaking. In such circumstances, all executory duties of the aggrieved promisor are discharged, including any running directly to third persons.

(b) The burden of pleading, proof, and risk of nonpersuasion of the trier of fact respecting any personal defense is that of the defendant/promisor.

> **Example:** Solomon Kate enters into a contract with Standard Sheeting Company for installation of an air conditioning unit in his home. Katz is to pay for the unit by giving a promissory note to Standard Sheeting. Several months later, while a large portion of the funds to Standard remained unpaid, Katz sells the house to Budwin Conn. One of the terms of the Conn/Katz contract is a promise by Conn to pay off the balance of the debt which Katz owed to Standard for installation of the air conditioner.
>
> After several payments Conn discovers that the air conditioner is inadequate to cool the house. He ceases to make the payments, and Standard brings an action asserting its status as an intended beneficiary of the Conn/Katz contract. Conn raises the defense of fraud in the inducement by Katz in the sale of the house to Conn.
>
> The trial court granted judgment for the nontrader, Standard. On appeal this was reversed. The court held that "one who promises to make a payment to the promisee's creditor can assert against the creditor any defense that the promisor could assert against the promisee." *See Rouse v. United States,* 215 F.2d 872 (D.C. Cir. 1954).

(3) Vicarious defenses may not be raised: The liability of the promisor stands or falls upon the binding nature of his contract with the promisee. The relationship between the promisee and the intended beneficiary is relevant only with respect to the "intention to benefit." Whether the promisee may have defenses to the asserted claims of a creditor beneficiary is irrelevant to the promisor's liability.

2. *Claims of the promisor:* The damage claim of an intended beneficiary is vulnerable to being reduced or extinguished by the amount of any counterclaim in the hands of the defendant/promisor. It is immune to any setoff.

   a. *Vulnerability to counterclaims:* A counterclaim is any cause of action which the promisor would have against the promisee for breach of the contract containing a direct undertaking to the intended beneficiary.

(1) Because the intended beneficiary's cause of action is derived from the contract of the traders, any damages claimed in consequence of a breach by the promisor may be reduced by the dimension of any counterclaim which the promisor has against the promisee for breach of that same contract.

> **Example:** If the consequential damages occasioned by the promisor's breach of his direct undertaking amount to $100,000, such a sum may be sought by the intended beneficiary. However, if the promisor can prove that he suffered $80,000 in consequential damages as a result of a breach by the promisee of that same contract, the amount which the intended beneficiary can collect is only $20,000. Remember, both the nature and dimension of her rights are wholly derived from the contract of the traders.

(2) No affirmative recovery against the intended beneficiary: If the damages recoverable by the promisor upon proof of his counterclaim exceed the liability to the intended beneficiary for breach of the direct undertaking, they nullify the beneficiary's claim. But because the beneficiary had no duties under the terms of the contract she cannot be held liable for the excess. Such a sum may be recovered from the breaching promisee.

b. *Immunity to setoff:* A setoff is any civil claim for damages which the promisor may assert against the promisee arising from any source other than the contract containing the direct undertaking to the intended beneficiary. Such claims are irrelevant to the intended beneficiary's right to seek an expectation remedy for breach of the direct undertaking.

E. **In the Event of the Promisor's Breach, the Secondary Rights of the Promisee:** As noted, the primary cause of action is that of the intended beneficiary. If she commences that action and is successful, the breach has been remedied and the promisee has no cause of action. If the intended beneficiary fails to commence the primary cause of action or is defeated other than on the merits, secondary rights accrue to the promisee who had bargained for the breached promise and supported it with valuable consideration.

1. ***An action at law for damages:*** As discussed in Chapter 7, "The Consequences of Breach," the common law protection for the expectation interest is the loss-of-bargain recovery of money damages at law. This will prove problematic for a promisee because, under the terms of the bargain, he was not to receive performance on the promisor's undertaking. It ran directly to an intended beneficiary.

a. *Loss-of-bargain recovery of damages precluded if injury to promisee is speculative:* An affirmative part of any plaintiff's quest for the loss-of-bargain recovery of money damages is proof of the loss to a certain dollar amount.

(1) If the intended beneficiary was a creditor of the promisee, breach by the promisor may leave the promisee able to establish his damages. They would be the consequences of having to pay off the debt directly to the intended beneficiary.

(2) If the intended beneficiary is not a creditor, proof of consequential damages would be speculative unless the aggrieved promisee formed a replacement contract obtaining a direct undertaking from another promisor. The difference between the cost of this replacement contract and the agreed-upon price of the contract with the defendant/promisor would be a certain measure of a loss-of-bargain damages.

b. *Standing to sue in equity:* In the event of the promisor's breach of the direct undertaking, if the promisee is unable to prove his loss-of-bargain damages with the certainty demanded by the common law, he has no "adequate remedy at law." In such circumstances he has standing to sue in equity.

(1) Suit for specific performance: The usual goal of a promisee suing in equity is to obtain a decree compelling the defaulting promisor to carry out the direct undertaking to the intended beneficiary.

(2) Nature of relief discretionary: As with any prayer for equitable relief, a remedy cannot be claimed as of right but is addressed to the sound discretion of the court.

c. *Quest for rescission and restitution at law:* If the loss-of-bargain measure of money damages is speculative, and an equity court unwilling to lend assistance, an aggrieved promisee who has bestowed anything of value upon the defaulting promisor can reclaim it or its market value in quasi-contract.

II. **THE ASSIGNMENT OF CONTRACT RIGHTS: Faced with a demand for performance by a nontrader who has received a present, operative, and nonrevoked assignment, a promisor must perform the duties assigned or answer for material breach in an action maintained by that assignee.**

THE ASSIGNMENT OF CONTRACT RIGHTS

Problems in perspective: A promisor can never claim surprise when faced with a demand for performance by an intended beneficiary. At the formation stage, he undertook a promissory obligation running directly to that nontrader. Far more startling is the prospect of a demand for performance made by a complete stranger to the formation of the contract and thereafter introduced by the unilateral decision of the other trader. Yet such is the concept of an "assignee of contract rights." Assuming that the steps required for a present assignment have been observed, the right to receive the performance of the promisor has been extinguished in the other original trader and transferred immediately and exclusively to the assignee.

Terminology: Because we must again keep track of three actors, it will be useful to unite on the following descriptive terms. The parties who formed the contract as offeror and offeree are referred to as "the traders." In the formation of an executory bilateral contract, each trader is the "obligor" of his own duty of performance, and the "obligee" with a right to expect to receive the performance of the other. If, in her capacity as obligee of the other trader's duty of performance, that trader seeks to introduce a stranger and to transfer to that stranger the exclusive right to receive the performance of the other trader as obligor, we call the obligees an "assignor." The stranger to whom she would transfer the right to the performance of the obligor is the "assignee."

In dealing with the materials on assignment, it may assist you to focus on three key propositions:

> First, modern statutory and common law positively favors the freedom to assign contract rights and is increasingly tolerant of the freedom to delegate contract duties.
> Second, the assignment of the right to receive, in whole or in part, the performance of the obligor is a wholly unilateral legal privilege of the obligee. It does not depend upon the prior, contemporaneous, or subsequent consent of the obligee.
> Third, because it represents exercise of a unilateral legal privilege, an assignment may never be used to materially add to or vary the contract duties of the nonconsenting obligor nor to vary the dimension of the risks which he assumed at the formation stage.

Article 9 of the U.C.C. contains an extensive codification of the law of assignment which is treated in a course on Secured Transactions. Our review will concentrate on the common law, noting areas in which Article 2 has expressed a position with respect to the assignment of rights in a contract for the sale of goods. We will proceed in the following order. First, we will examine the elements of a present assignment. Second, our inquiry will be whether the present assignment is "operative" to create in the stranger the legally valuable status of assignee. We will focus upon the impact of the present assignment upon the duties and risks of the obligor, as well as the presence of any restrictive terms in the contract. Assuming that the assignment is both present and operative, we will review the circumstances in which the assignor may revoke it either by reacquiring the legal interest in the subject matter, or setting it up in a rival, subsequent assignee who may turn out to have the exclusive right tothe obligor's performance. Finally, with problems of present assignment, operative assignment, and revocation sorted out, we will examine the status of the sole or prevailing assignee. If she commences litigation at law or in equity alleging breach of the duties assigned, what defenses may the obligor raise so as to defeat or diminish liability to this stranger?

A. **Present assignment:** In order to achieve a present assignment, the obligee must manifest an intention to make a present assignment, take steps sufficient to achieve a present transfer, and that intention and those steps must relate to a suitable present subject matter.

Problems in perspective: What makes the topic of a present assignment recur in litigation is the failure of the common law to insist upon any particular form to accomplish the result. An assignment need not employ magic words such as "I hereby assign." It need not be in writing, and it need not be supported by consideration. Yet if the process leaves considerable latitude for individuality or experimentation, the elements which must be incorporated are fixed. A failure to include any of them is fatal to achieving a present assignment, meaning that the purported assignee acquires nothing by way of a claim as against the obligor.

1. *The intent to make a present assignment:* Either by words, deeds, or a combination thereof, the obligee must manifest a present intention to act in the present so as to extinguish all right, title, and interest in the subject matter in himself and to transfer the same immediately and exclusively to the designated assignee. *Buck v. Illinois National Bank & Trust Co.,* 79 Ill. App. P.2d. 101, 223 N.E.2d. 167 (1967).

   Example: Paula Producer declares to her faithful executive assistant, Tim Worthing: "Tim, given your years of faithful service, next week I will assign to you the right to receive 5% of the funds owed to me for distribution rights under my new film, *Milktrain Doesn't Stop in Biggsville Anymore.*"

   It would be imprudent for Worthing to change his lifestyle predicated on this statement. The declaration of an intent to act next week flunks the legal requirement that a present assignment must take place right here, right now or it has not occurred. *See Restatement, Second,* § 324.

2. *Acts of present assignment:* In addition to manifesting an intent to create the assignment in the present, the assignor must clearly identify the subject matter, the designated assignee, and take such steps as are necessary to transfer the legal interest in the subject matter without further action. *McCown v. Spencer,* 8 Cal. App. 3d 216, 87 Cal. Rptr. 213 (1970). *Accord Restatement, Second* § 324.

   a. The assignment must amount to a complete transfer of the entire interest of the assignor in the designated subject matter and divest the assignor of all control over the thing assigned. Unless the assignor has parted with such control, he has not achieved a present assignment.

      Example: Ted Taxpayer became involved in a contest with the Internal Revenue Service over an alleged tax liability. Before the IRS had taken steps to attach his assets, Taxpayer entered into an agreement with a foreign bank to transfer to it the right to receive the royalty payments owed Taxpayer by an oil company. Under the terms of the agreement the bank was to pay to Taxpayer a sum equal to 95% of all royalty payments it received from the oil company.

      When the United States sought to attach this account, the bank asserted that it had received a present assignment of the funds prior to the attachment with the consequence that they were no longer the funds of the Taxpayer. The oil company, as obligor, paid the disputed funds into court and inaugurated an interpleader action.

The federal district court concluded that irrespective of the intent of Taxpayer to constitute the bank his assignee, his effective retention of control over 95% of the funds meant that he had not surrendered all right title and interest in the subject matter. There had been no present assignment in the eyes of the law. *Continental Oil Co. v. United States,* 326 F. Supp. 266 (S.D.N.Y. 1971).

   b. *No writing is required:* An oral assignment, if it expresses the requisite intention of the assignor to act in the present, is effective. *Buck v. Illinois National Bank & Trust Co,* 79 Ill. App.2d. 101, 223 N.E.2d. 167 (1967).

   c. *Partial assignment permissible:* An obligee may assign the right to receive clearly defined portions of the obligor's performance to several noncompeting assignees, or retain a portion of the subject matter herself while assigning the balance. Vindicating the rule that an assignment may not add to the contract burdens of the nonconsenting obligor, he may require the joinder of all partial assignees in one demand so as to be able to perform his contract duty in the same time, place, and circumstances as originally pledged to the assignor. *See Restatement, Second,* § 326.

Example: On February 1, John Newman forms a contract with Ronald Knox under the terms of which Knox is to pay Newman the sum of $10,000 on March 20. On February 5, Newman states to John Keble, "I hereby assign to you the right to receive $1,000 of the $10,000 owed to me by my obligor, Ronald Knox, on March 20." On February 7, Newman declares to E. B. Pusey: "I hereby assign to you the right to receive $1,000 of the $10,000 owed to me by my obligor, Ronald Knox, payment to be made on March 20."

Newman has made two nonconflicting partial assignments which, when combined, total $2,000 of the $10,000 owed by Knox under the executory terms of the Newman/Knox contract. Newman has made no assignment of the balance of $8,000. With respect to both attempted assignments, Newman's intent to act in the present, to divest himself of the partial interest, and to vest the same immediately exclusively in the designated assignees is plain. We have both the requisite intent and acts to constitute a present assignment. The only complication resulting from the partial nature is that Knox can insist that Newman, Keble, and Pusey all join together on March 20 so that he may perform his promise to pay $10,000 without any alteration of the time or place to which he had originally consented.

  3. *Present subject matter:* The assignor's intent and actions effecting a present assignment amount to an exercise in futility unless they relate to a suitable present subject matter.

a. *Future rights under an existing contract are freely assignable in the present:* If those rights are conditional, being dependent upon the satisfaction or excuse of conditions precedent or concurrent, the assignee takes them subject to those conditions. *Speelman v. Pascal,* 19 N.Y.2d 313, 178 N.E.2d 723 (1961). *Accord Restatement, Second,* § 321.

b. *Future rights in future contract not presently assignable at law:* Future rights in a not-yet-existing future contract may not be assigned at law for the simple reason that there is, at present, no suitable subject matter.

c. *Future rights in future contract potentially assignable in equity:* If the attempted present assignment of rights in a future contract takes place in the context of an expectation predicated upon an established, though informal economic relationship which generates the hope of the contract, a present assignment has taken place in the eyes of an equity court.

   (1) Assignee achieves present transfer of equitable interest: The equitable title to the anticipated future subject matter is immediately passed to the assignee.

   (2) In the event of subsequent contract formation, assignor holds the subject matter in trust for assignee: In the event that the existing relationship does generate the anticipated contract, the assignor holds only the bare legal title. The assignee may sue in equity to claim that legal title. *Speelman v. Pascal,* 19 N.Y.2d 313, 178 N.E.2d 723 (1961). *Accord Restatement, Second,* § 321.

   Example: On February 1, Floyd Obie, a rice farmer, approaches the Biggsville National Bank with an application to borrow $30,000. Obie explains that with these funds he will be able to purchase seed and equipment necessary to dramatically expand his rice production. The Bank is interested in security. Obie has been a farmer in Goshen County for twenty years and each year has sold his rice crop to Consolidated Elevator. Obie tells the Bank that he is willing to make an assignment to them in the amount of $35,000, a sum sufficient to cover both the principal and interest on the loan, of the $125,000 he expects to earn in a contract with Consolidated which he anticipates forming in late May.

   The Bank cannot gain an assignment which will be recognized by a court at law because on February 1, Obie has no contract with Consolidated. Put bluntly, there is nothing to assign. However, there is a substantial history of an established economic relationship between Obie and Consolidated that makes Obie's anticipation of a future contract much more than a mere dream. An equitable assignment can be created on February 1. The Bank will immediately achieve equitable title to the $35,000 subject matter. In the event the anticipated contract with Consolidated is formed, Obie will hold bare legal title to those funds. Should he refuse to surrender them, the Bank may sue to specifically force him to disburse them to the equitable owner.

B. Unless the Attempted Present Assignment is Operative, the Purported Assignee Achieves No Claim or Standing as Against the Promisor: Depending upon the nature of the subject matter and terms of the contract, the attempted assignment, no matter how perfect in present form, is inoperative, meaning that the purported assignee acquires no status. *See Restatement, Second,* § 317.

Problems in perspective: We now focus upon the third of our key propositions. At common law, an obligee may not use the machinery of assignment to unilaterally impose upon the obligor any material change in the nature of the duties or dimension of the risk to which the promisor had consented at the formation stage. If the assignment threatens such a material alteration in either duties or risk, it is inoperative. An inoperative assignment confers no rights or status upon the purported assignee.

Protection against material alteration is provided by law, but at the formation stage a promisor may have sought a greater degree of security from the threat of having to perform to the demand of a stranger. He may have insisted upon contract provisions which restrain or preclude the right of the other trader to set up rights in a stranger. If that has happened, you may be surprised to learn that an operative assignment has been accomplished. As noted, modern statutory and decisional law positively favors freedom of assignment.

1. *Common law restraints on the freedom of assignment:* An assignment which would materially alter the nature of the nonconsenting promisor's contract duties or materially enlarge the dimension of his risk is not operative, and the purported assignee acquires no rights.

   a. Assignments which would materially vary the contract duties of the nonconsenting obligor are not operative. *Accord* U.C.C. § 2-210(2).

      (1) The right to receive the personal services of another under an existing contract may not be assigned without a material alteration of the nature of the employee's duties.

      Example: Jean DeFratis, a Biggsville lawyer, enters into a contract to provide legal counsel to Frank Kraus, a real estate developer. Kraus paid DeFratis a retainer of $25,000 for a right to call upon up to 200 hours of her time over the next twelve months. Three months later, Kraus is interested in selling his business to Joan Parson. Among the assets he wishes to transfer to Parson is an assignment to receive the legal services of Jean DeFratis for the remaining nine months of the retainer term.

      The assignment, no matter how perfect in present form, would not be operative. The rendition of legal advice is generally deemed personal in nature, and to force DeFratis to accept as a client someone of Kraus' selection who may or may not operate the business in a similar manner is to threaten DeFratis with a material alteration of her contract duties. This may not be accomplished without her consent.

(2) Requirement and output contracts: If the contract measures the quantity term by the output of the seller or requirements of the buyer, there is substantial common law authority hostile to the operative consequence of an attempted present assignment.

    (a) Traditional view: The duties of an obligor in an output or requirements contract may not be assigned. No two buyers are likely to generate identical requirements, nor are two manufacturing sellers likely to produce identical output. An obligee of such a contract may not make the unilateral decision to impose that risk upon the obligor.

    (b) Potential for operative assignment under U.C.C.: The treatment of outputand requirements contracts under U.C.C. § 2-306(1) requires good-faith dealing and makes unenforceable a tender of output or demand for performance "unreasonably disproportionate to any stated estimate or in the absence of a stated estimate to any normal or otherwise comparable prior output or requirements."

        (i) Since the Code assumes that reasonable fluctuations in output or demand are to be tolerated, an assignment which threatens no unreasonable fluctuation would not seem to materially alter the dimension of the obligor's right.

        (ii) The use of stated estimates or prior history as a benchmark would appear to provide an objective test for reasonable fluctuation. *See* Official Comment 2.

(3) Cannot alter material terms: An assignment which would alter a material term of the contract is not operative. Thus if the terms of the assignment purport to alter the nature of the subject matter, quantity, time, or place of performance, the nonconsenting obligor may ignore the demands of the purported assignee.

   b. Assignments which do not threaten material alteration of the obligor's duties, but which do materially alter the dimension of the risk he had assumed in forming the contract are also inoperative. *Accord* U.C.C. § 2-210(2). Three types of risk must be considered here:

    (1) Alteration of the risk of having to perform a dependent promise: If the obligor has made the maturing of his performance obligation dependent upon the satisfaction or excuse of a condition precedent or concurrent, an assignment which would enhance the chance of maturing that promise is inoperative. It has materially varied the dimension of the risk of having to perform. Common examples include:

        (a) Insurance: The coverage in a policy of automobile insurance may not be assigned by a person deemed by the carrier as an acceptable risk to a stranger of that party's choosing.

(i) **Coverage may not be assigned:** The carrier has calculated the risk of having to perform on its dependent promise to indemnify for a casualty loss upon the driving record, age, sex, and locality of its insured.

(ii) **Proceeds of insurance policy freely assignable:** The carrier can have no objection if the insured party merely changes the beneficiary to be paid in the event that the insured does suffer a casualty loss.

(b) **Covenants not to compete:** An employee covenant not to compete may not be assigned without a material alteration in the dimension of the risk to the employee that working conditions under a new employer may prove less agreeable to either party, thereby exacerbating the risk of terminating the employment and triggering the covenant.

Example: Philip Cullins entered into a written contract of employment with the Smith & Bell Insurance Agency as an insurance broker. The contract recited that in his employment capacity Cullins would be privy to much confidential and proprietary information. Declaring that its object was to protect the employer from an employee's defection and use of such data in a competitive venture, the contract stipulated that in the event Cullins resigned or was discharged, he would not compete in the insurance business within the county for a period of three years. The contract also declared that the employer was not guaranteeing any minimum period of employment.

After several years of harmonious relations, during which time Cullins became both well-known and respected in the community for his abilities as a broker, Smith & Bell arranged the sale of their agency to one Hauck. The contract of sale purported to assign to Hauck all assets of the agency, including the right to enforce the covenants of its employees not to compete in the event of separation. Hauck thereafter offered to retain Cullins in his same job at his same salary. Cullins declined and took steps to form his own agency.

Hauck commenced suit to enjoin Cullins from competing in the insurance business in violation of the express covenant not to compete. He alleged his standing as assignee of all assets of Smith & Bell, including the contract of employment with Cullins.

Both the trial and appellate courts rejected the application. They held that the assignment, no matter how perfect in form, was not operative because it materially altered the dimension of Cullins' risk that he would find his employment satisfactory to his employer or agreeable to himself. *See Smith, Bell & Hauck, Inc. v. Cullins*, 123 Vt. 96, 183 A.2d 528 (1962).

(2) Alteration of the risk inherent in attempting performance: Emphasis upon exacerbating the risk inherent in attempting performance is a rejection of the doctrine prohibiting a material alteration in the nature of the obligor's duty. Thus, if the assignment would call upon the obligor to perform at a different time or in a different place, it would be inoperative. It would have altered both the nature of the obligor's duties and risk.

(3) Alteration of the risk of not receiving the same full measure of counter-performance from the assignor as obligee: The most common example of an assignment rendered inoperative on this theory is an assignment of a right to receive payment for the rendition of yet-to-be-performed personal services. If the assignor is able to part with the financial return, there is a fear that she will lack the same full measure of incentive to perform the services at her highest level. This idea has been given the nonflattering label, "the dead horse theory."

2. ***The fate of contract provisions purporting to forbid or restrict the right to create an assignment:*** They are disfavored by the law.

Problems in perspective: Three reasons support this hostility. First, there is concern for the rights of an innocent person who, in ignorance of the fact that the purported assignment is violative of a contract provision, pays value for the assignment. Second, there is a frank recognition that the assignment of the right to receive future performance under present contracts is a major part of our gross national product. Closely allied is the third reason, which tended to be emphasized in earlier cases. Restraints on the alienation of personal property were politically unpopular in nineteenth-century America. The hostility of the law manifests itself in many forms:

a. There is a presumption that a contract clause prohibiting or restricting a right to assign "the contract" is intended only to preclude the delegation of contract duties, not the assignment of rights by an assignor who retains the burden of performing his own duties. *Detroit Greyhound Employees Fed. Credit Union v. Aetna Life Ins. Co.,* 381 Mich. 683, 167 N.W.2d 274 (1969). *Accord* U.C.C. 2-210(3), and *Restatement, Second,* § 322.

b. Only the plainest possible language can drive a court to the conclusion that a clause prohibiting assignment means more than a prohibition on delegation. This is especially true when the subject matter of the assignment is merely the payment of money by the nonconsenting promisor. *Charles L. Bowman & Co. v. Erwin,* 468 F.2d 1293 (5th Cir. 1972).

c. Language as preventing the right to make a licit assignment as opposed to extinguishing the power to make an operative assignment.

(1) If the contract restraint is the form of a covenant not to assign, the legal effect is to prevent an obligee from making a licit assignment.

(a) Status of innocent assignee: If the purported assignee is innocent, without knowledge or reason to know that the assignment is in violation of a contract term, and she has paid value for the assignment, she will acquire status as one holding a present, operative assignment.

(b) Rights and duties of the nonconsenting obligor: The obligor must perform to her demand at peril of breach, although he will have a cause of action against the faithless assignor for breach of the covenant not to assign.

(2) If the contract restraint takes the form of expressly treating the attempted assignment of rights as an offer to the nonconsenting obligor to rescind the contract, or makes such an attempt an express condition subsequent discharging the contract duties of the obligor, it has extinguished the power as well as the right to make a present, operative assignment.

(a) The purported assignee acquires no legally enforceable claim against the nonconsenting obligor, who may now rescind the contract or consider his duties discharged.

(b) Rights of purported assignee against faithless assignor: If the purported assignee is innocent of knowledge or reason to know that the assignment violated contract prohibitions and he paid value to the assignor, he will now recover against the faithless assignor for breach of an implied warranty which is attached to every assignment given for consideration.

(c) Terms of the implied warranty attending every assignment forconsideration: The assignor warrants that he has both the right and power to make a present, operative assignment and thereafter will do nothing to interfere with the assignee's quiet enjoyment of the subject matter. *See Restatement, Second,* § 333.

d. *Countervailing values:* A restraint on alienation of property by way of assignment will be respected if it is clearly drafted to embrace the assignment of rights as well as the delegation of duties, and if the restraint is reasonably designed to attain or encourage accepted social or economic ends. *Hanigan v. Wheeler,* 19 Ariz. App. 49, 504 P.2d 972 (1972).

Example: In *Gale v. York Center Community Cooperative, Inc.,* 21 Ill. 2d 86, 171 N.E.2d 30 (1960), the court upheld a partial restraint on the assignment of property interests of members. It was recognized that restraining the right of members to assign their interests in the cooperative was essential if the cooperative housing association was to continue as a viable economic entity.

e. *Some restraints are void, as being contrary to statutory policy*

(1) **Claim to damages assignable:** Under U.C.C. § 2-210(2), a right to damages for breach of a contract for the sale of goods may be assigned notwithstanding an express term in the contract precluding such assignment.

(2) **Right to receive payment of money assignable:** U.C.C. § 9-318(4) broadly invalidates an express term of a contract which purports to restrict the assignment of the right to receive payment of monies due.

C. The Consequences of a Present, Operative Assignment and the Potential for Destruction of the Assignee's Status by Revocation

1. ***The status of an assignee:*** Assuming that he can prove the elements of a present assignment and defeat any contention by the obligor that it is not operative, all right title and interest in the subject matter of the assignment has been extinguished in the assignor and is now vested exclusively in the assignee.

   a. The obligor must tender performance of the assigned duties to the assignee at peril of material breach.

      (1) An attempt by the obligor to ignore the status of the assignee and tender performance to the original obligee/assignor is totally ineffective in discharging his contract duties. *See Framingham Welding and Engineering Corp. v. Bennie Cotton, Inc.,* 361 Mass. 866, 281 N.E.2d 236 (1972).

      (2) If the obligee/assignor accepts a tender of the performance which had been assigned, she exposes herself to a triple battery of legal consequences.

         (a) An equity court will regard the subject matter as impressed with a trust in favor of the assignee who may demand surrender.

         (b) At common law, the obligee/assignor may be targeted in an action for monies had and received or in tort for conversion. *See Patrons State Bank & Trust Co. v. Shapiro,* 215 Kan. 856, 528 P.2d 1198 (1974).

   b. In the event of the obligor's failure, refusal, or defective performance, the primary cause of action to seek recovery of the loss-of-bargain measure of money damages at law belongs to the assignee. If a remedy at law is not adequate to place her in the position she would have occupied had there been full and timely performance by the obligor, the assignee has standing to seek relief in equity.

2. ***Revocation — a potential destruction of the assignee's status:*** Before an assignee may be secure in her status she must consider the possibility that it has been destroyed by the obligee/assignor.

Problems in perspective: Destruction of the assignee's status may occur in two possible ways. In a very limited number of instances, the assignor has both the right and the power to revoke the assignment and reacquire legal dominion over the subject matter. Far more common are fact patterns in which the assignor has no right to revoke but may have the apparent power to accomplish that result by creating a successor assignee of the same subject matter who turns out to have a superior claim to the performance of the obligor.

a. *An oral gratuitous assignment is revocable:* If the assignment was both oral in form and gratuitous in nature, the assignor has a right to change his mind and reacquire legal dominion over the subject matter to the exclusion of the assignee. *See Restatement, Second, § 332.*

   (1) Revocation — how accomplished: If the assignor has the right to revoke the assignment, he may exercise it by notice given to either the gratuitous assignee or obligor, or the simple act of creating a subsequent, conflicting assignment to a second assignee. Acceptance by the assignor of performance by the obligor has also been held to revoke the gratuitous assignment, as has bankruptcy of the assignor. This last result is clearly for the protection of the assignor's creditors.

   (2) A gratuitous assignment is irrevocable, meaning that the assignor has no legal right to reacquire legal dominion over the subject matter, under any of the following circumstances [*See Restatement, Second, § 332*]:

      (a) If the assignor's declaration of an intent to make a present assignment is in writing, delivery of that writing to the gratuitous assignee makes the assignment irrevocable. The analogy is to the common law of gifts. We have a donative declaration coupled with constructive delivery of the subject matter to the donee.

      (b) If the subject matter of the assignment is intangible, the only legal evidence of a claim is termed a "token chose." Delivery of the token chose by the assignor to the gratuitous assignee renders even an oral assignment irrevocable. The assignor has placed the only means of asserting possession in the hands of the assignee.

         Example: Herb Jackson owns fifty shares of common stock in Globe Mining Corporation. He makes an oral declaration of a present intention to assign his interest in Globe to his nephew. In carrying out the act of present assignment, Jackson endorses the certificates and hands them as a gift to his nephew.
         Even though the assignment by Jackson to his nephew was both oral in form and gratuitous in nature, the delivery of the endorsed stock certificates was that of a token chose. Jackson

is now without power to reacquire the interest or to assign it to a rival assignee.

    (c) Estoppel: If the gratuitous assignee changes position in detrimental reliance upon the oral assignment, the assignor will be estopped to revoke it.

    (d) Performance: If the gratuitous assignee obtains performance from the obligor, it is obviously too late for the assignor to revoke.

(3) Consequences of wrongful revocation of a gratuitous assignment: If an assignor without a legal right achieves the *de facto* revocation of an irrevocable gratuitous assignment by creating a subsequent assignee with a superior claim to the obligor's performance, he is liable to the aggrieved gratuitous assignee in tort for conversion.

b. *Assignments made for consideration are irrevocable:* Whether oral or written in form, if the assignee has paid value (incurred bargained-for legal detriment) for the assignment, the assignor never has a right to revoke it.

    (1) Power to achieve *de facto* revocation by creation of successor assignee of same subject matter: Notwithstanding that he has no legal right to revoke the assignment, a faithless assignor may attain this result by the expedient of creating a subsequent assignee of the same subject matter who, depending on the law in the jurisdiction respecting the claims of rival assignees, turns out to have the superior claim to the performance of the obligor.

    (2) Consequences of a wrongful revocation of an assignment made for consideration: If a faithless assignor creates multiple, conflicting assignments for value, only one of the assignees may prevail in claiming the performance of the obligor. His disappointed rivals have no recourse against the obligor but may recover against the treacherous assignor for breach of the implied warranty which attends every assignment made for consideration.

        (a) Terms of the implied warranty: The assignor warrants that she has both the right and power to make a present, operative assignment of the subject matter and that having done so, will do nothing to interfere with the assignee's quiet enjoyment of the subject matter.

        (b) Breach: The nature of the breach will be dependent upon which of the rival assignees prevails under the law of a given jurisdiction.

            (i) If the dispute between conflicting assignees is resolved in favor of the one first in time, the subsequent rivals can establish breach of the implied warranty of a right and power to make a present, operative assignment.

(ii) If the dispute is determined in favor of a subsequent assignee, the disappointed rival first in time may recover for breach of the warranty that the assignor would do nothing to interfere with the assignee's quiet enjoyment.

c. *Priority among conflicting assignees:* Partial assignments do not present this problem, for the claims of what may be several assignees do not conflict. Each is entitled to a clearly defined portion of the obligor's performance. But if the assignor has created numerous rivals as assignees of the same subject matter, in the words of Holmes to Watson: "The game's afoot!"

(1) A gratuitous assignee holding a revocable assignment is eliminated from the race: The mere creation of a subsequent rival while his claim remains revocable accomplishes revocation.

(2) As among competitors with irrevocable assignments the assignee with the superior equity will prevail: Common law solutions seem agreed that as among rival assignees, the one with a superior equity will prevail.

(a) Fate of irrevocable gratuitous assignment: The pragmatic consequence of this rule is to subordinate the claim of a gratuitous assignee with an irrevocable assignment to a subsequent rival who paid consideration for her assignment.

(b) Economic value of consideration irrelevant to determination of superior equity: Vindicating the position of the common law that "value" lies in bargained-for legal detriment and not economic equivalency, an assignee who paid $5,000 for an assignment has a status equal to that of a rival who paid $20,000.

(3) Conflicting common law positions where rivals have equivalent equities: Three competing common law positions have emerged over time in the United States to resolve the priority as among rival assignees with equivalent equities.

Problems in perspective: An obligee who sells the right to the obligor's performance to multiple innocent parties will rarely be so accommodating as to await the inevitable action for breach of warranty and then respond in damages! Thus, the most vital problem facing the rivals is gaining priority in their bid to obtain the performance of the obligor. Each of the rival common law rules for resolving this conflict of innocent victims begins with the proposition that the assignee first in time is presumptively first in right. Where they differ is with respect to the fate of an assignee junior in time who has taken such self-protective steps as being the first to give notice to the obligor.

There is a sense in which much of the drama of this conflict has been removed by the adoption in every state except Louisiana of the

Uniform Commercial Code. Article 9 provides a comprehensive statutory treatment of security interests in contract claims which grants priority to the first purchaser who makes a public recordation of his interest. If that purchaser happens to be the last to have "attached the security interest," she clearly prevails. If none of the holders of a security interest has complied with the statutory steps for recording, the holder first in time is first in right.

(a) The New York Rule: Sometimes termed the "American Rule," offers the most certain and simple solution. The assignee first in time is first in right. The rationale is that once an irrevocable assignment has been made, there is no existing subject matter for a successive assignment.

   (i) It is the clear position of jurisdictions adopting this solution that the mere fact that an assignee junior in time may have been first to notify the obligor grants no priority over the assignee first in time.

   (ii) Under the most extreme version of this rule, no amount of self-protective steps by a subsequent assignee will suffice to dislodge the claim of the first. Thus if the obligor has innocently rendered his performance to a junior assignee, the subject matter is held impressed with an equitable trust in favor of the assignee first in time. *See Superior Brassiere Co. v. Zimetbaum,* 214 App. Div. 525, 212 N.Y.S. 473 (1925).

(b) The English or California Rule: Begins with the presumption that the assignee first in time is first in right. However, if a junior assignee, who obtained her assignment without knowledge or reason to know that it was in violation of rights previously assigned, is first to give notice to or make demand upon the obligor, she prevails. The rationale of this rule is that it imposes no great burden on an assignee and reduces the likelihood of the faithless assignor's ability to victimize others. *See Haupt v. Charlie's Kosher Market,* 17 Cal. 2d 843, 112 P.2d. 627 (1941).

(c) The Massachusetts Rule: Given the sharp division between the New York and California positions, it was inevitable that some jurisdiction would strive for a compromise.

   (i) Begins with the presumption that the assignee first in time is first in right and rejects the idea that mere giving of notice by a junior assignee can alter that priority.

   (ii) However, there are four other self-protective steps a junior assignee can take any one of which can give him priority.

      a) Obtain performance from the obligor

        b) Obtain a judgment against the obligor for breach of the assigned duty

        c) Obtain from the assignor a tangible token representing the claim or

        d) Secure a novation from the obligor

    (d) *Restatement* view: Both the original *Restatement* and the *Restatement, Second* (§ 342) have endorsed the Massachusetts Rule.

D. The Assignee's Claim in Litigation: In the event that the obligor fails, refuses, or defectively performs the duty which had been assigned to the sole or prevailing assignee, the remedial consequences all flow from the proposition that he alone had the exclusive right to receive the breached performance.

1. *No claim against the obligee/assignor:* Unless the assignor is guilty of interfering in the assignee's quiet enjoyment by attempting a wrongful revocation, or unless his own material breach has discharged the obligor on a theory of failure of consideration, he has no liability to the assignee in the event that the obligor breaches the terms of the contract.

2. *Breach by obligor is not a violation of the implied warranty attending an assignment for consideration:* By implication of law, every assignment for which consideration is paid is attended by an implied warranty that the assignor has both the right and power to make a present, operative assignment and thereafter will do nothing to interfere with the assignee's quiet enjoyment. This warranty does not cover breach by the obligor for which the assignor is not responsible.

3. *Rights of the aggrieved assignee against the breaching obligor:* A failure or refusal on the part of the obligor to perform a contract duty which has been assigned is a present material breach of the contract. So, too, is a defective attempt to carry out the terms of such a promise. In each instance the primary cause of action to remedy this material breach, at law or in equity, belongs to the assignee.

4. *Defenses available to the defendant/obligor:* The common law phrase that the assignee "stands in the shoes of the assignor" makes the emphatic point that the machinery of assignment can never create rights or status in the assignee which exceed those of the obligee/assignor.

    a. Burden is upon the purported assignor as plaintiff to establish a present assignment and a material breach by the obligor of a fully matured contract duty.

       (1) If the promise of the obligor which was assigned was dependent upon the satisfaction or excuse of a condition precedent or concurrent, the obligor has no duty to perform and thus no occasion to breach unless those conditions have been removed.

(2) Whether issues of the operative nature of the assignment are treated as part of the plaintiff's case in chief or matters of affirmative defense by an obligor is a matter for civil procedure.

b. If the present assignment and its operative nature are either conceded or established, an obligor may raise any real or personal defense to the formation or enforcement of the contract which is the source of the assignee's claim.

(1) Any real defense precludes formation of that contract and is a total defense to the claims of the purported assignee.

(2) Any personal defense, including failure of consideration, renders the contract duties of the obligor voidable. If asserted in a timely manner, they defeat the claim of the assignee.

(3) Defenses precluded by status of assignee as holder in due course, or waiver by the obligor: A common law status, or a promise by the obligor not to assert defenses, may preclude full exploitation of the general rule that an assignee is vulnerable to personal defenses available against the obligee/assignor.

(a) Holder in due course: If the assignment is embodied in a negotiable instrument such as a check or promissory note and the assignee pays value for the assignment without notice of any defense available to the obligor as maker, her status cuts off the ability of the obligor to raise personal defenses. Real defenses, which preclude contract formation, are generally deemed available.

(b) Waiver: Subject to state and federal statutory and regulatory rules designed to protect consumers, an obligor may promise not to assert defenses against an assignee. If that has been consciously done by the obligor, he has waived the defense and may not change his mind and reclaim it.

(4) Status of counterclaims and setoffs: Unlike an intended third-party beneficiary who is immune to setoffs, an assignee standing in the shoes of the assignor is vulnerable to both.

(a) A counterclaim is any cause of action for damages in the hands of the obligor against the obligee/assignor for breach of the contract upon which the assignee founds her rights.

(i) Faced with litigation by the assignee, the obligor may assert and prove this counterclaim, whether it arose before or after notice of the assignment had been given.

(ii) If the dollar dimension of the counterclaim equals or exceeds the consequential damages flowing from the obligor's breach, the claim of the assignee is totally defeated.

(iii) If the dollar dimension is less than the consequential damages occasioned by the obligor's breach, liability to the assignee is reduced by that amount.

(iv) Under no circumstances is the assignee liable for any excess dimension of the damages established by the counterclaim. They are recovered against the breaching obligee/assignor.

(b) Limited vulnerability to setoffs: A setoff is any civil claim the obligor has against the obligee/assignor which does not arise out of a breach of the contract which is the source of the assignor's status.

(i) Setoffs may be proven and their damages used to negate or reduce liability to the assignee provided that they had accrued *before* the effective date of the assignment.

(ii) The effective date of an assignment is the date upon which the assignor gives notice of his status to the obligor.

III. **THE DELEGATION OF CONTRACT DUTIES: An attempt by an obligor to place primary responsibility for the performance of his executory duties under the terms of a contract in a nontrader is termed a "delegation."**

Problems in perspective: There is an alternative role for a stranger to play in living out the terms of a contract made by others. Assignees are strangers imported for the limited, and generally pleasant, purpose of receiving the performance owed to the obligee/assignor by the obligor. Radically different is the mission and fate of a "delegate," a stranger imported at the unilateral behest of a contract obligor to assume the primary responsibility for the performance of contract duties then owed to the other trader as obligee.

The material on delegation is much less complicated than that on assignment. If the modern statutory and decisional law displays a positive bias in favor of freedom of assignment, it is far more reluctant to sanction wholesale a unilateral privilege to set up in some stranger the primary obligation to perform duties so that the other trader is exposed to the performance of a person not of her choosing.

Terminology: We term the trader who seeks to transfer the primary obligation to perform his duties the "delegor." The other trader, who was to have received the performance of those duties under the terms of the contract, is the "obligee." And the stranger who assumes the primary responsibility is termed, not surprisingly, the "delegate." If the delegation complies with the legal requirements and it does not violate contract prohibitions or operate to the demonstrable prejudice of the interests of the obligee, it is termed "effective." If the delegate has promised to undertake primary responsibility for performance of the delegor's contract duties, we speak of his "assumption" of those duties. This will have a major impact upon the rights of an obligee in the event the delegate fails, refuses, or defectively performs the delegated duties.

A. The Mechanics of Delegation: The requirements for an effective delegation are quite simple, and no formality need attend their accomplishment.

1. *If no assumption of the duty on the part of the delegate is desired:* An obligor need only clearly identify the intended delegate and to that person manifest a consent to permit the delegate to perform certain or all of the contract duties owed by the obligor/delegor to the other trader under an existing contract.

2. *If an assumption of duty by the delegate is desired, a contract of delegation must be formed:* If the delegor/obligor wishes to create a legal responsibility in the delegate to assume primary responsibility for the performance of duties owed to the obligee, he must bargain for a promise from the delegate and support that promise with valuable consideration.

   a. *Terms explicit:* Usually the promise by the delegate to assume primary legal responsibility for the contract duties of the obligor/delegor will be explicit.

   b. *Assumption implied from overall transaction:* Both the U.C.C. and the *Restatement* recognize that general language such as "I hereby assign my contract" effect an assignment of rights and delegation of the duties of the party importing the nontrader. If the nontrader accepts this arrangement without protest, he will be deemed to have implicitly promised to assume legal liability for the duties of the assignor/delegor. *See Restatement, Second,* § 328(2), and *U.C.C.* § 2-210(4).

B. Restraints on Effective Delegation: Like assignment, the power to delegate is a unilateral legal privilege which does not depend upon the prior, contemporaneous, or subsequent consent of the other trader. However, it has long been clear that delegation represents a far more direct threat to the other trader than the mere assignment of the right to receive that party's performance. The terms of the bargain, or the nature of the contract duties, may render the attempted delegation "ineffective" given the impact upon the other trader as obligee.

1. Contract terms prohibiting or restraining delegation will always be enforced. None of the hostility which marks the common law attitude toward contract restraints on assignment is evident when a party has taken the self-protective step of prohibiting or restraining delegation by the terms of the contract. *See U.C.C.* § 2-210(1) and *Restatement, Second,* § 318(1).

2. If the delegation has taken place in the context of a contract for the sale of goods, U.C.C. § 2-210(5) expressly provides that the obligee may treat it as creating reasonable grounds for insecurity. Such insecurity then triggers the provisions of § 2-609.

   a. The insecure obligee may make written demand upon the delegate for adequate assurance of performance.

b. A failure on the part of the delegate to provide adequate assurances of both a willingness and capacity to perform the delegated duties of the obligor/delegor is, itself, a material breach of the contract. [*See* discussion of rights of an aggrieved obligee, *infra.*]

3. If the obligee has not taken the precaution of inserting contract restraints or prohibitions respecting delegation, whether the delegation is effective will depend on the nature of the duties and the impact upon the reasonable expectations of the obligee.

a. *Contract duties of a "personal character" may not be effectively delegated without the consent of the obligee:* If the commercially reasonable expectations of the obligee founded on the contract include not only what is to be performed but who is to perform it, those duties are "personal." Older cases termed a fact pattern in which the personal reputation, skill, taste, or discretion of the obligor formed a material part of the benefit of the obligee's bargain as centered on the *"delectus personas"* ("the choice of person") of the obligor.

Examples: Paul O'Cullen commissions Budwin Conn, a noted portrait painter, to render a likeness of his infant daughter. Conn may not delegate the duties of this contract to another artist. Any attempt to do so could be resisted by O'Cullen as not effective. *See Restatement, Second,* § 318.

A manufacturing firm engages a particularly popular and successful advertising agency to prepare a fall promotion of its line. Both parties are aware that the market for these products is very competitive, and the manufacturer regards itself as having achieved a major success in obtaining the services of an agency which normally deals only with well-established and prestigious clients.

Any attempt by the agency to delegate the performance of its duties to another firm would probably be ineffective. This would be particularly true if the techniques of the agency were proprietary or otherwise easily recognized by important persons in the marketplace. *See Eastern Advertising Co. v. McGaw & Co.,* 89 Md. 72, 42 A. 923 (1899).

b. If the contract duty is dominated by mechanical or utilitarian qualities or other criteria readily judged for reasonable completion, the subject matter is not personal. *Macke Co. v. Pizza of Gaithersburg, Inc.,* 259 Md. 479, 270 A.2d 645 (1970).

Example: A developer and earth-moving contractor entered into a contract providing for the grading and leveling of new streets in the city of San Francisco. Later the contractor attempted to assign "the contract" to another earth-moving firm. When the developer learned that the attempt was to assign not only the contractor's right to receive payment but also its duties with respect to the grading project, it refused to recognize the delegation.

The Supreme Court of California held that the subject matter was not personal. It declared:

> All painters do not paint portraits like Sir Joshua Reynolds, nor landscapes like Claude Lorraine, nor do all writers write dramas like Shakespeare or fiction like Dickens. Rare genius and extraordinary skill are not transferable, and contracts for their employment are therefore personal, and cannot be assigned. But rare genius and extraordinary skill are not indispensable to the workmanlike digging down of a sand hill or the filling up of a depression to a given level, or the construction of brick sewers with manholes and covers, and contracts for such work are not personal.

Taylor v. Palmer, 31 Cal. 240, 247–48 (1866).

    c. *Waiver by obligee of right to object renders delegation effective:* If an obligee accepts installment performance by the delegate of contract duties which might well have been personal in quality, such acceptance without complaint constitutes a "waiver" of the right to decline further performance which has continued at the same quality standard previously accepted. *Bewley v. Miller,* 341 A.2d 428 (App. D.C. 1975).

C. The Consequences of an Effective Delegation: The obligee must cooperate in the delegate's attempt to discharge the duties of the obligor/delegor.

    1. ***Failure to cooperate in the face of an effective delegation is a repudiation of the contract by the obligee:*** Absent an ability to successfully contest the effective nature of the delegation, the obligee must cooperate in receiving the performance efforts of the delegate. To refuse is tantamount to a repudiation of the contract. *See Devlin v. Mayor of New York,* 63 N.Y. 8 (1875).

    2. If that attempt is successful in gratifying the reasonable expectations which the obligee had in the contract, performance by the delegate discharges the duties of the obligor/delegor.

    3. The obligor/delegor is not relieved of her contract duties, but recedes to a posture of secondary liability.

D. Remedies Open to an Aggrieved Obligee: In the event that the delegate falls, refuses, or defectively carries out the delegated duty, the obligor/delegor is in present material breach of the contract. *Accord* U.C.C. § 210(1).

    1. ***Rights as against the obligor/delegor:*** In the event of such material breach, the aggrieved obligee may commence an action against the obligor/delegor seeking recovery of the loss-of-bargain measure of money damages at law, or if that remedy is unavailable, may sue in equity.

    2. ***Rights as against the delegate:*** Whether the aggrieved obligee may have an election to remedy the loss of bargain by action at law or suit in equity against the delegate depends upon whether there had been an assumption by the delegate of the obligor/delegor's duty.

5

a. If the delegate had not assumed the obligor/delegor's contract duties, he is not liable to the aggrieved obligee.

b. If there had been a contract of delegation between the obligor/delegor and delegate, the obligee is an intended third-party beneficiary of that contract and may commence an action against the delegate in that capacity. *See Rose v. Vulcan Materials Co.*, 282 N.C. 643, 194 S.E.2d 521 (1973).

    (1) Faced with such an action, the delegate may raise any real or personal defense arising out of the contract of delegation.

    (2) The delegate may also assert any counterclaim arising from a breach by the obligor/delegor of the contract of delegation. Setoffs may not be used to defeat or diminish liability to the obligee.

3. The aggrieved obligee may elect as between the obligor/delegor or the delegate who has assumed duties. There can be only one full recovery.

a. If the aggrieved obligee elects to seek his remedy as against the obligor/delegor, the defendant may implead the delegate who had assumed her duties as a third-party defendant. The theory would be one of material breach of the contract of delegation.

b. An obligor/delegor, who has been forced to perform the contract duties assumed by a delegate to pay damages to the delegate or to form an alternative contract of delegation to secure their performance, may recover for any loss sustained from the defaulting delegate. *See Imperial Refining Co. v. Kanotex Refining Co.*, 29 F.2d 193 (8th Cir. 1928).

EXCUSABLE NONPERFORMANCE

▶ **CHAPTER SUMMARY**

6

EXCUSABLE NONPERFORMANCE

Scope: Assuming that a contract duty has fully matured, a failure or refusal to carry out its terms is not a breach if the law has excused the obligation. Any system which builds wealth upon the strength of promises must reserve excuse for the most extraordinary fact patterns. In this chapter we will review the three doctrines which, in the turbulent period surrounding the Arab oil boycott and since, have been repeatedly claimed as relieving parties of otherwise binding contract duties. The doctrines are: objective impossibility, commercial impracticability, and frustration of purpose. We will first survey the status of these doctrines at common law. Part II of this chapter will examine their formulation under Article 2 of the Uniform Commercial Code.

Problems in perspective: A central purpose of the bargain is the allocation of risk concerning the shape and content of the future. Prudent traders are encouraged to contemplate the potential hazards implicit in or surrounding their promises and to guard against them by using express conditions. Yet for all of the emphasis upon the "reasonable person" and the allocation of foreseeable risk, it has never been the literal case that "a deal was a deal come hell or high water." In the materials which follow you will see three themes constantly repeated and occasionally interwoven. At some point, physical or legal barriers to the accomplishment of a promised performance are so great that the promisor is excused. In a departure from the law of physics, there will come a point at which the cost of keeping a promise becomes so disproportionate to common sense and the rational allocation of scarce goods and resources that the promise should no longer command conduct. Least likely is a situation in which the goal which motivated the bargain has been so totally robbed of its assumed utility or worth that, in utter frustration, the quest should be called off.

Acting as a balance against granting excuse predicated upon any of these pleas is the recurrent expectation that the law should distinguish between the fate and fortune of the far-sighted and prudent when contrasted with the myopic and the foolish. How relevant is the foresight and caution of the reasonable person? Finally, there is the expectation interest of the other party which will be nullified if excuse is granted. Does that expectation interest stem from a superior skill at anticipating risk and resisting its assumption? Or is it merely chance that would now permit him to reap where he did not consciously sow? It makes for interesting classroom discussion.

I. EXCUSABLE NONPERFORMANCE UNDER THE COMMON LAW

A. Impossibility — the Promised Performance Cannot Be Done: The earliest appeal for excusable nonperformance was mounted upon the contention that, subsequent to formation, physical barriers had arisen which made performance of one of the bargained promises impossible. The request for relief has not met with a generous common law reception.

1. *Elements of excusable nonperformance predicated upon a claim of impossibility:* In order to set the stage for relief, it is necessary for the party seeking excuse to demonstrate that subsequent to formation, factors neither foreseen by the parties nor reasonably foreseeable have rendered performance of the promised task objectively impossible.

a. *Role of foreseeability:* As early as the 1820s the common law was settled that if the factual development cited as a source of claimed impossibility had been foreseeable at the formation stage of the bargain, and no provision of the contract had been made to guard against it, the promisor was bound to perform or answer for breach. *Fowler v. Bott,* 6 Mass. R. 62 (1809). *Accord United States Fidelity & Guaranty Co. v. Rob Homes, Inc.,* 323 So. 2d 105 (Miss. 1975).

Example: Adams entered a contract with a builder, Nichols, under the terms of which Nichols promised to construct a dwelling house for Adams by a date certain. In order to secure himself against breach, Adams insisted, and the contract provided, that Nichols purchase a surety bond from one Selkirk. Under the terms of that bond if Nichols failed to complete the house by the promised date, Selkirk was to pay $400 to the disappointed Adams.

Nichols commenced construction, and, when the house was about halfway completed, a fire of unknown origin destroyed the structure and a large quantity of supplies maintained by Nichols. The builder did not offer to begin anew. Adams commenced an action to recover the $400 promised on the bond. The defense was one of physical impossibility.

The defense was disallowed. The court regarded the law as settled that when the law imposes a duty upon an individual, a failure to perform resulting from an accident without fault may provide an excuse. But things were fundamentally different when the duty had been created by contract. If performance of contract duties was rendered physically impossible by foreseeable causes, and the promisor had not taken the trouble to protect himself by conditioning his liability, he remained fully liable to perform or respond in damages. To those who complained of a harsh result, the court had a ready answer: "In these and similar cases, which seem hard and oppressive, the law does no more than enforce the exact contract entered into. If there be any hardship, it arises from the indiscretion or want of foresight of the suffering party. It is not the province of the law to relieve persons from the improvidence of their own acts." *Adams v. Nichols,* 36 Mass. (19 Pick.) 275 (1837).

b. *Consequence of unforeseeable physical barrier must have produced objective impossibility*

(1) Subjective impossibility — the promisor cannot perform — not a source of excuse: If the only consequence of the unforeseen and unforeseeable barrier is to make it personally impossible for the promisor to accomplish performance, there is no excuse. At common law each party warrants his or her own subjective capacity to perform the terms of the contract or answer for breach.

(2) Objective impossibility — the performance cannot be done: If the consequence of the unforeseen and unforeseeable barriers would

preclude any person from accomplishing the promised performance, the specific promisor is excused. *See B's Company, Inc. v. B.P. Barber & Associates, Inc.*, 391 F.2d 130 (4th Cir. 1968).

2. ***Contract to remodel as example of objective impossibility:*** In contrast to a contract to construct a building, which has rarely been excused on grounds of impossibility, contractors who engage to do repairs or remodeling on existing structures have found it fairly easy to claim excuse if the building is destroyed without their fault. Faced with destruction of the building, the impossibility of painting its exterior is truly objective: The task cannot be accomplished by anyone.

    a. *Supporting rationale — failure of an implied-in-fact condition:* The most common rationale for discharging the contractor from liability for failing to complete the promised repairs is that there was an implied-in-fact condition that the building should continue to exist. *See Tripp v. Henderson,* 158 Fla. 442, 28 So.2d 857 (1947).

    b. *Recovery in quasi-contract:* In what has to be one of the more highly fictional concepts of "benefit," courts have held that a contractor discharged from his executory duties on grounds of objective impossibility may recover from the owner the reasonable value of any performance bestowed on the project up to the point of destruction. Such a contractor bears the loss of his expectation in completing the now impossible task, and the loss of any materials which may have been destroyed prior to their incorporation into the project.

B. **Impracticability — After-arising Factors Have Rendered the Cost of Performing a Contract Promise Grossly in Excess of What Had Been Assumed by the Parties at the Formation of the Contract:** Excuse predicated upon a plea of impracticability is not mounted on a theory of literal physical or legal impossibility, but rather is focused upon the costs of performing the promise. The concept of equating a gross increase in the cost of performance, occasioned by unforeseen after-arising developments, with impossibility has been sanctioned by the *Restatement, Second, § 261.*

Problems in perspective: At the formation stage, both parties have a rough idea of the costs of performing the exchanged promises. Indeed, the "benefit of the bargain" is the degree to which a promisee has been able to obtain a marginal saving on the normal, or "market" value (cost) of the performance being purchased from the other trader. What if after-arising developments dramatically restructure the costs of only one trader? Is it fair that the other may demand performance at peril of breach? At some point, the answer is "no."

    The doctrine of impracticability evolved from an economic analysis of the bargain and grew out of efforts to arrest the binding force of promises later proven to be badly out of touch with market realities. The development was summarized by Judge Skelly Wright in discussing one of the more famous of the cases arising out of the havoc to international trade produced by the closure of the Suez Canal in 1956:

The doctrine of impossibility of performance has gradually been freed from the earlier fictional strictures of such tests as the "implied term" and the parties' "contemplation". . . It is now recognized that "[a] thing is impossible in legal contemplation when it is not practicable; and a thing is impracticable when it can only be done at an excessive and unreasonable cost. . . ." The doctrine ultimately represents the ever-shifting line, drawn by courts hopefully responsive to commercial practices and mores, at which the community's interest in having contracts enforced according to their terms is outweighed by the commercial senselessness of requiring performance. . . .

Transatlantic Financing Corp. v. United States, 363 F.2d 312 (D.C. Cir. 1966).

The desire to focus upon economics and to take a broader perspective than the immediate interests of a single set of traders has made the doctrine of impracticability the vehicle of choice for drafters of Article 2 of the Uniform Commercial Code. As a result, most of the common law development of this doctrine has been taken over by construction of U.C.C. § 2-615. *See* the discussion of this and other theories of excusable nonperformance under the Code in Part II of this chapter, *infra.*

1. ***Elements of impracticability:*** While not all courts have agreed on an analytical framework, Judge Wright declared an ability to recognize "at least three reasonably definable steps" which a party seeking excuse predicated upon this doctrine must plead and prove.

    a. An unexpected contingency must have arisen subsequent to formation of the contract.

    b. The risk of the unexpected occurrence must not have been allocated to the party seeking excuse either by the terms of the bargain or by custom in the marketplace.

    c. The consequence of this unexpected and unallocated contingency must have rendered performance commercially impracticable.

2. ***The unexpected after-arising contingency:*** Here the focus is essentially upon the subjective assumptions of the parties. Did they bargain with a conscious view toward what has, in fact, been a subsequent factual development? If they did not, the after-arising contingency was "unexpected."

3. ***Risk of the unexpected development must not have been allocated to the party seeking excuse either by the terms of the contract or custom of the marketplace:*** If the express terms of the bargain made one of the parties clearly responsible for the after-arising contingency, it could hardly be said to have been unexpected. Thus the terminology here is not a happy one.

a. An implied assumption may be established by proof that risks of the general variety were contemplated by the parties and yet the trader gave an unconditional undertaking.

b. The customs and mores of the marketplace may cast an assumption of the type of risk later identified as including the after-arising contingency upon one class of traders. A specific contract made against that setting which says nothing to shift this general allocation may be fatal to the party seeking excuse.

4. *Consequence of an unexpected and unallocated after-arising contingency must have rendered performance impracticable:* Here the emphasis is upon the distortion in the promisor's cost of performance.

a. The test is "objective" in the sense that the cost must have become so distorted that no promisor could reasonably be expected to perform. Proof that the added costs were onerous given the circumstances of the particular promisor, without proof that they would have been regarded as senseless by others in the marketplace, would be "subjective impracticability" and no excuse.

b. *Failure to utilize insurance:* In passing upon a plea of grossly enhanced costs, it is appropriate for the court to consider the potential availability of general or specific insurance. If the party seeking excuse could have protected itself in this manner and failed to do so, the impracticability is subjective.

Example: On October 2, 1956, only ten weeks after Egypt had ignited an international crisis by nationalizing the British and French interests in the Suez Canal, Transatlantic Corporation entered a contract with the United States under the terms of which it obligated itself to carry a cargo of surplus food from a Texas port to Bandar Shapur in Iran. While the contract did not specify the route to be followed, it was the intention of Transatlantic to follow well-established custom and sail via the Canal. On October 27, 1956, the *SS Christos* was dispatched by Transatlantic with those sailing instructions. Two days later war between Israel and Egypt began. On October 31, both France and Britain invaded the Suez Canal Zone. On November 2, Egypt obstructed the Canal with sunken vessels, closing it to traffic.

Faced with these developments, Transatlantic contacted officials of the Department of Agriculture seeking new instructions. When it was clear that the *Christos* had both fuel and supplies for a longer voyage around the Cape of Good Hope, she was instructed to proceed using that alternate route. When Transatlantic sought payment of the original contract price plus additional sums for its added expenses, the United States refused to pay more than the contract price. Transatlantic then commenced an action claiming that its original contract had been excused on grounds of impracticability.

Transatlantic's claim of impracticability was rejected by both the federal district and court of appeals. In seeking to apply the three-step analysis, the opinion of the court of appeals demonstrates the soft focus of analysis in marking what it candidly termed an "ever shifting line" between fact patterns succeeding or failing in a bid for excusable non-performance.

The court conceded that the first element was established. There had been an after-arising contingency in fact unexpected by these traders. Silence as to the route was consistent with an assumption of using the shortest and traditional route — the Suez Canal.

The second element, that the risk of closure must not have been allocated by the contract or custom, was closer. The contract was silent, and the Canal had never been closed. Yet there had been remarkable tension in the area for weeks with corresponding increases in international shipping fees. At a minimum, Transatlantic made an unconditioned undertaking in circumstances where the marketplace (and thus reasonable traders) were reacting to perception of enhanced general risk. But the opinion did not rest on this proposition, since the court recognized that it was one thing to foresee risk in general and another to provide against a specific contingency such as closure.

The third element was proof of objective impracticability. The court held that Transatlantic failed to establish this. Besides a general indisposition to find excuse in mere increased cost, there was the fact that the vessel was seaworthy and provisioned for the longer journey round the Cape. Custom deemed it an alternative to the Canal. Finally, the fact that the contract was made in the face of at least the foreseeability of generally enhanced risk caused the court to exact a greater proof of ruinous economic consequences than might have been accepted had there been no such setting. *Transatlantic Financing Corp. v. United States,* 363 F.2d 312 (1966).

5. ***Rights of the parties in the wake of excuse:*** If impracticability is established, the executory duties of the promisor are excused. So, too, are the rights and duties of the other trader. The contract is discharged.

   a. *Quasi-contractual adjustments:* A party who has rendered performance prior to the discharge may not recover on the contract but may obtain the market value of such performance on a theory of quasi-contract. The restitution interests of the parties are thus fully protected.

   Example: In *Transatlantic, supra,* the court of appeals ridiculed the plaintiff for seeking both the contract price plus an award for extra costs in carrying out the duties of a contract it contended had been excused. The only consistent position was that if excused the contract price was legally irrelevant. The only recovery would have been for the market value of the services rendered by a party who no longer was bound by contract.

   b. *No protection of the reliance interest:* Any expenses incurred by either trader in preparing for performance may not be recovered. Each party bears his or her own loss.

6

C. Frustration of Purpose — After-arising Factors Have So Depleted the Value or Utility Thought to Inhere in the Other Trader's Performance That the Contract Duties of the Party Seeking Excuse No Longer Warrant Incursion of Their Original Cost: In a frustration fact pattern, performance by the party seeking excuse is quite possible, and its cost is unchanged from the assumption of the promisor on the day he gave his promise. What has been altered by after-arising developments is the value or utility to the promisor of the other trader's performance. The claim is that with his goal no longer obtainable, the promisor should be excused on a theory of frustration from the duty to perform his own obligations. The *Restatement, Second,* § 265 sanctions such a result.

1. *Elements of a frustration case:* A party seeking excuse from the obligation to perform contract duties at peril of breach must establish three elements.

   a. That subsequent to formation some event or contingency neither foreseen nor reasonably foreseeable has occurred.

   b. That the event was not within a class of risk which the parties were tacitly assigning to the promisor by their failure to address them explicitly.

   c. That the consequence of this after-arising development is that the value of the other party's performance has been totally or nearly totally destroyed.

2. *The role of foreseeability:* As noted, a party seeking to establish frustration must allege and prove that the after-arising event was neither foreseen (subjective concept) nor reasonably foreseeable (objective concept) at the formation stage.

   a. *Risk foreseen:* If it was foreseen, the failure of the trader to guard against the risk by an appropriate condition is fatal.

   b. *Risk foreseeable:* If the after-arising circumstances could have been foreseen through the exercise of reasonable contracting skills, the same result follows but for the policy reason of holding traders to objective standards.

   c. *Risks too remote or too obvious as unforeseeable:* The earliest cases adopting the doctrine of frustration presented some problems in terms of the foreseeability analysis. How could parties forming an agreement to acquire temporary use of an apartment affording an excellent view of the coronation procession of Edward VII, a prince noted for being overweight and well beyond middle age, claim frustration when the King's illness required cancellation of the announced event?

   Problems in perspective: The first half of this proposition is easy to grasp. At the formation stage the parties are expected to use reasonable efforts and bring to bear reasonable talents in anticipating the risks inherent in carrying out and receiving performance of the contract promise. But the power of the brain to anticipate the future, termed "foresight," is limited in much the same manner as the power of the eye to transmit an image to the brain. Some objects are simply too far away to be seen at all or, if glimpsed, to be recognized. A person who fails to appreciate their presence is not negligent. She is human. So too with risks so unusual and unexperienced that to anticipate them is to guess, and to list them would be endless.

Continue to indulge the analogy to the human eye and you will quickly appreciate that some risks are not reasonably foreseeable because they are too close, too obvious. If you hold a book one inch from your eye, the organ cannot focus. As a consequence, the information on the page cannot be transmitted to the brain. Likewise, the brain rebels at having to provide against dangers which are so obvious that they form part of the unexpressed, common-sense expectation of both traders. But if after-arising events frustrate one of these assumptions, there will be no contract language guarding the interest of the affected trader. And yet would it not be unfair to expect him to perform?

Examples: In August 1941, Otis Melton enters a contract with Roger Taylor to lease Taylor's business premises at the intersection of Main and A streets in Biggsville. The term of the contract is five years. Melton's use of the premises is restricted to the sale of "new and used automobiles, the servicing of cars in need of repair, and the sale of gasoline." On January 1, 1942, the government of the United States promulgates wartime regulations prohibiting the sale of new automobiles. The production of new cars for civilian use is suspended. The 1942 offering from Detroit is a one-door, twenty-ton tank!

Faced with these developments, Melton claims frustration of purpose. He contends that his primary purpose in leasing the premises was to sell new cars. This he can no longer do. Taylor responds that he is willing to relax the contract restrictions on use given the new circumstances. Melton refuses this offer and abandons the premises claiming excusable nonperformance.

Melton's bid for a decree of frustration is doomed. He can establish neither element. The potential for United States involvement in war and for the disruption of civilian production of automobiles was clearly within the realm of the reasonably foreseeable in the fall of 1941. Indeed, war had already broken out in both Europe and Asia. Further, in assessing the alleged frustration, the fact that used cars and gasoline could still be sold, and the landlord, Taylor, had announced a desire to cooperate in easing Melton's plight meant that the dealer had not proved total or near total destruction of the value or utility of the premises. *See Lloyd v. Murphy,* 25 Cal. 2d 48, 153 P.2d 47 (1944).

Paul Prentice enters a contract to sell two highly prized tickets to the Super Bowl to Fred Barnes. The agreed price is $500. Two days prior to the date for the game, a players' strike is announced. The game is canceled. There had been no warning in the media of an impasse between the owners and players.

In these circumstances Barnes, the purchaser, seeks excuse on a theory of frustration. Prentice responds that no provision in the contract relieved Barnes of the duty to purchase in the event the game was not played as scheduled. If the court before which the Prentice/Barnes case is tried were to follow the famous coronation case, *Krell v. Henry*, 2 K.B. 740 (1903), Barnes will be excused. The major element of "value" known to both parties in forming an agreement to buy two tickets to a football game at such an extraordinary price was the idea that they provided admission to the Super Bowl, not an empty stadium on the designated date. The risk that the game might not be played was so obvious that the neither these traders nor the mythical reasonable person would have bothered to expressly condition the buyer's obligation upon that assumed circumstance continuing to obtain.

Recently a subcontractor brought an action for breach of contract against a general contractor which had been awarded a road repair and reconstruction contract by the Commonwealth of Massachusetts. The contract called for the tearing out of a grass median between opposing lanes of traffic and replacement with a concrete barrier. Plaintiff had subcontracted to supply the barriers. After construction began, citizen protests brought to the project to a halt. The Commonwealth settled with angry residents by agreeing to abandon the removal of the grass median and the installation of concrete barriers. At this point the plaintiff had supplied about half of the barriers originally required in the project. Defendant paid for these but declined to recognize further liability. When faced with an action for breach it claimed frustration of purpose. The defense was sustained. The court concluded that subsequent to formation an unanticipated event (the citizen protest) had led to the abandonment of the concrete barrier feature of the prime contract. Such an event had not been foreseen at formation and was not within the class of risks impliedly assigned to the general contractor by the silence of the parties. *Chase Precast Corp. v. John J. Paonessa Co.*, 409 Mass. 371, 566 N.E.2d 603 (1991).

3. ***Consequences of frustration:*** A party able to establish the two elements of frustration of purpose is excused from all executory duties. The analogy is to failure of consideration. Neither trader may recover from the other the expectation interest which lay in the future on the day the contract was frustrated.

   a. *Restitution for any performance to date:* The dominant American view is that a party who has partially performed at the point of frustration may not recover on the contract but may claim in quasi-contract for the reasonable value of any performance bestowed upon and consumed by the other trader.

   b. *Reliance interest not protected:* Any expenses which either of the parties had incurred in preparing to perform but which had not been bestowed upon the other trader are lost and may not be recovered.

II. **EXCUSABLE NONPERFORMANCE UNDER THE U.C.C.:** Article 2 expressly treats three recurrent situations in which a seller may be tempted to seek excusable nonperformance. The first surrounds casualty to the goods intended by the seller as his means of performing his contract obligation. The second addresses after-arising conditions which do not affect the goods but substantially prejudice the manner or mode he had intended to employ to deliver the goods, or the means or specie he expected the buyer to use to pay for them. Finally, the Code takes over development of the common law concept of commercial impracticability with an innovative treatment of "excuse by failure of presupposed conditions."

Problems in perspective: Because the Code provisions are aimed at commercial transactions, their focus is upon adjusting the marketplace, as well as the immediately affected traders, to such fundamental alterations as government regulations, war conditions, or sudden and massive disruptions in pattern of supply and demand. Two very important consequences flow from the "forest conservation" mentality of the Code when contrasted with the tree pruning attitudes of common law decisions.

The all or nothing — excused or bound — dichotomy is rejected. A feature of common law decisions was a choice between a decree of excuse "yes" or "no." Such an outcome is not prohibited under Article 2, but the parties and a court are given a third choice: to adjust the terms of their bargain so as to accommodate the new realities. The Official Comment states the proposition as follows:

> In situations in which neither sense nor justice is served by either answer when the issue is posed in flat terms of "excuse" or "no excuse," adjustment under the various provisions of this Article is necessary, especially the sections on good faith, on insecurity and assurance and on the reading of all provisions in light of their purposes, and the general policy of this Act to use equitable principles in furtherance of commercial standards and good faith. (§ 2-615, Comment 6)

> In making a good-faith adjustment to the changed circumstances, a seller must fulfill his contract to the extent which the supervening factors permit, and if the consequences are such as to generally affect his customers, he must take into account the needs of all in seeking to supply one. Thus it is both right and proper for such a seller to spread the consequences of the changed circumstances over the broad network of affected commercial relationships rather than concentrating either its burdens or benefits on a single selected party. (§ 2615 (b) and Official Comment 11.)

Terminology: The Code does not employ the terms "impossibility" or "frustration," electing to include them within a broadened meaning of "impracticability." The Official Comment to § 2-615 declares that this change in vocabulary is not intended to eliminate the distinctions articulated by common law terminology but "to call attention to the commercial character of the criterion chosen by this Article."

A. **Casualty to Identified Goods:** Unlike common law cases which usually had the luxury of dealing with the fate of a particular building or talents of a specific individual, the contract for the sale of goods has as its subject matter something that is often "fungible," meaning that any unit of the goods can serve as a replacement for any other.

Problems in perspective: If the building burned or the opera star developed tonsillitis, the *impact* upon the contract might be debated, but there could be no debate as to whether the *contract* was under assault. By contrast, if the subject matter of the contract was an obligation of the seller to deliver 1,000 bushels of #2 Durham Wheat to the buyer, the destruction or deterioration of any particular bin of wheat may or may not have been the subject matter of that contract. The attitudes of the seller desiring excuse and the buyer desiring wheat conforming to the contract description will rarely agree on the initial premise — *was this particular contract affected?*

1. *Identification:* The Code attempts to resolve the threshold question by a concept of "identification." While many key terms are defined by the Code, this one is not. The closest thing to a definition emerges from § 2-501, which enumerates the manner in which goods may be regarded as having become "identified" to the contract in the absence of explicit agreement advancing or postponing such a result.

   a. *The concept of identification:* Though unstated in so many words, the concept is one of an intention of *both parties* to regard specific, existing goods as the subject matter of their contract.

   b. *The techniques for identification of specific goods:* Section 2-501(1) declares that this can be accomplished "at any time and in any manner explicitly agreed to by the parties." In the absence of such explicit agreement, identification occurs:

      (1) When the contract is made if it is for the sale of goods already existing and designated by the parties as the subject matter.

      (2) If the contract is for the sale of future goods, when the goods are shipped, marked, or otherwise designated by the seller as goods to which such contract refers.

      (3) When the crops are planted or the young of animals are conceived if the contract is for the sale of crops or the young of animals.

2. *Excusable nonperformance or modification predicated upon casualty to identified goods:* Where the contract requires for its performance goods identified when the contract is made, casualty without fault of either party before the risk of loss has passed to the buyer leaves the issue of discharge or modification to the election of the buyer.

   a. *Qualification for excuse:* Under § 2-613, neither party must have been "at fault" in the casualty to identified goods.

      (1) If one of the traders is guilty of negligent or willful conduct which produced the casualty, the obligations of that trader are not ex-

cused: The Official Comment makes it clear that fault embraces negligence as well as willful misconduct.

Example: On May 20, Leslie Taber, a manufacturing seller of doll house furniture, enters into a contract with Karl Berger for the sale of a specified assortment from her existing inventory. Berger makes his selection, and Taber agrees to deliver those goods on June 15. On June 6, those identified goods are destroyed or damaged owing to the negligence of the seller. Taber may not claim excuse, and Berger can treat any failure on the part of Taber to supply those goods on June 15 as a material breach.

(2) If the identification of goods has been by the seller subsequent to contract formation because they were not existing on the date of formation, seller may substitute other goods at any time prior to the date for her performance and in this manner keep the terms of the contract binding upon both buyer and seller.

Example: Assume the facts in the preceding example with this change: On May 20, when Taber forms the contract to sell doll house furniture to Berger, the sale is not from existing inventory but is to be satisfied from production which Taber will generate prior to June 15. On June 5, Taber completes production of goods conforming to the contract description and designates them by internal memorandum to her shipping department as those to be sent to Berger on June 15. Those goods have now been identified to the contract. *See* § 2-501(b).

On June 8, those goods are destroyed when one of Taber's employees backs a truck over them. Taber is at "fault" under § 2-613 and may not claim excuse. However, if she is able to produce replacement goods conforming to the contract description prior to June 15, she has a privilege to identify them in substitute for the original production. If she does so, Berger must purchase the goods tendered (assuming they conform to the contract description) on June 15 and pay the contract price.

b. *Consequences of casualty without fault*

(1) If the loss is total, the contract is avoided and the right of the buyer to the goods and the seller to payment are both discharged.

(2) If the loss is partial or the goods have deteriorated so as to no longer conform to contract specifications of quality, the buyer has an election to inspect them and an option to treat the contract as discharged or to accept the goods "as is" with due allowance from the contract price.

B. Substituted Performance Rather than Excuse Where Casualty Is Not to the Goods, but to the Manner or Mode of Delivery or Specie of Payment: Consistent with its goal of promoting the formation and performance of contracts for the sale of goods, the Code distinguishes between casualty to identified goods and after-arising factors which merely affect the mode or manner of delivery by the seller or payment by the buyer. In the later circumstances, "avoidance" (destruction) of the affected contract is a last resort. If a commercially acceptable substitute remains both available and practicable, it must be tendered and accepted. *See* § 2-614.

1. *Substituted manner or mode of delivery:* Where, without fault of either party, the agreed loading, berthing, or unloading facilities fail, or an agreed carrier becomes unavailable, or the agreed manner of delivery becomes otherwise commercially impracticable, the bargain is threatened but may be salvaged. If a commercially practicable substitute is available, the seller must tender performance in this means and the buyer must accept it as discharging the seller's contract duties. *See* U.C.C. § 2-614(1).

2. *Substituted means or manner of payment:* It sometimes happens that subsequent to formation, a government in whose jurisdiction the parties must perform interferes to make the manner or means of payment illegal. The consequence to the parties will depend upon whether the goods have already been tendered by the seller and passed into possession of the buyer.

   a. If, subsequent to formation, the agreed-upon means of payment fails because of some domestic or foreign regulation, the seller may withhold or stop delivery unless the buyer provides a means or manner of payment that is a commercially reasonable equivalent.

   b. If the goods have already been delivered, the buyer's payment obligation is performed by a tender of the purchase price in a means or manner which remains legal unless the regulation is discriminatory, oppressive or predatory.

      Example: If the intervening governmental regulation by the state in which the buyer resides would force the seller to accept as payment script which could not be converted into foreign currency or specie reasonably suited to foreign exchange, it would be likely deemed "discriminatory, oppressive, or predatory." If the goods had yet to be delivered, the seller could refuse. If the regulation showed no sign of being relaxed or repealed within a commercially reasonable period, the seller could treat the contract as excused. If the goods had already been delivered, the seller could refuse to regard a tender by the buyer of that nonconvertible script as payment of the contract price. A cause of action for breach could be pursued against the seller in any other jurisdiction which would accept the case.

C. **Excuse by Failure of Presupposed Conditions:** By its terms, § 2-615 provides for the potential excuse or modification of the contract duties of a seller but not a buyer.

   1. *Impracticability of performance:* Subject to his having expressly or impliedly assumed a greater obligation (risk) and subject to the Code provi-

sions on substituted performance if the after-arising factors affect the manner of delivery or payment, a seller is excused by subsequent factual developments or governmental intervention.

a. *After-arising contingency contradicting basic contract assumption:* A seller may claim refuge in § 2-615(a) if performance "as agreed has been made impracticable by the occurrence of a contingency the nonoccurrence of which was a basic assumption on which the contract was made."

b. *Governmental intervention:* The seller complies "in good faith with any applicable foreign or domestic governmental regulation or order whether or not it later proves to be invalid." U.C.C. § 2615(a).

c. *Burden of proof is upon seller who would claim excuse:* The burden of establishing the elements of a case under § 2-615's concept of impracticability is upon the seller. *Ocean Air Tradeways, Inc. v. Arkay Realty Corp.,* 480 F.2d 1112 (9th Cir. 1973).

2. **Role of foreseeability:** The term is not used in the verbal formulation of § 2-615, but the Official Comment makes it clear that § 615 is directed to circumstances in which the seller's performance "has become commercially impracticable because of unforeseen supervening circumstances not within the contemplation of the parties at the time of contracting." Section 2-615, Official Comment 1.

a. *Comment 8 further clarifies the point:* If the after-arising factual development or government intervention was foreseeable at the formation stage and the contract was silent in making the obligation of the seller dependent upon some protective condition, the foolish seller will be deemed to have impliedly assumed a greater liability and precluded from claiming either partial or total excuse.

b. *Objective or subjective test of foreseeability:* Some commentators have claimed that in § 615 the issue is not what a reasonable person would have foreseen as elements of risk, but whether this particular set of buyer and seller foresaw it. The language of Official Comment 8 does not support that reading:

> The provisions of this section are made subject to assumption of greater liability by agreement and such agreement is to be found not only in the expressed terms of the contract but in the circumstances surrounding the contracting, in trade usage and the like. Thus the exemptions of this section do not apply when the contingency in question is sufficiently foreshadowed at the time of contracting to be included among the business risks which are fairly to be regarded as part of the dickered terms, either consciously or as a matter of reasonable, commercial interpretation from the circumstances . . .

Holding the ability of the parties to the standard of reasonable, commercial capacity given the practices, customs and mores of the marketplace would appear to be an objective "reasonable person" test.

Example: In 1972, Gulf Oil Corporation renewed a contract with Eastern Airlines to supply jet fuel to Eastern's fleet in numerous southern airports. The contract contained an escalator clause tied to a specified grade of domestic crude oil. At the time the price of such oil was controlled by federal regulation. In 1973 the Arab oil-producing nations declared a boycott against the United States. The price of oil on the international markets began a swift and dramatic climb. In reacting, the United States government drastically revamped its controls in order to provide incentives for new domestic oil production.

All of these moves were monitored with alarm by Gulf. The contract pricing term was tied to a trade paper quotation which continued to publish only the control price of $5 per barrel. Notwithstanding, in less than four months following September 1973, the price on the international markets and the decontrolled price for "new" domestic crude went from $5 to $11 and showed no signs of anything but further steep increases.

Gulf sought to be excused from its contract duty to sell Eastern's requirements at the designated airports claiming commercial impracticability under U.C.C. § 2-615. In rejecting the claim the court held: "If a contingency is foreseeable, it and its consequences are taken outside the scope of U.C.C. § 2-615, because the party disadvantaged by fruition of the contingency might have protected himself in his contract."

c. *Gravity of the disruption:* Official Comments 3, 4, and 5 seek to explain the gravity of the after-arising developments which, alone, can be relied upon by a seller as a source of excusable nonperformance or a right to modify the terms of his promise.

(1) Contradiction of "basic assumption of the parties." While the disruptive factor may affect only the seller, its nonoccurrence must have been a basic assumption of both buyer and seller.

(2) Increased costs, as well as a rise or collapse of the market in which the contract was formed and is to be performed, are not presumptively a source of excuse. The comments declare that these are the core risks which every contract confronts.

Examples: In *Shafer v. Sunset Packing Co.,* 256 Or. 539, 474 P.2d 529 (1970), the court held that notwithstanding subsequent events which had doubled the seller's cost, rendering performance unprofitable, there was an insufficient showing to warrant excuse. "A mere showing of unprofitability, without more, will not excuse the performance of a contract."

In *Neal-Cooper Grain Co. v. Texas Gulf Sulfur Co.,* 508 F.2d 283 (7th Cir. 1974), the seller sought excuse contending that unforeseen factors had arisen, rendering its cost of performance burdensome. The court of appeals rejected the proposition out of hand. "We will not allow a party to a contract to escape a bad bargain merely because it is burdensome . . . . [T]he buyer has a right to rely on the party to the contract to supply him with goods regardless of what happens to the market price. That is the purpose for which contracts are made."

(3) By contrast, a severe shortage of raw materials occasioned by war, embargo, crop failure, or an unforeseen shutdown of major sources of supply which result in a market increase in the seller's cost of performance or prevent the seller from obtaining crucial supplies necessary to that performance present the types of failure of presupposed conditions covered by § 615.

(4) The status of contract for the sale of agricultural produce: a recurring problem both under the common law and the U.C.C. has been the claim of excuse by a farmer or rancher who had agreed to sell agricultural produce only to suffer a crop failure or casualty to the herd.

(a) Common law position: The common law drew a distinction between contracts which had expressly restricted the seller's obligation to the produce of a designated tract of land as opposed to those which simply expressed the seller's obligation generally.

(i) If the seller had taken the precaution of restricting his obligation to a particular source, a failure without fault of that source provided a potential excuse on a theory of objective impossibility. The cases are not consistent in insisting that the cause have been unforeseeable.

(ii) If the seller had merely undertaken a general obligation, the failure of the source he had intended was treated as merely subjective and not a candidate for excusable nonperformance.

(b) Under U.C.C. § 2-615: Both the results and analysis are consistent with the common law. A seller who has taken the precaution of restricting her liability to the produce of a designated tract or herd is protected by failure without fault of that source. Those who have not must either obtain the goods on the general market or answer for breach. *See Bunge Corp. v. Miller*, 381 F. Supp. 176 (W.D. Tenn. 1974).

d. *Assumption of greater obligation:* All of the protections potentially available under § 2-615 may be precluded if the court determines that at the formation stage the seller had assumed the risk now cited as the basis for claimed relief.

(1) Unless it expressly conditions its liability, a manufacturing seller assumes risk that the most cost-effective means of production may

prove unworkable. *See Natus Corp. v. United States,* 371 F.2d 450 (Ct. Cl. 1967).

(2) If the contract sees the seller promise the fabrication of innovative products, the seller assumes the risk of achieving the technological breakthroughs.

Example: In *United States v. Wegematic Corp.,* 360 F.2d 674 (2d Cir. 1966), a manufacturing seller had promised to develop and supply the Federal Reserve Board with a computer described in its bid as "a truly revolutionary system utilizing all of the latest technical advances." When it found itself unable to produce a machine which lived up to contract specifications, the seller sought a decree of excusable nonperformance. The district court awarded the government a loss-of-bargain recovery.

In affirming, the court of appeals declared: "We see no basis for thinking that when an electronics system is promoted by its manufacturer as a revolutionary breakthrough, the risk of the revolution's occurrence falls on the purchaser; the reasonable supposition is that it has already occurred or, at least, that the manufacturer is assuring the purchaser that it will be found to have when the machine is assembled."

e. *Consequences of failure of presupposed conditions may not be total excuse:* The Code emphatically rejects the necessity of electing between holding the contract duties of a seller beset with failure of presupposed conditions wholly discharged or fully binding.

(1) Noting that parties to a sale of goods contract are bound by the implied covenant to deal in good faith, Official Comments 5, 6, and 7 declare that if the supervening factors do not totally destroy the seller's capacity she must work in good-faith cooperation with the buyer to reschedule or modify the tender of that performance which remains commercially practicable.

(2) Allocation of remaining seller's capacity: A seller faced with a failure of presupposed conditions affecting only a part of her capacity to perform must allocate production and deliveries among her customers.

(a) Seller may not discriminate between or among customers. Official Comment 11 declares that "[a]n excused seller must fulfill his contract to the extent which the supervening contingency permits, and if the situation is such that his customers are generally affected he must take account of all in supplying one."

(b) Option to include in the allocation regular customers not currently under contract: While not forced to do so, a seller may include customers in the allocation of his diminished capacity who are not under current contract. However, inclusion of such customers so as to claim the higher prices which future contracts may command would not be consistent with good-faith obligations toward parties to current contracts.

(3) Notice of allocation: A seller purporting to modify his contract duties or seeking total excuse must give seasonable notification to any contract buyer of his decision. If allocation or adjustments are to be made, the timing and dimension of the newly promised deliveries must be estimated.

(4) Election of the buyer: Assuming that the seller is privileged within the coverage of § 2-615(a) and has given the notice required by § 2-615(b), the election to accept modified performance without further recourse against the seller or treat the contract as discharged is that of the buyer. U.C.C. § 2-616(1).

(a) A buyer who finds that the prospective deficiency substantially impairs the value of the contract to him may elect to terminate it, in which case neither party has recourse against the other for any yet to be performed terms of their bargain.

(b) A buyer who elects to receive the modified performance of the seller is, in effect, agreeing to a binding modification of the contract and has no recourse on the terms of the original bargain against the seller.

(c) A buyer failing to expressly respond to the seller's notice within a reasonable time (not exceeding thirty days) is deemed to have elected to let the contract lapse.

f. *Potential application to buyers:* Though they are unmentioned in the text of U.C.C. § 2-615, some courts have extended the statute to provide relief to buyers. *See Nora Springs Cooperative Co. v. Brandau,* 247 N.W.2d 744 (Iowa 1974).

NOTES

THE CONSEQUENCES
OF BREACH

▶ **CHAPTER SUMMARY**

CONSEQUENCES OF BREACH

Scope: This chapter centers on three allied topics, each related to the disappointment of the expectations created by the contract. The first topic is breach, where we must distinguish a fatal, "material breach" from the "minor breach" which does not destroy the relationship. Assuming that the breach is material, our second and third topics concentrate on the consequences as viewed from the vantage point of the disappointed or "aggrieved" party. What are the affirmative obligations of that party? Finally, what remedial rights accrue to the aggrieved party?

Problems in perspective: In the first chapter it was suggested that the formation of contracts be viewed as an attempt by individuals to allocate the risks and hazards inherent in carrying today's promise into future performance. What made that exercise rational was the hope of gaining the performance pledged by the other trader. We now come to a final risk: The danger of overreaction to an alleged defect in the quality or quantity of that party's performance, or in the timing of her efforts to perform. It is human nature in such situations to desire to simply walk away from the disappointing bargain. At a minimum, the party who deems himself "aggrieved" desires to be free from the obligation to absorb the cost and burdens of performing his own promises. But, unless the defect in the performance of the other trader has resulted in a failure to satisfy a condition precedent or concurrent, or has triggered a condition subsequent which discharged the contract duties of the aggrieved party, the difficult lesson is that only a "material breach" can justify repudiation of one's obligations. The Supreme Court of Michigan put the judgment call, and the danger inherent in making it, quite clearly:

> Repudiation is one of the weapons available to an injured party in event the other contractor has committed a material breach. But the injured party's determination that there has been a material breach, justifying his own repudiation, is fraught with peril, for should such determination, as viewed by a later court in the calm of its contemplation, be unwarranted, the repudiator himself will have been guilty of material breach and himself have become the aggressor, not an innocent victim.

Walker & Co. v. Harrison, 347 Mich. 630, 81 N.W.2d 352 (1957).

It should come as no surprise that the bias of both the modern common law and the Uniform Commercial Code in favor of contract formation, the protection of commercially reasonable expectations, the enjoyment by nontraders of valuable rights, and the use of conditions to create a clear order for the maturing of the exchanged promises now culminates in a set of policies which require a calm and mature attitude toward the subject of breach and its consequences.

Perhaps the reason why the law requires calmness and maturity from the aggrieved party is because of the harsh and one-sided nature of the remedies which courts have devised to deal with the "party in breach." If the breach is material, the aggrieved party suffers an immediate failure of consideration which excuses him from performance of his own contract duties. He now turns to litigation in quest of the "loss-of-bargain" measure of money damages. By definition this is a sum of money which, insofar as money can approximate it, aims to place the aggrieved party in the position which would have been occupied had there been full and timely performance. The breaching party receives no further performance and foots what may be a staggering cash bill! If you remember the one-sided nature of the damage remedy at law, you can easily see the necessity of conditions to fix the time and order of performance, and the variety of doctrines reviewed in this chapter which lessen the draconian consequences to the party who has failed to gratify the reasonable expectations created by her contract promise.

For more than a century, the common law has required that the injured party take reasonable, self-help steps to minimize the damages threatened by the material breach. Recent decades have expanded the duties of the aggrieved trader. Focusing upon the premise that a contract seeks performance and not status in litigation, modern doctrines steer the injured party toward the marketplace rather than the courthouse. The first obligation may be to cooperate with the other trader's attempt to correct the defect in her performance. If that can be accomplished, the goals of the bargain are achieved without the intervention of either litigation or third parties. If the party in default will not or cannot correct the material flaw in her performance, the aggrieved party will be redirected to the marketplace in search of a substitute buyer or seller. Only if the cost of a replacement contract exceeds that of the original bargain are there "consequential damages" which may be recovered at law. Items of cost incurred by the aggrieved party in seeking out a favorable replacement contract may be recovered as "incidental damages" from the trader in breach. An aggrieved party who fails to take these affirmative steps must prove them to have been futile at peril of seeing the damage remedy dramatically curtailed, if not reduced to the cruel joke of an award of a nominal sum, such as one dollar.

Terminology: Contemporary opinions use potentially confusing terms to express the affirmative duties of the aggrieved party. The duty to take reasonable self-help steps to minimize the loss or injury threatened by the breach is termed the duty to "mitigate damages." The duty to cooperate with the other party in correcting any defect in that party's performance when such correction is offered, is referred to as a "cure effort." The replacement contract under which an aggrieved buyer returns to the marketplace to purchase like goods from a substitute seller is termed a "cover contract."

I. **BREACH — A DISAPPOINTMENT OF THE REASONABLE EXPECTATIONS CREATED BY THE TERMS OF THE EXECUTORY CONTRACT:** It is possible for a party to breach a contract in advance of the circumstances or date which would otherwise mature it as a matter of present obligation. In Chapter 4, we reviewed the doctrines of breach by anticipatory repudiation, voluntary disablement, and (for contracts for the sale of goods), the U.C.C. concept of breach by a failure to provide adequate assurances of a willingness or ability to perform. In this concluding chapter we concentrate on a much more common development — the "present breach."

BREACH: A DISAPPOINTMENT OF REASONABLE EXPECTIONS CREATED BY TERMS OF THE EXECUTORY CONTRACT

A. **Breach of Contract Defined:** If a contract promise is unconditional (meaning that it was not dependent on any condition) or all conditions have otherwise been satisfied or excused and no doctrine of excusable nonperformance can be claimed, the promisor's failure or refusal to perform constitutes a "present breach." A defective rendition of the performance attempt called for by terms of the contract is also a present breach.

B. **Present Breach as Material or Minor:** Faced with a failure or refusal to perform, the consequences to the other trader are quite clear. Such a total abandonment of the obligation created by the contract is clearly material, meaning that it has extinguished the essence of the expectations created in the aggrieved party. But if the promisor had attempted performance, a claim of disappointment by the promisee is far more problematic. The disappointed party, and ultimately a reviewing court, must determine whether the breach is so serious as to terminate the contract for all purposes other than an assessment of an adequate remedy, or is merely "minor," impairing the expectations of the aggrieved party but not destroying the relationship. This distinction is critical if, at the date of the alleged breach, the aggrieved party has contract duties of her own left to perform. If the breach is material, those duties are excused. If it is minor, they must be performed lest the alleged victim turn into the ultimate aggressor.

1. *Material or "total" breach:* If the defect in the promisor's performance seriously disappoints the reasonable expectations of the aggrieved promisee, the breach is "material," or, as the *Restatement, Second,* terms it, "total."

    a. *Question of fact:* Whether or not the defect in the quality, quantity, or timing of the promisor's attempted performance has seriously disappointed the reasonable expectations of the promisee is an issue of fact. The requirement that the impact be serious is the standard of law. The burden of proving this essential quality is that of the promisee who claims the privileges accorded to the victim of a material breach.

    b. *Consequences of a material, total breach:* A promisee faced with a material breach may elect to treat it as totally destructive of the contractual relationship for all purposes except a remedy at law or in equity seeking to protect her disappointed expectation interest. *See Restatement, Second,* § 236(1).

        (1) Executory duties of the aggrieved promisee are discharged: Any contract performance owed by the promisee on the date she suffers the material breach is now discharged on a theory of failure of consideration.

        (2) Duty to mitigate: While abandoning all efforts to carry out the terms of the contract, the aggrieved party will be required to take reasonable self-help steps designed to minimize the damages occasioned by the material breach. [For a discussion of the affirmative duty to mitigate, *see* Part II of this Chapter, *infra.*]

        (3) Litigation to secure the expectation interest of the aggrieved promisee: The promisee will now commence an action at law seeking the "loss-of-bargain" measure of money damages from the breaching promisee. If an adequate remedy at law cannot be obtained, the aggrieved promisee has standing to sue in equity for such extraordinary intervention as a specific performance decree or injunctive relief.

2. *Minor or "partial" breach:* Any default or defect in the promisor's performance which does not seriously disappoint the reasonable expectations of the promisee amounts to a present breach, but it is only of a minor or partial quality.

   a. *Consequences of a minor or partial breach:* The contractual relationship is not threatened with destruction by a breach of this lesser magnitude.

      (1) Relationship to the doctrine of substantial performance: If the defect in the promisor's performance attempt is minor only, then there has been substantial performance of that contract duty. If the obligations of the promisee are protected by constructive — as opposed to express — conditions, substantial performance satisfies those implied-at-law conditions.

      (2) The contract duties of the aggrieved party are not discharged, and the substantial performance by the other party matures those duties as matters of present obligation. The aggrieved party must now perform her own matured duties or commit a material breach of the contract.

      (3) Right of aggrieved party to suspend counterperformance: In an effort to furnish the aggrieved party with a self-help remedy, some courts have concluded that a partial breach may justify a suspension of counterperformance by the aggrieved party in efforts to force the promisor to correct the defect. However, if the defect remains uncorrected and yet it still does not extinguish the reasonable expectations of the aggrieved party, that party must perform her own contract promises at peril of falling into material breach.

   b. *Role of the damage remedy:* The aggrieved party, having performed her own contract duties, may now resort to litigation seeking an assessment of damages sufficient, when added to the substantial performance received from the defendant-promisor, to fully protect her expectation interest. *See Restatement, Second,* § 236(2).

C. **Distinguishing a Material from a Minor Breach:** As noted, the initial determination respecting the gravity of the breach must be made by the aggrieved promisee in reckoning her rights and obligations. The danger is obvious. If a disappointed promisee treats as material a breach later deemed "minor" by a reviewing court, the attempt to treat the contract as terminated will, itself, have produced the material breach. If the aggrieved party hesitates before committing herself to this perilous election, that hesitation may prove decisive.

   1. Failure of the aggrieved party to treat a breach as material waives the right to subsequently use it as a pretext for terminating the contract.

   2. *Criteria used in making the distinction:* Section 275 of the first *Restatement* listed six criteria which were to be evaluated in determining the materiality of any claimed present breach. The mix of factors reveals two

concerns. There is an obvious focus on the reasonable expectations of the aggrieved party and the degree to which they have already been achieved, threatened, or defeated. But there is also an explicit interest in the hardship which will be suffered by the breaching party should the default be deemed material and the aggrieved party given the election to terminate the contract while seeking the loss-of-bargain award of money damages.

a. The extent to which the injured party will obtain the substantial benefit which he could have reasonably anticipated

b. The extent to which the injured party may be adequately compensated in damages for lack of complete performance

c. The extent to which the party failing to perform has already partly performed or made preparations for performance

d. The greater or lesser hardship on the party failing to perform in terminating the contract

e. The willful, negligent, or innocent behavior of the party failing to perform

f. The greater or lesser uncertainty that the party failing to perform will perform the remainder of the contract. *Accord Restatement, Second,* § 242.

3. ***The added problems of determining the materiality of a breach if the contract calls for one of the parties to perform in installments:*** It often happens that the contract calls for the seller to deliver the goods in installments or for the buyer to make payments in this manner. What is the legal consequence of a present breach of one of these installment obligations? Can it ever justify the other party in treating the entire contract as terminated and seeking a loss-of-bargain award for her entire expectation interest?

a. *Test for determining material impact upon the entire contract:* In order to justify such a dramatic response, the aggrieved party must be prepared to demonstrate that the consequences of the failure, refusal, or defective performance of an installment obligation has defeated her expectations with respect to the entire bargain or severely hampered her ability to carry out her own contract obligations.

Example: Earl Sato, a homebuilder, enters into a contract with Bob Ortega under the terms of which Sato is to construct a three-bedroom dwelling for Ortega. The contract price is $120,000, payable by Ortega in four installments of $30,000. The first installment is due when the foundation has been completed, the second when the framing is up, the third when the house is roofed, and the final installment is to be paid five days after completion of the house.

Sato promptly commences work and completes the foundation after three weeks of effort. Notwithstanding written notice that the payment is due, Ortega does not make it. There is simply a failure to make the payment. Ortega makes no statement which could be interpreted as a repudiation of the contract, nor has he taken any step which has prospectively disabled himself from an ability to comply with its terms. May Sato (1) declare the contract terminated, (2) abandon all further performance efforts, and (3) commence an action against Ortega for $46,000 upon proof that this would have represented his net profit or expectation interest in the entire contract?

Almost certainly not immediately. Using the criteria from the *Restatement, First,* the seeds of a material breach on the part of Ortega are clearly present, but the burden of proving this ultimate quality of the breach is that of Sato. To date Sato has received none of Ortega's performance. Furthermore, it would appear reasonable to conclude that Sato intended to finance his cost of performance of the next stage of the construction project out of the funds paid by Ortega for the just completed one. Thus a failure or refusal by Ortega to make that payment adds burdens to Sato's performance obligations which he may establish as significant. It may threaten Sato's ability to perform his own contract obligations to Ortega, to his workers, and to his suppliers.

What is unknown at this time is Ortega's reason for failing to perform and the degree to which it indicates that he will be unwilling or unable to perform future installment obligations as the framing and roofing are completed. If Sato can prove that the breach of the first installment augurs a series of breached future installments, the materiality of a breach of the contract considered as a whole becomes apparent. The longer Ortega persists in his failure to pay with neither explanations for his default nor assurances that it will be corrected, the stronger is Sato's ability to establish material breach.

b. *Bias of the law is in favor of isolating the breach to the single installment rather than finding a material breach of the whole contract:* Unless driven to recognition of a total breach by the aggrieved party's positive evidence, the bias of the common law is to permit the aggrieved party to recover damages for that disappointment while preserving the balance of the contract between them.

Example: A film studio entered a contract with a motion picture distributor under the terms of which it was to supply one motion picture per month for a year to the licensee, who was to have the exclusive right to exhibit them in the United States. The licensee was to pay an exhibition royalty to the studio within thirty days after each film's release for exhibition. The studio made due delivery of the first film, which was promptly exhibited by the licensee, who failed without explanation to make the first royalty payment. After assuring itself of these facts, the studio declared the contract to have been materially breached and commenced an action for the royalty on that installment plus its profits on the eleven further installments of the contract which were now not to be performed.

Both the trial and appellate courts refused to find proof of a material breach of the entire contract in the mere fact that the licensee failed to make the first installment payment. Declaring that it was the plaintiff-studio's burden to establish that this default was "'so material' as to affect the contract as a whole," the New York Court of Appeals concluded that the fact of a missed first payment was inconclusive in proving the ultimate quality of the breach. The policy of the court was akin to the ambition of the Mikado. "We have established a new test, which weighs the effect of the default, and adjusts the rigor of the remedy to the gravity of the wrong." It was possible for a breach of a single installment to justify termination of the entire contract and enforcement of the one-sided damage remedy, but such a consequence would never be presumed nor proven by "inconclusive facts." *See Helgar Corp. v. Warner's Features, Inc.*, 222 N.Y. 449, 119 N.E. 113 (1918).

4. ***Installment contracts under the U.C.C.:*** The ambition of the common law to keep installment contracts alive is intensified by the U.C.C. Consistent with what the comment terms good faith and commercial standards and the sense of the situation, § 2-612 takes a functional attitude toward recognition that a contract is of an installment nature and the rights and obligations of an aggrieved party arising out of a present breach of one or more of those installments. Such attitudes are to prevail over "any uncommercial and legalistic interpretation" of the agreement.

   a. *Installment contract defined:* Section 2-612(1) defines an installment contract as one which expressly or by commercial understanding requires or authorizes the delivery of goods in separate lots to be separately accepted by the buyer.

   b. *Consequence of nonconformity of one or more installments:* Under U.C.C. § 2-612(2) the rights of the aggrieved buyer are presumptively limited to the defective installment or installments, not the entire contract.

      (1) Right to reject a nonconforming installment: The buyer may reject any installment which is nonconforming with respect to quality, quantity, or time if the nonconformity substantially impairs the value of that installment and cannot be cured.

      (2) Effect of the seller's cure or assurance of cure as precluding rejection of that installment: If the seller gives adequate assurances that the nonconformity will be cured (corrected), the buyer must accept that installment.

   c. *Right to terminate the entire contract:* Section 2-612(3) declares that whenever nonconformity with respect to one or more installments substantially impairs the value of the whole contract, there is a breach of the whole.

(1) Burden of proof that there is substantial impairment to the value of the whole contract must be borne by the party seeking to terminate the entire agreement.

(2) Waiver of right to terminate entire contract: If the aggrieved party accepts a nonconforming installment without seasonable notification of cancellation, brings an action with respect to that installment or installments only, or demands further performance from the other trader, the ability to treat those installments as a breach of the whole contract has been waived.

> **Examples:** A fabricator of cassette tapes entered a contract with a manufacturing seller to purchase custom made plastic housings for its products. The contract called for six million units to be delivered at the rate of 500,000 per month. At the time of formation the product was new and the manufacturer was known by the buyer to be inexperienced.
>
> At no time during the ensuing production effort did the seller ever deliver the promised 500,000 units per month. The reaction of the buyer was one of apparent understanding and a declared greater interest in quality rather than quantity. But there were quality problems as well. At least five separate defects in the product were detected by the buyer who provided prompt notice to the seller. Each defect was quickly corrected although one recurred a second time. After one year's experience, the buyer attempted to treat the entire contract as having been breached by the seller.
>
> The buyer was deemed unable to prove substantial impairment of the value of the entire contract to the satisfaction of the trial court. The nonconformity with respect to quantity (500,000 units per month) was deemed insubstantial given the buyer's repeated display of a tolerant attitude and continued acceptance of short tenders. The quality defects presented a "closer question." The fact that the seller had been able to correct each defect after notice, and they were different rather than repeated instances of the same problem ultimately persuaded the court that the buyer had failed to prove that this history of nonconformity as to installments had impaired substantially the value to the buyer of the entire contract. *See Holiday Manufacturing Co. v. B. A. & F Systems, Inc.*, 380 F. Supp. 1096 (D. Neb. 1974).
>
> Repeated instances of the same defect can have a cumulative effect which impairs the value of the entire contract. In *Sunray D-X Oil Co. v. Great Lakes Carbon Corp.*, 476 P.2d 329 (Okla. 1970), the court found that the buyer was justified in treating the entire contract as having been breached when the seller tendered nine consecutive installments of the goods suffering from the same flaw. In each case the buyer had given prompt protest and notice of the nonconformity.
>
> If the circumstances of the buyer are such that defects in one or only a few installments substantially impair the commercial interests of the buyer, he is justified in treating them as having impaired

the whole contract. In *Graulich Caterer, Inc. v. Hans Holterbosch, Inc.,* 101 N.J. Super. 61, 243 A.2d 253 (1968), the buyer had a booth at the New York World's Fair. The seller had contracted to deliver food to this pavilion. The intense need for large quantities of food occasioned by the Fair had put a severe strain on the area's network of catering firms. When the food delivered by the seller was defective on two consecutive days, the court held the buyer justified in treating the whole contract as having been breached.

(3) Right to demand adequate assurances: The official comment to § 612 points to an intermediate step which may be taken by a party who cannot demonstrate a present impairment of the value of the whole contract, but who has been rendered insecure by the nonconformity in an installment with respect to the other party's ability or willingness to avoid nonconformity in future installments.

(a) Such an insecure party may make a written demand upon the other trader under the terms of § 2-609 seeking assurance of due performance with respect to future installments.

(b) A party who has made such a written demand may, if it is commercially reasonable, suspend any further performance of her own pending receipt of adequate assurances.

(c) Failure of the other trader to provide adequate assurances within a reasonable time not exceeding thirty days following receipt of a justified written demand amounts to a repudiation of the entire contract terminating the bargain for all purposes except a remedy adequate to protect the aggrieved party's expectation interest. *See* § 2-609(4).

AFFIRMATIVE OBLIGATIONS OF THE AGGRIEVED PARTY

II. THE AFFIRMATIVE OBLIGATIONS OF THE AGGRIEVED PARTY: Until relatively recently, the affirmative obligation of a party faced with a breach of contract was a simple one of taking reasonable steps to minimize the resulting harm. Recent common law trends, now codified if the contract was for the sale of goods, go far beyond this avoidance of avoidable injury to impose upon the aggrieved party a duty to cooperate with the other trader in "curing" (correcting) the breach. Finally, if the aggrieved party is a buyer in a contract for the sale of goods, Article 2 of the U.C.C. requires a battery of common sense steps to preserve the economic value of any nonconforming goods tendered by the seller who is unwilling or unable to cure the defective tender.

Terminology: Reflecting generations of convention, courts speak of a "duty to mitigate" and, more recently, of a "duty to cooperate in cure efforts" or "duty to preserve nonconforming goods." The use of the term "duty" is not free from difficulty in that it suggests that a party who fails to follow its dictates will be exposed to some form of legal compulsion. This will not happen. Instead, the law articulates the expectations and then places compliance with them in the self-interest of the aggrieved party. This is done by the simple expedient of cutting any recoverable damages occasioned by the breach to the amount which could not have been avoided had the affirmative duties of the aggrieved party been reasonably met. Even more dramatically, the U.C.C. treats a failure on the part of an aggrieved buyer to follow certain of its affirmative duties as a "waiver" of the nonconforming aspects of the seller's tender, resulting in an obligation to pay the contract price for the goods "as is."

A. **The Duty to Mitigate:** The duty to avoid avoidable elements of loss or injury flowing from a breach of contract is established by a long line of common law decisions.

Problems in perspective: The genesis of the duty to mitigate was recognition that every contract involved an attempted exchange of mutually desired performance. In the event that these desires were thwarted by a failure or refusal to perform, or by a level of performance which did not gratify reasonable expectations, the social institution most immediately able to relieve the disappointment was the marketplace, not a courthouse. Thus, depending upon the ability of the marketplace to serve as a source of substitution for the breached subject matter, the duty of the aggrieved party to replace it there at peril of having damages reduced to what could have been avoided by a timely replacement was advanced with vigor.

If the subject matter was unique — the seller breached a contract to convey the Hope Diamond — the marketplace affords no replacement opportunity to the aggrieved buyer. The affirmative dimension of his duty to mitigate would be limited to attempting to settle on favorable terms any contracts of his own which had been dependent upon his status as owner of such an item. For very different reasons, the more interesting questions arise in the far more frequent contexts of a breach, by the buyer or seller of a contract covering fungible goods, and a breach by an employer of a contract for personal services by the employee.

1. ***The duty in general:*** The doctrine and its rationale found clear expression in a dissenting opinion by a member of the California Supreme Court:

   The familiar rule requiring a plaintiff in a . . . contract action to mitigate damages embodies notions of fairness and socially responsible behavior which are fundamental to our jurisprudence. Most broadly stated, it precludes the recovery of damages which, through the exercise of due diligence, could have been avoided. Thus, in essence it is a rule requiring reasonable conduct in commercial affairs. *Parker v. Twentieth Century-Fox Film Co.*, 3 Cal. 3d 176, 474 P.2d 689 (1970) (Sullivan, J., dissenting).

2. ***Aggrieved employee's duty to mitigate in the face of a breach of a contract for personal services:*** The essence of a contract for the rendition of such services is that the time and talent of the employee are exchanged for compensation paid by the employer. A breach by the employer liberates both the time and talent of the aggrieved employee. A general observance of the duty to mitigate obliges the employee to turn to the marketplace to resell those assets.

a. *Special concern for status of employee:* While in essence an exchange, a contract for personal services differs from a bargain to sell a horse or a house. A human being is involved. For more than a century American courts have been solicitous of the security and status of men and women who labor in the marketplace. This solicitude takes the form of three classical exceptions which limit the dimension of the aggrieved employee's duty to form a replacement contract.

(1) There is no affirmative duty to seek out, or to accept if it is offered, a replacement contract involving work of a different nature than covered by the breached contract.

(2) The duty to mitigate does not embrace work of the same nature if it is offered at a substantially inferior grade of pay.

(3) Finally, work of comparable nature and pay does not fall within the duty to accept at peril of a reduction in recoverable damages if acceptance would involve relocation to a different locale. *See Hussey v. Holloway,* 217 Mass. 100, 104 N.E. 471 (1914).

Example: In 1966 the film star, Shirley MacLaine, signed a contract to play the female lead in a song and dance extravaganza entitled "Bloomer Girl." A term of that contract required MacLaine to be on location at the defendants' Burbank, California, studio for some fourteen weeks. Her salary was to be $750,000. Seven weeks prior to the date set for her services, the studio determined that the public had lost its affinity for motion pictures of this type. It unilaterally canceled production of "Bloomer Girl" and instead offered MacLaine the female lead in a dramatic western, "Big Country, Big Man." The period of time required was fourteen weeks. The salary was to be $750,000. Filming was to be partially in Burbank and partially on location in Australia.

MacLaine flatly refused this offer of replacement employment and commenced an action against the studio for the full contract price, $750,000. Her argument was that "Bloomer Girl" was a singular opportunity to reinforce the public's appreciation of her multi-faceted talent as a dramatic actress, singer, and dancer. A female lead in a dramatic western was thus work of a substantially inferior quality. Less emphasis was placed on the change of location. The issue of compensation was not an issue, being the same for both films. Over Justice Sullivan's strong dissent, the California Supreme Court affirmed the trial court's grant of summary judgment to the effect that as an aggrieved employee, MacLaine's duty to mitigate did not embrace "Big Country, Big Man." The studio was held liable for the full contract price, $750,000, plus interest. To the majority, the fact that MacLaine admitted that she had made no effort to seek replacement work in the movies or on the stage as a singer or dancer was not unreasonable. Perhaps only a California court could be certain that stars do not seek employment employment seeks stars! *See Parker v. Twentieth Century-Fox Film Co., supra.*

b. Burden of proof rests with the employer to prove that replacement opportunities reasonably within the aggrieved employee's duty to mitigate were available and ignored. *See Levy v. Tharrington,* 178 Okla. 276, 62 P.2d 641 (1936).

3. ***The duty to mitigate in the face of a breach of a contract for the sale of goods:*** Perhaps because it is so well established at common law, the U.C.C. does not explicitly mention the duty to mitigate in the event the buyer or seller breaches a contract for the sale of goods. Notwithstanding, the assumption that the marketplace will serve as a ready source of a substitute supply of fungible goods or an alternative buyer exacts a strong allegiance to the duty to resort to that institution if the aggrieved party's expectation interest is to be protected.

a. *The buyer's duty to mitigate in the event of the seller's breach:* In the event breach by the seller goes to the whole of the contract, the first remedy provided under the Code is the buyer's right to cover by obtaining conforming goods from a substitute seller and then recovering, as consequential damages, any difference between the contract price and the cost of the cover contract. *See* § 2-711(1)(a).

(1) Section 2-712(1) defines a cover as a purchase or contract to purchase substitute goods undertaken by the aggrieved buyer in good faith and without unreasonable delay, following the seller's breach of the whole contract.

(2) If the aggrieved buyer has made such a cover, he may be assured of a recovery of loss-of-bargain damages as the difference, if any, between the cost of the cover and the terms of the materially breached contract. *See* § 2-712(2).

(a) Any reasonable cover will be respected in computing the damages of the aggrieved buyer. Official Comment #2 declares: "The test of proper cover is whether at the time and place the buyer acted in good faith and in a reasonable manner, and it is immaterial that hindsight may later prove that the method of cover used was not the cheapest or most effective."

(b) The privilege of resorting to a cover contract is not limited to merchant traders but may be used by consumers to gain the object of their bargain (the desired goods) while fixing the dimension of their consequential (loss-of-bargain) damages. *See* Official Comment #4.

(3) Failure to cover does not preclude the aggrieved buyer from a loss-of-bargain remedy at law, but it will now become his duty to prove the difference between the contract price and market value of the goods at the time and place when the defaulting seller should have performed. *See* §§ 2-713 and 2-723. Further, comment 3 to § 2-712 limits the buyer's loss-of-bargain recovery "to such as could not

have been obviated by cover." Here is a clear vindication of the duty to mitigate. If items of the buyer's damage could have been avoided by a timely cover, they may not be recovered in an action against the defaulting seller.

b. *The aggrieved seller's duty to mitigate:* In the event of the buyer's wrongful refusal to accept a tender of the goods, to pay for them, or the failure of the manner of payment tendered by the buyer (his check bounces), a seller who is still in possession of the goods or who is able to regain possession is free to form a substitute contract for their "resale" in the marketplace.

(1) Effect of a resale contract: If the seller avails herself of the self-help remedy of resale, she immediately accomplishes the objective of the breached contract by converting the goods into a purchase price. She also fixes the dimension of her consequential damages as the difference, if any, between the price term of the breached contract and the amount realized in a "resale made in good faith and in a commercially reasonable manner." *See* § 2-706(1).

(2) Danger of abusing the defaulting buyer: Further content of § 2-706 addresses the not infrequent instance in which the seller abuses the defaulting buyer by arranging a collusive resale of the goods and then seeks to use the large difference between the contract price and the amount apparently realized on this resale as a measure of the, buyer's liability for consequential damages. *See Bache & Co. v. International Controls Corp.,* 339 F. Supp. 341 (S.D.N.Y 1972), and *Wurlitzer Co. v. Oliver,* 334 F. Supp. 1009 (W.D. Pa. 1971).

(3) The Code's solution is to require that if the resale is to be other than open and advertised to the public, the defaulting buyer must be notified in advance of the time, place and manner of the contemplated resale. *See* § 2-706(3) and (4).

B. **The Affirmative Duties of the Aggrieved Buyer Faced With a Seller's Tender That Is Not Conforming to the Terms of the Contract:** The general concept of mitigation centers on the aggrieved party's attainment of the subject matter of the breached contract from a substitute party in the marketplace by a resale or cover contract. Under the influence of U.C.C. Article 2, an even more obvious response has emerged. In the event of a seller's defective tender, the most obvious source of correction is not a stranger in the marketplace, but the defaulting seller himself. If he corrects or "cures" the defect within the time allowed by the contract, there are no damages, and the fact of breach is part of the technical history of their dealings. The concept of cure may well spread by analogy to other areas of contractual dealings, as may the other affirmative obligations of the potentially aggrieved buyer.

Problems in perspective: In order to understand the rather elaborate set of affirmative duties of a disappointed buyer, it is necessary to center on the "perfect tender doctrine." The framers of the U.C.C. adopted Justice Learned

Hand's assertion that in the world of commerce there is no room for the doctrine of substantial performance. Thus a buyer may reject the seller's tender for any nonconformity to the terms of the contract. The potentially devastating consequences of placing the buyer in such a commanding position are curtailed by the affirmative duties of the buyer to inspect the goods, give prompt and specific notice of any alleged nonconformity, and to cooperate in any cure effort announced by the seller.

In default of a cure effort or its success, the seller's interests are further protected by the buyer's affirmative obligations with respect to the rejected nonconforming goods. Any reasonable instructions from the defaulting seller with respect to their disposition must be followed by a buyer who will later be compensated for any expenditures incurred. If no such instructions are forthcoming, a merchant buyer must use reasonable self-initiated efforts to preserve the economic value of any rightfully rejected goods that are perishable or threatened with a speedy deterioration in value. There is both a carrot and stick. Any funds realized by the aggrieved buyer in reselling such goods for the defaulting seller's account may be retained to the extent necessary to compensate for any consequential and incidental damages. The buyer avoids the bother and expense of litigation.

Let's review this ingenious sequence one step at a time. When this survey is completed, we will examine a hypothetical which will illustrate the operation of nearly all of these rules.

1. ***Seller's tender of delivery:*** Both the rights and obligations of a buyer commence with the seller's effort to deliver the goods. Under U.C.C. § 2-503(1), that effort is referred to as a "tender." The seller is required to put and hold goods conforming to the contract description at the buyer's disposition and give the buyer any notice reasonably necessary to enable the buyer to take delivery.

   a. The tender must be at a reasonable hour and the goods held available to the buyer for a period reasonably necessary to permit the buyer to take delivery.

   b. Unless otherwise agreed, it is the buyer who must furnish any facilities reasonably necessary for receipt of the goods.

2. ***Legal effect of seller's tender:*** Under § 2-507, if the seller has made a tender in compliance with § 2-503, a constructive condition to the buyer's duty to make payment is satisfied and that payment obligation matures. The seller is entitled to acceptance of the goods by, and payment at the contract price from, the buyer.

3. ***The buyer's right to a perfect tender:*** The obligation of the seller under § 2-503(1) is to make a tender of *conforming goods*. Under § 2-601 the mirrored image of the seller's duty is the buyer's right to insist that the goods and the manner of their delivery conform perfectly to the terms of the contract.

a. *Buyer's right to inspection of the goods:* In order to protect the buyer's interest, § 2-513 grants the buyer an absolute right to inspect the goods before payment can be demanded or an acceptance decision required.

b. If this inspection reveals that either the goods or the tender is "non-conforming" *in any respect,* the buyer may, under the terms of § 2-601:

(1) Reject the whole,

(2) Accept the whole, or

(3) Accept any commercial unit or units and reject the balance.

c. An acceptance in whole or in part of nonconforming goods by the buyer does not preclude the buyer's right to subsequently assert a claim for damages for any difference between the market value of the goods accepted and the contract price of what were to have been conforming goods.

d. *Partial acceptance must be in commercial units of the goods:* Beyond a general limitation that the buyer act in good faith in exercising an election under the perfect tender doctrine, a partial acceptance must be in commercial units.

4. ***Manner and consequences of rightful rejection:*** A buyer determined to exercise rights under the perfect tender doctrine must reject any nonconformity within a commercially reasonable time following the seller's tender.

a. *Manner of rejection — seasonable and specific notice to the seller of any claimed nonconformity:* Under U.C.C. § 2-602, the buyer's rejection is ineffective unless, within a commercially reasonable time following the tender, the seller is given specific notice of any claimed nonconformity.

b. *Nonseasonable notice of rejection is a* de facto *acceptance of the goods:* Failure on the part of buyer to act swiftly in providing notice of the claimed nonconformity to the seller is treated as an acceptance of the goods under § 2-606(1)(b), in which case the buyer is obligated to pay the contract price for the goods as tendered.

c. *Nonspecific seasonable notice treated as a waiver of any unmentioned defect which seller could cure:* A seasonable notice which is not specific in informing the seller of any nonconformity ascertainable by reasonable inspection is treated as a waiver of that nonconformity under § 2-605(1). The buyer is precluded from using the nonspecified ground to justify a rightful rejection, if the defect was one which the seller could have cured if given specific notice.

d. *The meaning of "seasonable":* Section 1-204(3) defines an action as taken "seasonably" when it is taken at or within a time agreed or, if no time is agreed, within a reasonable time.

(1) Thus for all practicable purposes, "seasonable" and "seasonably" are U.C.C. synonyms for "reasonable" and "reasonably."

(2) Factors to be considered: While ultimately a question of fact in any given case, the official comment to § 1-204 bids the court to look to the "circumstances of the transaction, including course of dealing or usages of trade or course of performance."

(3) Terms defined: As explained in § 1-205, "course of dealing" is a sequence of previous dealings between the parties. "Course of the transaction" refers to their conduct under the immediate bargain. "Usages of trade" is any practice or method of dealing regularly observed by traders in the relevant market.

5. ***The seller's right to cure a nonconforming tender:*** Thus far we have reviewed two affirmative obligations of a buyer faced with the seller's tender: To make a determination of conformity and, if nonconformity is discovered, to provide the seller with prompt and specific notice of the claimed defect. The third affirmative obligation of the buyer is to cooperate with the seller in any cure effort.

a. *Cure a matter of right if the time for the seller's performance has not yet expired:* Under § 2-508(1), a seller who has received notice of nonconformity has a right to correct the defect if time for the seller's performance has yet to expire. In order to perfect this right to cure, the seller must give seasonable notice to the buyer of the intention to make a conforming delivery.

b. *Time for cure may be extended beyond contract term if seller is surprised by buyer's rejection:* If, in good faith, the seller claims to have been surprised at the buyer's rejection of the goods, he may react to that decision with a prompt notice of an intention to cure the defect. In these circumstances, the seller is to be granted a reasonable extension of time to substitute a conforming tender if that extension is not harmful to the buyer's commercial interests.

(1) Section 2-508(2) requires that before an extension of time can be claimed, the seller must have "had reasonable grounds to believe" the tender would prove acceptable to the buyer.

(2) Such reasonable grounds could arise from a course of prior dealings between the parties or trade usages which would sanction the reasonable conclusion that the tender conformed to the seller's obligations under the contract.

c. *Effect of a successful cure:* If the seller succeeds in making a conforming replacement tender under the terms of § 2-508, it is an academic question whether the earlier nonconforming tender represented a breach. Receipt of conforming goods within the time allowed by the contract or within an extended period which was not injurious to the commercial interests of the buyer would leave the buyer without any consequential damages and thus no motive to litigate the earlier tender.

6. ***Disposition of nonconforming goods in a merchant buyer's possession:*** The duties to ascertain conformity, make an election under the perfect tender doctrine, provide prompt and specific notice to the seller of any alleged nonconformity, and cooperate in cure efforts are exacted of both merchant and nonmerchant buyers. If the buyer is a merchant, further provisions of the Code now address the buyer's responsibility with respect to rightfully rejected goods.

Problems in perspective: If the seller's tender has left the merchant buyer in possession of goods which have been effectively rejected under § 2-602 and there has been no cure effort by the seller (§ 2-508) or that effort has failed, a major complication arises in that the buyer is in possession or control of goods which belong to the seller. While these goods do not conform to the contract, and hence the buyer is relieved of any right to pay for them, they do have economic value. As you might suspect, the buyer will be expected to behave in a commercially reasonable manner to preserve that value.

Whether that expectation will rise to a level of a duty to act depends upon the merchant status of the buyer and whether there is an immediate threat to the value of the goods in the face of inaction. In typical Code fashion, there is both a carrot and a stick. As we shall see, if the buyer is forced to sell the goods for the defaulting seller's account, any proceeds may first be applied as a self-help remedy to gain any consequential or incidental damages. A failure of a merchant buyer to comply with the steps we now review would constitute bad-faith dealing and would itself be a breach of the implied covenant in every contract for the sale of goods that the traders will observe good-faith and commercial standards. *See* § 1-203.

a. *Merchant buyer's duty to seek and follow reasonable instructions from the defaulting seller in disposing of the nonconforming goods:* Under § 2-603(1), a buyer in possession or control of rightfully rejected goods must follow any reasonable instructions from the seller with respect to their disposition.

b. *Merchant buyer's duty to act on own initiative if the nonconforming goods are threatened and the seller fails or refuses to provide instructions:* If the goods are perishable or are threatened with a rapid deterioration in value, the merchant buyer must make reasonable efforts to sell them for the defaulting seller's account. Section 2-603(1).

c. *General buyer's privilege to act in the absence of seller's instructions:* Section 2-604 addresses the rights of both merchant and nonmerchant buyers to dispose of nonconforming goods which are not threatened with imminent destruction or deterioration. The buyer may store them for the seller's account, ship them back to the seller, or resell them for the seller's account.

(1) Any good-faith election by the buyer will be respected: In electing as among these alternatives, the buyer is held only to standards of good-faith dealing. Any reasonable decision will be respected even if, in hindsight, it proves not to have been the most economical. Section 2-604.

(2) Buyer entitled to offset consequential and incidental damages against fruits of resale: A buyer who sells for a defaulting seller's account under either § 2-603 or § 2-604 is entitled to be reimbursed for any expenses incurred in that effort. Such funds may be withheld from the proceeds of the resale as incidental damages occasioned by the seller's breach. If the fruits of the resale are sufficient, they may also be used to make the aggrieved buyer whole for any consequential damages occasioned by the breach of contract.

(a) In both instances, the buyer is able to make herself whole without the necessity of resorting to any form of litigation.

(b) Any excess of the proceeds over the buyer's consequential and incidental damages must be remitted to the defaulting seller.

7. ***The aggrieved buyer's interest in forming a cover contract:*** The final obligation of an aggrieved buyer is to turn to the marketplace to form a replacement or cover contract for the goods. *See* § 2-712(1).

a. Any difference between the cost of the cover contract and the contract terms may be recovered against the defaulting seller as a certain measure of consequential damages. Any cost incurred in seeking an advantageous cover may be taxed against the defaulting seller as items of the buyer's incidental damages. Section 2-712(2).

b. The amount of the incidental and consequential damages represents the injury to the buyer's expectation interest. An award of that sum places him in exactly the monetary position which he would have enjoyed had there been full performance and no breach. *See* § 2-715.

Example: On March 10, Kraley's Supermarkets enters a contract to purchase 10,000 cartons of navel oranges from Pick Sweet Farms. Under the terms of the contract, Pick Sweet is to deliver all of the goods to Kraley's suburban warehouse facilities on or before March 25. The contract price for the oranges is $3 per carton.

Tender by the seller: On March 18, trucks bearing 10,000 cartons of citrus fruit, each marked "navel oranges," are dispatched by Pick Sweet for the Kraley warehouse. They arrive at 2:00 p.m. By 4:00 p.m. the off-loading has been accomplished. One of the Pick Sweet drivers gives an oral notice that delivery has been completed to the Kraley warehouse superintendent. At this point, the goods are sitting on the Kraley loading dock.

Analysis: Pick Sweet, as seller, has made a tender of the goods within the meaning of U.C.C. § 2-503. Under § 2-507, the legal consequence of the seller's tender matures a constructive condition concurrent to the liability of the buyer to pay the contract price, $30,000.

[Note: Some opinions and text writers refer to this constructive condition concurrent as a "constructive condition of exchange."]

VARIATION #1: Buyer's duty to ascertain conformity: Although in receipt of the oral notification by the Pick Sweet driver, the Kraley superintendent decides that it is too late in the day to inspect the goods. On the following day several other larger orders are received from suppliers. It is not until the morning of March 20 that Kraley's staff begins to inspect the goods. By noon it has been discovered that, while all of the cartons are marked as containing oranges, 100 cartons contain lemons. This nonconformity is reported to Kraley's superintendent. Pressed by other matters, the superintendent pays no heed to the inspection report until the following morning, March 21. At that time he telephones Pick Sweet's headquarters, located about one hundred miles away from his office, and announces: "We are rejecting the goods you sent here a couple of days ago."

Analysis: There is a strong likelihood that Kraley's has failed to "make an effective rejection" under the perfect tender rule. If this is true, it has accepted the goods within the meaning of § 2-606(2) and is currently liable to pay the entire contract price to Pick Sweet.

Unreasonable delay in inspection: Kraley's problems begin with the issue of inspection. As a buyer, Kraley's had an absolute right under § 2-513 to inspect the goods to determine the conformity of the seller's tender. No provision in the Code sets a time limit on the buyer's exercise of this right of inspection. However, a failure to inspect within a reasonable time will leave the buyer unaware of the nonconformity and thus unable to act within the explicit constraints of the Code respecting seasonable and specific notice to the seller of the claimed nonconformity. Absent such seasonable and specific notice, there is no rightful rejection.

Tardy notice of rejection ineffective: Even if a court were to agree that the delay in inspecting the tender of perishable foodstuffs was "reasonable," there is a major problem with the further one-day delay in the buyer's attempt to act on the information that the Pick Sweet tender contained nonconforming lemons. The qualities of an effective rejection are spelled out in § 2602(1). The act of rejection must take place within a reasonable time after delivery or tender of the goods and it must be accomplished by seasonable notice to the seller. The goods had been tendered on March 18. They were not inspected until March 20. Notice of the attempted rejection was not given until the morning of March 21.

It is ultimately a question of fact if, given the perishable nature of the goods, the course of prior dealings of these parties, and the customs of the marketplace, Kraley's has waited too long to act. If it has, the rejection is not effective. Section 2-606(1)(b) draws a conclusion fatal to the buyer's interest: "Acceptance of the goods occurs when the buyer . . .fails to make an effective rejection, but such acceptance does not occur until the buyer has had a reasonable opportunity to inspect them." *See Robinson v. Jonathan Logan Financial,* 277 A.2d 115 (D.C. App. 1971).

Nonspecific notice: A nonseasonable notice of rejection is always fatal to the buyer who, *de facto,* accepts the goods as is with full liability to pay the contract price. A seasonable notice which is not specific as to the claimed nonconformity is not *per se* fatal but is unfair to the seller, who is deprived of the information upon which to make a cure decision. For this reason, if the unspecified ground could have been discovered by a reasonably prompt inspection, the buyer will be deemed to have waived it and precluded from using it to justify the attempted rejection.

In our fact pattern, Kraley's failure to make reference to the 100 cartons of nonconforming lemons doubtless precluded Pick Sweet from exercising its absolute right to cure since time remained for it to perform under the contract. Kraley's will now be barred under § 2-605(1) from reliance upon this nonconformity. Since there were no other flaws in Pick Sweet's tender, Kraley's is precluded from rejecting under § 2-601. Again, it must pay the entire contract price for the goods as tendered.

VARIATION #2: Assume that instead of the facts given in Variation #1, Kraley's reacts to Pick Sweet's tender on March 18 with a prompt inspection of the goods. That inspection reveals nonconformity in the presence of 100 cartons of lemons in mismarked containers. On March 19, Kraley's telephones Pick Sweet and gives a specific report of this defect. It also announces an intention to invoke its right under the perfect tender doctrine to reject the entire tender (the conforming oranges as well as the nonconforming lemons). In reply, Pick Sweet announces an intention to cure the defective tender by replacing the lemons with conforming oranges.

Analysis: Because six days still remain under the terms of the contract for the seller's performance, a cure effort by Pick Sweet may be asserted as a matter of right. Section 2-508(1). Kraley's has no choice but to allow Pick Sweet to substitute conforming oranges for the nonconforming lemons. If this is accomplished on or before March 25 (the last day for the seller's performance under the terms of the contract), Kraley's will be liable to pay the full contract price, having received exactly what was desired when desired from the seller, Pick Sweet.

Note that in these circumstances there is no need for Pick Sweet to seek an extension of time for its performance. If it had been forced to do so and could make a good-faith claim to have been surprised by the nonconformity, Kraley's would have been obliged to grant a reasonable extension of time for the cure effort unless an extension was demonstrably prejudicial to Kraley's commercial interest. *See Traynor v. Walters,* 342 F. Supp. 455 (M.D. Pa. 1972).

A good-faith basis for a claim of surprise on the part of the seller could be that its labeling facilities had not malfunctioned in the ten years since installation. The burden would be on the buyer to demonstrate prejudice to its commercial interests in granting any extension. As a retailer of grocery products, the fact that Pick Sweet's tender had provided 9,900 cases of conforming oranges would suggest that a brief extension of time would not harm Kraley's commercial interests.

VARIATION #3: Assume that in response to a seasonable and specific notice of nonconformity, Pick Sweet declares that it is either unable or unwilling to cure the defective tender. Kraley's now asks for instructions from Pick Sweet as to the disposition of the rejected tender. Pick Sweet refuses to provide these instructions.

Analysis: Pick Sweet is now in breach of the contract. The refusal to cure makes the breach "total," liberating the buyer, Kraley's, to seek an appropriate remedy and to make a replacement, cover contract in the marketplace. There remains the vexing fact that Kraley's is in physical possession of the rejected lemons. As a merchant buyer, Kraley's is under an affirmative obligation to seek instructions from the defaulting seller as to the disposition of these goods. Section 2-603(1). When the seller refused to supply those instructions, the buyer must reckon with the fact that the goods are perishable. In order to preserve their economic value, Kraley's is obligated to make reasonable efforts to sell the goods for Pick Sweet's account.

VARIATION #4: Kraley's now returns to the produce market. It has determined to restrict its rejection to the nonconforming lemons. It decides to accept the conforming oranges. It now forms a cover contract to acquire 100 additional crates of oranges to replace the nonconforming lemons. It pays $3.50 per crate for the replacement goods. It also sells the nonconforming lemons for $2.50 per carton. Kraley's is able to prove that it has incurred $50 in additional costs by the necessity of making the cover and sale efforts.

Analysis: The actions of Kraley's in seeking a prompt cover and in selling the nonconforming goods for the defaulting seller's account are fully justified under the Code. The difference between the contract price of $3 per crate and the $3.50 per crate cost of the cover contract yields a certain measure of the buyer's consequential damages. They are $50 (100 x $0.50). In addition, the aggrieved buyer has sustained incidental damages of $50 in costs incurred by the cover and sale efforts. When these two figures are totaled, the damages sustained by Kraley's is $100. But it has in hand from the sale of the nonconforming lemons $250. Kraley's is now privileged to deduct its damages of $100 from the proceeds of the resale. Kraley's will then send the balance of $150 to Pick Sweet.

Note what has been accomplished. Without the use of any legal talent, and without recourse to litigation, the aggrieved buyer has taken self-help steps which have given it quick access to the goal of its original bargain: 10,000 crates of oranges at a net figure which is exactly the same as the contract price, $30,000.

C. **Revocation of Acceptance in Whole or in Part:** Section 2-608 provides two circumstances in which it is proper for a buyer to revoke acceptance.

1. Where the nonconformity in the goods escaped detection by a buyer who had made a reasonable preacceptance inspection, the buyer may revoke the acceptance.

a. Revocation of acceptance must occur within a reasonable time after the buyer discovers or should have discovered the nonconformity.

b. The buyer's revocation must also take place before any substantial change in the condition of the goods which is not caused by the previously undetected defects.

2. If the buyer accepted what were known to be nonconforming goods in reliance upon the seller's express assurance that the defect would be cured, a failure of the seller to cure within a seasonable time entitles the buyer to revoke the acceptance.

3. **Means of revocation:** In either instance, the buyer now determined to revoke acceptance must give notice to the seller.

a. The official comment to § 2-608(2) makes it clear that this notice requirement applies to both merchant and nonmerchant buyers. However, the degree of specificity of the grounds for a claimed right to revoke is "less stringent in the case of a nonmerchant buyer."

b. The buyer who elects to revoke acceptance has the same rights as afforded initially under the perfect tender rule. Revocation may be as to the entire tender or restricted to any commercial unit of the goods.

4. **Affirmative duties of the revoking buyer:** Section 2-608(3) declares that a buyer who revokes has the same duties as if the goods had initially been rejected.

a. In all circumstances, these duties would include acting in a commercially reasonable manner to preserve the economic value of the seller's tender and mitigate any loss which could be avoided by a timely cover.

b. If the revocation is occasioned by a discovery of a hidden nonconformity, the affirmative duties of the buyer may extend to cooperating in the seller's effort to cure the defect.

Example: Frank Trigleth entered into a contract with Frontier Mobile Home Sales to purchase, from among the seller's display units, a mobile home. The contract obligated the seller to furnish the home according to specifications and to install a refrigerator and an air conditioning unit. When the seller delivered the unit, Trigleth immediately noticed that some of the furnishings were not the ones ordered. Also, there were areas of defective construction, neither the refrigerator nor the air conditioner had been included, and there was a hole in the front end of the home. Frontier immediately promised to correct all of these omissions and defects and, on that basis, Trigleth accepted the home and moved his family into it.

Some three months later, most of these defects had not been corrected. Trigleth informed Frontier in writing that he "reserved an election to cancel the contract" unless the defects were repaired immediately. In return, Frontier made further assurances but ineffective repair efforts. Five months later, with such glaring defects as the hole in the front of the home still uncorrected, Trigleth sought to revoke his acceptance.

The trial court noted that it was dealing with a nonmerchant buyer under § 2-608. It then held that the assurances of the seller of a forthcoming cure effort had justified the patience of the consumer so that, notwithstanding the fact that the claimed nonconformity was either discovered or discoverable upon the initial tender and there had been a lapse of nearly seven months, the revocation was timely. The court ordered a refund of all monies paid to that point by the buyer, a cancellation of the installment debt and note, and awarded Trigleth a security interest in the rejected home as a means of protecting the buyer's interest. The Arkansas Supreme Court affirmed. *Frontier Mobile Homes Sales, Inc. v. Trigleth*, 256 Ark. 101, 505 S.W.2d 516 (1974).

D. The Duty to Mitigate Limits the Election of a Buyer or Seller Faced with Anticipatory Repudiation: Consistent with its emphasis upon commercially reasonable behavior, the U.C.C. has dramatically limited the option of the aggrieved party to affirm the contract in the face of an anticipatory repudiation and thus postpone the date of breach to the one fixed in the contract for the repudiating party's performance.

1. *The common law election of the aggrieved party:* The earliest common law rulings granted an aggrieved party who still had executory duties of her own on the date of the repudiation an absolute election between two dramatically different responses.

   a. Treat the anticipatory repudiation as a present breach and bring an immediate cause of action for loss of bargain; or

   b. Affirm the contract and await the original due date for the repudiating party's performance before seeking a loss-of-bargain remedy.

2. *Danger to the breaching party:* If the repudiation was in the face of a rising market for the subject matter, the decision of the aggrieved party to await the due date for performance and to treat the contract as breached on that date would increase the dimension of consequential damages. This is because the formula was the difference between the contract price and the market price of the subject matter on the date the defendant should have performed.

   a. If the aggrieved party treated the repudiation as accelerating that date, damages were computed as of the date the action was commenced.

   b. If the aggrieved party affirmed the contract, the computation was made as the difference between the market value and contract price on that later date.

Example: Paul Deer, a farmer, enters a contract on February 10 to sell 100,000 bushels of wheat to Sophie Smith. Delivery is to be made by Deer between June 15 and 25. The contract price is $0.31 per bushel. In mid-April, weather conditions are so adverse to planting a wheat crop that Deer informs Smith that he cannot and will not comply with his obligations under their contract. The market price for June delivery wheat contracts on the date of this communication is $0.34 per bushel.

Smith reacts by informing Deer that their contract had not tied his sales obligation to the produce of his particular farm and that she expected him to deliver wheat as per their contract even if he had to purchase the grain which he was to sell to her. By early May the price for a June wheat contract rose to $0.42 per bushel. By the first week in June the price had advanced to $0.48. On June 25, Smith forms a cover contract purchasing 100,000 bushels of wheat at $0.54 a bushel. She now commences an action against Deer for a loss of bargain computed as the difference between the contract price, $0.31 per bushel, and the cost of the cover contract, $0.54. Multiplied by the 100,000 bushels called for in their contract, Smith seeks to recover $23,000 as her actual, out-of-pocket loss.

Deer protests that if Smith had accepted the fact of his repudiation at the time it was made in mid-April she could have formed a cover contract for $0.34 per bushel. This would have limited her consequential damages to $3,000. In the alternative, he contends that if she had acted within a reasonable time after the date of his repudiation, the cost of a cover contract would have been no more than $0.40 per bushel, limiting her damages to $9,000.

The validity of Deer's contention that the great bulk of Smith's damages could have been avoided by a timely acceptance of his breach was unclear at common law. It is quite clear that he would succeed in dramatically limiting the size of Smith's recovery under Article 2.

3. ***Anticipatory repudiation under the U.C.C.:*** Section 2-610 provides that when either party repudiates the contract with respect to a performance not yet due, the loss of which will substantially impair the value of the contract to the other, the aggrieved party may:

   a. Resort immediately to any remedy for breach including seeking a loss-of-bargain recovery, forming a resale or cover contract; or

   b. Await performance by the repudiating party for a reasonable period of time.

   c. A refusal by the buyer to accept the seller's breach in the face of a rising market, or by the seller to accept the buyer's breach in the face of falling market conditions, would be manifestly unreasonable. Any actual loss sustained beyond what could have been avoided by a timely acceptance of the repudiation would not be recoverable. *See Oloffson v. Coomer,* 11 Ill. App. 3d 918, 296 N.E.2d 871 (1973).

E. A resale of the subject matter by a seller with an elastic supply curve need not be counted as mitigation because the buyer's breach has liberated any additional sales opportunity for the seller.

1. In the great majority of cases, a material breach by the seller liberates goods which the seller would have otherwise been unable to offer to another buyer. If these goods are sold, it is elementary justice that their price should be deducted from the damages occasioned by the buyer's breach.

2. A very different fate awaits a seller who has many standard price goods and few buyers. A breach of contract by Buyer *A* does not liberate any asset which the seller needs if she is to deal with Buyer *B*. Had Buyer *B* come along, the seller could have accommodated both.

3. *Proper measure of damages is loss of net profit:* In such circumstances the proper measure of damages is not the difference between the contract and market price but the net profit the seller would have made on the breached contract. *See* U.C.C. § 2-708(2).

REMEDIES
FOR BREACH
OF CONTRACT

III. REMEDIES FOR BREACH OF CONTRACT

A. The Interests of the Aggrieved Party: Whenever a party suffers a material breach of contract, at least three interests are immediately threatened.

1. *The restitution interest:* If, on the date of the breach, the aggrieved party has already wholly or partially performed his own contract obligations, a material breach on the part of the other trader leaves the breaching party unjustly enriched by the value of that performance and the aggrieved party unjustly impoverished by its cost.

2. *The reliance interest:* If, on the date of the breach, the aggrieved party has not yet performed his own contract obligations but has incurred expenses or foregone other opportunities in reliance upon the expectation that the other would perform, the breaching party is not unjustly enriched, but the out-of-pocket loss to the aggrieved party represents present unjust impoverishment.

3. *The expectation interest:* If, on the date of the breach, the aggrieved party has neither performed his own contract obligations nor changed position in detrimental reliance on the promise of the breaching party to perform, there is neither unjust present enrichment of the breaching party nor unjust present impoverishment of the aggrieved party. There is, however, a disappointment of expectations of future wealth or future advantage which would have been gained had the breaching party performed.

Problems in perspective: There is, in truth, only one remedy available at law for breach of contract. It is an award of money damages. And yet, depending upon the measure deemed appropriate by the court, that award can range from an attempt to place the aggrieved party in approximately the position which would have been occupied had there been full and timely performance, to the cruel joke of a nominal sum such as one dollar. While there are technical requirements which often dictate the choice, a student interested in grasping more than the mechanics of remedies must absorb a basic understanding of modern social attitudes toward these three interests. There are surprises.

If we compare the consequences of breach to the situation of the two parties immediately before they formed the contract, a clear hierarchy would appear to arise:

> Restitution interest most pressing: From the vantage point of the aggrieved party, the restitution interest presents the most pressing claim for relief. When contrasted with the preagreement status quo, the aggrieved party has suffered a net decline in his assets (the cost of his performance). Even worse, the breaching party has achieved a net increase in his assets (the value of the aggrieved party's performance).

> Reliance interest presents a middle case: Here the breach does not result in any element of unjust present enrichment of the breaching party. Yet the out-of-pocket expenses undertaken by the aggrieved party since the date of formation were predicated upon the expectation that the promise or promises of the other trader would be kept. When the promisor breaches, these reliance expenditures are wasted, turning into unjust present impoverishment of the promisee.

> Expectation interest appears least serious: Here neither the aggrieved nor the breaching party has suffered or gained any net decrease or increase in assets when contrasted with the precontract status quo. What has been upset is the aggrieved party's expectation of future advantage.

Looking at these interests, one might assume that society would exhibit greatest concern for the restitution interest and be least distressed by the plight of a plaintiff unable to claim more than a broken expectation. This was surely the preference of what we today term "ancient civilizations." Among the English-speaking, it would explain the development of the doctrine of quasi-contract to protect the restitution interest and the emergence of promissory estoppel as a means of vindicating the reliance claim. Whatever the merits of this assessment as accurate history, it is totally at odds with the goals of contemporary practice.

The objective of the modern damage remedy is not the limited, backward-looking agenda of restoring the preagreement status quo. The loss-of-bargain measure of money damages has no other purpose than to vindicate the expectation interest of the aggrieved party. The potential intervention of equity can only be sought if the damage remedy is "inadequate," meaning that it fails to vindicate the expectation interest.

Upon reflection, the preference of modern contract law for rescuing the future rather than restoring the past is inevitable, not surprising. The primary goal of the objective theory of contract formation, the protection of commercially reasonable expectations, the potential rights of nontraders, and the use of conditions to order the performance of promises has been the attainment of future wealth on the strength of today's promises. If those promises are broken, damage remedies which strive to rescue that goal represent a harmonious conclusion to the modern commercial law.

A broader understanding may be achieved by noting that much modern economic theory sees protection of private expectation interests as vindicating society's need for an efficient allocation of scarce goods and services. The genius of the private bargain is that in exchanging promises each trader gives up an asset which he values less to gain an asset which he values more. The resulting redistribution of assets to persons who place optimal value on their acquisition is the essence of an efficient (productive) distribution of wealth.

Let us first survey the damage remedy and its classical limitations. We will then take an elaborate example which will allow you to apply your understanding.

B. Punitive or Exemplary Damages Not Recoverable: The goal of the damage remedy at law is to compensate the aggrieved party, not to inflict a punishment upon the party in breach. And this is true regardless of the moral blame incurred by the defendant in breaching the contract. *See Addis v. Gramophone Co.,* [1909] A.C. 488 (H.L.). *Accord* U.C.C. § 1-106(1).

C. The Loss-of-Bargain Measure of Money Damages: The damage remedy at law accepts the fact of a material breach as having destroyed the contract for all purposes save for the computation and award of a sum of money sufficient, insofar as money can approximate it, to place the aggrieved party in the position that would have been occupied had there been full and timely performance. This is clearly the goal of the U.C.C.. *See* § 1-106. It is reflected in *Restatement, Second,* § 344.

1. *Presumptive measure of award:* In the absence of special circumstances, the loss of bargain is measured as the difference, if any, between the contract price and market value of the breached performance at the time and place when, under the terms of the contract, it should have been performed.

   a. *Objective quality of expectation:* By measuring the damages as the difference between the contract price and the cost of performance at the time and place the breached obligation should have been performed, recovery is both objective in nature and exposed to the realities of what actually happened between the formation and performance dates.

      (1) The measure is objective in that an aggrieved party may not recover the value of his hope or optimistic assessment about the future. The only benefit of his bargain compensable at law is the difference, if any, between what he had promised to pay for that performance in the future and the cost of that performance from another source on the day it should have been furnished.

      (2) The measure is realistic since, if the market value of the subject matter has actually declined between the formation and performance dates, recovery is limited to the lesser sum.

2. *Loss-of-bargain award is a one-sided approximation of performance:* The major flaw in the loss-of-bargain award of money damages is also its greatest strength. By settling for an approximation rather than performance of the broken bargain, the remedy is within the capacity of a judiciary possessed of limited human and financial resources. But the price is the totally one-sided nature of the outcome. The aggrieved party is placed in a position akin to that which would have been achieved by performance. The breaching party forfeits all expectation in the bargain and pays what may be a staggering damage award.

3. *Limitations designed to protect the interest of the breaching party:* Aside from creating the distinction between material and minor breach and placing the aggrieved party at risk of any overreaction, the common law has been slow to protect the expectation interest of the aggrieved party. Such an interest could be protected by a decree of specific performance, for the aggrieved party would then have to pay the contract price as an equitable condition to relief. Such decrees are, however, quite rare. In the great majority of cases of material breach, the only protection of the defendant is to be found in four classical limitations on the damage remedy.

   a. *Consequential:* In order to be compensable at law, damages must be a consequence of the defendant's breach. This is a rather obvious doctrine, for unless the damages are caused by the breach, they are beyond the realm of a loss-of-bargain recovery.

     (1) Unlike a tort recovery, the damage remedy is not subjected to a proximate cause limitation. An essentially similar restriction is to be found in the doctrine of foreseeability which we shall review in a minute.

     (2) Formation expenses disallowed: The major element of a plaintiff's claim likely to be disallowed in the initial test for causality are all expenses incurred in forming the contract. If those expenses would have been wasted had the defendant refused to assent to the bargain, they are part of the price of forming a contract, not damages for its breach.

   b. *Foreseeable:* In order to be compensable at law, damages in fact caused by the breach must have been either generally or specially foreseeable at the formation stage. With the introduction of the concept of foreseeability, the common law consciously accepted a result wherein the defendant's liability could fall short of the aggrieved party's actual loss. *Hadley v. Baxendale,* 9 Ex. 341, 156 Eng. Rep. 145 (1854). Yet the limitation is objective. It is no defense that the particular defendant did not foresee the particular injury. Consistent with the objective theory of contract formation, the inquiry is with respect to the anticipatory skills of the "reasonable person." The distinction between generally and specially foreseeable losses is made on the information available to the reasonable person at the formation stage.

(1) Generally foreseeable elements of loss: To test whether a particular loss or injury was generally foreseeable, the question is posed in the following way: "Would a reasonable person, standing in the shoes of the defendant on the date of formation and knowing only the terms of the contract have, had he paused to consider the question, foreseen this injury as a probable consequence of breach?"

(2) Specially foreseeable losses: The magnitude of potentially recoverable losses may be dramatically increased if the special needs or circumstances of the promisee are revealed to the potential promisor prior to the formation of the bargain.

   (a) In order to set the stage for the recovery of special elements of damage, the communication by the promisee to the promisor prior to formation of the bargain must have been such as to alert a reasonable person to both the nature of the added risk and its likely dimension. *Kerr S.S. Co. v. Radio Corporation of America*, 245 N.Y. 284, 157 N.E. 140 (1927).

   (b) Assuming that there has been adequate notice, the test as to whether a specific element of the aggrieved party's loss was specially foreseeable is formulated as follows: "Would a reasonable person, standing in the shoes of the defendant on the day the bargain was formed and aware not only of the terms of that contract but the disclosed special needs or circumstances of the promisee have, had he stopped to think about it, foreseen this injury as a probable consequence of breach? *Victoria Laundry (Windsor) Ltd. v. Newman Industries, Ltd.,* [1949] 2 K.B. 528, 1 All Eng. Rep. 997.

(3) Actual thought not required: Damages are not rendered non-foreseeable merely because the particular defendant did not stop to contemplate their potential occurrence. Nor must the plaintiff prove that a reasonable person would have actually foreseen them. It is sufficient that had the reasonable person paused to consider the matter, the losses would have been foreseeable.

(4) Loss need only have been probable; it need not have been foreseen as an inevitable consequence of breach.

   Example: Chelsea Shipping contracted with Holly Sugar to transport a cargo of sugar from Contanza to Basrah in the Middle East. Chelsea was aware that Holly was a sugar merchant and that there was a market for sugar in Basrah. It did not know that Holly intended to sell the sugar as soon as possible after its arrival. Chelsea breached the contract of carriage when they diverted their ship with the consequence that it was nine days late in arriving in Basrah. During that brief period the price of sugar fell dramatically in Basrah.

Holly sold the sugar on the day of its late arrival. It was then able to calculate that had the sugar arrived as per the contract promise of Chelsea, it would have fetched nearly $20,000 more than the amount realized from the late sale. It commenced an action against Chelsea, contending that $20,000 represented its consequential losses. Chelsea conceded that the damages had been caused by its breach but defended on the grounds that they were not foreseeable.

In an appeal to the House of Lords, the plaintiff was held entitled to the $20,000 as generally foreseeable damages. Lord Reed declared: "[The shipowner] knew there was a market in sugar at Basrah, and it appears to me that, if he had thought about the matter, he must have realized that at least it was not unlikely that the sugar would be sold in the market at market price on arrival. And he must be held to have known that in any ordinary market, prices are apt to fluctuate from day to day." Lords Morris and Hudson coined the phrase, "the result was liable to be." Lord Pearce preferred to see the market fluctuation as "a serious possibility." Lord Upjohn termed it "a real danger." *Koufos v. Czarnikow Ltd.,* [1969] 1 A.C. 350 (House of Lords).

The entire appeal would have been unnecessary had Holly disclosed to Chelsea its plan to sell immediately on the open market before the shipper agreed to deliver the cargo by a certain date.

c. *Unavoidable:* Of those losses in fact caused by the defendant's breach and either generally or specially foreseeable at the formation of the contract, plaintiff may recover for only those elements of injury which proved unavoidable given an expenditure of reasonable efforts to mitigate damages. [*See* the discussion of the Duty to Mitigate, Part II.A, this chapter.]

d. *Certain in dollar amount:* Finally, of those losses in fact caused by the defendant's breach and either generally or specially foreseeable at the formation of the contract, and unavoidable given reasonable efforts by the aggrieved party to mitigate, only those damages which can be proved to a certain dollar amount may be compensated at law.

Problems in perspective: All limitations on the damage remedy would be meaningless if, in the final analysis, the finder of fact were left to speculate as to their dimension. For this reason, American courts were among the first to fashion the common law requirement that damages had to be proved with a fair degree of certainty. Where this limitation was most lifting was in contracts essential to the formation of a new business venture. It was undoubtedly true that a breach would diminish or even extinguish profits. But how large would the profits have been had the contract been performed? With no track record, the new business was the typical example of a deserving party turned aside with a nominal award. Better that than a guess. The requirement remains but has been relaxed of late. Both the *Restatement, Second,* and Uniform Commercial Code reject the notion that the plaintiff must prove damages with mathematical certainty. Still, they must be far more than a guesstimate. *See Ericson v. Playgirl, Inc.,* 73 Cal. App. 3d 850, 140 Cal. Rptr. 921 (1977).

(1) If the marketplace is a ready source of substitution for the breached subject matter, certainty will pose little problem.

    (a) If the aggrieved buyer formed a cover contract, his certain damages are the difference, if any, between the cost of the cover contract and the terms of the breached contract.

    (b) If the aggrieved party is the seller, a resale contract will fix a certain measure of consequential damages. It is the difference between the fruits of the resale and the price the breaching buyer was to have paid under the terms of the contract.

    (c) If the aggrieved party fails to make a substitute contract, consequential damages may still be established with a requisite certainty by measuring the difference between the terms of the breached contract and the market price of the subject matter at the time and place performance should have been rendered.

(2) The modern trend is to hold plaintiff to proof of consequential damages only to a "reasonable certainty." *See Restatement, Second,* § 352.

(3) U.C.C. position: The official comment to § 1-106 declares that the drafters rejected "any doctrine that damages must be calculable with mathematical accuracy. Compensatory damages are often at best approximate: They have to be proved with whatever definiteness and accuracy the facts permit, but no more."

Example: On March 13, 1926, the Chicago Coliseum Club, a sports promoter, signed a contract with William Harrison ("Jack") Dempsey, the then-reigning heavyweight boxing champion of the world. Under the terms of the contract, the Club was to stage a defense of Dempsey's title against the ranking contender, Harry Wills. The sum of $10 was paid to Dempsey on the signing, and the Club promised to pay him a minimum of $800,000 plus a percentage of the gate receipts. The contract specified that the title defense would take place in Chicago during the month of September, 1926. Two provisions of the contract obliged Dempsey to do nothing between the signing and the projected date of the Wills match to jeopardize either his health or the title. He also promised to permit the Club to take out a policy of life insurance on his person as security against the major expenditures they would incur in performing their duties to promote and stage the event. Prior to signing with Dempsey, the Club had entered a contract with Harry Wills, as well as with the promoter Andrew Weisberg.

    On July 10, physicians from the insurance carrier which was to write the policy of life and health insurance on Dempsey's person arrived at his training camp to conduct a physical examination. Dempsey refused to permit the examination and dispatched a telegram to the Club declaring that he was "[e]ntirely too busy training for my coming Tunney match to waste time on insurance representatives stop as you have no contract suggest you stop kidding yourself and me also."

The Club treated this telegram, coupled with Dempsey's behavior, as a breach by anticipatory repudiation. They immediately dispatched a team of lawyers to Indiana, where Dempsey was visiting his mother. Personal service was obtained over Dempsey and the Club sought an equity decree declaring that a contract did, indeed, exist between them, and enjoining Dempsey from risking the title in a defense against Tunney. The Indiana equity court obliged with both the decree and an injunction. Dempsey simply fled Indiana and went to Pennsylvania, the state in which the Tunney match was being promoted. An attempt to enforce the decree in Pennsylvania proved unsuccessful. Dempsey fought Tunney and lost the title. Years later, Dempsey made the mistake of returning to Illinois, where service was obtained and the Club commenced an action for a loss-of-bargain recovery.

The Club divided its prayer for damages into four categories: (1) loss of profits which would have been earned by the plaintiff had the Dempsey/Wills match been fought, (2) expenses incurred by the Club prior to signing the agreement with Dempsey, (3) expenses incurred subsequent to formation of the contract in the Club's efforts to carry out its promotion obligations, and (4) expenses incurred in obtaining the declaratory judgment, the injunction, and attempting to enforce it in Pennsylvania.

1. The loss of profits: plaintiff claimed $1.6 million; the court awarded $1 million. The court concluded that the loss of profits was consequential upon the Dempsey breach, generally foreseeable, and unavoidable (there is only one heavyweight champion so a replacement fight could not be staged). Notwithstanding, the Club's prayer for $1.6 million in loss-of-bargain damages was deemed speculative. The Club had failed to prove these losses with sufficient certainty.

2. Expenses incurred prior to Dempsey's having signed the contract on June 13: plaintiff claimed $150,000; the court awarded nothing. Not $0.01 of these expenses could be recovered, for they were not consequential upon the breach. They represented the cost of obtaining a contract which Dempsey could have refused to sign. They were not damages flowing from its breach.

3. Expenses incurred subsequent to signing in attempting to carry out the Club's promotion obligations: plaintiff claimed $100,000; the court awarded $20,000. Of the more than $100,000 in expenses alleged by the Club, the court awarded less than $20,000. It determined that at least $80,000 represented ongoing payroll and overhead which would have been incurred whether Dempsey had signed or not. These recurrent items were not consequential upon the breach. Special and specific expenditures which were nec-

essary to carry out the Club's responsibilities under this fight could be recovered.

4. Expenses incurred by the Club in attempting to restrain Dempsey from breaching the contract in general or fighting Tunney: plaintiff claimed $90,000; the court awarded nothing. The court disallowed the entire bill. A major portion of these expenses were attorney fees. The court noted that they were not provided for in the contract. More fundamentally, these expenses were deemed avoidable. It reasoned that any rational response to a breach by Dempsey would have seen the ultimate futility of depending upon Pennsylvania's equity courts to frustrate the desires of local sports fans or specifically order Dempsey to step into a ring so that Harry Wills might seek to beat him senseless!

Spontaneously, the court added a fifth item to the plaintiff's quest for damages: return of the $10 paid to Dempsey on the date of signing. This was fully recoverable as it represented the Club's restitution interest.

So for a complaint that sought nearly $2 million in loss-of-bargain relief, the court was willing to award $20,011 as the consequential, foreseeable, unavoidable, and certain damages. *See Chicago Coliseum Club v. Dempsey,* 265 Ill. App. 542 (1932).

D. **When Money Fails to Right the Wrong:** The potential for equitable intervention.

Problems in perspective: *Chicago Coliseum* is merely an example of a court forced to award damages which all concerned knew to be far less than the actual consequential loss inflicted upon the plaintiff. Yet the court's view that the Club had merely compounded its difficulties by resorting to the equitable proceedings in Indiana and Pennsylvania alerts you to the idea that equity does not extend a secure safety net for persons unable to obtain an adequate remedy at law. As we shall see, the burden is upon the plaintiff to secure "standing." Victory there only assures the right to address a "prayer" to the equity court. Relief is not a matter of right, but of grace meted out by a "court of conscience."

Terminology: In the Alice in Wonderland world of equity, there was a time when the litigant was obliged to resort to an entirely separate judiciary. Today, in all but two American states, the jurisdiction over both law and equity has been merged into a single judicial system. Notwithstanding, many states prefer different terms for litigation conducted "in equity." The aggrieved party is the "complainant," not the "plaintiff." Litigation is commenced with a "bill" rather than a "complaint." The target of this exercise is not a "defendant" but rather a "respondent." The entire proceeding is a "suit in equity." By contrast, one brings an "action at law."

1. *Inadequacy of the damage remedy as a standing prerequisite to sue in equity:* An aggrieved party may not choose between equitable relief and the damage remedy. That choice has been made by society, and it has opted for the damage remedy as the remedy of preference. Equitable rem-

edies are thus reserved as a potential response only for those cases in which the complaining party can prove the inadequacy of the remedy at law.

a. Proof of the inadequacy of the damage remedy to vindicate the expectation interest of the aggrieved party is a standing prerequisite to a plea for equitable intervention. Proof of this inadequacy must be to the satisfaction of the equity court. *See Klein v. Pepsico*, 845 F.2d 76 (4th Cir. 1988).

b. Where a market exists offering a replacement opportunity to the aggrieved party, the remedy at law is presumptively adequate. Damages can be measured as the difference between the contract terms and the market price for the subject matter of the breached bargain. The presumption of adequacy is rebuttable.

> **Example:** George Catts, a farmer, entered a written contract with a local fruit-canning concern to sell to it his entire crop of tomatoes. The canning concern operated in a seasonal market in which it had a short time to process a highly perishable commodity. This required the hiring of temporary help and competing with other canners for such items as containers and shipping space.
>
> Shortly before his crop was ready for harvest, Catts repudiated his contract. The buyer then commenced suit for specific performance, claiming that the economics of its entire operation were dependent upon a minimum crop for which it had entered forward contracts with farmers such as Catts. Plaintiff claimed that there were no tomatoes within the relevant market which were not already presold. Catts contended that his had been a contract to sell goods, presumptively not unique and therefore within the ability of the damage remedy to redeem the plaintiff's expectation interest. He thus contested the plaintiff's standing to sue for specific performance.
>
> The chancery court affirmed the operating assumption but concluded that where a plaintiff was able to demonstrate that the market could not serve as a source of substitution, there could be no cover contract. In its absence, damages would be speculative. Nominal damages were clearly inadequate, and thus plaintiff had standing to complain in equity. The community interest in jobs coupled with the abhorrence of wasting food were strong motivating factors urging an equity court to grant relief.
>
> The initial relief ordered was an injunction forbidding Catts from disposing of his crop in any way other than by honoring his contract obligation to the plaintiff. If the injunction failed to secure the desired performance, the court indicated that it was prepared to appoint a receiver who would harvest the crop and deliver it to the plaintiff. *Curtice Brothers Co. v. Catts,* 72 N.J. Eq. 831, 66 A. 935 (1870).

c. Where no market exists or the subject matter is unique, the presumption is reversed, and the inadequacy of the legal remedy is assumed. The major beneficiaries of this presumption are buyers of real estate.

d. *The U.C.C. view:* Comments 1 and 2 to Section 2-716(1) frankly seek an enhanced role for the remedy of specific performance. "[W]ithout intending to impair in any way the exercise of the court's sound discretion. . .this Article seek to further a more liberal attitude than some courts have shown in connection with the specific performance of contracts of sale. . . ." Uniqueness is rejected as the sole basis for an equitable remedy. "Specific performance may be decreed where the goods are unique or in other proper circumstances." The official comment explains that the Code's emphasis upon "the commercial feasibility of replacement" requires that courts rethink the definition of "unique" goods. If there is no ready market to which the aggrieved party may turn, specific performance is an appropriate remedy.

Example: In *Laclede Gas Co. v. Amoco Oil Co.,* 522 F.2d 33 (8th Cir. 1975), the buyer was successful in a bid for a decree of specific performance of a long-term contract to supply requirements of propane gas. The defendant-seller had argued that the commodity was available on the spot market for individual transactions. In Amoco's view this rendered the goods not "unique." The court disagreed. A major benefit to the buyer in the contract arrangement was a stable, long-term commitment from the seller. It was very uncertain whether the market would generate replacement long-term contracts. In the absence of such certainty as to its own supply, Laclede could not function with respect to its own customers. Such factors satisfied the "other proper circumstances" concept of § 2-716.

2. A plaintiff able to demonstrate standing has no right to relief in equity, merely a prayer addressed to the sound discretion of the court. The factors which influence the court are beyond the scope of a first-year survey of contracts and are generally studied in a remedies course. A quick sketch of the more prominent factors would include:

a. *Laches:* As a court of conscience, equity tribunals deem themselves beyond the regulation of such standard norms as a statute of limitations. The court will, itself, determine if the complaining party was timely in asserting "his equity." There is more than arrogance in this rule, for an equity court needs to worry not only about stale proof, but about enforcement difficulties which may be compounded by a tardy bid for relief.

b. *Concern for third parties and public interest:* Equity courts seek to view the exercise of their jurisdiction in the broader context of how a remedy may affect innocent third persons or even the public.

Examples: Sometimes such factors counseled intervention. *Curtice Brothers v. Catts, supra,* was such a case. The court was obviously concerned with the well-being of the labor force which would be unemployed if the cannery did not operate. More broadly, it abhorred the waste of food.

At other times, these considerations bid the court to deny relief to an otherwise deserving party. In *Seaboard Air Line Railway Co. v. At-*

lanta, Birmingham & Coast Railroad Co., 35 F.2d 609 (5th Cir. 1929), it was clear that the defendant had breached a contract which required it to maintain a rural crossing. Defendant conceded that it had failed to honor its obligation to control traffic through the crossing both "night and day." However, it also proved that it was short of operating funds, and that any money spent on what was an increasingly unused route would be at the expense of the maintenance of its more popular routes. The court deemed the public interest better served by placing the limited resources of the defendant in the service of the greatest number of passengers. The district court's refusal to grant specific performance was approved.

c. *Complaining party must have clean hands:* Equity courts are not only interested in the defaulting party and the breach, they are also concerned with the conduct of the allegedly aggrieved party. If his formation tactics or subsequent conduct fail to meet the court's expectations of "conscientious" behavior, relief will be denied.

d. *Equity courts are interested in the pragmatic "adequacy" of consideration:* Allied to their concern with the clean hands of the complaining party, equity courts have insisted that the mere presence of bargained-for legal detriment ("valuable consideration") is insufficient to warrant discretionary relief. Only if the bargain was "fair" in the distribution of benefits and burdens will the court be inclined to intervene.

e. *Enforcement difficulties must not over-tax the resources of an equity court nor undermine its insistence that its decree be obeyed:* Here, the concern is mixed.

(1) Court must be able to frame a precise decree or it will not act: Equitable relief differs from the damage remedy in that it seeks to keep the contract alive for performance purposes. Unless the court is confident that it understands the bargain and can frame an appropriate decree, it will not act.

(2) Supervision of that decree must not be too burdensome: Unless the court is confident that it can detect and correct any resistance to its decree and that the cost of such detection and correction will not overstrain its resources, it will refuse relief.

Examples: In 1833, a New York impresario had created an opera company for that emerging metropolis. Having obtained a suitable house, props, and licenses, he assembled a cast. Among the last to sign was an Italian tenor of great reputation. A written contract was signed obliging the tenor to perform in New York for the 1833 season. Shortly before it was to begin, the impresario got wind of the tenor's plans to sail for Havana there to undertake engagements which were in direct conflict with his time commitments.

Contending that no adequate remedy existed at law, the impresario applied for a writ of *ne exeat* to physically restrain the respondent from leaving the jurisdiction. The writ was refused and the tenor discharged with the following comments by the chancellor:

"In this case it is charged in the bill, not only that the defendant can sing, but also that he has expressly agreed to sing, and to accompany that singing with such appropriate gestures as may be necessary and proper to give an interest to his performance. And from the facts disclosed, I think it is very evident also that he does not intend to gratify the citizens of New York, who may resort to the Italian opera, either by his singing, or by his gesticulations. Although the authority before cited shows the law to be in favor of the complainant, so far at least as to entitle him to a decree for the singing, I am not aware that any officer of this court has that perfect knowledge of the Italian language, or possesses that exquisite sensibility in the auricular nerve which is necessary to understand, and to enjoy with a proper zest, the peculiar beauties of the Italian opera, so fascinating to the fashionable world. There might be some difficulty, therefore, even if the defendant was compelled to sing under the direction and in the presence of a master in chancery, in ascertaining whether he performed his engagement according to its spirit and intent. It would also be very difficult for the master to determine what effect coercion might produce upon the defendant's singing, especially in the livelier airs; although the fear of imprisonment would unquestionably deepen his seriousness in the graver parts of the drama." *DeRivafinoli v. Corsetti,* 4 Paige Ch. 263 (N.Y. Chancery 1833).

In 1939, the Maryland judiciary found itself faced with a prayer for a decree of specific performance by a lady who had been hired as a nurse, companion, and chauffeur by an elderly and infirm man. She alleged that they had formed an oral agreement under the terms of which she promised to care for his health and property during the balance of his lifetime. In return for these services, she was to receive $8 per week and a home in his residence. Upon the defendant's death, she was to inherit a life estate in his residence and title to the automobiles. It was then alleged that plaintiff had faithfully performed all of these services and was desirous of continuing. However, relatives were claimed to have poisoned the defendant's mind against her with the consequence that he had sought first to evict her and then to starve her out of his house.

A remedy at law was foreclosed by the Statute of Frauds. What triggered the statute was the promise to convey an interest in his real estate. Plaintiff sought to evade the statute by alleging part performance as an evidentiary substitute. The validity of this strategy depended upon her ability to qualify for relief in equity. Such relief was denied. The personal nature of the services caused the court to doubt its ability to cement by a decree a human bond which had been shattered. Further, it could not ensure that, if the defendant were forced to accept plaintiff as a nurse, her services would be unaffected by the disaffection that now existed between them. With knowledge that it was turning away a deserving victim of a breach of contract, the court declined to grant either specific performance or any form of injunction. *Fitzpatrick v. Michael*, 177 Md. 248, 9 A.2d 639 (1939).

3. ***Equity courts not bound by precedent:*** Because they are possessed of a discretionary power reacting to very specific fact patterns, equity courts have long held themselves not bound by the rule of *stare decisis.*

4. ***Nature of equitable relief:*** If an equity court does decide to accept jurisdiction and to intervene on behalf of the complaining party, its remedial powers are awesome.

   a. *Decree of specific performance:* The defendant will be ordered to literally carry out the terms of the broken bargain.

      (1) Imprisonment for equitable contempt: If there is defiance, classical equity courts were wont to imprison the defendant for contempt. The term was indeterminate. The prisoner held the key to his cell in his pocket. All he had to do was bow to the will of the Chancellor and obey the court's decree.

      (2) Modern preference for fictional performance: It is rare today for an equity court to invoke the power to imprison. An easier and more effective strategy is to simply appoint a court officer who will harvest the crop or sign the deed. In the meantime the court will treat the actions of its officer as those of the defendant!

   b. *Injunctive relief:* If enforcement difficulties dissuade the court from granting the affirmative specific performance decree, an effective substitute may be to enjoin the defendant from disposing of the subject matter in any manner other than in compliance with the terms of her contract. The economic needs of the defendant then become the source of compulsion.

      If the damages for breach will prove difficult to calculate, the issuance of an injunction restraining a breach has several strategic benefits. Recently Judge Richard Posner noted that such a remedy may force the party seeking to breach into fruitful negotiations with the potential victim. In the facts before the trial court, Walgreen, a discount chain of pharmacy stores, had been a long-standing tenant in the Southgate Mall in Milwaukee. The lease contained a promise by the landlord that it would not locate any other tenant which operated a pharmacy. The landlord faced a crisis when the largest tenant in the mall closed and it became necessary to locate a new "anchor tenant." After some negotiation, the landlord located a prospect which included a deep discount pharmacy operation. Walgreen was granted an injunction by the district court. On appeal, the Seventh Circuit affirmed, noting:

      The benefits of substituting an injunction for damages are twofold. First, it shifts the burden of determining the cost of the defendant's conduct from the court to the parties. If it is true that Walgreen's damages are smaller than the gain to Sara Creek [the landlord] from allowing a second pharmacy into the shopping mall, then there must be a price for dissolving the injunction that will make both parties better off. Thus the effect of upholding the injunction would be to substitute for the costly process of forensic fact determination the less costly processes of private negotiation. Second, a premise of our free-market system, and the lesson of experience here and abroad as well, is that the prices and costs are more accurately determined by the market than by government. A battle of experts is a less reliable method of determining the actual cost to Walgreen of facing new competition than negotiations between Walgreen and Sara Creek over the price at which Walgreen would feel adequately compensated for having to face that competition.

Walgreen Co. v. Sara Creek Property Co., 966 F.2d 273 (7th Cir. 1992).

E. Restitution and Reliance Recoveries: Consolation prizes at law. An aggrieved party unable to obtain a loss-of-bargain recovery at law and refused equitable relief has failed to protect her expectation interest. Her only recourse is to return to the common law, seeking the backward-looking measures of damage which aim to restore her to the preagreement status quo.

1. *Recovery in restitution:* A party who has conferred his own performance on the other trader before that party breaches the contract has, at a minimum, a restitution claim.

   Problems in perspective: Over the years a variety of terms have been employed to surround this elementary exercise in undoing a wrong. After-the-fact theories have sought to harmonize the assertion of a restitution claim with society's anticipation that a loss-of-bargain recovery would be sought. Those with a predilection for catchy phrases explained the result by asserting that the aggrieved party had "waived the contract and sued in tort."
   A more logically convincing explanation is that the aggrieved party may treat the material breach as an offer to rescind the contract. That offer may then be "accepted" by initiating a reliance recovery. With the contract thus neatly eliminated, the court can concentrate directly upon the fact that the defendant is in possession of a benefit obtained from the plaintiff, who expected payment. Recovery can then be had on an implied-at-law promise to restore that benefit or pay its market value. This explanation and the outcome were then encapsulated in the idea that the plaintiff may recover in "quasi-contract."

   a. *Defendant in material breach:* As an alternative response to seeking to vindicate his expectation interest at law or in equity, the aggrieved party may treat the material breach as an occasion to rescind the contract. Any performance which the aggrieved party had rendered to the breaching party may then be recovered in quasi-contract.

      (1) If the defendant can restore performance in the form received (*e.g.,* return the goods or reconvey the real estate) literal restitution may be achieved.

(2) If the defendant cannot restore the plaintiff's performance as received (because it has been consumed, conveyed to an innocent third person, or deteriorated) there will be liability for the "value" of the plaintiff's performance. The determination of "value" can be difficult.

    (a) Measure is not the plaintiff's cost: Although a restitution claim features unjust present impoverishment of the plaintiff and unjust present enrichment of the defendant, the measure of damages is the enrichment of the defendant, not the cost to the aggrieved party.

        Example: If the cost to plaintiff was $50,000 but the same performance could have been purchased at the same time and place from rival sellers for $45,000, the plaintiff will be limited to a restitution recovery of $45,000.

    (b) If the defendant is able to prove that the "value to him" is actually less than the market value of the performance, courts are divided on the proper measure of damages. The *Restatement, Second,* § 371 simply declares that "as justice may require," a court may choose between the general market value of the plaintiff's performance and the actual value as experienced by the defendant.

b. *Claimant in breach:* Defendant's restitution claim as a means of avoiding forfeiture. In a clear recognition that the doctrines of material breach and loss-of-bargain remedy are totally one-sided, the common law has permitted a party who has breached after first rendering part performance to offset, as against the aggrieved party's claim for loss of bargain, the value of any part performance which the defendant has rendered and which the plaintiff has consumed or retained. *See Restatement, Second,* § 388.

2. ***Reliance expenses as a measure of damages:*** The *Restatement, Second,* § 349, recommends that the aggrieved party be allowed to opt for a reliance claim as an alternative to seeking a loss-of-bargain recovery.

a. *Traditional refusal to recognize a reliance claim as an appropriate remedy for breach of contract:* The position of the *Restatement, Second,* is contrary to the traditional common law view that reliance damages are not a remedy for breach of contract.

b. *Limitations:* Under the *Restatement* scheme, the plaintiff's claim would be subject to the requirements of foreseeability, unavoidability, and certainty which have limited the defendant's exposure to the loss-of-bargain measure of money damages. Naturally, the losses also had to be consequential in the sense that they must have been incurred by the plaintiff after the defendant had promised to perform.

F. Stipulated Remedies Provisions: The degree to which the terms of the contract may determine the nature and extent of available remedies. The fate of a stipulated remedies provision contained in a contract has been less than generous at the hands of courts.

Problems in perspective: It will come as no surprise that parties may not confer standing to seek equitable intervention by the terms of their contract. But what if the parties have merely sought to fix a sum of damages? Such a strategy has an obvious advantage to the immediate parties in assisting them in preparing attempts for the future. It also offers society the potential benefit of reducing the number of cases which compete for attention on increasingly crowded judicial dockets. Notwithstanding, such attempts have met with nearly two centuries of resistance from common law courts.

The problem is that remedies represent a *social* rather than a *personal* response to a breach of contract. If the parties are allowed to dictate the consequences of breach, they may transgress the societal decision that damages are not intended to punish or compel the breaching party, but only to compensate the aggrieved trader. Modern economic theory supports this social convention. Put bluntly, some uneconomic bargains are better breached than performed. If the parties were able to mask the inherent inefficiency of their bargain by building in some damage equivalent of a nuclear deterrent to breach, the bargain would be likely performed with the consequent waste of scarce goods and services.

1. *Liquidated damages clause vs. penalty:* The inherent suspicion of common law courts toward stipulated remedies clauses has resulted in their classification under two labels:

   a. *Liquidated damages clauses respected:* If the provision is a "liquidated damages clause," it is valid and will be respected as the measure of damages without any judicial inquiry into the actual damages.

   b. *Penalty clause void:* By contrast, if the provision is deemed a "penalty clause," it is unconscionable as an affront to public (legal) policy.

2. *Criteria for making the distinction:* Two criteria must be satisfied before a stipulated remedies provision will be deemed a "liquidated damages clause."

   a. *Loss of bargain reasonably deemed unavailable in the event of breach:* At the formation stage both traders must have come to the reasonable conclusion that, in the event of breach, the loss-of-bargain remedy would not be available. If the loss-of-bargain remedy was likely to have been available, the parties had no business attempting to oust its application by stipulating a different remedy.

   b. *Goal must be reasonable compensation:* Acting on this mutual and reasonable recognition, the parties must have adopted as a stipulated consequence of breach a provision which sought to fairly compensate the aggrieved party, not to penalize the other for failing or refusing to perform.

EXAM PREPARATION

Exam Preparation   EP-2

EXAMINATIONS IN PERSPECTIVE

Scope: In this chapter we will discuss the course material from the perspective of preparing for a mid-term or final examination. The comprehensive nature of these exercises presents an opportunity to put the individual doctrines of contract law into a "big picture." While I am not so foolish as to suggest that they are fun, examinations can be a valuable part of your learning process.

Contracts in perspective: For many, the contracts course presents a marked challenge as examinations draw near. The problem is the rule-laden quality of the discipline. We have rules, exceptions to the rules and (to border on the perverse) exceptions to the exceptions. Given this quality, it is not surprising that many intelligent persons fear an ability to adequately prepare for the examination, or to work with the material on the day of that exercise. Let me suggest an alternative perspective.

In the final analysis, there are only seven major issues which can be raised on a contracts examination: After years of teaching, it dawned on me that there are really only seven major subjects which can be raised on a contracts examination. Few essay questions manage to raise more than three of these seven issues, and a good many center on only two! If a student could quickly isolate which of the seven possible issues were being questioned in a given fact pattern, she could focus her energies and craft what is almost certainly a superior response. I will shortly identify these seven possible major subjects. You should not be surprised to find that they correspond rather closely to the chapter organization of this book. Before I do that, let me speak with candor of the two most common disasters facing a first-year law student about to sit for a final examination.

Few things are more sad from my perspective than the following laments:

(1) "I really knew the law and yet I did so poorly on your examination."
(2) "I was doing fine, but ran out of time."

"The facts ma'am, just the facts." Joe Friday was a detective in a television series you are too young to have viewed. The point he made to each victim or potential witness is equally applicable to every law school examination. The first student did poorly because he did not grasp a major feature of a law school examination: the exercise is not an abstract inquiry into legal concepts; it tests the emerging ability of a law student to perform the task of a lawyer — to review a fact pattern and to identify in those facts the legal issues which will structure the client's fate.

"If I had had a longer time, this would have been a shorter letter." Such was the lament of Mark Twain respecting the added pressure of a time limitation on the completion of any human project. His statement is surely worth recollecting by anyone facing a law school examination. Nearly all are set within a limited time. The typical contracts final allots three hours. Nothing is too obvious if saying it will help one student. On an examination featuring three questions, there is no way in which excellence on questions one and two can prevent a disaster for a student who fails to write a response to question three. You must manage your time and accept the idea that your first priority is to respond to each of the questions.

I.   **STRATEGIES FOR SUCCESS ON LAW SCHOOL EXAMINATIONS: Beyond making a good-faith effort to keep up with your assignments, there are some steps which you can take which will significantly enhance your** chance to have a successful experience. You have spent a good deal of time acquiring knowledge and skills. Your primary goal should be to give yourself a fair chance to demonstrate what you have accomplished. My suggestions break down into things to do in the week or weeks preceding the examination as well as steps to take in confronting the actual exercise.

A. **What to Do in the Week or Weeks Before:** As the academic term draws to a close, your task is to dispel the mystery which can surround an exercise you are approaching for the very first time.

Step #1: Ask your instructor to tell the class the nature of the examination format. Most law school examinations are in an essay format, but it is not unknown for instructors to use multiple choice or even true-false propositions.

Step #2: Go to the library or student bar association and determine if past examinations by your contracts instructor are on file for your inspection. Nearly every law school does this, and yet I am surprised by the number of students who fail to take this preliminary opportunity to probe the mind of the instructor!

Step #3: Consider asking a classmate or two to join you in going over these past examinations. You now have an advance opportunity to use the facts in prior questions to spot the issues and structure your analysis of an actual law school final. Give yourself several hours for this exercise. Begin by separately reading the entire examination and preparing an outline of a response you would write for each question. Then compare and discuss your work products.

B. **A Day of the Examination Strategy:** Here is a strategy designed to avoid both the issue omission and out-of-time disasters.

Step #1: Put the examination in perspective. If the examination consists of more than one fact pattern, my initial suggestion is that you read the entire examination. Recognizing that your instructor has attempted to write a comprehensive examination, your task is to figure out where each of the seven major issues was raised. As noted earlier, on a multiple question examination, no one question will likely contain all seven issues. Most will contain no more than two. It is also possible that one or more of the seven major issues will not be raised at all on your examination. But before you can safely conclude that this is the case, you must have the entire examination in perspective.

Step #2: Recognize that the facts generate the issues. If you will work with the facts, they will inevitably betray the issues which the instructor is expecting you to discuss.

Step #3: Become comfortable with the proposition that there is rarely one "correct" answer. Unlike examinations in other disciplines, there is rarely a single "correct" answer to an essay-type question on a law school final. Instead, the exercise is in issue spotting and analysis. Thus it is entirely possible for a paper which has concluded that the buyer has no cause of action to score as highly as one which has reached a liability conclusion! What the two papers will have had in common is recognition of the same legal issues which structure that inquiry and a logical application of the "law" to the facts.

Step #4: Follow the examination instructions. Your effort to make productive use of your limited time begins with the determination to follow the examiner's instructions. If you are told to discuss the plaintiff's potential theories of liability, confine your answer to that subject. As a general proposition, credit on a examination cannot be earned for information or analysis which is volunteered and beyond what the question has sought.

Step #5: Know what you want to say before you begin to write. Once you have spotted the issues raised by the fact pattern, your task is to create a "legally logical," tightly organized and clearly expressed essay. Such a product is nearly impossible unless you first outline your answer before you begin to write.

I cannot overstress the advantages of a preliminary outline of your answer to each question on the examination. If you have three hours for the exercise and three essay questions to write, begin by outlining all three answers. This exercise lets you concentrate on the "big picture" and dramatically reduces the possibility that you will overlook a major issue. The second advantage is that you can now rationally allot your time. You now know that the most complex task will be to craft an answer to, let us say, the second question. Budget a bit of extra time for that question before you begin to write. Far better to know in advance that it will take a few more minutes than to stumble across this fact an hour and a half into the exercise! If you do that, you are likely to have spent too much time on question one and be thrown into a panic. Needless to say, such a mental attitude is not conducive to your best performance on question two. And you risk not getting to question three.

Step #6: Organize your response in a legally logical manner. Suppose an examination fact pattern is followed by the direction that you determine if a buyer has a cause of action against a seller. Your analysis of the facts reveals that there are issues surrounding the presence of an offer, certain measure of money damages, excusable nonperformance, and a conditional promise to sell. This summary reads like the directions to a tossed salad. An essay response amounting to a ten-page expansion of this order would have "spotted the issues" but would have revealed the author as fundamentally confused respecting their resolution. A grade of "C" would be an ambitious goal.

But there is an "A" alternative. Suppose you were to begin your essay with the following statement to the reader:

> The Buyer's recovery of a loss-of-bargain award of damages depends upon whether a contract was formed between the parties and materially breached by the Seller. The Buyer's first task will be to prove that the Seller made an offer of a present contract. Assuming that can be done, the facts suggest that the duty to sell was conditional. The Seller cannot breach such a duty until that condition has either been satisfied or excused. Even more difficult for Buyer, there are facts suggesting that the Seller may be able to claim excusable nonperformance premised upon commercial impracticability. If this is established, his refusal to deliver the goods is legally privileged. Finally, if each of these issues is resolved in the Buyer's favor, the Seller's refusal to perform is a present material

breach. In order to recover a loss-of-bargain measure of damages, the Buyer will have to establish his loss to a reasonably certain dollar amount. I will begin by discussing the presence of an offer.

The advantages which flow from this paragraph begin with the very positive initial impression made upon the reader. Immediately, she can determine that you have spotted each of the issues in the fact pattern.

Equally impressive, you have presented the issues in a legally logical manner. You have shown that if there was no offer the contract case is over. If there was an offer but the seller's duty never matured because an express condition precedent had neither been satisfied nor excused, the seller's duty to perform would never have matured. He could not be in breach. If it had matured, commercial impracticability may have excused the seller's duties. Finally, if the buyer establishes the presence of a fully matured seller's contract duty and the seller fails in efforts to prove excusable nonperformance, the buyer's ability to claim a loss of bargain requires proof of the dollar loss with reasonable certainty. By merely adding a paragraph explaining each of these propositions, you will have created a model answer.

Step #7: Never abandon a question on the strength of your conclusion respecting a preliminary issue. An examination tactic which can rival the failure to spot a major issue as a road to disaster involves what a judge might term mooting out the balance of the issues on the strength of a preliminary decision. To continue our example, suppose you were to decide that the duties of the Seller were subject to an express condition precedent which had been neither satisfied nor excused. As a judge you could now dispose of the litigation. The issues of excusable nonperformance and certainty of damages would be moot. On an examination you recognize that if the facts present these issues you must discuss them. Thus if you conclude that the Seller's obligation never matured, you immediately state: "But if the Buyer should prevail on this issue, the Seller may still deny breach by seeking to establish commercial impracticability."

C. **Seven Issues from Which All Contract Examinations Are Ultimately Crafted:** As you read the fact patterns which make up your final examination, seek out the presence of these issues:

1. *Did the parties form an agreement?* Here you will look for three major aspects of the course:

   a. Offer and acceptance:

      (1) Do you find an offer?

      (2) If so, at the time acceptance was attempted, was that offer still outstanding?

      (3) Was there an effective acceptance?

   b. Does ambiguity of language preclude the formation of an agreement?

    c. Do the mistakes of the parties, or those of third-party intermediaries, preclude the formation of an agreement?

2.   ***If the parties formed an agreement, is their bargain a contract?***
Private parties may form an agreement, but a contract is a legal status, and whether it has come into existence depends upon two factors:

    a. Is there "valuable consideration" (bargained-for legal detriment on both sides of the exchange)?

    b. Do the facts suggest the presence of any real defenses precluding formation or personal defenses rendering the obligations of one of the parties voidable?

EP

3.   ***Do the terms of the contract, or the subsequent conduct of either of the traders who formed it, confer any rights or impose any duties upon nontraders?***

    a. Is there an intended beneficiary?

    b. Is there an assignee of rights?

    c. Is there a delegate of duties?

4.   ***Have the performance obligations created by the contract matured?***

    a. Have all conditions precedent or subsequent either been satisfied or excused?

    b. Are there any express conditions subsequent, and if so, have they been triggered?

5.   ***If performance obligations have matured, have they been discharged on any theory of excusable nonperformance? Can either party claim:***

    a. Objective impossibility?

    b. Commercial impracticability?

    c. Frustration of purpose?

6.   ***If a party with a fully matured obligation which has not been excused fails, refuses, or defectively performs, you are in the presence of breach.***

    a. What is the impact of the breach upon the contract duties of the aggrieved party?

    b. What remedial rights accrue to the aggrieved party?

7. *If the aggrieved party cannot recover her expectation interest on a breach of contract theory, may she claim money damages on any alternative theory measured by:*

    a. Her restitution interest recovered in quasi-contract?

    b. Her reliance interest recovered on a theory of promissory estoppel?

PRACTICE EXERCISE #1:

On December 4, Sally Fields and her father, Professor Franklin, were driving along the California coast when their car became engulfed in dense fog. Shortly thereafter it collided with a bus. While no one on board the bus was hurt, Professor Franklin sustained a severe head wound and was rendered unconscious. Among the passengers on the bus was Dr. Terrance Devers, an Irish physician making his first visit to the United States as a tourist. Devers offered his assistance to Ms. Fields, who was uninjured but somewhat hysterical. Together they managed to hail a passing automobile and in this manner Professor Franklin was transported to a small community hospital about ten miles inland from the scene of the accident. Upon their arrival they discovered that the town's only physician had departed by helicopter to assist at the scene of a drowning accident. In his absence Dr. Devers examined Franklin. To an attending nurse he expressed the fear that unless emergency brain surgery was immediately performed, Franklin was in danger of death.

That remark was overheard by Ms. Fields. Quite frantic, she seized Dr. Devers by the shoulders and said intensely: "Doctor, you must operate! Money means nothing to me with Daddy's life at stake. I will see that you are paid a fee of $50,000 . . .or $60,000. . .or whatever it takes. Oh, Doctor, I promise!" Dr. Devers responded that he had no professional status in an American hospital and thus could not treat patients, let alone perform surgery.

Ms. Fields continued her entreaties, and, at length, Dr. Devers relented and performed the operation. The surgery was completed with professional competence, and Dr. Devers remained at the hospital for several days monitoring what appeared to be an improving Professor Franklin. On the day after Dr. Devers had resumed his vacation, Professor Franklin died of heart failure, a factor unrelated to his injury or the surgical procedure. Ms. Fields thereupon wrote Dr. Devers: "You will receive nothing but contempt from me for that operation on my poor father. Try to collect anything, and I will fight you every step of the way."

Dr. Devers has consulted you relating the above facts. He asks for advice concerning his rights, if any, against Ms. Fields. Kindly prepare an opinion letter for your client.

YOUR INITIAL ANALYSIS: Please note that you have received an instruction that is at once open-ended and limited. You are to assess all theories which may generate a legal claim by Dr. Devers against Ms. Fields. You are not asked to discuss any potential liability that Professor Franklin's estate might have to the physician.

Does Devers have a contract claim? It is at this point that you evaluate the fact pattern for the potential presence of the first six of the seven possible issues.

EP

#1 ***Did the parties form an agreement?*** Two issues to discuss: The facts suggest two immediate problems with an offer — the state of mind of Ms. Fields and the price term of the alleged offer. There do not appear to be difficulties with an acceptance by Devers if he was faced with an offer. He acted promptly and, according to the facts, performed the requested act with professional competence.

#2 ***If the parties formed an agreement, is their bargain a contract?*** One issue to discuss: There would not appear to be any difficulty with valuable consideration assuming that Ms. Fields intended a bargain. There was legal detriment on both sides of the exchange. But what about defenses? There is a major issue of illegality given the unlicensed status of Dr. Devers in the United States.

#3 ***Do the terms of the contract, or the subsequent conduct of either of the traders who formed it, confer any rights or impose any duties upon nontraders?*** No issues to discuss. Clearly, Professor Franklin was an intended third-party beneficiary of the contract in which Devers assumed the direct undertaking, and Fields had an intention to benefit. The facts appear to preclude any claim by Franklin's estate that the operation was done in an incompetent manner, and the examination instructions put these issues out of bounds.

#4 ***Have the performance obligations created by the contract matured?*** If there is a contract here, it was formed in the unilateral mode. No issues to discuss. The facts stipulate that Devers has done an act which would constitute a timely and effective acceptance. If Fields had made an offer, her duty to pay has clearly matured.

#5 ***Is Fields able to claim any theory of excusable nonperformance?*** No issues to discuss. No; the doctrines of objective impossibility, commercial impracticability and frustration of purpose are not applicable here.

#6 ***If Fields is in breach of a contract formed in the unilateral mode, what is the impact upon the duties and rights of Devers?*** One issue to discuss: Devers has no executory duties, no occasion to mitigate. He would have a loss of bargain, assuming that he could establish a price term.

Are there any alternative measures of recovery which Devers might press? Issues to discuss: If the operation had been performed on Ms. Fields, she might be liable for its market value in quasi-contract. But it was not, and the liability of the estate is not in issue. If Devers fails to establish a contract, he may recover on a theory of promissory estoppel for any out-of-pocket expenses he can establish as being in consequence of Ms. Fields' promise.

YOUR OUTLINE:

Devers' contract claim:

1. ***Offer of a bargain vs. an hysterical reaction to a tragic situation:*** Solution — whether a reasonable person in Devers' position would have concluded that

Ms. Fields was extending an offer of a present contract to be formed in the unilateral mode.

2. ***Essential terms:*** Facts hedge price set in "offer." Unless the essential terms can be resolved to the court's satisfaction, there is no offer as a matter of law.

3. ***Major issue of the legality of the subject matter:*** A surgical procedure by a physician who lacks professional credentials in the United States. Mixed social values. On the one hand, we don't want unlicensed persons to engage in medical practice. On the other, we do not want a competent physician to stand by and watch a human being die. Clearly not a *malum in se* situation.

4. If there is a contract and the court has not resolved the price term, Devers will have a difficult time establishing his loss of bargain.

Devers' claim in promissory estoppel:

1. Fields made a promise, issue as to whether in the circumstances it would be foreseeable that it would induce detrimental reliance.

2. If it was, it is clear that Devers did change position.

3. Fields has now breached her promise.

4. Devers may recover on a reliance theory for any expenses he incurred in attending Professor Franklin or in absenting himself from his vacation plans. He may not recover an expectation claim for the value of the surgery.

PRACTICE EXERCISE #2:

On May 10, 1989, Fred Barnes contracted with Stanley Decker under the terms of which Decker promised to construct a dwelling house for Barnes in accordance with plans and specifications created by Pam Sterling, a Biggsville architect. Under the terms of the written contract, the price of the construction was to be $100,000. Barnes was to pay this amount in monthly installments, each of which would be in an amount equal to 80% of Decker's costs incurred during the preceding month for labor and materials as certified by architect, Sterling. The remainder was to be disbursed to Decker thirty days after completion of the structure, which was scheduled for not later that October 1.

Decker promptly commenced performance. The payments which matured on June 1 and July 1 were promptly paid by Barnes. On July 15, Decker wrote his son, Sam, declaring: "You may have the payment which will be due about August 1st or 2nd on the Barnes' construction project." A few days later Decker met Sterling at the construction site and mentioned that he wanted the August payment made to his son. Sterling reported this conversation to Barnes, who was most distressed. At this point in time his house is about half-completed. He does not want to pay any funds to Decker's son and has instructed his friend, Sterling, to refuse the certificate.

Barnes consults you and relates the above facts. You have promised to act quickly to provide him with an opinion letter as to the liability, if any, that he may face to Decker's son, Sam.

YOUR INITIAL ANALYSIS: The instructions provided for this question are a dead giveaway as to the major issues. Sam Decker is obviously a nontrader, not having been party to the formation of the contract between his father and Fred Barnes. Your only duty is to discuss the claims, if any, which this nontrader may have against Barnes.

Does Sam Decker have any legally enforceable claim? Again, I suggest that you do a quick mental check against the six possible contract law issues.

#1 *Did the parties form an agreement?* No; Sam Decker was not a party to the formation of an agreement which the facts stipulate was formed on May 10 between his father, Stanley, and Fred Barnes. Other than noting this fact, there are no formation issues.

#2 *If the parties formed an agreement, is their bargain a contract?* There are no formation issues since the facts stipulate that the agreement formed between Stanley Decker and Fred Barnes was a contract.

#3 *Do the terms of the contract or the subsequent conduct of either of the traders who formed it confer any rights or impose any duties upon nontraders?* Here is a major issue. The terms of the contract formed on May 10 conferred no such rights. Thus there could never be an intended beneficiary. Sam Decker does not enter the picture until July 15, when his father wrote to him. Sam is obviously not a potential delegate since the letter sought to impose no duties on Sam. It did, however, speak of an intention to confer upon the son a right to receive the August payment due from Barnes. Sam is a potential assignee of contract rights.

#4 *Have the performance obligations created by the contract matured?* No; here is a second issue. The express terms of the contract make the liability of the owner for an installment payment subject to a condition precedent that the architect, Pam Sterling, issue a certificate of conformity to plans and specifications. Sterling has yet to issue the certificate and may be conspiring with Barnes to withhold it because of the owner's unhappiness at facing the demands of an assignee.

#5 *Is Barnes able to claim any theory of excusable nonperformance?* No issues to discuss. The doctrines of objective impossibility, commercial impracticability, and frustration of purpose are not applicable here.

#6 *If Barnes fails or refuses to perform to the demands of Sam Decker and young Decker can establish his status as an assignee, Barnes will be in breach.* What would be the impact of such a breach on the rights of Sam Decker? Here you will need to discuss the litigation posture of an assignee.

Are there any alternative measures of recovery which Sam Decker might press? No; as a purported assignee, Sam Decker has not received any direct promise from Barnes, nor has he conferred any element of performance upon Barnes. He would thus have no claim sounding in either promissory estoppel or quasi-contract.

YOUR OUTLINE:

Sam Decker's contract claim:

1. Formation of a bargain between Decker's father and Fred Barnes is specified in the facts. It is also specified that the agreement has the status of a present contract. Note that as of July 15 it is partially executed.

2. Major issue as to Sam Decker's status as an assignee of his father's claim. First issue: Was there a "present assignment?" The statement by the father may suffice to manifest an intention to make a present assignment, but is the letter a sufficient act of present assignment? Assuming that Sam Decker could convince a court that it was, there is no problem with a present subject matter. The right to the August payment is a future right under an existing contract. Second issue: assuming a present assignment, was it operative to extinguish the right in Stanley and set it up immediately and exclusively in Sam? There is no prohibitory term of the contract offended by the attempted assignment. Nor does it seem to materially alter the nature of Barnes' duty. It may threaten a material alteration in his risk that Stanley Decker will render the same measure of performance once he has parted with the right to the payment. After all, the house is only half-finished, and Decker has not completed the work scheduled for July. There are no problems with attempted revocation of the assignment.

3. Barnes' duty to pay funds on August 1 is dependent upon an express condition precedent. Pam Sterling must first issue a certificate of completion. She has yet to do so. However, if she refused on grounds other than her professional assessment of Decker's performance, that would be "bad faith" and would excuse the condition. This would mature Barnes' liability to make the payment.

4. If Sam Decker can establish a present, operative assignment, he will stand in his father's shoes. He will thus have to await the maturing of Barnes' duty. If Sterling issues the certificate, that liability will mature on a theory of satisfaction. If she refuses on grounds of objection to the quality of the work, Barnes' duty will not mature and the assignee would have no claim. If she refuses on any other ground, the condition will be excused.

PRACTICE EXERCISE #3: What follows is a substantially longer fact pattern and yet, when we have applied our approach, it simply yields a slightly longer list of issues which we must discuss.

Mary Gonzales, Grace Kirk, and Sue Tang have been friends for more than thirty years. For nearly a decade, they have worked every Thursday afternoon as volunteer receptionists at the Danville Hospital. It has been their custom to have lunch together before spending four hours on duty at the hospital. Starting about a month ago, Gonzales began to monopolize conversations at these lunches with complaints that efforts to sell her home had been unsuccessful. She noted that it had been very difficult to convince her husband, Joe, to agree to the sale of the house which he had built in 1970. Mary is now 66; Joe is 68. Neither is in the best of health, and the extensive grounds require maintenance, which Joe is no longer able to perform. They listed the home with a Danville realtor in July, 1994, for $300,000.

EP

Two weeks ago, at their Thursday lunch, Kirk, a retired real estate agent, asked how much the local banks had agreed to lend on the property. Gonzales replied that the house had been appraised at $325,000 and that an 80% loan ($260,000) was probably the maximum which could be obtained given the age and condition of the property. Kirk then stated that she had always adored the house and with a "little creative financing" thought that she might be able to afford the purchase. Later that afternoon, with Tang no longer present, Kirk outlined her plan to Gonzales. Kirk would apply for a loan from the Last National Bank representing the sales price of the house as $325,000. An 80% loan on this amount would raise $260,000. Actually, the price that Kirk would pay Mary and Joe Gonzales would be $280,000. Kirk assured Mary that in this manner she would be obtaining the size of loan she required, Mary and Joe would sell a house they had been unable to market for more than a year, and no one would be the wiser or injured by their little secret. Mary Gonzales promised to consider this proposition and discuss it with her husband.

On Monday, May 8, Grace Kirk received the following letter from Mary Gonzales. It was hand delivered by Sue Tang, who volunteered to drop it by Kirk's residence when she called to return a borrowed book:

Saturday, May 6, 1995

Dear Grace,

Ever since our conversation last Thursday, I have been thinking about your saying that you would like to buy our home. Joe and I love the old place and want to see it go to someone who feels the same way about it we do. Joe is particularly concerned that the grounds be kept intact so that his flower gardens will be preserved and the little children in the neighborhood will have a place to play and enjoy nature. Both of us agree that there is no one we would rather see own it than you.

With these thoughts in mind we are prepared to let you have the house for the $280,000 figure under the arrangement you mentioned. I have not detailed it to Joe for he has been ailing of late and probably would not understand it. We have been looking for a smaller place and have our eye on the Conlon property on the west side of town. Old man Conlon told Joe he wanted $140,000. We think that we can reach an agreement with him. Naturally, we cannot agree to let our home go until we have made a deal for a new one. I would say that we would be willing to give you a deed and receive payment as soon as that happens. We would let you have possession within a month after that.

I hope you will be as happy about this as we are. I'll be talking with you.

As ever,

Mary

Kirk was delighted with Mary's letter. She immediately went to the Danville branch of the Last National Bank and made a loan application for an 80% loan on the Gonzales house. The application asked for the sales price of the property. Kirk filled in the amount as "$325,000." Clement Kong, the loan officer, indicated that he saw no problem obtaining a commitment from the bank within 10 days. Later that day, May 8, Kirk encountered Sue Tang on the street. She told Tang the contents of the letter from Mary Gonzales and how delighted she was with the prospect of purchasing the Gonzales home. She also told Tang that she was anxious to close the transaction as quickly as possible since she had plans to subdivide the property, a step which she knew would upset Joe Gonzales. She asked Tang to keep the matter of the planned subdivision their secret.

The next morning, Kirk prepared a letter in which she agreed to purchase the Gonzales home "just as outlined in your letter to me of May 6." She put the letter in her purse but forgot to mail it until Wednesday, May 10.

In the meantime, Joe Gonzales discussed the proposed sale with his neighbor, Robert Odgers. Odgers indicated that he had heard that Kirk had hired a local planning consultant to develop a plan to subdivide the Gonzales property into three residential lots and to lobby the City Planning Commission for the requisite approval. Greatly agitated, Gonzales confronted his wife, Mary. Seeing that her husband was very upset, Mary indicated that such a plan had never been mentioned notwithstanding hours of conversation in which the women had debated the problem of selling the home. She told her husband that the only thing she could think of that would motivate Kirk was a shortage of money. At this point she confessed the scheme of informing the bank of a sales price of $325,000 so that the loan proceeds would be inflated, easing Kirk's ability to make the purchase for $280,000.

The letter from Kirk, mailed on May 10, was delivered to the Gonzales residence on May 11. While it remained unnoticed in their mailbox, Joe Gonzalez telephoned Kirk to tell her that under no circumstances would he consent to sell their home to her or to participate in her "double-cross of the bank." He did not reach Kirk but left that message on her answering machine.

Joe and Mary Gonzales have just received a registered letter from Grace Kirk in which she informs them that they have a binding contract to sell their home for $280,000, that she has obtained independent financing enabling her to make the purchase without the participation of the Last National Bank or any other local lender, and demanding vacant possession by June 1st. Joe and Mary have brought both of Kirk's letters to your office and recited the above facts. They ask whether they are bound to a contract with Kirk. They are pleading with you to find some way to stop this sale but at the same time caution you that they want to be advised in a realistic manner as to their potential rights and liabilities. You have promised to respond in an opinion letter. Kindly draft that letter.

YOUR INITIAL ANALYSIS: Again, the instructions center on the major issues raised in this fact pattern. You are asked to advise the Gonzaleses as to whether they have formed a contract with Kirk. You are also prompted to discuss potential defenses they might have to any asserted liability. Once again, simply go down your mental check list:

#1 ***Did the parties form an agreement?*** There are clearly problems with an "offer" here. We have two candidates: the oral proposal made by Kirk to Mary Gonzales, and the letter of May 6 written by Mary Gonzales to Kirk. We also have an issue with an "acceptance." If the oral statement by Kirk constituted the offer, the letter from Mary added terms prompting application of the common law rejection/counteroffer rule. If, however, the offer was contained in the letter from Mary, we have an interesting issue of the life of the offer given the mode of acceptance (mail), the two-day delay in posting it, and the fact that Joe attempted to revoke the offer before he was actually aware that it had been delivered. These are deposited acceptance rule issues. But the content also raises a problem, for on its face it is a mirrored image, but subsequent facts tell us that it hides the true intent of Kirk.

#2 *If the parties formed an agreement, is their bargain a contract?* Two issues here: valuable consideration and defenses. There does not appear to be a problem with consideration insofar as Kirk having supplied it. But for the attempted bargain with the Gonzaleses, she was under no obligation to purchase the house. There are clearly at least three issues with respect to potential defenses. First is the proposed fraud upon the Last National Bank. Note that Mary is in on the plot, but Joe is not. Also, factually, Kirk does not need bank financing, but was a term of the agreement illegal? These are interesting issues that impact on whether this should render it unenforceable. Here is where we can discuss Kirk's hidden plan to subdivide tho property. If she had stated this in her "acceptance," there would have been no agreement. Hiding it may well have set the stage for a claim of fraud in the inducement. Also, note the factual stress on the thirty-year close relationship and Kirk's status as a retired relator. Any possible defense of "constructive fraud" here?

#3 *Do the terms of the contract or the subsequent conduct of either of the traders who formed it confer any rights or impose any duties on nontraders?* No.

#4 *Have the performance obligations created by the contract matured?* No, they have not. If we treat Mary's letter as the offer which Kirk accepted, then it is vital to note that Mary conditioned liability on the sale of the home to their ability to successfully purchase the "Conlon place." Factually that has not happened, though the Gonzaleses would be under a good-faith duty to attempt it: interesting issue as to how the discovery of Kirk's bad faith with respect to the subdivision would impact the duty of the seller to fulfill a condition precedent. There is a second issue of lesser importance. Assuming that the Conlon place was purchased, the liability to surrender vacant possession would not mature for another month. The facts tell us that the imperious Kirk is demanding vacant possession on June 1.

#5 *If performance obligations have matured, have they been discharged on any theory of excusable nonperformance?* No.

#6 *If a party with a fully matured obligation which has not been excused fails, refuses, or defectively performs, you are in the presence of a breach.* Since this question focuses on formation issues and defenses, it will not be necessary to spend a good deal of time on breach and remedies. But it is worthy of a quick summation. In the unlikely event that a court finds the Gonzaleses bound to a contract with no defenses to enforcement, then the fact that real estate is the subject matter suggests that the damage remedy will be inadequate. Kirk would then have the option of seeking relief in equity which, as a court of conscience, would likely look askance at her formation tactics and also take into account the fact that Joe appears to be a moral innocent.

#7 *If the aggrieved party cannot recover her expectation interest on a breach of contract theory, may she claim money damages on any alternative theory?* Clearly, Kirk has no restitution interest, for she has conferred nothing of value on the Gonzaleses. She had apparently undertaken expenses in retaining the services of the planning consultant. Here is a potential reliance claim, but it is not clear on the facts whether she obtained his services before or after attempting to accept Mary's letter. If before, there is no claim. If after, the issue would be whether, given her duplicity, they were claims which a reasonable person in the position of Mary Gonzales might have foreseen and whether "justice" would require any protection of Kirk's interests.

YOUR OUTLINE:

Having completed this mental check list, note how "small" the outline turns out to be. You must discuss offer, life of the offer, acceptance and defenses centered on illegality, fraud in the influence, and constructive fraud. You will also wish to briefly discuss the condition precedent attached by Mary as well as the performance date which, under no circumstances, has matured. If time permits, you will note the potential remedies to which it appears that Kirk is *not* entitled.

EP

NOTES

GLOSSARY

Glossary   G-2

GLOSSARY

A

Aggrieved party: A term used to describe the victim of a material breach of contract.

Assignment: A unilateral legal privilege whereby a party to an executory contract, termed an "assignor," extinguishes the right to receive the performance of the other party in himself and transfers that right immediately and exclusively to a nontrader, termed an "assignee."

B

Bilateral: One of two alternative means of contract formation. A contract is said to be formed in the "bilateral mode" when the offer and acceptance each take the form of a promise. A promise standing against a promise forms a bargain in this bilateral mode.

Breach: The failure, refusal, or defective performance of a duty created by the terms of a contract.

C

Contract: A social status, a contract consists of a promise or set of promises which the law will enforce or, in some way, regard as the source of legal obligation.

Cover: A replacement contract formed by an aggrieved buyer who seeks the subject matter from an alternative seller in efforts to mitigate damages.

Cure: An effort by a seller who has tendered goods which do not conform to the contract description to eliminate the nonconformity. If successful, a cure effort precludes breach on the part of the seller.

D

Dependent promise: If a contract promise will not mature unless a condition precedent or concurrent is either satisfied or excused, it is termed a "dependent promise."

Direct undertaking: In the formation of a contract conferring legal status upon an intended third-party beneficiary, the promise of one of the parties which, while given to the other, requires that performance efforts be conferred directly upon the intended beneficiary.

E

Executory: A promise is termed "executory" when it has been exchanged in the course of contract formation but has yet to be performed.

Executed: A promise is termed "executed" when, having been exchanged in the course of contract formation, it is performed by the promisor. *See Fully executed and Partially executed.*

Excusable nonperformance: Under both the common law and Uniform Commercial Code, doctrines have been devised which will render the failure or refusal of a party to carry out the terms of a contract promise a matter of legal privilege rather than breach. Such a party is able to claim "excusable nonperformance." At common law the doctrines are: objective impossibility, commercial impracticability, and frustration of purpose. The Uniform Commercial Code adds a concept of casualty to identified goods.

Excuse of condition: If a condition precedent or concurrent is removed as a barrier to maturing liability on a dependent promise by a doctrine other than satisfaction, it is said that the condition was "excused."

F

Failure of consideration: A personal defense which arises if one party to an executory bilateral contract materially breaches the obligations of that bargain. Such a material breach discharges the obligations of the aggrieved party on a theory of "failure of consideration."

Fully executed: If the reasonable expectations which the promisee had in a contract have been satisfied by performance of the promisor, the obligation of that party is said to be "fully executed."

I

Illusory promise: A promise which contains no element of bargained-for legal detriment and is thus not "valuable." If, in the course of attempted contract formation, one of the parties gives only an illusory promise, the other has the defense to formation "want of consideration."

In pari delicto: A Latin term indicating that both parties to a bargain which is *malum prohibitum* were actively aware that it offended an executory or legislative prohibition. Such persons are generally precluded from a quasi-contractual adjustment following any attempted performance.

Inadequacy of consideration: Aside from contracts formed between persons who are party to a fiduciary or confidential relationship, "inadequacy of consideration" is merely a plea that one of the parties made a bad bargain. It is no defense to enforcement of those terms. The protected person in a fiduciary relationship, or the subservient party in a confidential relationship, may raise a plea of economic or pragmatic unfairness in the terms of a bargain as a personal defense.

Independent promise: A contract promise is said to be "independent" if it is not circumscribed by any condition.

M

Malum in se: If the subject matter of an attempted contract is intrinsically evil, the wrongfulness could be appreciated by reference to personal conscience. Such an attempted bargain is void.

Malum prohibitum: Here the illegality does not spring from an intrinsically evil bargain, but by virtue of an offense to some legislative or executive governmental regulation. Such an attempted bargain is void, but a party who renders goods or services unaware of the *malum prohibitum* may recover in quasi-contract.

Material: A breach is said to be "material" if it goes to the essence of the reasonable expectations which the contract promise had created in the aggrieved party.

O

Obligee: A synonym for "promisee," the term is used to designate the party to whom executory duties are owed at the time of a delegation of those duties. If A and B form a bilateral contract and thereafter B seeks to delegate his duties to Y, A is the "obligee" of those duties.

Obligor: A synonym for "promisor," the term is generally used by courts to refer to the party whose executory contract duties are assigned. If A and B form a bilateral bargain and thereafter A seeks to assign her rights to B's executory performance to X, B is the "obligor" of those contract duties.

P

Partially executed: If a promisor has accomplished some, but not all, of the performance necessary to carry out the terms of his compromise, it is said to be "partially executed" and "partially executory."

Perfect tender doctrine: The privilege of the buyer, in any contract for the sale of goods, to reject a tender by the seller that fails to conform in any particular to the terms of the contract.

Promisee: If the contract is formed in the bilateral mode (exchange of promises), each of the parties is the "promisee" of the obligation pledged by the other.

Promisor: If the contract is formed in the bilateral mode (exchange of promises), each party is the "promisor" of his or her own obligation of performance.

S

Substantial performance: A level of performance which is flawed in meeting the expectations of the promisee by only a slight defect in quality or quantity or suffers from an insignificant time delay. Such an accomplishment will mature the duty of the other party to render her counterperformance if that promise is protected by a constructive condition.

U

Unilateral: A contract is formed in the "unilateral mode" if the offer seeks acceptance in the form of the offeree's performance of a designated act or endurance of a specified forbearance. A promise standing against a bargained-for act or forbearance forms a contract in the unilateral mode.

V

Vested or vesting of rights: A legal status achieved by an intended third-party beneficiary which puts it beyond the power of the parties who created the contract to rescind, modify, or novate it without her positive consent.

Void: If the formation effort founders upon a real defense, the resulting agreement is "void" as an attempted contract.

Voidable: If one party to an executory agreement can assert a personal defense to enforcement of its terms, a contract is formed but is said to be "voidable" at the option of that party.

W

Want of consideration: A real defense precluding formation of a contract. Want of consideration arises when one of the parties incurs no element of bargained-for legal detriment.

TABLE OF AUTHORITIES

TABLE OF CASES

TA

TA

TA

TABLE OF STATUTES, CODES AND OTHER AUTHORITIES

CONTRACTS ◄ casenote law outlines

Restatement, Second of Contracts

TA

NOTES

CROSS-REFERENCE CHART

Casebook Cross-Reference Chart   CR-2

CR

CONTRACTS Casenote Law Outline Cross-Reference Chart	Calamari 2nd Ed. 1989	Dawson 6th Ed. 1993	Farnsworth 5th Ed. 1995	Fessler 1982	Fuller 5th Ed. 1990	Hamilton 2nd Ed. 1992	Kessler 3rd Ed. 1986	Knapp 3rd Ed. 1993	Murray 4th Ed. 1991	Murphy 4th Ed. 1991	Rosett 5th Ed. 1994
CHAPTER 1: THE AGREEMENT PROCESS											
I. Manifesting Mutual Consent	28-30, 783-785	330-373, 425-435, 508-515, 531-542	138-153	348, 355	328-358	519-542		35-51	41-50	252-276	520-523
II. The Offer	22-27, 259-263	349-360, 370-414, 422-425, 450-451, 612-614	151-215	248-261	359-410	416-489	315-370, 689-694	51-80	71-139	276-306, 373-410	523-582
III. The Acceptance	83-140	216-233, 370-396, 402-458, 422-451	179-248	267-307	428-470	489-597	247-272, 348-370	51-80	139-206	306-373	582-611
IV. Impact of Ambiguity and Mistake on the Bargain	356-361, 368-369	360-373, 402-409, 495-498, 615-658	795-830	402-452	654-695, 696-743	599-638, 658-671, 342-367	862-886	272-307, 729-751	419-421, 431-452	479-511	175-185, 199-200, 668-669
CHAPTER 2: THE QUALITIES OF A CONTRACTUAL RELATIONSHIP											
I. Valuable Consideration: The Bargained-for Incursion of Legal Detriment	146-149, 206-214, 675-676	193-233	45-73, 116-137, 346-347	36-124	2-189	157-326	279-314	82-132	212-283	97-193	14, 202-208, 214-229

CONTRACTS *Casenote Law Outline* Cross-Reference Chart	Calamari 2nd Ed. 1989	Dawson 6th Ed. 1993	Farnsworth 5th Ed. 1995	Fessler 1982	Fuller 5th Ed. 1990	Hamilton 2nd Ed. 1992	Kessler 3rd Ed. 1986	Knapp 3rd Ed. 1993	Murray 4th Ed. 1991	Murphy 4th Ed. 1991	Rosett 5th Ed. 1994
II. Substitutes for Valuable Consideration as Grounds for Imparting Liability Consequences For Breaching a Promise	241-246, 261-263, 270-276	233-293	62-137	130-145	19-53	159-168, 219-235, 469-489, 576-598	223-225, 308-314	135-227	283-325	193-251	229-293
CHAPTER 3: THE BARGAIN IN LITIGATION											
I. Defective Formation as a Defense	356-367, 368-369	219-221, 370-373, 621-639	795-862	402-459	654-695	599-638, 658-671	875-880	729-751	419-421, 431-452	479-511	175-185, 199-200, 668-669
II. Defenses Related to the Capacity of One of the Parties	313-325	235-240, 297, 546-568, 964-965	325-336	201-203, 209-211, 412-416		764-767		171, 585-601	261	512-528	119-134
III. Defenses Rooted in Social Objection to the Content of the Bargain	817-831	516-538, 700-725	386-482	97-100, 146-175	53-77	205, 723-757	76-78, 95-98	660-698, 698-724	466-481, 497-523	582-682	83-102, 142-163, 873-884
IV. Defenses Centered on the Deceptive or Coercive Formation Tactics of One of the Parties	340-352	483-489, 570-603, 647-658	336-386	179-208, 211-217	47-53	198-208, 623-628, 699-702, 750-777	84-98, 657-663, 674-678	601-660	455-481	528-622	134-175
V. Defenses Arising from the Form of the Bargain	370-378	457-508, 957-974	286-323, 565-663	223-242	527-579, 596-653	110-113, 682-722, 889-912	564-623	451-493, 351-412	327-431	683-802	300-334

CR

CONTRACTS *Casenote Law Outline* Cross-Reference Chart	Calamari 2nd Ed. 1989	Dawson 6th Ed. 1993	Farnsworth 5th Ed. 1995	Fessler 1982	Fuller 5th Ed. 1990	Hamilton 2nd Ed. 1992	Kessler 3rd Ed. 1986	Knapp 3rd Ed. 1993	Murray 4th Ed. 1991	Murphy 4th Ed. 1991	Rosett 5th Ed. 1994
CHAPTER 4 THE ALLOCATION OF RISK INHERENT IN THE BARGAIN											
I. Classification of Conditions According to Their Impact upon the Modified Promise		734-741	679	629-634	910-914, 958-961	810-814	976-990	817-818, 866-870	539-545	809-810	643-644
II. Sources of Conditions in a Bargain	379-388, 480-483	727-773, 786-826	665-698	542-572	899-982	782-794	976-990	499-510, 809-825	549, 550, 581-588	804-827, 846-924, 987-1008	624-635, 645-646
III. Maturing of Contract Duties: Satisfaction or Excuse of Conditions	539-586	615-859	121-125, 677-685, 692-695, 751-788	600-614			861-971				
CHAPTER 5 THE RIGHTS AND DUTIES OF NON-TRADERS											
I. The Status and Right of an Intended Beneficiary	689-710	877-917	863-912	775-791	744-794	838-861	1384-1418	1197-1231	753-802	1335-1389	780-802
II. The Assignment of Contract Rights	722-740	917-956	913-958	793-800, 813-816	795-838	164-168, 862-888	1500-1558	1231-1259	803-849	1279-1322	802-843
III. The Delegation of Contract Duties	730-755	917-956	913-958	822-828	805-811	164-168, 862-888	1500-1558	1231-1259	803-849	1322-1334	802-843
CHAPTER 6 EXCUSABLE NON-PERFORMANCE											
I. Excusable Nonperformance under the Common Law	542-552, 571-584	615-859	534-546, 805-851	471-491, 504-522	696-742	645-681	861-971	729-807	613-652	924-987	548, 663-668

CR

CONTRACTS Casenote Law Outline Cross-Reference Chart	Calamari 2nd Ed. 1989	Dawson 6th Ed. 1993	Farnsworth 5th Ed. 1995	Fessler 1982	Fuller 5th Ed. 1990	Hamilton 2nd Ed. 1992	Kessler 3rd Ed. 1986	Knapp 3rd Ed. 1993	Murray 4th Ed. 1991	Murphy 4th Ed. 1991	Rosett 5th Ed. 1994
II. Excusable Nonperformance under the UCC	542-552, 571-584	641-856	705-706, 714-720, 811-812	491-504	723-738	723-738	861-971	751-784	618-644	949-983	666-667
CHAPTER 7 THE CONSEQUENCES OF BREACH											
I. Breach - Disappointment of Reasonable Expectations	419-423	1-8, 31-32	735-754, 788-794	471-504	983-1027	51-53	106-110	848-890	567-588	1010-1036	690
II. Affirmative Obligations of the Aggrieved Party	606-613	38-51, 71-73, 830-834	693-735	715-744	229-249	19-23, 96-100	1134-1138	938-960, 1158-1176, 1184-1194	686-693, 711-725	1069, 1106, 1247	370-387, 855-860
III. Remedies for Breach of Contract	16-22, 588-603	1-192	483-564	644-711	192-325	1-156	1069-1108, 1138-1165, 1172-1201	891-1135	657-752	1036-1152, 1171-1244	335-519

NOTES

INDEX

ID

ID

ID

ID

NOTES

LAW OUTLINES from CASENOTE™

the Ultimate Outline

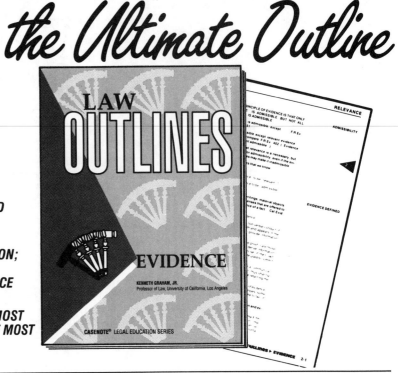

▶ WRITTEN BY NATIONALLY RECOGNIZED AUTHORITIES IN THEIR FIELD.

▶ FEATURING A FLEXIBLE, SUBJECT-ORIENTED APPROACH.

▶ CONTAINS: TABLE OF CONTENTS; CAPSULE OUTLINE; FULL OUTLINE; EXAM PREPARATION; GLOSSARY; TABLE OF CASES; TABLE OF AUTHORITIES; CASEBOOK CROSS REFERENCE CHART; INDEX.

▶ THE TOTAL LAW SUMMARY UTILIZING THE MOST COMPREHENSIVE STUDY APPROACH IN THE MOST EFFECTIVE, EASY-TO-READ FORMAT.

REF #	SUBJECT	AUTHORS	RETAIL PRICE
#5260 —	ADMINISTRATIVE LAW by **Charles H. Koch, Jr.,** Dudley W. Woodbridge Professor of Law, College of William and Mary. **Sidney A. Shapiro,** John M. Rounds Professor of Law, University of Kansas. (1994)	(effective 7/1/96) **$18.95**
#5040 —	CIVIL PROCEDURE by **John B. Oakley,** Professor of Law, University of California, Davis. **Rex R. Perschbacher,** Professor of Law & Associate Dean, Academic Affairs, University of California, Davis. (1996)	**$19.95**
	COMMERCIAL LAW (see 5700 SALES • 5710 SECURED TRANS. • 5720 NEG. INSTRUMENTS & PMT. SYST.)	
#5070 —	CONFLICT OF LAWS by **Luther L. McDougal, III,** W.R. Irby Professor of Law, Tulane University. **Robert L. Felix,** James P. Mozingo, III Prof. of Law, Univ. of S. Carolina. (1992)	**$18.95**
#5080 —	CONSTITUTIONAL LAW by **Gary Goodpaster,** Prof. of Law, Univ. of California, Davis. (1994 w/'95 supp)	**$21.95**
#5010 —	CONTRACTS by **Daniel Wm. Fessler,** Professor of Law, University of California, Davis. (1996)	**$18.95**
#5050 —	CORPORATIONS **AND ALTERNATIVE BUSINESS VEHICLES** by **Lewis D. Solomon,** Arthur Selwin Miller Research Prof. of Law, George Washington Univ. **Daniel Wm. Fessler,** Prof. of Law, University of California, Davis. **Arthur E. Wilmarth, Jr.,** Assoc. Prof. of Law, George Washington University. (1994)	**$20.95**
#5020 —	CRIMINAL LAW by **Joshua Dressler,** Professor of Law, McGeorge School of Law. (1996)	**$18.95**
#5200 —	CRIMINAL PROCEDURE by **Joshua Dressler,** Prof. of Law, McGeorge School of Law. (1993 w/'95 supp.)	**$17.95**
#5800 —	ESTATE & GIFT TAX **INCLUDING THE FEDERAL GENERATION-SKIPPING TAX** by **Joseph M. Dodge,** W.H. Francis Prof. of Law, University of Texas at Austin. (1993)	**$18.95**
#5060 —	EVIDENCE by **Kenneth Graham, Jr.,** Professor of Law, University of California, Los Angeles. (1996)	**$19.95**
#5300 —	FEDERAL COURTS by **Howard P. Fink,** Isadore and Ida Topper Prof. of Law, Ohio State University. **Linda S. Mullenix,** Bernard J. Ward Centennial Prof. of Law, Univ. of Texas. (1996)	**TBA**
#5210 —	FEDERAL INCOME TAXATION by **Joseph M. Dodge,** W.H. Francis Professor of Law, University of Texas at Austin (1994).	**$19.95**
#5300 —	LEGAL RESEARCH by **Nancy L. Schultz,** Assistant Dean and Dir., Research and Writing, George Washington Univ. Nat'l Law Center. **Louis J. Sirico, Jr.,** Professor of Law and Director of Legal Writing, Villanova University. (1996)	**$18.95**
#5720 —	NEGOTIABLE INST. & PMT. SYST. by **Donald B. King,** Professor of Law, Saint Louis University **Peter Winship,** James Cleo Thompson, Sr. Trustee Prof., SMU. (1995)	**$18.95**
#5030 —	PROPERTY by **Sheldon F. Kurtz,** Percy Bordwell Professor of Law, University of Iowa.	**TBA**
#5700 —	SALES by **Robert E. Scott,** Dean and Lewis F. Powell, Jr. Professor of Law, University of Virginia. **Donald B. King,** Professor of Law, Saint Louis University. (1992 w/'96 supp.)	**$18.95**
#5710 —	SECURED TRANSACTIONS by **Donald B. King,** Professor of Law, Saint Louis University. (1995 w/'96 supp.)	**$17.95**
#5000 —	TORTS by **George C. Christie,** James B. Duke Professor of Law, Duke University. **Jerry J. Phillips,** W.P. Toms Professor of Law & Chair, Committee on Admissions, University of Tennessee. (1996)	**$19.95**
#5220 —	WILLS, TRUSTS & ESTATES by **William M. McGovern,** Professor of Law, University of California, Los Angeles. (1996)	**$19.95**

TOTAL *the* STUDY *Team*

CASENOTE LEGAL BRIEFS

America's best selling legal briefs

Features: CASENOTE® CASE CAPSULES
States essence of the case at a glance

▶ **COMPLETE BRIEFS** *The most comprehensive briefs; concurrences and dissents are never omitted; judge's names are included; no sketchy summaries; editor's analysis discusses case relevance.*

▶ **ALL MAJOR CASES BRIEFED** *All cases appearing in bold face titles in casebook are briefed in your CASENOTES.*

▶ **TRUE-TO-CASE EXCERPTS** *Cases are briefed according to the way in which they are edited by your casebook editor.*

▶ **FREE SUPPLEMENT UPDATE SERVICE** *CASENOTES are always made complete whenever a casebook supplement is issued.*

▶ **OVER 170 TITLES**

and

LAW OUTLINES from CASENOTE™

the Ultimate Outline

▶ *WRITTEN BY NATIONALLY RECOGNIZED AUTHORITIES IN THEIR FIELD.*

▶ *FEATURING A FLEXIBLE, SUBJECT-ORIENTED APPROACH.*

▶ *CONTAINS: TABLE OF CONTENTS; CAPSULE OUTLINE; FULL OUTLINE; EXAM PREPARATION; GLOSSARY; TABLE OF CASES; TABLE OF AUTHORITIES; CASEBOOK CROSS-REFERENCE CHART; INDEX.*

▶ *THE TOTAL LAW SUMMARY UTILIZING THE MOST COMPREHENSIVE STUDY APPROACH IN THE MOST EFFECTIVE, EASY-TO-READ FORMAT.*

REF #	SUBJECT	AUTHORS	RETAIL PRICE
#5260 —	ADMINISTRATIVE LAW by **Charles H. Koch, Jr.,** Dudley W. Woodbridge Professor of Law, College of William and Mary. **Sidney A. Shapiro,** John M. Rounds Professor of Law, University of Kansas. (1994)	(effective 7/1/96)	$18.95
#5040 —	CIVIL PROCEDURE by **John B. Oakley,** Professor of Law, University of California, Davis. **Rex R. Perschbacher,** Professor of Law & Associate Dean, Academic Affairs, University of California, Davis. (1996)		$19.95
	COMMERCIAL LAW (see 5700 SALES ● 5710 SECURED TRANS. ● 5720 NEG. INSTRUMENTS & PMT. SYST.)		
#5070 —	CONFLICT OF LAWS by **Luther L. McDougal, III,** W.R. Irby Professor of Law, Tulane University. **Robert L. Felix,** James P. Mozingo, III Professor of Law, University of South Carolina. (1992)		$18.95
#5080 —	CONSTITUTIONAL LAW by **Gary Goodpaster,** Prof. of Law, Univ. of Calif., Davis. (1994 w/1995 supp.)		$21.95
#5010 —	CONTRACTS by **Daniel Wm. Fessler,** Professor of Law, University of California, Davis. (1996)		$18.95
#5050 —	CORPORATIONS by **Lewis D. Solomon,** Arthur Selwin Miller Research Prof. of Law, George Washington Univ. **AND ALTERNATIVE BUSINESS VEHICLES** **Daniel Wm. Fessler,** Professor of Law, University of California, Davis. **Arthur E. Wilmarth, Jr.,** Associate Professor of Law, George Washington University. (1994)		$20.95
#5020 —	CRIMINAL LAW by **Joshua Dressler,** Professor of Law, McGeorge School of Law. (1996)		$18.95
#5200 —	CRIMINAL PROCEDURE by **Joshua Dressler,** Prof. of Law, McGeorge School of Law. (1993 w/'95 supp.)		$17.95
#5800 —	ESTATE & GIFT TAX by **Joseph M. Dodge,** W.H. Francis Professor of Law, University of **INCLUDING THE FEDERAL GENERATION-SKIPPING TAX** Texas at Austin. (1993)		$18.95
#5060 —	EVIDENCE by **Kenneth Graham, Jr.,** Professor of Law, University of California, Los Angeles. (1996)		$19.95
#5360 —	FEDERAL COURTS by **Howard P. Fink,** Isadore and Ida Topper Prof. of Law, Ohio State. Univ., **Linda S. Mullenix,** Bernard J. Ward Centennial Prof. of Law, Univ. of Texas. (1996)		TBA
#5210 —	FEDERAL INCOME TAXATION by **Joseph M. Dodge,** W.H. Francis Professor of Law, University of Texas at Austin (1994).		$19.95
#5300 —	LEGAL RESEARCH by **Nancy L. Schultz,** Assistant Dean and Dir., Research and Writing, George Washington Univ. Nat'l Law Center. **Louis J. Sirico, Jr.,** Professor of Law Villanova University School of Law. (1996)		$18.95
#5720 —	NEGOTIABLE INSTRUMENTS & PMT. SYST. by **Donald B. King,** Prof. of Law, St. Louis Univ. **Peter Winship,** James Cleo Thompson Sr. Trustee Professor, Southern Methodist University. (1995)		$18.95
#5030 —	PROPERTY by **Sheldon F. Kurtz,** Percy Bordwell Professor of Law, University of Iowa.		TBA
#5700 —	SALES by **Robert E. Scott,** Dean and Lewis F. Powell, Jr. Professor of Law, University of Virginia. **Donald B. King,** Professor of Law, St. Louis University. (1992 w/'96 supp.)		$18.95
#5710 —	SECURED TRANSACTIONS by **Donald B. King,** Professor of Law, St. Louis Univ. (1995 w/'96 supp.)		$17.95
#5000 —	TORTS by **George C. Christie,** James B. Duke Professor of Law, Duke University. **Jerry J. Phillips,** W.P. Toms Professor of Law & Chair, Committee on Admissions, University of Tennessee. (1996)		$19.95
#5220 —	WILLS, TRUSTS & ESTATES by **William M. McGovern,** Professor of Law, University of California, Los Angeles. (1996)		$19.95

CASENOTE™ LEGAL BRIEFS

PRICE LIST — EFFECTIVE JULY 1, 1996 ● PRICES SUBJECT TO CHANGE WITHOUT NOTICE

Ref. No.	Course	Adaptable to Courses Utilizing	Retail Price
1265	ADMINISTRATIVE LAW	BONFIELD & ASIMOV	16.00
1263	ADMINISTRATIVE LAW	BREYER & STEWART	18.00
1266	ADMINISTRATIVE LAW	CASS, DIVER & BEERMAN	16.00
1260	ADMINISTRATIVE LAW	GELLHORN, B., S., R., S. & F.	16.00
1264	ADMINISTRATIVE LAW	MASHAW, MERRILL & SHANE	17.50
1262	ADMINISTRATIVE LAW	SCHWARTZ	17.00
1290	ADMIRALTY	HEALY & SHARPE	20.00
1291	ADMIRALTY	LUCAS	17.50
1350	AGENCY & PARTNERSHIP (ENT.ORG)	CONARD, KNAUSS & SIEGEL	20.00
1351	AGENCY & PARTNERSHIP	HYNES	19.00
1281	ANTITRUST (TRADE REGULATION)	HANDLER, B. P. & G.	16.50
1283	ANTITRUST	SULLIVAN & HOVENKAMP	17.00
1611	BANKING LAW	MACEY & MILLER	17.00
1610	BANKING LAW	SYMONS & WHITE	14.00
1303	BANKRUPTCY (DEBTOR-CREDITOR)	EISENBERG	18.00
1440	BUSINESS PLANNING	HERWITZ	12.50
1040	CIVIL PROCEDURE	COUND, F., M. & S	19.00
1043	CIVIL PROCEDURE	FIELD, KAPLAN & CLERMONT	19.00
1041	CIVIL PROCEDURE	HAZARD, TAIT & FLETCHER	18.00
1047	CIVIL PROCEDURE	MARCUS, REDISH & SHERMAN	18.00
1044	CIVIL PROCEDURE	ROSENBERG, S. & D.	19.00
1046	CIVIL PROCEDURE	YEAZELL, LANDERS, & MARTI6	16.00
1311	COMM'L LAW	FARNSWORTH, H., R., H. & 7.	18.00
1312	COMM'L LAW	JORDAN & WARREN	18.00
1310	COMM'L LAW (SALES/SEC.TR./PAY.LAW)	SPEIDEL, SUMMERS & WHITE	20.00
1313	COMM'L LAW (SALES/SEC.TR./PAY.LAW)	WHALEY	17.00
1320	COMMUNITY PROPERTY	BIRD	16.50
1630	COMPARATIVE LAW	SCHLESINGER, B., D., & H.	15.00
1048	COMPLEX LITIGATION	MARCUS & SHERMAN	16.00
1072	CONFLICTS	BRILMAYER	16.00
1071	CONFLICTS	CRAMTON, CURRIE & KAY	16.00
1070	CONFLICTS	REESE, ROSENBERG & HAY	19.00
1086	CONSTITUTIONAL LAW	BREST & LEVINSON	17.00
1082	CONSTITUTIONAL LAW	COHEN & VARAT	20.00
1088	CONSTITUTIONAL LAW	FARBER, ESKRIDGE & FRICKEY	17.00
1080	CONSTITUTIONAL LAW	GUNTHER	18.00
1081	CONSTITUTIONAL LAW	LOCKHART, K., C. & S.	17.00
1085	CONSTITUTIONAL LAW	ROTUNDA	19.00
1087	CONSTITUTIONAL LAW	STONE, S., S. & T.	18.00
1017	CONTRACTS	CALAMARI, PERILLO & BENDER	22.00
1101	CONTRACTS	CRANDALL & WHALEY	19.00
1014	CONTRACTS	DAWSON, HARVEY & HENDRESON	18.00
1010	CONTRACTS	FARNSWORTH & YOUNG	17.00
1011	CONTRACTS	FULLER & EISENBERG	19.00
1100	CONTRACTS	HAMILTON, RAU & WEINTRAUB	18.00
1013	CONTRACTS	KESSLER, GILMORE & KRONMAN	22.00
1016	CONTRACTS	KNAPP & CRYSTAL	19.50
1012	CONTRACTS	MURPHY & SPEIDEL	21.00
1018	CONTRACTS	MURRAY	21.00
1015	CONTRACTS	ROSETT	20.00
1019	CONTRACTS	VERNON	19.00
1502	COPYRIGHT	GOLDSTEIN	17.00
1501	COPYRIGHT	NIMMER, M., M., & N.	18.50
1218	CORPORATE TAXATION	LIND, S. L. & R	13.00
1050	CORPORATIONS	CARY & EISENBERG (ABR. & UNA8R.)	18.00
1054	CORPORATIONS	CHOPER, MORRIS & COFFEE	20.50
1350	CORPORATIONS (ENTERPRISE ORG.)	CONARD, KNAUSS & SIEGEL	20.00
1053	CORPORATIONS	HAMILTON	18.00
1057	CORPORATIONS	O'KELLEY & THOMPSON	17.00
1056	CORPORATIONS	SOLOMON, S., B., & W.	19.00
1052	CORPORATIONS	VAGTS	16.00
1300	CREDITOR'S RIGHTS (DEBTOR-CREDITOR)	RIESENFELD	20.00
1550	CRIMINAL JUSTICE	WEINREB	17.00
1020	CRIMINAL LAW	BOYCE & PERKINS	21.00
1024	CRIMINAL LAW	DIX & SHARLOT	16.00
1028	CRIMINAL LAW	DRESSLER	20.00
1027	CRIMINAL LAW	JOHNSON	19.00
1021	CRIMINAL LAW	KADISH & SCHULHOFER	18.00
1026	CRIMINAL LAW	KAPLAN & WEISBERG	17.00
1023	CRIMINAL LAW	LAFAVE	14.00
1022	CRIMINAL LAW	WEINREB	14.00
1205	CRIMINAL PROCEDURE	ALLEN, KUHNS & STUNTZ	16.00
1202	CRIMINAL PROCEDURE	HADDAD, Z., S. & B.	19.00
1200	CRIMINAL PROCEDURE	KAMISAR, LAFAVE & ISRAEL	18.00
1204	CRIMINAL PROCEDURE	SALTZBURG & CAPRA	16.00
1203	CRIMINAL PROCEDURE (PROCESS)	WEINREB	17.50
1303	DEBTOR-CREDITOR	EISENBERG	18.00
1302	DEBTOR-CREDITOR	EPSTEIN, LANDERS & NICKLES	17.00
1300	DEBTOR-CREDITOR (CRED. RTS.)	RIESENFELD	20.00
1304	DEBTOR-CREDITOR	WARREN & WESTBROOK	18.00
1224	DECEDENTS ESTATES	RITCHIE, ALFORD, EFFLAND & DORIS	20.00
1222	DECEDENTS ESTATES	SCOLES & HALBACH	20.50
1231	DECEDENTS ESTATES (TRUSTS)	WAGGONER, WELLMAN, A. & F.	19.00
	DOMESTIC RELATIONS (see FAMILY LAW)		
1670	EMPLOYMENT DISCRIMINATION	FRIEDMAN & STRICKLER	16.00
1671	EMPLOYMENT DISCRIMINATION	ZIMMER, SULLIVAN, R. & C.	17.00
1660	EMPLOYMENT LAW	ROTHSTEIN, KNAPP & LIEBMAN	18.50
1350	ENTERPRISE ORGANIZATION	CONARD, KNAUSS & SIEGEL	20.00
1342	ENVIRONMENTAL LAW	ANDERSON, MANDELKER & TARLOCK	15.00
1341	ENVIRONMENTAL LAW	FINDLEY & FARBER	17.00
1345	ENVIRONMENTAL LAW	MENELL & STEWART	16.00
1344	ENVIRONMENTAL LAW	PERCIVAL, MILLER, S. & L.	17.00
1343	ENVIRONMENTAL LAW	PLATER, ABRAMS & GOLDFARB	16.00
	EQUITY (see REMEDIES)		
1217	ESTATE & GIFT TAXATION	BITTKER & CLARK	14.00
1214	ESTATE & GIFT TAXATION	KAHN & WAGGONER	16.00
1213	ESTATE & GIFT TAX (FED. WEALTH TRANS.)	SURREY, MCDANIEL & GUTMAN	15.00
	ETHICS [see PROFESSIONAL RESPONSIBILITY]		
1065	EVIDENCE	GREEN & NESSON	19.00
1063	EVIDENCE	LEMPERT & SALTZBURG	11.00
1066	EVIDENCE	MUELLER & KIRKPATRICK	16.00
1064	EVIDENCE	STRONG, BROUN & MOUSTELLER	21.50
1062	EVIDENCE	SUTTON & WELLBORN	21.00
1061	EVIDENCE	WALTZ & PARK	19.00
1060	EVIDENCE	WEINSTEIN, M., A & B.	21.50
1244	FAMILY LAW (DOMESTIC RELATION)	AREEN	21.00
1242	FAMILY LAW (DOMESTIC RELATION)	CLARK & GLOWINSKY	18.00
1245	FAMILY LAW (DOMESTIC RELATION)	ELLMAN, KURTZ & BARTLETT	19.00
1243	FAMILY LAW (DOMESTIC RELATION)	KRAUSE	23.00
1240	FAMILY LAW (DOMESTIC RELATION)	WADLINGTON	19.00
1231	FAMILY PROPERTY LAW (WILLS/TRUSTS)	WAGGONER, WELLMAN, A. & F.	19.00
1360	FEDERAL COURTS	BATOR ET AL. (HART & WECHSLER)	18.00
1362	FEDERAL COURTS	CURRIE	16.00
1363	FEDERAL COURTS	LOW & JEFFRIES	15.00
1361	FEDERAL COURTS	MCCORMICK, C. & W.	19.00
1364	FEDERAL COURTS	REDISH & NICHOL	16.00
1510	GRATUITOUS TRANSFERS	CLARK, LUSKY & MURPHY	17.00
1650	HEALTH LAW	FURROW, J., J., & S.	16.50
1640	IMMIGRATION LAW	ALEINIKOFF, MARTIN & MOTOMURA	15.00
1371	INSURANCE LAW	KEETON	20.00
1372	INSURANCE LAW	YORK, WHELAN & MARTINEZ	18.00
1370	INSURANCE LAW	YOUNG & HOLMES	16.00
1394	INTERNATIONAL BUSINESS TRANSACTIONS	FOLSOM, GORDON & SPANOGLE	14.00
1393	INTERNATIONAL LAW	CARTER & TRIMBLE	15.00
1392	INTERNATIONAL LAW	HENKIN, P., S. & S.	16.00
1390	INTERNATIONAL LAW	OLIVER, F., B., S., & W.	21.00
1331	LABOR LAW	COX, BOK, GORMAN & FINKIN	18.00
1333	LABOR LAW	LESLIE	17.50
1332	LABOR LAW	MELTZER & HENDERSON	19.00
1330	LABOR LAW	MERRIFIELD, S. & C.	18.00
1471	LAND FINANCE (REAL ESTATE TRANS)	BERGER & JOHNSTONE	17.00
1620	LAND FINANCE (REAL ESTATE TRANS)	NELSON & WHITMAN	18.00
1470	LAND FINANCE	PENNEY, B. & C.	15.00
1451	LAND USE	CALLIES, FREILICH & ROBERTS	16.00
1450	LAND USE	WRIGHT & GITELMAN	22.00
1421	LEGISLATION	ESKRIDGE & FRICKEY	14.00
1590	LOCAL GOVERNMENT LAW	VALENTE & McCARTHY	21.00
1480	MASS MEDIA	FRANKLIN & ANDERSON	14.00
1312	NEGOTIABLE INSTRUMENTS (COMM. LAW)	JORDAN & WARREN	18.00
1313	NEGOTIABLE INSTRUMENTS (COMM. LAW)	WHALEY	17.00
1570	NEW YORK PRACTICE	PETERFREUND & McLAUGHLIN	24.00
1541	OIL & GAS	KUNTZ, L., A & S.	17.00
1540	OIL & GAS	MAXWELL, WILLIAMS, M. & K.	17.00
1560	PATENT LAW	FRANCIS & COLLINS (CHOATE)	22.00
1310	PAYMENT LAW (COMM LAW, SALES & SEC.TR.)	SPEIDEL, SUMMERS & WHITE	20.00
1313	PAYMENT LAW (COMM.LAW / NEG. INST.)	WHALEY	17.00
1431	PRODUCTS LIABILITY	KEETON, O., M., & G.	19.00
1091	PROF. RESPONSIBILITY (ETHICS)	GILLERS	12.00
1093	PROF. RESPONSIBILITY (ETHICS)	HAZARD, KONIAK, & CRAMTON	17.00
1092	PROF. RESPONSIBILITY (ETHICS)	MORGAN & ROTUNDA	12.00
1033	PROPERTY	BROWDER, C., N., S & W.	19.50
1030	PROPERTY	CASNER & LEACH	20.00
1031	PROPERTY	CRIBBET, JOHNSON, FINLEY & SMITH	20.50
1037	PROPERTY	DONAHUE, KAUPER & MARTIN	17.00
1035	PROPERTY	DUKEMINIER & KRIER	17.00
1034	PROPERTY	HAAR & LIEBMAN	19.50
1036	PROPERTY	KURTZ & HOVENKAMP	18.00
1032	PROPERTY	RABIN & KWALL	19.00
1038	PROPERTY	SINGER	17.50
1621	REAL ESTATE TRANSACTIONS	GOLDSTEIN & KORNGOLD	17.00
1471	REAL ESTATE TRANS. & FIN. (LAND FINANCE)	BERGER & JOHNSTONE	16.00
1620	REAL ESTATE TRANSFER & FINANCE	NELSON & WHITMAN	17.00
1254	REMEDIES (EQUITY)	LAYCOCK	19.00
1253	REMEDIES (EQUITY)	LEAVELL, L., N. & K/F.	20.00
1252	REMEDIES (EQUITY)	RE & RE	22.00
1255	REMEDIES (EQUITY)	SHOBEN & TABB	21.50
1250	REMEDIES (EQUITY)	YORK, BAUMAN & RENDLEMAN	24.00
1312	SALES (COMM. LAW)	JORDAN & WARREN	18.00
1310	SALES (COMM. LAW)	SPEIDEL, SUMMERS & WHITE	20.00
1313	SALES (COMM. LAW)	WHALEY	17.00
1312	SECURED TRANS. (COMM. LAW)	JORDAN & WARREN	18.00
1310	SECURED TRANS.	SPEIDEL, SUMMERS & WHITE	20.00
1313	SECURED TRANS. (COMM. LAW)	WHALEY	17.00
1272	SECURITIES REGULATION	COX, HILLMAN, LANGEVOORT	17.00
1270	SECURITIES REGULATION	JENNINGS, MARSH & COFFEE	17.00
1271	SECURITIES REGULATION	RATNER	17.00
1680	SPORTS LAW	WEILER & ROBERTS	16.50
1215	TAXATION (BASIC FED. INC.)	ANDREWS	20.00
1217	TAXATION (ESTATE & GIFT)	BITTKER & CLARK	14.00
1212	TAXATION (FED. INC.)	FREELAND, LIND & STEPHENS	17.00
1211	TAXATION (FED. INC.)	GRAETZ & SCHENK	16.00
1214	TAXATION (ESTATE & GIFT)	KAHN & WAGGONER	16.00
1210	TAXATION (FED. INC.)	KLEIN & BANKMAN	17.00
1218	TAXATION (CORPORATE)	LIND, S., L. & R.	13.00
1213	TAXATION (FED. WEALTH TRANS.)	SURREY, MCDANIEL & GUTMAN.	15.00
1006	TORTS	DOBBS	18.00
1003	TORTS	EPSTEIN	19.50
1004	TORTS	FRANKLIN & RABIN	16.50
1001	TORTS	HENDERSON, P. & S.	19.50
1002	TORTS	KEETON, K., S. & S.	22.00
1000	TORTS	PROSSER, W., S., K., & P.	23.00
1005	TORTS	SHULMAN, JAMES & GRAY	21.00
1281	TRADE REGULATION (ANTITRUST)	HANDLER, B., P. & G.	16.50
1230	TRUSTS	BOGERT, O., H., & H.	19.50
1231	TRUSTS/WILLS (FAMILY PROPERTY LAW)	WAGGONER, WELLMAN A. & F.	19.00
1410	U.C.C.	EPSTEIN, MARTIN, H. & N.	14.00
1580	WATER LAW	TRELEASE & GOULD	18.00
1223	WILLS, TRUSTS & ESTATES	DUKEMINIER & JOHANSON	18.00
1220	WILLS	MECHEM & ATKINSON	19.00
1231	WILLS/TRUSTS (FAMILY PROPERTY LAW)	WAGGONER, WELLMAN A. & F.	19.00

(SERIES XXXIX)

CASENOTES PUBLISHING CO. INC. ● 1640 FIFTH STREET, SUITE 208 ● SANTA MONICA, CA 90401 ● (310) 395-6500

PLEASE PURCHASE FROM YOUR LOCAL BOOKSTORE. IF UNAVAILABLE, YOU MAY ORDER DIRECT.*

4TH CLASS POSTAGE (ALLOW TWO WEEKS) $1.00 PER ORDER; 1ST CLASS POSTAGE $3.00 (ONE BOOK), $2.00 EACH (TWO OR MORE BOOKS)

*CALIF. RESIDENTS PLEASE ADD 8¼% SALES TAX